CW00816187

Shakespeare for Freedom

§

Shakespeare for Freedom presents a powerful, plausible and political argument for Shakespeare's meaning and value. It ranges across the breadth of the Shakespeare phenomenon, offering a new interpretation not just of the characters and plays, but also of the part they have played in theatre, criticism, civic culture and politics. Its story includes a glimpse of 'Freetown' in *Romeo and Juliet*, which comes to life in the 1769 Stratford Jubilee; the Shakespearean careers of the Leicester Chartist, Cooper, and the Hungarian hero, Kossuth; Hegel's recognition of Shakespearean freedom as the modern breakthrough; its fatal effects in America; the disgust it inspired in Tolstoy; its rehabilitation by Ted Hughes, and its obscure centrality in the 2012 Olympics. Ultimately, it issues a positive Shakespearean prognosis for freedom as a vital (in both senses), unending struggle.

Shakespeare for Freedom shows why Shakespeare has mattered for four hundred years, and why he still matters today.

EWAN FERNIE is Professor at the Shakespeare Institute (University of Birmingham) in Stratford-upon-Avon. He is joint editor of the *Shakespeare Now!* series and his books include *Shame in Shakespeare, Spiritual Shakespeares, Reconceiving the Renaissance, Redcrosse: Remaking Religious Poetry for Today's World, The Demonic: Literature and Experience, Thomas Mann and Shakespeare*, and the novel he co-authored with Simon Palfrey, *Macbeth, Macbeth*, which the philosopher Slavoj Žižek called 'a miracle, an instant classic'. In 2011, he co-wrote a civic liturgy for St George's Day which was performed in major cathedrals; and he is currently co-writing a play after Shakespeare's *Pericles* about immigration and sexual politics for the Royal Shakespeare Company. He is also working on the forgotten challenge of progressive culture in nineteenth-century Birmingham.

Shakespeare for Freedom

Why the Plays Matter

❦

EWAN FERNIE

The Shakespeare Institute, University of Birmingham

CAMBRIDGE
UNIVERSITY PRESS

University Printing House, Cambridge CB2 8BS, United Kingdom

One Liberty Plaza, 20th Floor, New York, NY 10006, USA

477 Williamstown Road, Port Melbourne, VIC 3207, Australia

4843/24, 2nd Floor, Ansari Road, Daryaganj, Delhi – 110002, India

79 Anson Road, #06–04/06, Singapore 079906

Cambridge University Press is part of the University of Cambridge.

It furthers the University's mission by disseminating knowledge in the pursuit of education, learning, and research at the highest international levels of excellence.

www.cambridge.org
Information on this title: www.cambridge.org/9781107130852
DOI: 10.1017/9781316452134

First published 2017

Printed in the United Kingdom by TJ International Ltd. Padstow Cornwall

A catalogue record for this publication is available from the British Library.

ISBN 978-1-107-13085-2 Hardback

For Theo and Kirsty

Contents

Figures

Acknowledgements

I have had the opportunity to present work-in-progress in many places, including the Kingston Shakespeare Seminar; the Global Shakespeare Seminar at the University of Warwick; the Deutsche Shakespeare Gesellschaft; the Shakespeare Association of America; the Universities of Durham, Munich, Verona, El Paso (Texas), Queensland, Sydney; and at British Council events in Belgrade and Budapest. I am grateful to my hosts and audiences for their hospitality and responses. Home events and colleagues at the Shakespeare Institute and the University of Birmingham have been equally helpful, and I owe as much as ever to my students, especially in this case Adam Seddon, Dave Paxton, Paul Hamilton, Richard O'Brien, Joy Leslie-Gibson, John Langdon and the graduates of the Shakespeare and Creativity MA. My shared projects with Paul Edmondson and Michael Dobson have made a crucial difference, and I've been buoyed up by Geraldine Collinge, Erica Whyman and Jacqui O'Hanlon at the RSC. Academic forebears in Shakespeare's fields of freedom, Peter Holbrook, Richard Wilson and Paul Kottman, have all offered generous encouragement. And my German collaborations with Tobias Döring have contributed richly, as have conversations with Bettina Boecker, Andreas Höfele and Claudia Olk. Zoltán Márkus was kind enough to welcome my Hungarian interests, and to check my Hungarian spelling. Lucy Kamenova also gave valuable help, particularly with my Kossuth researches. My mum and dad, Rab and Heather, and my in-laws, Shan and Charlie, have been stalwart supporters. And I am deeply grateful to encouraging angels Katharine Craik, Sally Baggott, David Fuller, Eric Mallin, David Ruiter, Rana Haddad, Kiernan Ryan, Zorica Bečanović–Nikolić, Liam Semler, Regina Schwartz, Margaret Tudeau-Clayton, Lucy Bailey and Annie Martirosyan – and my warm thanks also go to Annie for providing the index. Simon Palfrey tended to switch off when I tried to interest him in what he calls my forgotten men of history, but he's so entirely behind me and my projects that it didn't matter. Jane Grogan put me on to John Moriarty, and I benefited from rich exchanges with Richard Ashby and Brandon Chua. Jonathan Dollimore read some of my chapters even when he wasn't well, and I've tried to respond to his searching comments. Jeremy Newton read the whole book and his intelligent curiosity and enthusiasm have once more kept me going, as has the other life which he and Irene have so generously provided for me and my family at New Mills. I am indebted to the excellent anonymous readers at CUP and to the staff who helped me at the National Széchényi Library, the Folger Shakespeare Library, the Shakespeare Centre Library and Archive, the Cadbury Research Library of the University of Birmingham, Special Collections and Archives at the University of Leicester and the Shakespeare Institute Library. Peter Holland offered genial encouragement and printed the article which offers a kind of prospectus for this book in *Shakespeare Survey* (68). Some material from Chapter 9 was published in a collection of essays in honour of Andreas Höfele, *Acts of Crime: Lawlessness on the Early Modern Stage* (2015).

Profound thanks to my editor, Sarah Stanton, for her interest in the enterprise, and everything she did to help bring it to fruition, as well as for saying, 'Of course you're not free, Ewan; that's why you're writing a book about it!' Despite this, I tip my cap at Mida Zouhou for creating a little bit of freedom for me and others in Stratford. Prince died while I was completing the project, and I want to recall that his freedom really mattered to me when I was growing up in the 1980s. I also want to salute my mother's playful freedom, the freewheeling John Ford, and the vision of political freedom that so roused my grandfather, David Fernie. As always my deepest and most vital debt is to my wife, Deanna, who read the final manuscript and recommended cuts. The book is dedicated to our children, Theo and Kirsty, in the hope that they may always be free (in their own way of course . . .).

1

Reclaiming Shakespearean Freedom

§

What *good* is Shakespeare? The proliferation and specialisation of Shakespeare studies tend to have the unfortunate effect that we neglect the big question of why we bother with him at all. One of the great merits of Jonathan Bate's elegant and important book *The Genius of Shakespeare* was that it faced up to this question, but Bate's book is about twenty years old now, and we need to renew its effort.[1] After the World Shakespeare Festival that was central to the Cultural Olympiad of 2012, and the four-hundred-and-fiftieth birthday celebrations of 2014, as well as 2016's four-hundredth anniversary of the playwright's death, there is a real and frankly reasonable danger of everybody without a vested interest in the playwright simply getting sick of him. And there's no logical reason why that sickness shouldn't prove terminal, why Shakespeare shouldn't finally begin to die off in human culture. *If* Shakespeare matters – and I mean *still* matters – then in this context especially, we need a less academic reason than the 'aspectuality' and 'performativity' which Bate defines as salient qualities of Shakespeare's genius.[2] Bate is pointing to important truths – about Shakespeare's ambivalence, about his philosophical as well as aesthetic commitment to the realisation of character in action. But we now need a more direct and powerful way of expressing the poetry and reality of what Shakespeare has, in the past, given human life; in the wake of the 2012, 2014 and 2016 celebrations of Shakespeare, we need a better reason why we should continue to lavish such disproportionate attention on this long-dead Warwickshire poet-playwright. This book argues that Shakespeare means freedom. That is why the plays matter, and not just aesthetically but also in terms of the impact they historically have had and can continue to have on personal and political life in the world.

Of course Shakespeare's achievement – the beauty of his language and dramatic embodiment of life, the breadth of his insight – cannot be reduced to freedom, or to anything else for that matter; but in these pages, I will argue that in and through that breadth and beauty freedom nevertheless emerges as a supreme Shakespearean value, one which has played an important part in the history of culture and which we need to reclaim now. But what is freedom, and what does it mean to invoke it as a surpassing value in Shakespeare? It's impossible to formulate a satisfactory answer quickly. For in the plays as in life, freedom is richly various; if that's one reason for its complex appeal and poetry, it also makes it hard to get hold of. We might instinctively *know* what it means, but it's difficult to conceptualise and *say* what it means. Shakespeare's plays crystallise a number of different kinds of freedom dramatically, and that can give us a first steer on what it is and why it matters in general.

One central kind of freedom, in the Western tradition, is *the freedom to be yourself*. Such existential freedom is more comprehensive and profound than the freedom to *do what you like*, though that certainly contributes to it. As the famed creator of some of the world's most vital and substantial characters, Shakespeare affords excellent examples of this existential freedom. Take Falstaff, for instance. The very fatness of the fat knight expresses his condition of superabundant liberty, as becomes apparent the moment we meet him. Falstaff's first words in Shakespeare frame a question you'd think was innocent enough, 'Now, Hal, what time of day is it, lad?' But instead of saying five past three, for example, Hal lays bare Falstaff's freedom from such distractions. 'Unless hours were cups of sack, and minutes capons, and clocks the tongues of bawds, and dials the signs of leaping-houses, and the blessed sun himself a fair hot wench in flame-coloured taffeta,' he says, 'I see no reason why thou shouldst be so superfluous to demand the time of day' (*1 Henry IV*, 1.2.1–10).[3] Time, in this utterance, stands for duty, industry, self-control. Hal's Salvador-Dalí-like metamorphosis of its elements and appurtenances into the pleasures of drinking, eating and sex announces Falstaff's emancipation from such constraint. And yet, this speech does more than afford memorable images of Falstaff's freedom; it *participates* in that freedom in a crescendo of imagined indulgences – from drink, to food, to sex; from the tongues of bawds (a foretaste of tongues of whores), to 'leaping-houses' (whose name anticipates energetic release), to that 'fair hot wench in flame-coloured taffeta' (a phrase leaning towards luxurious climax). That such an irresistible creature has morphed out of 'the blessed sun himself' has a blasphemous implication; in the theatre, 'blessed sun' could be heard as 'blessed *son*'. This is a speech which doesn't just transgress against conventional religion but begins to remake it in the image of Falstaff's subversive and sensuous freedom, with the crucified messiah transmuting into a red-hot prostitute.

Falstaff is of course delighted by this. 'Indeed you come near me now, Hal,' he murmurs (1.2.11), before continuing the game with his own, differently alluring fantasy: 'when thou art king,' he says, 'let not us that are squires of the night's body be called thieves of the day's beauty. Let us be "Diana's foresters", "gentlemen of the shade", "minions of the moon"' (1.2.20–3). Such wistful phrasing has a cool and elegant dignity clearly meant to counterpoint Hal's hot whore. And it's an excellent joke of course – one where the fat knight reveals by cold juxtaposition Hal's warm imaginative involvement in his own supposed excesses, and even as he does so stakes hilarious claim to a stately composure that is patently quite beyond him. But it's not just a joke. It also intimates, however teasingly, a transvaluation of values, whereby Falstaff recasts unbridled freedom in such a way as asserts its potential for beauty and dignity.

In this conversation between Falstaff and Hal, we see how fertile freedom is, how Falstaff's unbridled life stimulates Hal's wit, which in turn provokes Falstaff's epiphany. Harry calls Falstaff 'fat-witted' (1.2.2). He means hung over, half-asleep; but he also, surely, means to acknowledge, stimulate and point out to the audience the expansive largeness of Falstaff's mind. When, in both parts of *Henry IV*, Falstaff takes up his own 'great belly' as a theme for comic celebration, he further encourages us to see his fatness as but the outward and visible sign of an uncontainable spirit of freedom (*2 Henry IV*, 1.2.133–4). 'Well, the truth is, Sir John,' says the Lord Chief Justice, 'you live in great infamy'; with his hands on his vast girth, Falstaff answers, 'He that buckles himself in my belt cannot live in less' (*2 Henry IV*, 1.2.125–7). Falstaff cannot be contained by ordinary decorums, nor can he even be confined by the play's end. More than any of Shakespeare's characters, he steps from play to play. And he steps through history too; that is why it's so easy to imagine him, even now, spilling out of his trousers while delightfully destabilising any given civic occasion, office function, family wedding. In Falstaff, we touch something essential: the unrestrained subversive freedom of Shakespeare's own imagination.

Falstaff not only nails the freedom to be yourself; he magnificently exemplifies its value. But freedom can also take an almost opposite form, that of *the freedom to be different*. The fat knight gives us the scandalous freedom of a mature person who lives his (or her) own life entirely beyond respectability, but Shakespeare equally speaks to the kind of freedom most associated in our time with adolescence or mid-life crisis. This is the freedom not of being (what you are) but *becoming* (what you might be), the freedom to cast off all that you have been till now in a sudden, insurgent desire to be otherwise. One Shakespearean character who exemplifies this self-subverting freedom is Rosalind. At the beginning of *As You Like It*, she clearly is a good girl, an obedient daughter; but this limits her freedom, which is why, when she's forced to leave home, she goes with such 'swashing', emancipated glee 'to liberty, and not to banishment' (1.3.114, 132). By assuming a male alter ego, she lays claim to a whole new self, one which sets her free not just from familial and social duty but even from her identity as a woman. For her, freedom isn't so much a charter to be and enjoy your self as the liberty to destroy your established identity in the act of stepping into a whole new existence. And this, too, is a very Shakespearean thing, exactly what any actor must do each time he (or she) throws himself (or herself) into a new part. Such freedom to be otherwise is hard-wired into the very technology of the form that Shakespeare works in.

A further, still more venturesome kind of freedom is *the freedom to enter evil*. Rosalind's and Falstaff's freedom is subversive in an enjoyable, relatively safe fashion. We experience Rosalind's new life as Ganymede as marvellous self-expansion; Falstaff, too, remains essentially delightful, because we are not encouraged to think too long or hard about those he is letting down or exploiting. And yet, Falstaff's freedom does have its cruelties – his indifference to his soldiers, the extra wound he dishes out to Hotspur's corpse. But if in Falstaff Shakespeare starts to open up the morally dubious side of freedom, elsewhere he goes much further. When at the beginning of *King Lear*, for instance, Edmund repudiates traditional constraints and beliefs – not least about his illegitimacy – he may remind us of Rosalind or Falstaff, but his is a wilfully illegitimate kind of freedom, one which spins a positively immoral vocation out of his illegitimate birth. It initiates a career of deliberate and murderous treachery, and it can't be excused as high spirits or recuperated into any kind of decency. If this darkens Edmund's dramatic life, at the same time it lends it an extra, glamorous power. Edmund puts it in tumescent terms: 'I grow; I prosper. / Now gods, stand up for bastards!' (1.2.21–2). Wicked freedom stands revealed as erotic intensification.

In Edmund, self-assertive freedom takes a turn for the worse, but freedom is equally found in Shakespeare in forms of life which are opposite to self-aggrandisement. Rosalind's 'swashing' liberation may be one of the glories of *As You Like It*, but Oliver's attempts at self-assertion in the same play are not at all successful. It is only when he is saved by the younger brother he has been jealously trying to put down that he is liberated – liberated *from self* into a life of love. Looking back on his earlier, unregenerate life, he ventures, beautifully:

> 'Twas I, but 'tis not I. I do not shame
> To tell you what I was, since my conversion
> So sweetly tastes, being the thing I am.
>
> (4.3.134–6)

Falstaff finds freedom in being what he is, whereas Rosalind finds it in becoming what she's not. Edmund forges a glamorous kind of freedom in wicked self-assertion, but Oliver tastes sweet freedom only when he's shocked out of self-interest. Freedom in Shakespeare is unpredictable, and the fact that we don't ever quite know where or when it might transpire makes an important contribution to the interest and appeal of the plays, both for the characters and the audiences.

I propose that Shakespeare can help us see freedom less as a substantial thing or concept and more as a specific and welcoming disposition towards life. For the plays suggest that the forms of freedom are as various as life is; they suggest freedom can be found wherever life is affirmed. As often as not in Shakespeare, freedom is a thrilling surprise, a kind of secular blessing or grace. You might expect to discover or secure it in triumph, but Antony and Cleopatra find it instead in death, 'which shackles accidents and bolts up change', and failure, which enables their splendid exit from the cramping conditions of culture and mortality (*Antony and Cleopatra*, 5.2.6). As we shall see in the course of this book, the same might be said for Hamlet.

Freedom in Shakespeare is an open question. We have only just begun to respond to its presence in the plays, but I hope I have done enough to demonstrate that it requires a wide-angled approach. I want this book to do justice to the difficult and differentiated breadth of Shakespearean freedom, not to narrow the lens a priori and make it sharper or neater. It is the complexity of freedom, including its moral complexity, that makes it interesting, alluring, sometimes tragic. In what follows, I will try to incorporate as much as I can of what freedom is in the plays, as well as something of what Shakespearean freedom becomes through the modern epoch, and what it might do for contemporary life and culture.

But I am leaving an important thing out. I have suggested that freedom of the most intense and existential kind is the freedom of being or becoming yourself. I have also suggested that freedom is self-sovereignty, self-possession and sheer enjoyment of life, that it is a welcoming and affirmative disposition towards life, wherever that is found. But so far I have been dealing only with examples of individual freedom, and freedom has an important collective aspect. Self-sovereignty and enjoyment of life work, I think, for national and larger political as well as subjective freedoms; they help explain something of the excitement and warmth of feeling which nationalism or broader identifications such as Zionism, Christendom or Pan-Slavism can involve. At the end of this chapter and elsewhere in the book, we will see that nationalism has often derived a powerful impetus from Shakespearean freedom. But there are tensions between subjective, familial, national and larger political identifications as alternative spheres of freedom, and these are tensions which sometimes tear apart the lives of individuals, families and nations. We don't have to look far for Shakespearean evidence. It is clear that Juliet transgresses against and compromises the Capulets' sense of themselves by falling for their enemy's son, and it's clear that this entails agonising consequences for her as well as them. *Coriolanus* presents a more complex case. The hero here becomes convinced that Rome is falling short of its own proper *Romanitas*, leaving him alone as the embodiment of its properly 'free contempt' for the mere needs and dispositions of the plebs (2.3.189). That is why when the city banishes him, Coriolanus feels able to say back to Rome, 'I banish you' (3.3.127). But what complicates this further is that Rome has banished Coriolanus at the behest of the people, who are agitating for a new, more democratic kind of freedom in a new kind of

Rome. The way they see it, Coriolanus doesn't stand for the freedom of the city at all but rather for the exclusive, unjust and outrageous freedom of his class.

All of Shakespeare's characters have to fight for their freedom through and sometimes against the larger freedoms of family, class, nation and so on; but beyond or perhaps below this, the basic sociality of Shakespeare's art – the fact that even his most splendid characters can only secure their freedom by interacting with others – lends Shakespearean drama an inherent political suggestiveness. How might such freedom be extended – even shared out equally – among the *dramatis personae*? What sorts of interaction, on and off stage, tend to promote the freedoms which Shakespeare dramatises? Some kinds of freedom (Oliver's) are clearly compatible with the free flourishing of others, but others (Edmund's) are actually forged by deliberately violating them. An *excessively* generalised freedom – which we might think of in contemporary terms of 'political correctness' – is likely to diminish the quality of freedom as a feeling for and identification with life. And if that's the case, as a society we need to know what scope, moral or otherwise, there is for the singular, amoral and even immoral freedom of the individual in relation to the politics of freedom in general.

This book will argue that freedom in Shakespeare is always a struggle for freedom. Freedom in Shakespeare is also a struggle between characters and from play to play over what freedom *means*. And it is a struggle that is played out time and again in the life and lives, and progressive political movements, which Shakespeare has stimulated or inspired. This struggle will never be over. Unlike Wagner, Shakespeare makes no attempt to give us an overarching myth. He offers only a series of plays. One comes to an end; another begins. There is no final, definitive synthesis. And in spite of the links and resonances between them, each play retains its own separate integrity. *The Tempest* cannot wholly absorb *King Lear*, or for that matter *Troilus and Cressida*, or *A Midsummer Night's Dream*. Shakespeare expresses the unavoidable and unending power of contingency. Even after Shakespeare – even after the four-hundredth anniversary of his death – life goes on. My hope in this book is that reclaiming Shakespearean freedom might at the same time encourage a creative and hopeful orientation to its ever-new possibilities, without evading the moral complexities and pitfalls that entails.

The time is ripe, I believe, for a bold new argument in favour of Shakespearean freedom. In recent years, there have been striking intimations of a new recognition of it in mainstream literary and popular culture, but these hopeful signs have been snuffed out by a crippling diffidence about the good of the arts in general, and of Shakespeare in particular – as we shall now see.

1 What Good Are the Arts?

John Carey raised that big question in his book of the same title in 2005, and the book's popular success suggests a new appetite for it.[4] If, on the one hand, this conveys a hunger in contemporary culture for aesthetic meaning and value, on the other, it probably confesses a creeping suspicion that the arts aren't really any good at all. Carey offers some uncomfortable and, I will suggest, ultimately unsatisfactory conclusions. But, at the same time, he leads us towards the case for Shakespeare I want to make in these pages, as well as demonstrating the difficulties which in our time we appear to have in making it.

What, asks Carey, is a work of art? 'My answer,' he writes, is 'A work of art is anything that anyone has ever considered a work of art, though it may be a work of art only for that one person.'[5] The trouble is that this gives no grounds on which to build the case for aesthetic value or appreciation. Is art morally improving then? Carey doubts it, citing the French dandy anarchist poet Laurent Tailhade (a friend of Wilfred Owen) who, when a bomb was thrown into the French parliament in 1893, said that the victims didn't matter so long as the gesture was beautiful. Carey points to Hans and Shulamith Kreitler's scientific assessment of the *Psychology of the Arts*, which concluded that 'the widely shared belief that art can instruct the public, and help to attain a better state of affairs, lacks any factual backing.'[6] And he gives short shrift to the mystical account whereby art facilitates in the beholder states of transcendent oneness with the Universe. This, he scoffs, is simply a fanciful invention of the mid-eighteenth century.[7] Moreover, where people do report being ravished by art into states of ecstasy, it tends to make them selfish and disengaged rather than better people, he suggests, pointing to a 1960s survey by Marghanita Laski.[8] To nail the point that art appreciation doesn't necessarily make you a better person, Carey then turns to Frederic Spotts's book

Hitler and the Power of Aesthetics, which puts paid to the comforting fiction that Hitler had no taste by showing how the worst moral monster of the twentieth century was simultaneously the greatest art collector of all time.[9]

But if he gives up on the arts in general, Carey still wants to make a case for the importance of literature, and of Shakespeare especially. He claims that 'literature gives you ideas to think with', but painting can also do that – think of cubism, and of the fact that much contemporary art is deliberately 'conceptual'.[10] Carey lauds Shakespeare's 'superior indistinctness', for being 'vivid and nebulous'.[11] But Beethoven is no less superior and vivid and, given the non-linguistic nature of his medium, he is more indistinct and nebulous (or, if we want to put it more positively, more suggestive, less tied to denotative meaning). As the last sally of his book, Carey writes, 'If I had to choose one single Shakespearean thought to cling to when all else fails, it would not be from any of the great plays or major characters but from Parolles in *All's Well that Ends Well*.' The Shakespearean thought that Carey has in mind is the one Parolles utters after being utterly humiliated and ruined: 'simply the thing I am / Shall make me live' (4.4.310–11). The very last sentence of *What Good Are the Arts?* reads as follows: 'That thought may be useful for all of us in the end, and it is a different thought for each of us, because each of us must read "the thing I am" in a different way.'[12] It's hardly a knock-down endorsement of Shakespeare's value, or of the good of the arts in general.

But what is interesting about it is the sheer tentativeness with which it intimates an argument about Shakespearean freedom which it somehow isn't ready or able to own. Carey appreciates Shakespeare's almost musical combination of vividness and openness to interpretation. 'Simply the thing I am / Shall make me live': the fact that he adopts this as his own last word on the question of aesthetic value suggests an irreducible freedom to be oneself is not just the hallmark of Shakespeare's achievement but the good of the arts in general. And Carey's gloss on the phrase – 'each of us must read "the thing I am" in a different way' – imputes a comparable freedom to Shakespeare's readers. All told, he implicitly evokes a Shakespeare who portrays free individuals and submits them to the free judgement of individuals whose freedom their freedom reflects and affirms, but he can't quite bring himself to say this. And we find this same powerful but disablingly abashed desire to affirm Shakespearean freedom in mainstream popular culture as well.

2   London 2012

Perhaps the most weirdly compelling and certainly the most public invocation of Shakespeare in our time occurred when Kenneth Branagh opened the Cultural Olympiad of 2012 watched by an estimated global TV audience of some 900 million.[13] Costumed in top hat and fake whiskers as the pioneering Victorian engineer Isambard Kingdom Brunel, Branagh nonetheless spoke these words: 'Be not afeard. This isle is full of noises, / Sounds, and sweet airs, that give delight and hurt not.' Since you're reading this book, you probably know that they originate from Caliban in *The Tempest* (3.2.135–6), and that they're nothing to do with the famous engineer. But one wonders what the watching millions who *didn't* know their Shakespearean provenance made of them.

The isle is full of noises?!

And even if you were one of the relative few, in the stadium or tuning in at home, who got the reference, you were likely to be bemused. As the first and most imposingly spoken words in the whole Olympic Opening Ceremony, they were meant to function as a kind of headline or even moral for the games, which moreover had a 'Caliban's Dream' theme song. And the enormous 'Olympic Bell' – struck by Team GB cyclist Bradley Wiggins to announce the stage was set for Branagh – was inscribed: 'LONDON 2012 / BE NOT AFEARD; / THE ISLE IS FULL OF NOISES'. In *The Tempest*, Caliban is the solitary indigenous inhabitant of an obscure island seemingly not much bigger than an indoor theatre, as well as, in Erin Sullivan's phrase, 'one of the most politically disenfranchised and dispossessed characters in all of Shakespeare's plays'.[14] Why was he speaking, through Brunel, for this unprecedentedly public presentation of Britishness? How was his poignant moment of aboriginal inwardness meant to relate to Brunel's achievements in engineering? And when Branagh positively hollered the climactic words of what was originally intended to be a quietly soothing as well as passionately inspired speech from the midst of Elgar's swelling 'Nimrod' variation 'in a manner', as

Sullivan rightly observes, 'more reminiscent of Henry V before his armies', what kind of triumph was being proclaimed and celebrated?[15] And how was Caliban's epiphany connected to the energetic dramatisation of the industrial revolution which succeeded it, seemingly to Branagh / Brunel's great pride and satisfaction?[16] What was going on in this strange appropriation of Shakespeare?

I should say at this point that it's not unusual, in modern times, for Caliban to stand for something beyond the purview of the play, and what he typically stands for is freedom. Aimé Césaire, the Martinique politician and poet of *negritude*, made him an icon of anti-colonialist resistance in his celebrated Shakespeare adaptation *Une tempête* (1969).[17] In Césaire's play, Caliban's 'first word is "Uhuru!" which, as Bate observes, is Swahili for "freedom" and 'his last utterance is a triumphant repetition of that word in French, "La liberté, ohe la liberté"'.[18] Of course in Shakespeare, this ecstatic freedom in fact boils down to Caliban's self-subjugation to a drunken sailor; but Laurence M. Porter comments on the way in which Césaire rescues it from this 'powerfully ironic context', turning it instead 'into the lucid affirmation of a new-found dignity'.[19] In a vein not untypical of *Shakespeare: The Invention of the Human* (1998), Harold Bloom fulminates that 'a poignant but cowardly (and murderous) half-human creature' has 'become an African-Caribbean heroic Freedom Fighter.' 'This,' he goes on, 'is not even a weak misreading; anyone who arrives at that view is simply not interested in reading the play at all.'[20] But Caliban's potential to speak to the struggle for freedom is unarguably present in the play itself when he says, 'This island's mine by Sycorax, my mother' (1.2.334–5). The most enthusiastically inspired critical response comes from Leslie Fiedler. 'Even drunk,' says Fiedler, 'Caliban remains a poet and a visionary, singing [a] new freedom in a new kind of song':

No more dams I'll make for fish
  Nor fetch in firing
  At requiring
Nor scrape trenchering, nor wash dish.
  'Ban, 'ban, Cacaliban
  Has a new master. – Get a new man!
Freedom, high-day! High-day, freedom! Freedom high-day, freedom!

(2.2.171–7)

Noting 'its Whitmanian long last lines,' Fiedler concludes rhapsodically: '[Caliban] has created something new under the sun, the first American poem.'[21]

Fiedler, writing in 1973, sees Caliban as not just 'the American Indian', but one who augurs a new epoch of sensual, aesthetic, cultural, racial and political freedom for all. What has happened in the critical tradition more broadly is that the historical struggle against imperialism has definitively let Caliban's potential for freedom out of the bottle and neither Bloom nor anyone else can get it back in.

Still, even in these liberal readings dating from the last half of the last century, Caliban remains a remote, marginal, oppositional figure, labouring far away from the centre of power to reclaim what is, aboriginally, his own. No-one, surely, expected him to turn up at the most public presentation of Britishness for decades, wearing a top hat, coolly passing himself off as Brunel, and as it were tapping his cane on British soil and saying, '*This island's mine.*' Certainly, in 1984, after race riots in Brixton, the St Lucian Nobel Laureate Derek Walcott imagined something very different:

> With the stampeding hiss and scurry of green lemmings,
> midsummer leaves race to extinction like the roar
> of a Brixton riot tunnelled by water hoses;
> they seethe towards autumn's fire – it is in their nature,
> being men as well as leaves, to die for the sun.
> The leaf stems tug at their chains, the branches bending
> like Boer cattle under Tory whips that drag every wagon
> nearer to apartheid. And, for me, that closes
> the child's fairy tale of an antic England – fairy rings,
> thatched cottages fenced with dog roses,
> a green gale lifting the hair of Warwickshire.
> 'I was there to add some colour to British theatre.
> 'But the blacks can't do Shakespeare, they have no experience.'
> This was true. Their thick heads bled with rancour
> when the riot police and the skinheads exchanged quips
> you could trace to the Sonnets, or the Moor's eclipse.
> Praise had bled my lines white of any more anger,
> and snow had inducted me into white fellowships,
> while Calibans howled down the barred streets of an empire

that began with Caedmon's raceless dew, and is ending
in the alleys of Brixton, burning like Turner's ships.[22]

Walcott's is a complex poem which struggles to reject Shakespearean
Englishness. Its imagery is fractious, discontinuous, hard to get a fix on.
We begin somewhere not in England, with lemmings: in the Arctic?
'Midsummer leaves' make a brief appearance only to be rushed unnatu-
rally fast to a contradictory 'extinction': by water hoses towards autumn's
fire. But if 'leaves' is a verb as well as a noun, and 'race' is a noun as well as
a verb, there is a chilling pun in 'midsummer leaves race to extinction',
which prepares us for the suggestion that the leaves are men 'as well as
leaves', and that they 'die for the sun': men from the tropics, black men?
At the same time, they remain leaves, their stems enchained, and so equally
slaves? The tree of race is somewhere behind all this. Its branches are said
to be 'bending like Boer cattle under Tory whips that drag every wagon
nearer apartheid'; and with that the poem's angry line of thought seems
itself to 'branch' out more clearly and simply, yet only for the branch of
pastoral poetry to snap off for good. In this poem, a recognition of the riots
gradually but inevitably overwhelms what remains of a Shakespearean
impulse to delight in a green and pleasant England. That fantasy, now
that it has been exposed as such, can be indulged and in terms that
delightfully suggest Anne Hathaway's cottage in Shottery: fenced with
dog roses, a fairy ring in the garden, a green gale lifting the hair of
Warwickshire. But it can be indulged only in valediction, as a lost thing
in a children's book which has to be shut forever. The Olympic Opening
Ceremony dramatised how green and pleasant England gave way to the
industrial revolution; for Walcott, its innocence is fatally compromised by
political failure. Walcott, also a playwright, was in the UK, his poem tells
us, in order 'to add some colour to British theatre'. At which point an
anonymous voice immediately objects – 'But the blacks can't do
Shakespeare, they have no experience' – and, surprisingly, the poem
concurs (because Shakespeare has to be forsworn for political reasons?).
It then shockingly proceeds to align Shakespeare's sonnets and plays with
'quips' (racist jokes?) traded between 'the riot police' and 'skinheads' acting
in favour of 'the Moor's eclipse'. In the context of what was then happening
in Brixton, this 'quip', a reference to *Othello*, is an especially horrible one,
a casually poetical euphemising of brutal race hatred. Behind it are black

men and women from Brixton, their thick heads, as the poem tells us, bleeding with rancour.

And Walcott evidently wants to stand with *them*, not with Shakespeare, the coppers and the skins; but he finds that his own verse has been blanched by praise, snow, 'white fellowships'. He wants to stand with the Calibans whom he so vividly pictures at the end of his poem urgently howling down the barred streets of an empire. And he wants to stand with them in solidarity not just with their suffering but also with their rage. Moot here is the ambiguity of the preposition 'down'; Walcott's Calibans are howling 'down' in the sense of *along* barred streets of empire, but they also are howling so violently as to bring those streets and that empire down, to an end. And with the empire, the poem insists, must come its literature, even if it is a tradition so venerable as to stretch as far back as Caedmon: the first Anglo-Saxon poet. The dewiness of this origin has its wistful beauty but only till we remember that pastoral has been exposed as a lie in this poem, and while it contemplates Brixton and its resonances with apartheid, it can no more accept that English literature is 'raceless'. And yet – Walcott cannot find or forge a place entirely outside English literature and culture. Caliban is his last figure of resistance, and the final, apocalyptical conflagration it imagines remains, at the same time, a spectacular Turner sunset. Walcott's poem demonstrates the cultural-historical reasons why Shakespeare should in fact to be associated with unfreedom, but at the same time it confesses that it can't find a way of imagining freedom which is not itself Shakespearean.[23]

For Césaire, Caliban is a Caribbean freedom fighter; for Fiedler, he is a liberated Native American, fighting for and exemplifying a condition of personal and political freedom which should be of interest to us all. The Caliban who comes home to London in Walcott's impressive poem does so as one of many, howling down the barred streets of an empire and setting it ablaze. It's true, then, that Caliban has had a further, politically significant life beyond the limits of *The Tempest*, but the nature of that life makes it more rather than less extraordinary that he should have turned up in a top hat to speak for the whole history and reality of British culture.

And yet, and as if to insist that the inclusion of Caliban's speech wasn't just a casual or thoughtless gesture, it was spoken again on the Olympic stage, at the Closing Ceremony, two weeks later. This time Caliban's words were voiced not by Branagh, but by Timothy Spall, another very established British actor, and Spall wasn't straightforwardly playing Caliban anymore than Branagh had. In fact, he outdid Branagh-as-Brunel in the guise of that acme of all British heroes, including Shakespeare: Winston Churchill. Spall-as-Churchill emerged from the top of a model of Big Ben to puff on a cigar and muse that the isle is full of noises; and it *was* full of noises, what with the excited crowd, the emphatically English music and the strange pageant of circling lorries, at least one of which was papered with a story headlined with the first line of a Shakespeare sonnet: 'My Mistress's Eyes Are Nothing Like the Sun.' Spall-Churchill-Caliban's delivery turned out to lack the clarity and authority of the otherwise equally bemusing Branagh-Brunel version, and the actor ultimately presented a rather pathetic prospect, subsiding into silence, marooned up Big Ben on an enormous roundabout, around which traffic continued to orbit senselessly . . .

But the Games still didn't give up on Shakespeare. They had another stab at incorporating Shakespearean significance into a third set-piece ceremony, though in terms of aesthetic confidence and impact this was the worst of the three. Its occasion, this time, was the Paralympic Opening Ceremony. Where Branagh and Spall had played Caliban at one remove, Ian McKellen now played Prospero more directly, but the words he spoke to a wheelchair-bound Miranda, played by disabled actress Nicola Miles-Wildin, weren't Shakespeare's:

Miranda! Miranda! Go out into the world! Will you be, for all of us gathering here, our eyes, our ears and our hearts? Shine your light on the beautiful diversity of humanity . . . Look up, stretch your wings and fly. Will you take this journey for all of us and will you set us free?[24]

These sentiments are admirable, but the vaguely iambic and heightened language is strained and repetitive: 'Miranda! Miranda!' 'our eyes, our ears and our hearts'. The last sentence is a bit coercive. I hope that reading Walcott's poem has suggested language sometimes has to come under strain in order to express experiential and political complexity, but McKellen's speech is strained by less than persuasive looseness. The worst phrase bears the most weight: 'beautiful diversity of humanity' is clichéd, excessively polysyllabic and awkward ('diversity', 'humanity'). But then this whole episode was perilously close to bathos throughout, and all the more so given the sentimentally overblown music and the fact that

Miranda and her wheelchair ultimately drifted off towards their brave new world in a sail boat that was simultaneously an upturned brick-red umbrella like something out of a children's TV show.

Branagh's was the best, but in truth none of these Shakespearean interludes really worked; certainly none of them had anything like the fierce power and resonance of the Walcott poem. It would be easy just to mock it all and have done with it, but I think it would be wrong to do so. Prospero, in *The Tempest*, talks of setting Ariel as 'free as mountain winds', and there is provocative potential in the idea of making Shakespeare's Miranda both a wheelchair user and an avatar of a different kind of freedom – a freedom which, presumably, doesn't so much transcend limitation as it is found within and transfigures limitation (*The Tempest*, 1.2.502–3). We have seen, earlier, that Caliban has inspired dissident critics and artists, 'howling down the barred streets of an empire', and in that context there's something exciting about him suddenly storming the centre and repossessing and even speaking for the history that has oppressed and excluded him. Indeed, it's a rather wildly exciting idea to imagine him seizing not the Bastille but Big Ben and assuming the authority of Churchill! My point is that Caliban's interventions at the Olympics nearly suggested a transformation of history and politics from within. Given his aboriginal credentials, making him politically exemplary does perhaps run the ideological risk of playing into a sinister ideology of blood and soil; but this danger is considerably minimised by the fact that the speech chosen as a central motif for the Olympics was one of soothing and tender susceptibility: '*Be not afeared . . .*'. Making it – rather than 'we shall fight them on the beaches' – Churchill's representative speech suggests a more peaceable kind of solidarity. As does making this same tender speech the stimulus to a revolution in industry. For all of the criticism I have offered, I also want to honour the fact that the use of Shakespeare within the ceremonies of the 2012 London Olympics got close to dramatising an extraordinarily comprehensive liberation, bringing the formerly excluded and despised to the centre of power and placing freedom at the heart of a gentler, more sensitive politics.

But if Caliban and the wheelchair-bound Miranda might have become Olympics icons of Shakespearean freedom, London 2012 muffled if it didn't altogether muff this; and it foundered on a crucial lack of confidence. Paul Prescott reports that Danny Boyle, the director of the Opening

Ceremony, told Culture Secretary Jeremy Hunt, 'the whole thing is based on *The Tempest*.'[25] When Frank Cottrell Boyce, the screenwriter who scripted the event, articulated the dearest, most serious message of the Opening Ceremony in the Olympic Programme, he called it:

A single golden thread of purpose – the idea of Jerusalem – of the better world, the world of real freedom and real equality, a world that can be built through the prosperity of industry, through the caring nation that built the welfare state, through the joyous energy of popular culture, through the dream of universal communication. A belief that we can build Jerusalem. And that it will be for everyone.[26]

Amen to that: however hard it would be actually to bring it to pass, it surely is a worthy aspiration. But you will notice that Shakespeare has entirely dropped out of it. Questioned specifically about Caliban's role, Boyce was evidently embarrassed: 'If you analyse why, I'd say I don't really know why – it's a madly inappropriate speech in a way. Why the hell would Brunel be quoting Caliban?'[27] Like Carey, the London Olympics wanted to commit powerfully and unequivocally to Shakespearean freedom but somehow it just couldn't.

3   The Robben Island Bible

Still, Shakespeare and freedom came together elsewhere in 2012, in 'Shakespeare: Staging the World': the impressive Olympic exhibition at the British Museum that ran from the 19th of July to the 25th of November, curated by Dora Thornton and Jonathan Bate. The prize and culminating exhibit there was the so-called Robben Island Bible, Sonny Venkatrathnam's copy of the Alexander Shakespeare, disguised as a Hindi religious text and signed by Venkatrathnam and thirty-three other South African political prisoners. It was opened at the page where the name 'N. R. Mandela' and the date 16.12.77 appear against this passage:

> Cowards die many times before their deaths,
> The valiant never taste of death but once.
> Of all the wonders that I yet have heard,
> It seems to me most strange that men should fear,
> Seeing that death, a necessary end,
> Will come when it will come.
>
> (2.2.32–7)[28]

If the Olympic Ceremonies flirted with but in the end failed definitively to commit to Shakespearean freedom, you'd think the Olympic exhibition would now make the most of the remarkable fact that the greatest and most celebrated freedom fighter of our time had signed his name to a passage of Shakespeare while in prison. But even though this was clearly the reason for exhibiting the Robben Island Bible in the first place, 'Shakespeare: Staging the World' did not do this.

In the last words of the exhibition catalogue, Bate and Thornton write about the Robben Island Bible, 'Shakespeare's life did not cease with the "necessary end" of his death in 1616: his plays continue to live, and to give life, four centuries on, all the way across the great theatre of the world.'[29] The trouble with this pleasingly emphatic confirmation of Shakespeare's universality and transcendence is that it pulls in exactly the opposite direction to Mandela's identification with Shakespeare's words. What Mandela recognises in the passage from Shakespeare he signs is the necessity of dying, and dying moreover what could very well be a violent death; what he *gets* from recognising this is presumably encouragement and the comfort of knowing that something like his experience has been imaginatively shared by the world's greatest writer. It is ironic that this heroic acknowledgement of death accomplished via reading Shakespeare becomes, for Bate and Thornton, a proof of the Bard's deathless universality. They prefer aesthetic transcendence to mortal risk – and who wouldn't? Well, the answer to that is Mandela wouldn't or, rather, didn't.[30] His reading of Shakespeare embraces mortal risk. Bate's and Thornton's immediate restatement of the myth that Shakespeare is deathless and universal to that extent betrays Mandela's reason for putting his name to the lines he chose. Neil MacGregor, the then director of the British Museum, in an overlapping book titled *Shakespeare's Restless World*, which presents a related exhibition of 'an unexpected history in twenty objects', also ends with the Robben Island Bible. And his conclusion? 'The Robben Island Bible resoundingly vindicates the great truth that everyone can see in Shakespeare the mirror of their own predicament.'[31] Maybe, but what about the great and much more urgently specific truth that you've got to find the courage to die, even if that means to die violently, a truth which Mandela apparently found in Shakespeare, and one which may very well have stiffened his resolve? What about the very particular meaning that Shakespeare had in a bleak South African prison in the 1970s where Mandela was still a political prisoner with no hope of release?

If Bate, Thornton and MacGregor pull too quickly away from Mandela's literally death-defying heroism into a more generalised celebration of Shakespeare's deathless universality, David Schalkwyk's sensitively rigorous treatment in *Hamlet's Dreams: The Robben Island Shakespeare* (2012) sells somewhat short the conjunction between Shakespeare and freedom which the Robben Island Bible suggests for opposite reasons. Himself a white South African as well as a Shakespeare professor, Schalkwyk's aversion 'to the exaggeration of Shakespeare's influence or importance' is redoubled by his sense of his own share of responsibility, despite an impressively liberal record, for South Africa's violent history.[32] This is a humbling quality of Schalkwyk's work, and I say so because you only have to think of the massive inequalities all across the globe to see that any of us in a position to write or read a book like this are ourselves guiltily complicit. To date, politically progressive cultural history has tended to be written in unproblematic solidarity with the victims – almost everyone will agree they were wronged and shouldn't have been. And of course such recognition matters; but if we are to change history in the future, what perhaps is needed more is recognition of our own guilt and a change of heart. What's needed in literary terms is a more repentant kind of cultural history, one written by the former oppressors, or at least by those who are associated with and have benefited from oppression. For Schalkwyk, the Robben Island Bible is a *temptation* – a temptation to a self-exculpating association of Shakespeare and freedom that will justify the way he has spent his life. Instead, and without in any way denying Shakespeare's aesthetic and moral interest – he in fact is a fine reader of the plays in the humanist tradition – Schalkwyk leaves us with a question, one which is as urgent as it is awkward: in the face of real, present-day oppression and suffering, what reason have we to continue praising the author who has already been praised above all others, and who, in South Africa, was moreover part of the assumed supremacy of white over black that fuelled and sustained oppression and suffering?[33]

And yet, Schalkwyk's sensitive anxiety about claiming too much for Shakespeare, and by extension for his own vocation as a white South African Shakespearean, perhaps prevents him from formulating the powerful connection between Shakespeare and freedom which the

Robben Island Shakespeare really does seem to suggest. Venkatrathnam has said: 'About six months before my due release date, I circulated *The Complete Works of Shakespeare* and asked my comrades there to select a line or passage that appealed to them and sign it. All of them chose lines of passages that inspired them and strengthened the resolve for the struggle.'[34] And as Schalkwyk notes, the first signature in the Robben Island is 'S. K. Venkatrathnam': 'His name appears in confident italics that expand across the space on the title page below the names of Shakespeare and the book's editor, Peter Alexander.'[35] Venkatrathnam's signature is thus, as Schalkwyk suggests, not just a simple assertion of ownership of the physical book but also a claim to moral parity with the two names it follows. I would add that, taken together with the other signatures which Venkatrathnam collected, it is an assertion on behalf of the political prisoners on Robben Island of equal ownership of and identification with the whole human world that Shakespeare depicted, which has since been recognised as one of the central achievements of Western art. Shakespeare, Venkatrathnam says, 'has a very peculiar place in the hearts and minds of people'; he 'uniquely represents the universal man'; he 'captures that essence.'[36] This may remind us of what Bate and Thornton, and MacGregor, say; but where their generalisations leave Robben Island behind, it is clear that this idea of a universal suffrage in the name of Shakespeare would have had real anti-apartheid edge actually on Robben Island. By finding themselves represented in this 'Bible' of Western secular culture, Venkatrathnam and the other prisoners who signed it were laying claim to the cultural and political representation which they were denied. By finding *themselves* in Shakespeare, those who did so were also implicitly signing up to Shakespeare's individualism, and in such a way as reveals the political implications of such a commitment more vividly than it might emerge in, say, an undergraduate tutorial in Oxford. Venkatrathnam is only secondarily making a claim about Shakespeare; his Robben Island Bible primarily lays claim to the human dignity which Shakespeare is taken to have expressed on behalf of the prisoners and the victims of apartheid more generally.

Schalkwyk is right to stress that many prisoners on Robben Island didn't sign up to Shakespeare; some signed for other reasons, because they had learned a speech in school, 'as witness to a sense of solidarity unconnected with the meaning of this speech or that sonnet', and so on;[37] many could not even read. He is also right to point out that even those who did sign often did not remember or continue to identify with what they had signed afterwards. And he's right that Mandela's own chosen passage is and is not well adapted to Mandela's heroic struggle for freedom inasmuch as Caesar is not, in Shakespeare, a heroic figure, and actually seems to be the enemy of freedom. Schalkwyk also comments on the uneasy fit between the Shakespearean tag which Mandela reached for at his trial 'when', Schalkwyk writes, 'the death penalty was a possible, even a likely, outcome'.[38] This is Mandela himself:

I was prepared for the death penalty. To be truly prepared for something, one must actually expect it. One cannot be prepared for something while secretly believing that it will not happen. We were all prepared, not because we were brave but because we were realistic. I thought of the line from Shakespeare: 'Be absolute for death; for either death or life shall be the sweeter.'[39]

Schalkwyk points out that the Shakespearean words that Mandela reaches for here belong in the original text, *Measure for Measure*, to 'a manipulative, Machiavellian politician', Duke Vincentio.[40] It prevents or at least disturbs any straightforward, optimistic alignment of the plays with Mandela's heroism.

Or does it? Of course none of the Robben Island signatories corresponds precisely to the character whose words he signs; and, in fact, this confirms both Shakespeare's individualism and their own. Mandela at his trial in Rivonia or on Robben Island is clearly not signing his personality away in favour of Caesar's or Duke Vicentio's; he is endorsing particular sentiments or ideas expressed by those characters which seem meaningful in relation to his own necessarily very different predicament. Coincident difference allows for identification.

One of the most moving moments in Schalkwyk's book is the following:

On 14 December 1977, two days before the book was signed by Mandela, Billy Nair marked a passage from the first play in the First Folio, an order that Alexander followed for Venkatrathnam's edition, *The Tempest*: 'This island's mine, by Sycorax my mother, / Which thou tak'st from me.' (1.2.331–2)[41]

Schalkwyk glosses this as follows:

At a time when almost all South African students, at university and school (and indeed students in the English-speaking world as a whole) would have been taught

Shakespeare's last singly authorized play as a representation of the conflict between the 'vile' and the 'non-vile', the 'noble' and the 'savage', a prisoner on Robben Island registered Caliban's claim as simply his own, and that of all the dispossessed inhabitants of South Africa.[42]

After all the morally troubled scrupulosity of his argument, there is a palpable sense of relief here. 'It is', as he writes, 'as direct and uncompromising a claim as one might find in Shakespeare', and it is one which offers a direct and uncompromising correspondence between Shakespeare and the struggle.[43] Otherwise, Schalkwyk deems that 'at most' his book has 'conjured a few shadows from the historical conjunction of Shakespeare's extraordinary text and the unique marks of the proper names inscribed in its pages'.[44] Certainly in no other case that he analyses is the correspondence between Shakespeare and the struggle as simple and satisfying as it is with Nair. Given the difficulty of these other cases, Schalkwyk is not even looking for simple correspondences. Instead, he sees himself as attempting to discern the individual and collective 'unconscious' of the Robben Island Bible.[45] The last sentence of *Hamlet's Dreams* expresses his fear that this unconscious has 'largely been my own'.[46]

In the end, I am not so sure as Schalkwyk that we need the concept of the unconscious to explain the Robben Island Bible. Instead I'd submit that the remarkable fact that those men signed their names on the collected works of a white sixteenth-century Englishman at that world-historical juncture constitutes a deliberate collective assertion, as Venkatrathnam's words intimate, of the human dignity which Shakespeare expressed and with which he is associated; it also quite plainly asserts that, in spite of their incarceration, they are as free to be themselves as Shakespeare's characters are. The beauty of the fact that the Robben Island Shakespeare asserts freedom by means of identification is that it implies freedom is more than a personal thing *all the way down*; it implies that freedom is always political, always a matter of asserting and protecting as well as identifying with the freedom of others and the possibility of freedom as such. The prisoners on Robben Island identify with Shakespeare's characters in the same way that Shakespeare's characters identify with one another in the erotic, ethical and political scenarios he dramatises. This, I think, can accommodate the fact that some of them identify with the speaker and the speech to which they put their names more fleetingly and even superficially than others. It also presents a larger and more durable claim for Shakespeare's political significance than the admittedly striking fact that he created a Caliban as well as a Prospero or a Caesar. The Robben Island Bible helps us see that Caliban's explicit struggle for freedom is related to the freedom of being expressed, enjoyed and fought for by Shakespeare's characters and readers.

It was an extraordinary, an almost unbelievable thing for Schalkwyk to hold in his hands the very copy of the Alexander Shakespeare, familiar from so many reading lists and classrooms, which thirty-four political prisoners on Robben Island, including Mandela, had signed. Encountering the book by chance at an exhibition mounted by the Shakespeare Birthplace Trust in Stratford in 2006, he arranged, through the good offices of Stanley Wells (honorary chairman of the Trust), to examine it after the exhibition closed. 'There was', he affirms, 'indeed something special about having touched and read the book that had passed through the hands of the people who had saved my country.' And yet, more 'especially striking' for Schalkwyk on that special occasion even than, say, the conjunction of Shakespeare and Nelson Mandela were 'the dessicated Eucalyptus leaves' and 'wild flowers' which he found still 'pressed between the pages' of the book and even 'still bearing the traces of their scent'. These, he writes, 'had presumably been picked on the way to the quarries where the prisoners had been subjected to hard labour' and 'preserved as a tiny form of sensory richness – a reminder of the outside to be savoured and recalled'. 'Shakespeare is important,' he reminds himself and us, 'but he's not everything.'[47]

Schalkwyk's reluctance to bring it all back to Shakespeare makes sense, and it is comparable to Walcott's similarly conflicted feelings about the Bard. Just as Mandela can't finally or completely be identified with Caesar or Vincentio, and just as Shakespeare is irreducible to the end of apartheid, so the end of apartheid exceeds Shakespeare.[48] Still, if it makes sense to observe and be moved by the trace and scent of eucalyptus which the leaves gathered by the political prisoners on Robben Island had left on the pages of Shakespeare's book, then it makes sense to observe and be moved by the trace of Shakespeare that the Robben Island Bible brought into the struggle against apartheid. It remains an extraordinary conjunction of Shakespeare and freedom.

4   Lajos Kossuth

If this book argues that Shakespeare's plays manifest and model the struggle for freedom, it further suggests that this struggle for freedom has been central to the Shakespearean tradition until recent times. And it suggests reconnecting with that lost tradition to affirm and renew Shakespearean freedom now. As a first indication of what we're missing, I want to take you more than a hundred and fifty years further back than the 2012 Olympics to an evening in the London Tavern on May the 13th, 1853, when ordinary English men and women made an extraordinary presentation to honour the Hungarian revolutionary Lajos (Louis) Kossuth (1802–94). My main source for this is a newspaper cutting, apparently from the *Illustrated London News*, titled 'Presentation of the Shakespeare Testimonial to Kossuth', in volume 11 of *Newspaper Cuttings Relating to Shakespeare*, which Lemuel Matthews Griffiths gifted to the Shakespeare Memorial Library at the Library of Birmingham.[49] The fact that Griffiths thought it worth collecting twenty-nine volumes of Shakespearean cuttings for a public library is itself eloquent of a higher estimation of what Shakespeare has to offer public life than we are used to. But the story he cut out and preserved of Kossuth and Shakespeare is especially remarkable, and I suggest that it reveals the potential of Shakespeare and freedom like nothing else.

What the people of England gave Kossuth in 1853 was far more physically impressive than the Robben Island Shakespeare. And insofar as it represents a more wholehearted, thought through and sustained commitment to Shakespeare's revolutionary potential, it is more metaphysically impressive as well. And yet, it's not nearly as well known. An article by the Hungarian historian Tibor Frank led me to suppose that it was held in the Kossuth Museum in Cegléd, and I made appropriate enquiries.[50] In fact, since 2004, it too has been held in the National Széchényi Library in Budapest, reunited with the handsome volumes, each emblazoned with the freedom fighter's coat of arms, that it housed when it was first given to Kossuth (Figures 1.1–1.3).

Apart from anything else, such a superb neglected work of craftsmanship deserves our attention. It presents an edition of Shakespeare's complete works, in the words of the *Illustrated London News*, 'superbly bound in mulberry-coloured morroco' and decorated with Kossuth's coat of arms

FIGURE 1.1 The Shakespeare Tribute to Louis Kossuth, courtesy of the National Széchényi Library, Budapest; photo by Adam Ackermann

FIGURE 1.2 Refer caption from figure 1.1

FIGURE 1.3　Refer caption from figure 1.1

'elaborately decorated in crimson, silk and gold'. The case containing the books is 'a model of Shakespeare's house, very delicately rendered by Messrs. Howitt of High Holborn'. The account in the paper gives further detail: 'The interior and exterior are of white holly, to represent lime-wash; the outside transverse timbers of black oak. The roof is made of birch, to represent thatch. The doors are of brown oak, with black oak graininess.' If examining the model suggests that the roof is actually made of the same wood as the walls, I would venture that the journalist can be forgiven an embellishment presumably intended to convey just how splendid a thing Kossuth had been given by the people of England. On a silver plate above the centre window is the following inscription: 'Purchased with 9215 pence, subscribed by Englishmen and women, as a tribute to Louis Kossuth, who achieved his noble mastery of the English language, to be exercised in the noblest cause, from the page of Shakespeare' (Figure 1.4).

These days Kossuth, perhaps, needs some introduction. A glamorous and romantic figure, he had wanted to become a writer, penning an account of the French Revolution in his youth, and even attempting

FIGURE 1.4   Refer caption from figure 1.1

a universal history. Drawn to both poetry and the stage, he translated a number of Western-language plays, at least one of which was staged in the provinces, then in Pest. Shakespeare interested and impressed him when he translated the first lines of *Macbeth*; and he made a good fist of them, according to a present-day Hungarian scholar: 'Though obviously dated and laden with antiquated elements of vocabulary, style and expression, Kossuth's *Macbeth* is written in strong, sophisticated and passionate terms.'[51]

But Kossuth's real genius was for politics. An ardent liberal, he longed for freedom for Hungary from Habsburg Austria. He was imprisoned for a year in 1837 and immediately sentenced to a further four years. Though he was freed in 1840, the confinement had damaged his health. And yet, the great epoch of Kossuth's life was about to begin. His literary and political talents came together as the editor of the increasingly radical paper *Pesti Hírlap*, which called for the freedom of the serfs, the cessation of systematic punishment beatings in law and in the family, the amelioration of poor conditions in prisons, an institute for the blind, orphanages and a children's hospital.[52] Subscriptions, by the standards of the time, went through the roof. Meanwhile Kossuth had married Terézia Meszlényi, who had visited him in prison; this represented 'another political and social breakthrough' since Kossuth was a Lutheran and Meszlényi a Catholic in a country where mixed marriage was forbidden by church and state.[53] Kossuth ultimately demanded a parliament for Hungary and a constitutional government for the rest of Austria, fighting a revolutionary war against the Habsburgs that was 'the largest, best organized and most determined insurrection of 1848 anywhere in Europe'.[54] In 1849, he became president-regent of the new Hungarian Republic, and the 'great reforms' he initiated included the emancipation of the serfs, the establishment of responsible government and the freedom of the press.[55] They also extended to a Jewish emancipation law, which 'was most enlightened by any measurement of the day'; 'it took the Habsburg administration almost twenty years before it would consent to, let alone initiate, a similar bill.'[56] But the Russians came to the aid of Austria, Kossuth's revolutionary project was defeated, and he was forced to flee his beloved country.

Some of Kossuth's generals, the so-called thirteen martyrs of Arad, died for the cause; that he himself did not is one of the things that tarnishes his reputation for some Hungarians to this day. Kossuth threw himself on the mercy of the Turks, who refused to give him up to the emperor. Finding his stand for liberty congenial to their own founding ethos, members of the U.S. Congress invited him to visit America, and Kossuth set sail for the land of the free, though not before first landing in England, in October 1851. Among those who met him when his ship docked at Southampton was the Birmingham activist, nonconformist preacher and Shakespeare lecturer George Dawson – also the moving spirit behind the establishment of the Birmingham Shakespeare Memorial Library, from where I derive this story. At Southampton, Dawson presented Kossuth with an address from the men of Birmingham, and he was prominent in securing Kossuth's subsequent visit to the city.[57] When the Hungarian freedom fighter arrived at Small Heath, between sixty and seventy thousand men were there to escort him to a city centre that was festooned with the Hungarian tricolour.[58] In Edgbaston, Kossuth's wife was presented with the following gorgeously bound and illuminated volume of *Sentiments and Similes of W. Shakespeare, selected from His Plays and Poems*, now also held in

FIGURE 1.5 *Sentiments and Similes of W. Shakespeare, selected from His Plays and Poems*, courtesy of the National Széchényi Library, Budapest; photo by Adam Ackermann

honour of 'the great statesman' by the National Széchényi Library (Figures 1.5 and 1.6).

Having arrived in the United States, Kossuth apologised, in a speech at Faneuil Hall, on April the 29th, 1852, for 'profaning Shakespeare's language'

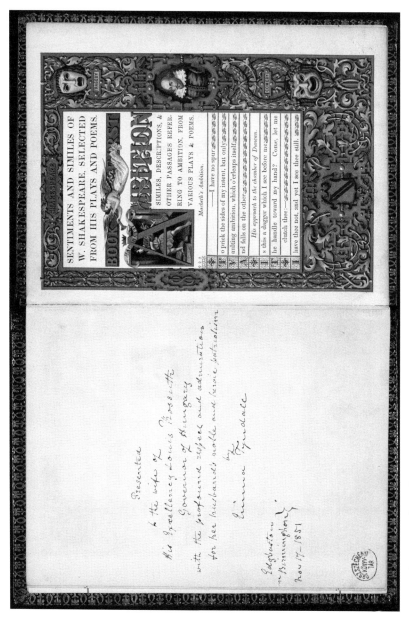

FIGURE 1.6   Refer caption from figure 1.5

in 'the cradle of American liberty'.[59] Abraham Lincoln recognised him as the 'most worthy and distinguished representative of the cause of civil and religious liberty on the continent of Europe'.[60]

There were limits to Kossuth's liberal credentials, however; as governor-regent of Hungary, he had been aggressively unsympathetic about extending the full political and cultural freedoms he had gained for ethnic Hungarians to the significantly numerous non-Magyar minorities of his country.[61] But that said, it is only fair to mention the nationality bill Kossuth passed intended to secure the position and safety of all ethnic groups in the new nation.[62] And then in exile, he devised more enlightened schemes for the self-government of the nationalities in Hungary, and for a Hungarian-Serbian-Romanian Danube Federation in Central Europe, which, had it been realised, might conceivably have prevented World War I.[63] A more straightforward moral failure was Kossuth's refusal openly to condemn American slavery because he wanted the support of the Southern (as well as the Northern) United States for the cause of Hungarian freedom, which the abolitionist leader William Lloyd Garrison denounced as criminally evasive.[64] But (as we shall see) Frederick Douglass nevertheless regarded Kossuth's Shakespeare-inspired struggle in Hungary as inspirational in the fight for black emancipation in America.

If there are real blemishes on Kossuth's record, Ralph Waldo Emerson afforded perhaps the most instructive as well as the most charitable response when he said to the Hungarian patriot at Concord: 'We know the austere condition of liberty – that it must be reconquered over and over again; yea, day by day; that it is a state of war ... always slipping.'[65] Emerson recognised that, in spite of his limitations, Kossuth remains a great hero of freedom, as well as a great voice, on the world stage, for the principles of freedom which his actions impressively if imperfectly illustrated. When he employed Shakespeare's language in Faneuil Hall, Kossuth did so to remind Americans that the 'nature of a privilege is exclusiveness, that of a principle is communicative. Liberty is a principle: its community is its security; exclusiveness is its doom.' In the same speech, he deplored the 'exclusive liberty' of the aristocracy, concluding as follows: 'As aristocracy should vanish within each nation, so should no nation be an aristocrat among nations. Until that ceases, liberty will nowhere be lasting on earth.' He was grateful, he said, for the warm reception he had received in America but, in accordance with his larger views, he did not wish to see this in merely personal terms. Instead, he approvingly quoted the man in a crowd in Worcester, Massachusetts, who had shouted out to him: '*We worship not the man, but we worship the principle.*' If he at times fell short himself of this principle, we may safely assume that he knew it. And as Emerson concluded at Concord, 'you, the foremost soldier of freedom in this age, – it is for us to crave your judgment; who are we that we should dictate to you?'[66] For Emerson, Kossuth still was 'the angel of freedom, crossing sea and land; crossing parties, nationalities, private interests and self-esteems; dividing populations where you go, and drawing to your part only the good'.[67]

Later in 1852 Kossuth returned to London. The Folger Shakespeare Library in Washington, DC, holds three letters which help recreate the excitement of the Shakespearean invitation to him in the London Tavern the year after. The prime mover in this enterprise was Douglas Jerrold, a playwright (his first great dramatic success had been *Black-Eyed Susan* in 1829) and radical journalist. A friend of Charles Dickens, Jerrold was, according to Peter Ackroyd, 'a small man with a massive head and sharp features', who was 'noticeable also for his intense nervous energy, tossing his long hair "like a lion does with its mane" at moments of excitement, and afflicted by a "peculiar restlessness of eye, speech and demeanour"'.[68] He was inspired by the report that Kossuth had learned English from reading Shakespeare in an Austrian prison. This convergence between Shakespearean eloquence and the Hungarian fight for freedom revealed to Jerrold an excitingly militant potential in the Bard: 'arrowy words that kindle as they fly – words that are weapons, as Austria will know'. Jerrold thought Kossuth was waking England up to its own Shakespearean vocation to liberty, by means of 'glorious words he has uttered among us, words that have been as pulses to the nation'. He was convinced that 'hundreds of thousands of Englishmen' would 'rejoice' to 'manifest their gratitude' for this new-found Shakespearean lease of life, and therefore he established a penny subscription so that England might bestow a suitably Shakespearean honour on Kossuth.[69] Frederick Douglass supported this in spite of Kossuth's pragmatic failure to condemn American slavery, and on the 8th of January, 1852 the *Frederick Douglass' Paper* duly declared, 'We hope to see [Jerrold's] excellent suggestion … at once acted upon', noting in addition that 'Mr. Jerrold has received numerous letters expressive of high approval of the proposition, and also several subscriptions.' 'He suggests,' Frederick Douglass concluded, 'that boxes be affixed to the offices of the liberal press throughout England.'[70] The real political passion which this conjunction of Shakespeare and Kossuth roused on both sides of the Atlantic helps measure how far we have come from such a militant view of the Bard.

Jerrold's penny subscription was so successful that he was able to commission a finely crafted casket to house the complete Shakespeare he intended to present to his hero, and when he received it, his grandson tells us, he 'took almost a boyish delight in showing the treasure to his friends'.[71] The first pertinent letter in the Folger's possession is from Jerrold to Thornton Hunt, editor of the radical periodical *The Leader*, which was also supported by George Dawson, the Shakespearean Birmingham progressive and Kossuth sympathiser we have met already. 'My dear Hunt,' Jerrold writes on the 21st of November, 1852, 'Will you not give a few lines on "Shakespeare and Kossuth," and will not the <u>Leader</u> open a box for pennies?' He notes, 'I am in the continual receipt of letters in the matter', and also that 'they are stirring at Manchester', suggesting that an actual political revolt might emerge from enthusiasm for the Shakespearean event he was plotting.[72]

Jerrold's next letter in the Folger's collection is addressed, on the 5th of December to Charles Gilpin, another confirmed supporter of Kossuth. A thoroughgoing Quaker and liberal, Gilpin was involved in movements to repeal the Corn Laws, abolish the death penalty, end slavery and establish world peace. Jerrold, Hunt, Dawson, Gilpin: the archival trail shows some of the big political players converging in the effort to yoke Shakespeare together with the international liberation movement. And the *Illustrated London News* reveals that further radical big hitters including Richard Cobden (co-founder or the Anti-Corn Law League), Sir Joshua Walmsley (president of the National Reform Association) and Alderman Wire (later lord mayor of London) were involved in the occasion itself. It is impossible to imagine as many public figures of comparable authority and stature getting involved in any bringing together of Shakespeare and radical politics today. Jerrold confided to Gilpin that the venue he had intended to host the presentation, the Whittingham Club, 'repudiate all and every matter bearing on Kossuth as political': a reminder that the attempt to link Shakespearean Englishness to Kossuth was seriously controversial, even dangerous.[73]

The third Folger letter is also addressed to Gilpin but comes this time from the great Hungarian himself. 'My dear Sir!' Kossuth writes from 21 Alpha Road, Regents Park on May the 3rd, 'It is Tuesday already, and I have yet no communication about the Shakespeare presentation meeting at which you desired my presence for Friday next.' Kossuth wants to know whether or not it's happening. And if it is, at what time? How political it is intended to be, and how public? Is he expected to speak? And will there be an address for him to answer? 'You know,' he reminds Gilpin gravely – if perhaps a tad disingenuously, given the eye-watering number of public engagements he had already undertaken on both sides of the Atlantic – 'that I but very hesitantly yield to any necessity of appearing in public; but if I must do it I would like to be acquainted with the particulars in time.' And he asks Gilpin kindly to 'make me informed about the matter' by the end of the day.[74] Presumably Gilpin (or someone else) did, because ten days later Kossuth knew his part sufficiently well to help make the presentation of the Shakespeare testimonial to him in the London Tavern on the 13th of May, 1853 a magnificent success.

Jerrold was always shy of public speaking, but on this occasion he took the chair in an exceptionally nervous and distracted mood; his son recalled 'his hair flowing wildly about him, his eyes starting, and his arms moving spasmodically'.[75] And yet, he managed to pull himself together enough to present Kossuth with the work he had commissioned and already taken much pleasure in.

It was clearly a very exciting occasion, and not only for the distracted Jerrold: one where literature and politics came together in the lives of ordinary people. When Kossuth rose to say thanks for his gift, the assembled company roared their approval. He had to stand on a chair, 'the better to be seen and heard'. Before he embarked on his speech, he admitted that he felt 'after an abstinence of some months from public speaking, almost the embarrassment of a debutant'.

But he needn't have worried. Unlike the poor chairman, he was always a brilliant speaker, and he certainly pulled the rabbit out of the hat on this occasion. He began by addressing Jerrold in the chair. 'My Lord,' said Kossuth,

I have received this evening a precious addition to the numerous tokens of friendship and sympathy to my country, with which people of different climates, different in origin, in language, religious worship, habits and political organisation, have honoured me; tokens worthy to adorn the national hall of a new-born Hungary, once the trials of national misfortune shall pass ... And may I sink or swim, may I live or die, I trust to God they will be placed there, to stand as memorials of the brotherly tie which unites the national members of mankind to one common family, which has one common father there above.

The value of Hungarian freedom Kossuth evokes is not a singularly private one – a matter for Hungary alone – but communicative and sympathetic: an instantiation of the irreducible particularity of freedom such as may appeal to all peoples. Liberty may be a principle, as the Hungarian had insisted in Faneuil Hall, and here he invokes it with religious hope and intensity, but it is a principle which comes to life in authentic and unimpeded self-realisation. That is how on the thirteenth of May in the London Tavern, Kossuth's own exotic flamboyance could convincingly combine with the freedom that Shakespeare had won for himself and his characters in such a way as to come to stand for nothing less than the value of freedom itself.

Warming now to his theme, Kossuth added,

To those memorials the old Magyar will lead the children of his children; to inspire them with the same just feeling of brotherly affection to their fellow-men; and tell them how we have merited those tokens of world-wide sympathy, by having fought bravely, and suffered ungrudgingly for freedom and fatherland; and admonish them to remain worthy of that sympathy by using wisely, and by maintaining resolutely, that freedom which we will have conquered for them.

In the speech he had made presenting the gift to Kossuth, Jerrold had said,

And, sir, hoping, believing, knowing that the day will come when you shall sit again at your own fireside in your own liberated Hungary, we further hope that sometimes turning the leaves of these word-wealthy volumes, you will think of Englishmen as of a people who had for you and for your cause the warmest admiration and deepest sympathy.[76]

Alluding to this, Kossuth now politely remarks that his plan to showcase his Shakespearean testimonial at the civic heart of a liberated Hungary 'will be a more adequate use of your valuable gift, than should I with selfish egotism of innocent joy only keep it to delight me and my children with at my own humble fireside'. The 'national hall of a new-born Hungary' he contrasts with Jerrold's picture of a contented and deserved domesticity is a kind of Valhalla of freedom: a synecdoche and quintessence for the free fraternity of humankind to which he had already appealed. But we need to keep the material occasion and spur for Kossuth's speech very much in mind – for his audience in the London Tavern, this brave new institution of Hungarian freedom which Kossuth was conjuring for them was conjured only in relation to and in a sense *out of* the splendid model of Shakespeare's birthplace that had both elicited his words and was presumably sitting before him on a table as he spoke.

Kossuth now went on to explain to the meeting that he literally did derive his knowledge of English from 'the page of Shakespeare'.[77] But he also insisted that Shakespeare had taught him not just English but politics. He had been forced to endure solitary confinement 'in a damp lonely chamber', 'seeing neither the sky nor the earth' and 'without a book to read, without a pen to write'. He was alone 'with God', 'my tranquil conscience, and with meditation'. 'But,' he goes on, 'it is fearful to be thus alone, with nothing to arrest the musing eye.' What he then says reveals his own, rather Shakespearean powers of fancy: 'Imagination raises his dreadful wings, and carries the mind in a magnetic flight to portentous regions, of which no philosopher has ever dreamt.' It was all Kossuth could do to get a grip: 'I gathered up all the strength of my mind, and bade him stop all that dangerous soaring.' 'It was done,' he confirms, but he admits he had grown 'afraid of myself'. That is why he petitioned his gaolers for something to read. 'Yes', they say, 'but nothing political'. 'Well, give me Shakespeare, with an English grammar and a dictionary', answered Kossuth; 'that you will take, I trust, not to be political. Of course not, answered they, and gave it to me.'

Kossuth now goes on to recall his days as an imprisoned student of Shakespeare's text. 'For months', he says, 'it was a sealed book to me, as the hieroglyphs were to Champolion, and as Layard's Assyrian monuments still are.' But then, he recalls, that at last: 'the light spread over me; and I drank, with never-quenched thirst, from that limpid source of delightful instruction.' He continues as follows:

Thus I learnt the little English I know. But I learnt something more besides. I learnt politics. What, politics from Shakespeare? Yes, gentlemen. What else are politics than philosophy applied to the social condition of men? and what is philosophy but knowledge of nature and of the human heart? and who ever penetrated deeper into the recesses of those mysteries than Shakespeare did?

I admit that I find this very moving. The inscription on Kossuth's presentation Shakespeare suggests that the Bard has given him a great political resource – 'his noble mastery of the English language, to be exercised in the noblest cause' – its phrasing implying a certain continuity between Shakespearean English and the cause of liberty, although it is worth noting that a Shakespearean mastery of language (noble) defers to the cause of liberty here (noblest). But Kossuth goes further than the English subscribers in extolling the merits of their national poet in his acceptance speech. Where Caliban snarls that Prospero taught him to speak and his profit on't is to know how to curse (cf. *The Tempest*, 1.2.366–7), Kossuth says that Shakespeare taught him not only to speak (English) but also 'something besides': politics. Kossuth knows that to claim to have learned his politics of freedom from a dramatic poet might be a surprising thing; it is the very claim, I have suggested, that London 2012 and its commentators so much wanted and yet, crucially, hesitated to make.

What, politics from Shakespeare?

But Kossuth is undeterred.

Yes, gentlemen.

Kossuth wasn't Nelson Mandela, but in his liberal nationalism, his (admittedly brief) leadership of a liberated nation and his international political celebrity he wasn't completely different from Mandela either – and both of them read Shakespeare in prison. In his preface to the third edition of *Radical Tragedy*, Jonathan Dollimore has suggested that the political criticism of our time has paid insufficient attention to liberal humanists such as Herman Hesse who opposed a defiantly non-political spirituality to the political barbarity of fascism, 'preferring instead easier targets in academic literary criticism'.[78] This is true, and important. But a hundred years before Hesse, Kossuth, and others like him, risked their lives, and the lives of others, for a vision of freedom that was more passionately political than it was personal and spiritual. In the London Tavern, Kossuth concurred with Jerrold and his audience that Shakespeare had made a real contribution to Kossuth's Hungarian revolution. Upon presenting his Shakespearean tribute to Kossuth, Jerrold said the Hungarian leader enjoyed 'not the acquaintance, but the lifelong friendship, of the men and women of our immortal Shakespeare'. He insisted that Shakespeare's characters were behind Kossuth and Hungary, and that they lent it more than just a personal authority as they were equally 'great proportions, solemn truths'.[79] In this remarkable conjunction of Shakespeare and politics, Jerrold is drawing on something like the apprehension of Falstaff, Rosalind and Edmund's vitality as sketched at the beginning of this chapter. Taken together, the vivid range of Shakespeare's characters stand for the variegated but unitary truth of freedom. That was why, in the London Tavern, Kossuth could claim to have derived from Shakespeare a revolutionary politics that was deeply responsive to the 'mysteries' of 'nature' and the 'human heart'. It was, Jerrold said, a 'glorious use' to make of 'a glorious weapon'.[80]

The night on which he received this splendid gift in the London Tavern Kossuth recalled that he had made six hundred speeches, and that he had been listened to and acclaimed by literally millions of people. This was because, he said, he had 'spoken for liberty' and 'held up the bleeding image of his country'. He implored the assembled company 'but to read the declaration of the independence of Hungary'; it is a mark of the political seriousness of the occasion that when he said he would get this document reprinted, it 'excited immense cheering'. After that, 'Alderman Wire, Sir Joshua Walmsley, and Mr. Cobden then addressed the meeting – the last named at some length – *in severe reprobation of the government*': one gets the impression of things building towards a political fever pitch. There is a vote of thanks to the Chairman Jerrold, who announces several further meetings to sympathise with Mr Kossuth: 'The meeting broke up with hearty cheering for Kossuth and his family.' Again the ripples reached America, with the *Frederick Douglass' Paper* more than doubling the number of 'English workmen' who had subscribed to the fund for purchasing Kossuth's Shakespearean tribute in its enthusiasm for the event.[81]

* * *

To my mind, this story about Shakespeare and Kossuth is one of the most extraordinary Shakespeare stories there is. And it is also one of the most significant, since it exemplifies the scope for and power of associating Shakespeare with freedom. So why has Kossuth disappeared so completely from the international political scene where once he loomed so large? Why has his intense and importunate association with Shakespeare been almost entirely forgotten?

One reason for Kossuth's eclipse is the current diffidence about freedom which I have pointed to throughout this chapter. Freedom is a potent political idea, as even the most casual consideration of history from the Greeks to the French Revolution and back to Mandela will suggest. And yet, for many years now, it has been pretty much off the agenda in the academy. This comes partly down to an unfortunate effect of nomenclature: the fact that 'neo-liberalism' has become the favoured critical term for that free-market fundamentalism which demonstrably works in the interests of the few at the expense of the many, and which was unleashed in a particularly virulent form on the world by the governments of Ronald Reagan and Margaret Thatcher. Neo-liberalism has, in short, given freedom a bad name. But of course recent intellectual distaste for freedom isn't *just* a matter of name calling. It was important in the 1980s to oppose Thatcher's position that 'there is no such thing as society', and the self-serving creed of 'greed is good' which was the other side of that, as Dollimore's affirmation of 'collectively defined goals' showed in the last sentence of *Radical Tragedy*.[82] But we have seen already that freedom in the sense of emancipation from externally imposed limits into a fully experienced and expressed life can be collective as well as individual, as it is in national liberation; and it arguably imposes the political obligation upon society in general to prioritise and enable as much freedom as possible for all. Certainly, I believe it is now time to remember and revive an important tradition of cultural critique that begins and ends with freedom. Freedom was the first aim of the French Revolution – which, according to Eric Hobsbawm, is the pattern of modern revolution as such;[83] it was freedom above all that inspired the American Revolution, and from 1829 to 1834 the idea of freedom drove a second wave of revolution in Europe, before igniting the 'spontaneous and general conflagration' of 1848 for which Kossuth was the major figurehead, and which Hobsbawm says was as near as we have ever come to 'the world-revolution of which the insurrectionaries of the period dreamed'.[84] Of course, enthusiasm for freedom can lead to suffering and evil. The French Revolution eventuated in chaos leading to mass innocent bloodshed (the Terror) and a new tyranny (Robespierre). Thomas Mann memorably recalls his experience during the Nazi period of listening to 'hysterical declamations of the German radio announcer about the "holy struggle for freedom against the soulless hordes"'.[85] Yet for Hannah Arendt, freedom still 'animates and inspires all human activities and is the hidden source of production of all great and beautiful things'.[86] And in this context, I would suggest, large-minded English enthusiasm for the Shakespeare-inspired insurgency of a progressive Hungarian freedom fighter is very much worth retrieving.

A more particular reason for the eclipse of the Shakespearean Kossuth is the understandable ethical suspicion in which Romantic nationalism is held, particularly after the catastrophe of Nazism. This connects with a salient issue in Shakespeare studies more broadly. Some years ago now, in one of his earliest books, Jonathan Bate ventured a bold comparison in order to describe and bring out the political value of Shakespeare's pluralism and openness: 'His "truth" cannot be defined or pinned down. He is always being appealed to, but he does not exist in an Authorized Version. He is open to perpetual reinterpretation and reappropriation. Shakespeare is like the English constitution.'[87]

Now that 'Global Shakespeare' is the watchword in international Shakespeare studies, it would be harder to get away with that. Given the crises of nationalism, empire and Anglo-Saxon cultural imperialism, the proponents of Global Shakespeare align themselves with Ania Loomba and Martin Orkin's pioneering assertion in *Post-Colonial Shakespeares*: 'The Shakespearean text, which for so long helped anchor a disciplinary formation called "English Studies", can become a means for discussing the nature of our diverse post-colonialities.'[88] In her defining article 'Global Shakespeares as Methodology', Alexa Huang confirms 'a degree of textual transparency that allows audiences to tell their own stories and thereby shape our knowledge base of world cultures'.[89] It is impossible not to notice how abstracted such professional statements seem after Kossuth's appeal from the heart, to the heart. It is also impossible not to notice that the accent is not so much on what Shakespeare is in himself than on what other cultures can do with him. Huang speaks for a utopian, post-national kind of liberalism, for which Shakespeare's Englishness is definitely off limits, and the heat and controversy of inter-national politics are politically regressive. To the extent that we may take such an approach as indicative, Shakespeare's association with an out-and-out nationalist such as Kossuth was bound to be passed over.

Now, clearly no sane and responsible person today would simply endorse Romantic nationalism. As Simon Winder writes,

There is no doubt that by many measures 1848 was a great watershed in European history – I am not sure anyone today would particularly fancy going back to a world where most of us would be tied labourers. But it is impossible not to feel a sense of dread about the gap between the excitement of 1848 and the degree to which we now know that it was firing a starting gun that would initiate some of Europe's most terrible events.[90]

Indeed, but I would maintain that we shouldn't rush to dismiss Kossuth. As we saw earlier, by the time he was in a position to, as he put it, 'profane Shakespeare's language' in Faneuil Hall, Kossuth had decided, 'Liberty is a principle: its community its security; exclusiveness is its doom.' As governor-regent of Hungary, he had emancipated the Jews; in exile, he had brought his formerly debased position on Hungarian minorities up towards the level of the principle he enunciated in America. Furthermore, Christopher Clark has shown that nationalism was more idealistic and sympathetic in Kossuth's period: 'Europeans could derive vicarious excitement from each other's national causes; liberals in Germany, France and Britain became enthusiasts of Polish, Greek and Italian liberty.' And:

Nationalism was a potentially radical force for two reasons. Firstly, nationalists, like liberals and radicals, claimed to speak for 'the people' rather than the crown ... Indeed, nationalism was in some respects more inclusive than liberalism, whose horizons were confined to a wealthy, educated and largely urban elite ... Secondly, nationalism was subversive because in many parts of Europe, the realization of the national vision implied fundamental transformations of the political map.[91]

That of course was absolutely the case for Kossuth, who sought to liberate his country from the Holy Roman Empire. And lest we should think that this is all very well but that progressive nationalism became a spent force in human culture after 1945, we should recall the post-colonial struggle for freedom, the liberation of various nationalities after the collapse of the Soviet Union and, most recently, the success of the Scottish National Party (SNP) in bringing Scotland to the brink of independence after the Scottish referendum of 2014.

Relevant here is a reticently fierce exchange in the *London Review of Books* about the late Scottish poet Edwin Morgan's poem, 'Louis Kossuth'. Morgan's lines imagine Kossuth in exile in Turin: 'The Danube can only flow through my dreams.' For all the excitement of his revolutionary life, all the hospitality he had enjoyed from liberal-minded foreigners, his 'longings / Are inextinguishable, exact, and sad'. He recalls a speech he had once made in Glasgow. In the melee after, he was 'buttonholed by a skelf of a man': the unprepossessing alcoholic Macfarlan, who attacked Kossuth for prioritising freedom over the material needs and welfare of the people.[92] In a subsequent letter to the LRB, Hugo Stolkin essentially chided Morgan for doing the same thing. The poet responded angrily, insisting he hadn't introduced Macfarlan to mock him and concluding as follows:

> The Scottish context is significant in the poem. Scotland has unfinished political business, with a devolved Parliament that pleases some and not others. Neither socialist nor nationalist aspirations can be ruled out. Stolkin says he is sad that 'Macfarlans [socialists] are in short supply these days.' I agree. But they are not in quite such short supply in Glasgow, where they may be nationalists as well.[93]

Now I am fundamentally arguing that Kossuth's brand of progressive nationalism opens into the broader cause of progressive politics as such, and for that reason should not be forgotten or neglected – and I should say, for the record, that I do not find Huang's hopes for a post-national politics unappealing, or even ultimately impossible. Nevertheless, what Morgan says stands as an intense little demonstration of the power that remains, even today, in Kossuth's specifically nationalist progressive challenge.

And yet, the English men and women who presented Kossuth with his Shakespeare testimonial in 1853 went decidedly beyond any restrictively nationalist view of Shakespeare. In making Kossuth a present of Shakespeare's house as well as his books, they symbolically gave away his birthplace and English origin in favour of claiming his relevance to the present-day political struggle abroad. This was not the England of Brexit isolationism. Nor was it Shakespeare as a mere pretext, for 'anchoring a disciplinary formation called "English Studies"'; for 'discussing the nature of our diverse post-colonialities'; for enabling 'audiences to tell their own stories'; for 'shaping our knowledge base of world cultures'. What happened on May the 13th, 1853 suggests instead that Shakespeare might actually and concretely exemplify freedom to the world. It can't completely purify Shakespeare of the sort of tainting historical associations that worry Walcott and Schalkwyk, nor will it disguise the fact that there is a successful, self-interested Shakespeare industry, but it might encourage us to renew the case that Shakespeare has an objective intellectual, existential and political contribution to make to global culture.

A further and perhaps most decisive reason for Kossuth's eclipse in contemporary culture is his theatrical individualism. Though Morgan is Scotsman enough to leave Shakespeare out of it, his Kossuth admits, 'Some say I am a showman.'[94] You'd think being a theatrical character would be no slur to Shakespeareans, but in fact there is a long-established prejudice against character in Shakespeare studies. This derives from the preference of modernist critics such as G. Wilson Knight for seeing the plays as comprehensive dramatic poems.[95] It has been re-stimulated in our time by the deconstruction of the self in postmodern approaches. And I suggest that it has been reinforced further by a certain distrustful puritanism involved in the professionalisation of English Studies as a respectably rationalist discipline. But what perhaps sealed the posthumous fate of Kossuth was Marxist scorn for a rival form of revolutionary politics. Karl Marx called Kossuth 'a swindler', 'a big-mouthed charlatan' and 'a tight-rope walker who does no dance on a rope but on his tongue'; but this is borrowing the scorn of the upper orders for 'low' commercial theatre, and Jonathan Sperber, Marx's biographer, points out that Marx was flattered and bribed into his hostility to Kossuth by undercover agents of the Austrian empire.[96] Though Marxists tend to reject 'bourgeois individualism', Terry Eagleton has recently insisted that 'the free flourishing of individuals is the whole aim of [Marxist] politics.'[97] And Sperber observes that the 'sole description of a communist society in the *Manifesto* was the assertion that it would be "an association in which the free development of each is the condition for the free development of all"'.[98]

Marx was a keen Shakespeare fan; his daughter called the works of Shakespeare 'our house Bible'.[99] Like Hegel, what he prized as Shakespeare's signal achievement was his really individuated characters. He recommended in a letter to an aspiring playwright that the man should '*Shakespearise*' his *dramatis personae*, explaining 'I miss what is characteristic in the characters.'[100] In ordinary language, when we say someone's 'a character', we mean that they live more distinctively and fully, and perhaps even that they exemplify character as such. The Shakespearean celebrity which Kossuth enjoyed in his own time demonstrates the potential political value of this. It shows that Brecht was wrong, that the magnetic richness of Shakespearean character is not always a distraction from history and politics.[101] To contemporaries such as Jerrold, the political promise of Shakespeare's powers of self-realisation and expression came to life vividly in Kossuth. Some leading Marxist thinkers, including Brecht, Marcuse and Dollimore, have worried that since Shakespearean character is most richly realised in tragic catastrophe and death, Shakespeare is a political pessimist.[102] And it is true that the failure of Kossuth's hopes and efforts to secure independence for Hungary suffuses his character with a historical pathos that seems truly Shakespearean; but Kossuth remained dauntlessly political unto death. His story therefore resonates more with Kiernan Ryan's argument that the Shakespearean hero who dies like a comet actually augurs a better future, where his (or her – I am thinking of Cleopatra) splendid self-realisation will be more possible and more shared.[103] For those who honoured him in the London Tavern, Kossuth's Shakespearean charisma revealed to the world something of the liberated condition he was fighting for. And as we have seen, Kossuth's was a character which stands for the larger, independent character of his nation, free from the Habsburgs. That was how he became Emerson's 'angel of freedom': the avatar of freedom as such.

What did Kossuth think when the meeting in the London Tavern dispersed and he was left to reflect on this extraordinary gift he'd been given? As an exile, he was presumably moved to have been given a model of a home, a birthplace. In fact, he would never again lay eyes on the home country for whose freedom he had given so much. Lovingly encasing Shakespeare's books in a model of the house of his birth in Stratford, as Jerrold and company had done in this tribute to him, eloquently testifies to a specifically English freedom to be oneself. But, as I've said, Jerrold and company also symbolically gave this away to Kossuth, thereby acknowledging that he was fighting for comparable freedoms in Hungary. And when they made a present of Shakespeare's books and house, they were also giving him the gift of an alternative birthplace, homeland and identity, and thereby decentring Shakespeare's Englishness. To that extent, the ceremony on May the 13th, 1853 dramatises a double conception of freedom, one which derives from nationality but also completely exceeds it, making Shakespeare and Kossuth unlikely brothers. Jerrold and the contributors to his Kossuth fund rejoiced that England had rediscovered itself in Kossuth, who had rediscovered himself in Shakespeare.

An extraordinarily comprehensive English unity had been achieved in favour of Hungarian freedom via a common link to Shakespeare. Jerrold insisted, in his presentation address, that to fund this tribute to Hungarian freedom, English 'pennies came in from men and women of all classes, from all parts of the country.'[104] 'Very curious would it be,' he opined, 'to consider the social history, the household history, of many of these pennies.'[105] In other words, Kossuth's Shakespeare house had been built from the very different pockets of a nation it had united with a foreign cause. What happened in the London Tavern affords a complex, reciprocal example of the way in which Shakespearean freedom renews itself beyond Shakespeare's nation. Neither Kossuth nor Shakespeare, neither England nor Hungary, had priority in this complex transaction, which may help us see that it's not necessary to throw the baby out with the bathwater when investigating Shakespeare's relevance to global culture. Shakespeare was a source of freedom, which Kossuth had brought to life now. And no-one present thought that the cause of liberty could or should just end there. Jerrold expressly looked forward to the day 'when the darkness that now benights the greater part of Continental Europe will be rolled away, dispersed by the light of liberty, like some suffocating fog', bringing freedom to France, to Austria and to Italy.[106] Here was a form of Shakespearean patriotism of an enthusiastically European and outward-looking kind.

Kossuth ultimately took his Shakespeare tribute with him into the last phase of his exile in Turin. He kept it in his study. And if, on one hand, this signified that he had kept faith with the struggle, it was also a sign that he remained every inch himself: a character. In what I have written in this chapter, I have tried to show that this was in no way at odds with his Shakespearean politics of freedom. Kossuth loved nature, climbing the high Alps when he was well into his eighties. His herbarium and collection of snail shells are in Budapest museums. Almost blind, he remained, Istvan

Deak tells us, 'upright, strong, dignified and argumentative'. Deak also tells us that he 'fell in love with a young Transylvanian-Hungarian girl, to whom he addressed pathetically beautiful letters'. Such irreducible, inimitable, no doubt sometimes infuriating life Kossuth found in the plays and fought to win for others. Shakespeare matters, this story suggests, because of his power to inspire others, including this Hungarian freedom fighter, to be or become themselves. In this my first attempt to do justice to Shakespearean freedom, it therefore seems perfectly appropriate to end not with Shakespeare but with Kossuth, who died on the 20th of March, 1894. His body was buried in Budapest. Millions showed up to welcome him home.[107]

2

Shakespeare Means Freedom

§

This book argues for a better reason to read, perform and celebrate Shakespeare. It argues that Shakespeare *means* freedom. Only the poet, according to Shakespeare's forebear Sir Philip Sidney, bursts out of 'the narrow warrant' of Nature to range 'freely . . . within the zodiac of his own wit'.[1] And Shakespeare quickly came to exemplify this, even in his own times. His plays were written for the suburbs or 'liberties' which lay beyond the legal limits of London's jurisdiction. His great rival Ben Jonson praised his 'open and free nature';[2] John Heminge and Henry Condell in their preface to the 1623 First Folio recalled how their late lamented colleague's writing hand had moved as freely as did his mind, in perfect, untrammelled self-expression. I shall argue in Chapter 4 that the Stratford Jubilee of 1769 – the event which more than any other established Shakespeare as 'the Bard' and world-champion poet – strengthened this association between Shakespeare and freedom. As we shall see, the Corporation of Stratford precipitated the Jubilee by making David Garrick its first ever 'Freeman'. And this was truly an honour Garrick deserved given the captivating freedom of his new, more naturalistic style of acting, which seemed to point to a fundamentally liberating truth: *that you could be whatever you liked*. As the official steward to the Jubilee, Garrick took Shakespeare out of the scholar's study, and even the theatre, and quite literally into the streets. He encouraged festival goers to wear a rainbow ribbon: 'The Shakespeare Ribband', which expressed the great variety of Shakespeare's genius in explicitly political terms of his openness and availability to all. In this context, it is not so surprising that James Boswell, in solidarity with the international liberation movement descended on the first great Shakespeare festival in the guise of a Corsican chief; nor that the songs that were sung for Shakespeare at Stratford were subsequently refitted for later jubilees in favour of the great political cause of the day: 'Wilkes and liberty'.

Today bardolatry is taken to be a conservative phenomenon, but this political dimension of Garrick's original Shakespeare Jubilee suggests that it is possible to construe it otherwise. Matthew Arnold's spiritualising rhapsody – 'Others abide our question. Thou art free' – can be read politically if the Shakespearean freedom to which it bears witness is taken to reveal the possibility and poetry of human freedom as such.[3] That certainly was the sort of bardolatry which appealed to the Chartists, who we shall see derived inspiration and strength from Shakespeare in their struggle for the political liberation of the English working class. We have already seen that Shakespearean freedom inspired the European freedom fighter Lajos Kossuth. That is the background against which the Working Men's Shakespeare Association's ceremonial tree planting on Primrose Hill in honour of the Shakespeare tercentenary of 1864 phased into a subversive political rally in favour of Italian emancipation under General Garibaldi. 'For Foucault, in the Collège de France lectures,' Richard Wilson tells us, 'it was because Shakespeare obstinately refused to sing "power's ode", dreaming instead of "the freedom to roam", and of "free genesis, self-accomplishment . . . a freedom against the world", that his dramas rank among the foundations of modern critical thought.'[4] Perhaps so, but I suggest that the inspiration modern critical thought takes from Shakespeare actually is a late iteration in a long lost tradition of associating Shakespeare with freedom which we urgently need to recover.

Of course Shakespeare is not *just* associated with freedom; I have mentioned the conservative tendency of bardolatry, and the truth is he is equally if not more associated with reactionary agendas. Jonathan Dollimore and Alan Sinfield's landmark collection *Political Shakespeare* (1985) was written explicitly against a general consensus that, in the words of the UK's then Chancellor of the Exchequer Nigel Lawson, 'Shakespeare is a Tory.'[5] Alvin Kernan, in *Shakespeare the King's Playwright*, presents the Bard as a hoarsely evangelical monarchist: 'the leading apologist for kings in his or any other time'.[6] In *The Genius of Shakespeare*, Jonathan Bate shows how Sir Walter Scott laid the modern foundations for such a view in his novel *Waverly* (1814), which co-opts Shakespeare for 'stability, passivity and a defence of property in the tradition of Edmund Burke's attack on the French Revolution'. 'Scott's Shakespeare,' Bate concludes, 'thus becomes a spokesman for nationhood in its most conservative form.'[7] In spite of the best efforts of Dollimore, Sinfield and a generation of other left-leaning academics, Scott and Lawson are still more in tune with the wider culture. As Peter Holbrook, current chairman of the International Shakespeare Association, wearily observes, 'Enthusiasm for Shakespeare today often implies bourgeois respectability.'[8]

But we don't just have to accept this. Walter Benjamin argues that to save the future we first have to save the past; if Shakespeare is now typically assumed to be conservative, his association with radical freedom can work as what Foucault calls a 'counter-memory', pulling in the other direction.[9] In his famous 'Theses on the Philosophy of History', Benjamin argues that the discipline of history should be a systematic sort of counter-memory: a revolutionary archaeology of the lost possibilities of the past. 'To articulate the past historically', he suggests, 'does not mean to recognize it "the way it really was"' but instead is 'to seize hold of a memory as it flashes up in a moment of danger', in order 'to wrest tradition away from a conformism that is about to overpower it'.[10]

According to Benjamin, the politically engaged thinker 'takes cognizance of [history as such] in order to blast a specific era out of the homogeneous course of history – blasting a specific life out of the era or a specific work out of the lifework'.[11] The pathos of this lost life redeemed from history re-motivates the struggle for a more fulfilled existence now. Such is the spirit in which this book attempts to retrieve and revive the association of Shakespeare and freedom.

And I'd venture to suggest that looking within history for promising alternative histories is actually a rather Shakespearean thing to do: think of the way that the Bard subversively – *and for so long!* – diverts momentum and attention from the official history of Agincourt in the Henriad (*Henry IV* Parts 1 and 2, and *Henry V*) to recover the life that precedes and was lost in it;[12] think too of the way that he contrives that 'losers' such as Hamlet, Antony and Cleopatra, and Coriolanus theatrically triumph over the worlds which in fact they lose. In other words, Shakespeare himself is an historian of counter-memory.

Benjamin's most famous thesis on the philosophy of history is number IX. There (following Gerhard Scholem's 'Gruss vom Angelus', and also Paul Klee's painting 'Angelus Novus') he imagines what he calls 'the angel of history' bending over the car crash of the past in an agony of compassionate desire to repair and save it. But before the angel is able to get on with this redeeming work, a storm gets caught in its wings, carrying it backwards into the future. The angel weeps, its hands close convulsively on nothing, and 'the pile of [historical] debris grows skyward'. The storm, Benjamin grimly comments, 'is what we call progress'.[13]

And yet, all is not lost. For, strange though it seems to say, Benjamin believes the situation can be saved by means of historical criticism; he writes in that European tradition which is much more optimistic and ambitious for critical thought than the Anglo-American tradition tends to be. If scholarship can break the spell of fake progress, this will simply put a stop to the storm. The angel will return in conducive, becalmed conditions, enabling it patiently to pick its way through the detritus of days, months and years.

Except of course that there isn't really an angel. If we need to break the spell of false progress, it is equally we who need to follow through and rescue from oblivion such things as the splendid model of the Birthplace which Jerrold and company presented to Kossuth in the London Tavern. And we need to rescue them not as antiquarian relics, but as auguries of that fuller, freer life which has yet to be realised and lived in history. Dust off Kossuth's Shakespeare tribute, Benjamin is saying, and bring it back to life today, yes, as a tribute to but also in the hope of dispelling all the suffering frustration of the living and the dead. What the image he derives from Klee intimates is that in the process, historical criticism will become not just a discipline of the schools but an *angelic* discipline.

I should admit at this point that the book you are reading is premised on a conviction that Shakespearean freedom not only permits but actually requires more creativity in criticism. Virginia Woolf said, 'It is rashness that we need in reading Shakespeare', because Shakespeare's 'fame intimidates and bores' – even in her time, when Shakespeare scholarship wasn't nearly so voluminous and professionalised, the Bard was apparently getting 'flyblown' with criticism.[14] Before Woolf, Goethe, one of the German architects of Shakespearean freedom we will meet in a later chapter, wrote,

A work of art, especially a poem, that leaves nothing to conjecture is not a true work of art, fully worthy of the name. Its highest function must always be to stimulate reflection, and it can only really commend itself to ... the reader by compelling him to interpret it in his own way, and to complete it, so to speak, by creative re-enactment.[15]

Within professional Shakespeare studies, my predecessor at the Shakespeare Institute, the late John Russell Brown, urged in *Free Shakespeare*, that 'we must seek *interplay* with the plays, explorations of an everchanging human image.'[16] I shall not disguise my own imaginative and intellectual investment in the case I make in these pages. Indeed, I would wish to encourage such commitment as a way of giving new life to Shakespearean freedom in the world today.

And yet, I would resist the imputation that Shakespearean freedom is a whimsical or historically misleading thing. To the contrary, I will demonstrate that freedom is objectively 'there' in both the form and content of Shakespearean drama, as well as in the responses to Shakespeare of some of the greatest European artists and writers. Freedom has in fact been more central than we realise to the historical interpretation of Shakespeare's legacy, and it also remains powerfully latent in the way in which Shakespeare is understood today. Shakespearean freedom, this book argues, is much more than an affecting counter-memory; it is a whole counter *tradition*, just waiting to be recovered and taken up by us.

And this does not entail a wishful utopianism. Freedom has its dark side, and Shakespearean freedom certainly does. As we'll see, some of the protesters at New York's Astor Place Theatre died for it, and it is obscurely involved in John Wilkes Booth's assassination of President Abraham Lincoln. According to Tolstoy, Shakespeare allowed too much; as a result, he gave up the discriminating critical distance needed to see what is wrong with the world and change it for the better. But if Tolstoy, consequently, sees Shakespearean freedom as a species of wicked licence, the English poet Ted Hughes – writing out of the horrors of the twentieth century, as well as those of his own private life – makes the opposite case. Hughes argues that Shakespeare is a poet of 'complete being' who heroically confronts and might help to redeem the violence of our lives. Such freedom involves risks, but they are, at least potentially, worth taking.

* * *

But if Shakespeare really means freedom, what is the intrinsic link between freedom and the plays? I suggest the association between Shakespeare and freedom is based on a fundamental connection between personal liberty and what is widely acknowledged as his greatest achievement as an artist – his creation of dramatic characters more spirited and alive than any who have been created before or since.

In his *Aesthetic Theory*, Theodor Adorno wrote of Shakespeare's 'breakthrough into mortal and infinitely rich individuality', but Adorno was really just reprising his great German forebear G. W. F. Hegel, who had in his own *Aesthetics* presented Shakespeare's characters as 'free artists of their own selves'.[17] A. C. Bradley very much follows Hegel in this, as in our own day does Harold Bloom. As major names such as Hegel, Bradley and Bloom indicate, this is the mainstream of Shakespeare criticism. And yet, most contemporary critics have found it harder to affirm Shakespearean freedom than Bloom does – and Bloom's own rage against them for setting social and ideological limits on Shakespearean freedom, from *The Western Canon* onwards, suggests the strain of his own position. And yet, I shall argue in a later chapter that it remains possible to understand the whole tradition of critical writing about Shakespeare after Hegel, including recent scholarship, as an extended intellectual struggle to affirm freedom. Recent, more sceptical accounts, from Stephen Greenblatt's epoch-defining *Renaissance Self-Fashioning* onwards, may be best understood not so much as attacks on freedom in Shakespeare but as a committed if admittedly embattled, even at times agonised effort to defend and renew it. Such work acknowledges and analyses the very conditions which prevent change in order to facilitate change.[18] As Antonio Gramsci so memorably put it: 'pessimism of the intelligence, optimism of the will'.[19] Or as I put it myself in these pages: get real but do not give up. The latest notable effort in this vein is Wilson's *Free Will: Art and Power on Shakespeare's Stage* (2013). Wilson suggests we should interpret Shakespeare's portrait of himself as 'our bending author' (*Henry V*, Epilogue 2) as the self-disclosure of one who 'bows to the power he bends': an artist who in his very act of submission actually does not so much honour sovereignty as subvert and disavow it.[20]

Wilson's use of the terminology of freedom is encouraging in this context, because so much other recent criticism has retreated into a vocabulary damagingly abstracted from life, partly in its efforts to distance itself from right-wing 'neo-liberalism'. I have already mentioned Bate's 'performativity', and Greenblatt's 'self-fashioning' also fits the bill: compare it for inspirational potential with Hegel's delighted recognition of 'free artists of their own selves'.[21] Admittedly, the vocabulary of 'agency' is well suited to the dramatic representation of an action, but it's less well adapted to personal and political life. 'Aspectuality', 'performativity', 'self-fashioning' or 'agency' are not what you cry when – at last, and throwing caution to the wind – you make your break for a better life. No, as Kossuth and Mandela both knew, what you cry instead is, '*Freedom!*'

And this isn't, I maintain, a superficial point. The word has an ontological vividness and comprehensiveness the other terms just don't share. That is the source of its inspiring poetry, as even a quick glance at the ways in which Shakespeare uses the word (and its cognate forms) will attest. The political watchword of *Julius Caesar*'s rebels is 'liberty, freedom, and enfranchisement!' (*Julius Caesar*, 3.1.80); but when we hear that 'Thought is free', in *Twelfth Night* and *The Tempest*, the emphasis is more intellectual (*Twelfth Night*, 1.3.58; *The Tempest*, 3.2.118). There are lines in *Henry VIII* (*All is True*) honouring academic freedom: 'All the clerks – / I mean the learnèd ones in Christian kingdoms – / Have their free voices' (2.2.91–3). But when Othello says, 'I would not my unhoused free condition / Put into circumscription and confine / For the sea's worth' (1.2.25–8), he gives us freedom as an inviolable state of being, as well as one that is more than oceanic in its magnitude. Human freedom here is spiritual freedom. It approaches that freedom that the magus offers Ariel in a passionate whisper: 'thou shalt be as free / as mountain winds' (*The Tempest*, 1.2.502–3). And yet, both Othello and Ariel have been slaves, and that should remind us not to oppose their spirituality of freedom to a politics which would enable its full expression. In this connection, it is worth remarking that the famous lines that follow from *A Midsummer Night's Dream* present a spiritual epiphany of something like feminist freedom:

> And the imperial votaress passed on,
> In maiden meditation, fancy-free.

> (2.1.163–4)

Leaving aside the delectable word-music, this presents a picture of richly self-exploratory and self-communing femaleness, a state where motion, thought and desire merge in pure liberty. And not just pure: *maiden* marks this liberty of the votaress as specifically a woman's as well as, crucially, unpossessed by men; and *imperial* connotes a similar self-sovereignty. It's worth recalling the context for the lines here: Cupid's arrow has whistled past, not at all disturbing the votaress's stately self-communing. She has escaped the imperative violence (and the violent imperatives) of love – or, at least, of love as we know it. *Fancy-free* transfers thought and desire from any given, objective world into *her own* secret freedom.[22] But for all their political suggestiveness, these lines equally intimate a natural conjunction of freedom and beauty, a connection evinced, elsewhere in Shakespeare, by Aeneas's assertion that Trojans in peacetime are 'Courtiers as free, as debonair, unarm'd / As bending angels' (*Troilus and Cressida*, 1.3.233–4). And if the votaress's freedom involves stepping away from love, a more helpful promise that eros might instead positively enable freedom can be heard in Othello's desire, before the green-eyed monster sinks its teeth in him, 'to be free and bounteous to [his new wife Desdemona's] mind' (1.3.264). 'Being free itself, it thinks all others so', says Flavius of open-handed bounty in *Timon* (2.2.227); it might be that freedom is the gift that goes on giving, bestowing itself on others only to return to the giver again. That, as we shall see, is the German philosopher Hegel's position. Unfortunately for Timon, it's not the way it turns out for him. Still, the ideal of a bounty that flows in a happy, unceasing process of what the Sonnets call 'mutual render' (125) arguably survives as the personal and political dream of which this particular play falls short.

All this richly various and affecting poetry of freedom lends both complex significance and emotional power to such utterances in Shakespeare as 'I was born free as Caesar, so were you' (*Julius Caesar*, 1.2.99); and of course Cassius is counting on that. Because freedom connotes so much life, even patently ideological assertions such as 'princes should be free' can't just be reduced to ideology (*1Henry VI*, 5.5.69). 'The jolly Briton / – your lord, I mean – laughs from's free lungs', we hear in *Cymbeline*: a fine phrase which escapes from its dastardly dramatic context (where Giacomo is attempting to seduce the virtuous Innogen) in identifying Shakespeare's own race and nation with a self-delighting liberty that exceeds both, and which will certainly appeal to non-Britons (1.1.68–9). This is also the spirit in which Falstaff, as A. C. Bradley suggests, 'walks about free and rejoicing'.[23] But even such joyous freedom remains eminently corruptible: Lucio, in *Measure for Measure*, tellingly talks of 'the foppery of freedom' (1.2.113). Still, he prefers this to 'the morality of imprisonment' (1.2.114–15). '*Tutto nel mondo è burla. L'uom è nato burlone*', everything in the world is a joke and man is born a joker: the joyous fugue at the climax of Giuseppe Verdi's

Falstaff – his final opera – celebrates such light-hearted freedom in a comic vision of the universal meaning and purpose of human life.

I have drawn attention to the poetry of freedom in order to bring out freedom's appeal and beauty, but writing specifically verse drama also helps Shakespeare express the politics of freedom. In *Contemporary Techniques of Poetry: A Political Analogy*, Robert Graves and Laura Riding insist on the political significance of verse, declaring, 'Metre considered as a set pattern approved by convention will stand for the claims of society as at present organised: the variations on metre will stand for the claims of the individual.'[24] But considerably before their book, George Saintsbury had, in an impressively sweeping history of English prosody, registered the more dialectical political implications of metre and variation, observing that the pentameter especially reconciles the 'claims of Order and Liberty'.[25] A more sophisticated view still is developed by the doyen of 'Shakespeare's metrical art': George T. Wright. According to Wright, the conflicted density of social life is musically reflected and reinforced in the 'almost infinite internal variation, and unpredictably enjambed or endstopped' lines of Shakespeare's verse.[26] But if metre is made of differences, it also organises them. Sometimes, Wright proposes, this 'pattern *is* life; order and design are fulfilling, satisfying, even redemptive'. But, at other times, it is just coercive and decorous 'and from it the vigorous and insistent human force rebels and flinches, asserts its powerful individuality in exceptional action and verse'.[27] What makes the mimetic texture of Shakespeare's art still thicker is the fact that, beyond the variations of metre, 'the sentence and the line, like human personalities, may [also] meet in inexhaustible combinations.'[28] And to these metrical and syntactic variations we have to add the creatively inconsistent play and contention of metaphors and figures that are so characteristic a feature of Shakespeare's language. Metre, syntax, metaphor: all of these variously intersecting orders of volatile energy express, rival and echo the way that character interacts and clashes not just with other characters, but also with larger forces of family, party and ideology – and that is to say nothing, at this point, of the way in which these larger forces themselves interact and clash. Wright's insightful analysis leads us towards a further, fuller recognition that, at the most basic, indeed mechanical level, life in the plays is constantly struggling for freedom within several dimensions that at once express, enable and delimit that struggle.

To step back from this complex, absorbing interest of Shakespeare's language is to see the actor and the stage, which are of course the fundamental material technologies involved in bringing Shakespeare's verse to life in the theatre. Perhaps the most curiously beguiling landmark in the philosophy of freedom is the brief but pungent reflection on the marionette theatre by the German Romantic writer Heinrich von Kleist (1777–1811).[29] Kleist saw that human freedom is limited when he found himself comparing it with the unselfconscious grace of a performing puppet: as he contemplated the easy beauty of the puppet, he understood that we, by contrast, are cursed with awkward self-reflection. Kleist concluded that if we are ever truly to become free, we will have to become puppets ourselves or, alternatively, as perfectly self-conscious and capable as gods. In his recent *The Soul of the Marionette: A Short Enquiry into Human Freedom*, the philosopher John Gray disagrees. Like Kleist, he isn't looking for freedom in what he calls 'the harlequinade of politics'; Gray too conceives only the possibility of a private, inner freedom. But for Gray this can be achieved by embracing our existential limitations: 'Übermarionettes do not have to wait until they can fly before they can be free. Not looking to ascend the heavens, they can find freedom in falling to earth.'[30]

But I propose that thinking about the Shakespearean actor can take us beyond Gray and this quietist, not to say defeatist, position, offering an alternative vision of freedom, and one which facilitates and resonates with the more politically engaged view of Shakespeare I present in this book. An actor is at the same time puppeteer and puppet. 'In character' he is realised as what he is not, expressing and indeed redoubling the self-inventing power with which Hegel saw Shakespeare had invested his characters. This business of finding oneself in another has the effect that actors evade their own clumsy psychological 'gravity', approximating something like the graceful freedom of movement that Kleist salutes in the marionette. Unlike Kleist's marionette, Shakespeare's actors give us an image of freedom in a hopeful and substantially realised shape of *our own humanity*. It's true that this manifestation is premised on its utter scriptedness, but even that isn't just a negative thing. The implication that freedom derives from an artificial system is encouragement to cultivate it politically. The fact, to which theatre history attests, that the personalities of star actors are able to emerge *through* such scriptedness – first as characters, then as stars – suggests that it doesn't so much prevent as enable self-realisation.[31] By focusing on the technology of the isolated puppet, Kleist and Gray neglect the interpersonal nature of drama, but the energetic liveliness of Shakespeare's plays, in which characters contend with one another and ideology to forge and manifest their freedom, evokes a more vital and populous life that can still serve as a beacon in a continuing struggle for political freedom.

A play convenes a community to watch a community constitute itself on stage. My argument in this book is that Shakespeare's plays convene an audience in the theatre to watch a community on stage constitute itself in terms of the struggle for freedom. Jürgen Habermas has suggested that Shakespeare's theatre, by bringing more elevated persons together in the playhouse with 'domestic servants, young clerks, and a *lumpenproletariat*', helped bring on 'the structural transformation of the public sphere'.[32] Crucial here is the fact that it offered 'every paying spectator a clear and unrestricted viewpoint'.[33] As a result, the on-stage struggle in Shakespeare played directly and equally to a newly enfranchised audience. It possessed an immediate physical power to affirm, rebuke and re-motivate whatever efforts for freedom that members of that audience were or were not making in their off-stage world. In addition, the Globe's thrust stage pitched the struggle for freedom in the plays right into the heart of this newly constituted public. It's not hard to see how the resulting experience of Shakespearean drama would have been politically exciting, and one of my objectives in these pages is to recover something of that original political excitement.

* * *

At first sight, it would seem that 2010 was a good year for Shakespeare and freedom. As the most prominent Shakespearean in the world today, Stephen Greenblatt, pronounced on the first page of a book actually titled *Shakespeare's Freedom*, 'Shakespeare as a writer is the embodiment of human freedom.'[34] You can't say it straighter than that, and it reads like a promise to reverse the scepticism of the same author's *Renaissance Self-Fashioning*; but *Shakespeare's Freedom* is too slight a sequel to Greenblatt's earlier and more substantial meditation on freedom to accomplish this. Its argument that the very limitations on freedom are also its enabling conditions – since such limits restrict

the freedom of power to dominate and destroy freedom – is a rather
indirect and equivocal affirmation (though it does constitute one of the
paradoxes of political freedom we will be considering in this book),
and it is much less densely and persuasively argued than is Greenblatt's
breakthrough title. Nor, to my mind, is *Shakespeare's Freedom* written
sufficiently from the heart of its topic. Consider what Greenblatt says
about Shylock's and Iago's 'radical individuation-through-loathing', for
instance – it's interesting but even he doesn't claim it is the mainspring
of freedom or of Shakespearean character.[35] And the extended attention which this short book gives to 'Shakespearean beauty marks'
seems tangential at best.[36] Greenblatt's praise for Shakespeare's freedom as an artist also remains ultimately gestural, since Shakespeare
demonstrably derived most dramatic material from others; it therefore
behoves any advocate of Shakespeare and freedom to explain just what
it is which makes Shakespeare free. Help is at hand in that the critical
tradition since Hegel has recognised that Shakespeare's freedom is
vested in the complex freedom with which he endows his characters;
but Greenblatt just doesn't give enough attention to this – he doesn't
even mention the philosopher who first proclaimed Shakespeare's
characters 'free artists of their own selves'.

In fact, a better augury for Shakespearean freedom was another work
published in 2010: Peter Holbrook's *Shakespeare's Individualism*.
Holbrook, too, just comes out and says it: 'We need to recognize that
Shakespeare's poetic personality is deeply wedded to one particular value:
individual freedom.'[37] And Holbrook brings back into focus something of
the poetry of freedom which has been so badly neglected in some more
sceptical theoretical treatments. He quotes a terrific formulation of John
Middleton Murry's: that Shakespeare can help us see that 'all things' are
good 'not with the goodness that is the opposite of badness, but each *with
the simple marvel of its own identity*'.[38] According to Holbrook, such
freedom has suffered from the academic 'deconstruction' of the integrity
and agency of the self. And it is now likewise suffering in the world beyond
academia, from the depredations of management culture, and the rise of
authoritarian powers such as China and Russia – as well as, we might add,
the Islamic State and the panicked culture of imprisonment and surveillance that is a salient feature of the so-called War on Terror.[39] This is the
context in which Holbrook asserts that Shakespearean truth to self has

become even more marvellous and, indeed, necessary than even Murry was able to see.

What Holbrook highlights is that central kind of Shakespearean freedom introduced in the previous chapter as *the freedom to be yourself*; but it needs supplementing, I suggest, with that almost opposite kind of freedom which we also touched on: *the freedom to be different*. We shall see in a later chapter that Hegel was the first to develop a view that Shakespearean freedom combines the sort of truth to self which Holbrook emphasises with an equally if not even more important freedom *from* it. Shakespeare's characters are free *artists* of their own selves because for all the self-realising power they derive from their own rich natures, they are equally possessed of an opposite, 'inventive power' which releases them from that nature. Shakespeare dramatically expresses the liberating truth that no-one simply coincides with what he or she is. Personality isn't static and emblematic; on the contrary, it is always in motion. The self in Shakespeare is a constitutively unfinished thing in dynamic process.

What this means for readers or theatre goers is that every moment in a play presents a self *in action*: a self more-or-less successfully realised, more-or-less successfully self-integrating and more-or-less securely self-possessed. Because of the vividness of Shakespearean character, you're always getting close to someone. But because Shakespearean character is always changing, you can't ever absolutely have that character. And so you remain eagerly engaged: in relationship, leaning – always curiously, sometimes anxiously, often excitedly – into the future of someone being freshly born not only to you, but also to him- or herself. Shakespeare takes us beyond identity; he takes *identity* beyond identity. And this is what makes his plays so intimately compelling.

But it also makes them harder to grasp intellectually. Indeed, it's true to say that we probably can't grasp Shakespearean character, because it is essentially unfixed. How then are we to do literary criticism at all? How are we to understand Shakespeare's aesthetic achievement, to which his characterisation is so unarguably central? One way forward might be to rethink character in terms of unfolding musical rather than static pictorial form. But if we want to contemplate Shakespearean character as such, in a single act of mind – if we still want to isolate and contemplate that 'X' which constitutes Shakespearean character – it will be helpful to resolve it into an image. And in that case, an abstract rather than a figurative image is liable to work best, because no figure could do justice to Shakespearean character's specifically shifting quality. I suggest that we might want to imagine Shakespearean character in terms of changing light or weather. And I suggest this because that is how one of Shakespeare's most famous characters pictures his own life and self in one of Shakespeare's most impressive passages of poetry:

ANTONY   Eros, thou yet behold'st me?

EROS   Ay, noble lord.

ANTONY   Sometime we see a cloud that's dragonish,
            A vapour sometime like a bear or lion,
            A towered citadel, a pendent rock,
            A forked mountain, or blue promontory
            With trees upon't that nod unto the world
            And mock our eyes with air. Thou hast seen these signs;
            They are black vesper's pageants.

EROS   Ay, my lord.

ANTONY   That which is now a horse even with a thought
            The rack distains, and makes it indistinct
            As water is in water.

EROS   It does, my lord.

ANTONY   My good knave Eros, now thy captain is
            Even such a body. Here I am Antony,
            Yet cannot hold this visible shape, my knave.

                              (*Antony and Cleopatra*, 4.15.1–14)

Here, I propose, one of Shakespeare's characters sees deep into Shakespearean character as such. Hegel argued that Shakespearean drama accomplished a fundamental historical breakthrough, moving beyond the essentially allegorical mode of classical theatre – where characters such as Antigone stand for a particular ethical value or 'pathos' – into a freer, specifically modern individuality. I propose that here, in progressing from his once imperturbable Roman heroism into the more fungible state he recognises in the changing clouds, Antony undertakes exactly that journey for himself. He indeed is 'lated in the world' in that he has gone beyond any sustainable antique conception of personality – and what makes this worse for Antony is that he has done so without quite attaining to the new, more liquid Shakespearean concept of modern selfhood that Hegel describes as characteristic of Shakespeare and modernity (3.11.3). Antony breaks into modern freedom but is unable to recognise and make this modern freedom the foundation for a new self and life. To that extent, it is true that what he experiences in this speech is really a kind of death. And yet, the *poetry* he speaks denotes more knowledge than Antony is intellectually capable of owning.

Antony assumes he is describing a revelation in the heavens of his own peculiar tragic state, but in fact he is unveiling something even more important: he is expressing a fundamental truth of being in Shakespeare in general. But if this is a truth of being, it is one where being is shifting into becoming, with the freedom to be yourself transitioning into the freedom to become something different. In this great speech, Antony reads the shiftingness written in the changing sky back into his own selfhood. That this isn't a purely negative thing is hinted at by the basic beauty of the metaphor: changing skies tend to be lovely, as the history of painting or photography attests. But in this speech, Antony, at least ostensibly, reads this cloudy mutability in terms of melancholy self-loss, even death: 'black vesper's pageants'. Throughout the play, we find him looking into what he calls 'the very heart of loss', waving goodbye to what Coppélia Kahn defines as 'the heroic Roman image of fixed and stable identity' (4.12.30).[40] And this is the point in his tragedy where Antony gives most sustained and insightful attention to what is happening to him. In doing so, I want to suggest, he at least partly recognises that his painful loss of secure identity at the same time potentially inaugurates a new life of freedom.

Antony's extraordinary existential poem appears at first to move from 'ish' and 'like' towards more solid and settled being. But then the mountain forks; the trees sway in and out of credible existence. The speech zooms in on the changing taking place between the changes in beautiful imagery of that 'which is now a horse' but which 'even with a thought the rack distains', making it 'indistinct as water is in water'. The nodding trees on their blue promontory mock our eyes with air because in fact they are only illusory trees, stirred by an illusory breeze. But then of course the whole pageant 'mocks our eyes with air' because all of it is equally insubstantial.

Or does it, is it? I have said that the simple beauty of a changing sky already works against Antony's mood of lamentation. Beyond that, the drift of his speech towards a melancholy exposure of vanity is entirely undermined by the persistent loveliness of his phrasing. The truth is that, in spite of the ostensibly tragic tenor of what he says, Antony negotiates his passage here into a deliciously shape-shifting deliquescence that it is impossible simply to bemoan or mourn.

'Eros, thou yet behold'st me?': his opening question indicates that even at the outset Antony is on the point of letting himself dissolve into another life. What follows is essentially justification for this, bringing him back to the brink of what now seems a more comprehensible and sympathetic release: 'Here I am Antony, / Yet cannot hold this visible shape, my knave.' What we have heard in between has primed us to imagine Antony melting into a succession of altered shapes that are parallel to the changing cloud formations he has so beautifully evoked. That is why his speech, in the end, does not leave a pitiable impression of failure. Instead, it subtly but potently insinuates the absolute unsustainability of the old life of simple and secure identity that Antony is leaving behind, while subversively hinting that going to pieces might in fact initiate a finer and more beautiful form of being – one which transcends any simply knowable identity in favour of not only incorporating but positively identifying with mutability and change.

Antony professes to feel lost in the flux of corruption, but his exquisite responsiveness to the change he is supposed to be lamenting suggests that, at some less than altogether conscious level, he identifies not so much with the confoundingly contradictory images he pictures – dragon, bear, promontory, and so on – as with the magical and encompassing process of shifting between them. Therefore, and at the same partly unconscious level, Antony feels on the pulses and comes close to seeing for himself what Hegel perceives about Shakespeare's characters: that they are free artists of their own selves. He almost recognises that human personality isn't condemned to be what it is, and so *re-cognises* himself and human personality as such. And if only he could, it would instantly enable him to step decisively out of the ruins of his antique identity and into a new, modern era of subjective freedom.

But at this point Antony doesn't seem at all up to that. He sees himself as simply and completely out of control. Of course, he is partly in denial. His

Roman self is decomposing not so much of its own accord but because, time and again, he has chosen not Rome but his gorgeous Egyptian lover. At times, he has imagined a grandly alternative, Egyptian Antony – 'Let Rome in Tiber melt, and the wide arch / Of the ranged empire fall. Here is my space.' (1.1.35–6); but here he is simply trying to exchange one fixed identity for another. He proves unable to incorporate his movement between Rome and Egypt in an overall conception of who he is. Now, as he contemplates the changing clouds in his mood of awed recognition, he does see into this shiftingness; but he still can't actively, positively and unambiguously embrace it.

But if he can't, Cleopatra can. She is very able to welcome and identify with her 'becomings', and in a mode of life that is elastic enough to encompass nothing less than 'infinite variety' (1.3.97, 2.2.241). Cleopatra is a woman able to shimmer at Cydnus and hop through the public street. Moreover, she is able to redeem her capsized captain into a perfect visionary fulfilment of the new life we have seen him break into but which he fails more consciously and thoroughly to make his own. She achieves this by reimagining him after his death as magnificently one with the creative process of the universe – his reared arm cresting the world, his delights – dolphin-like – showing his back above the element in which he lives (5.2.78 ff.). 'Most sovereign creature,' Dolabella murmurs, and well he might. But Cleopatra denies that Antony is any kind of dream; or if he is, he is *nature's dream*, outstripping fantasy and realising in and as a man what is most deeply valuable and real about human being. Maybe, so long as we add that Cleopatra is speaking not just for but as great creating nature here.

Middle-aged man, besotted adulterer, public failure: Antony does not, perhaps, seem the most auspicious avatar of Shakespearean subjective freedom. But between them, he and Cleopatra nevertheless fit him up as an example of such Shakespearean freedom at its most sublime and exciting, as a sovereign creature who at the same time is the font and fount of creativity itself.

But, as we have seen, Antony is a bridge from allegorical antique personality into modern Shakespearean selfhood. As such, he's not so much 'lated in the world' as he is before his time. And although Cleopatra manages to rescue him in death, Antony's self-realisation while he is alive is always shot through with melancholy failure. In *As You Like It*, Rosalind lives out more joyously and fully the freedom that Antony only half discovers. By leaving her given social and gender identity behind, she gains a world of freedoms in Arden. As she puts it, 'I can do strange things' (5.2.43). And of course the strangest thing she does is to adopt a new, transgendered life as the youth Ganymede, cup-bearer and lover of Zeus. Rosalind's original reason for becoming Ganymede is to avoid being raped on the road, which itself rather neglects the associations with homosexual domination which the alias she has chosen implies. In any case, the pleasure she takes in assuming her 'swashing' male disguise tellingly exceeds this sensible motive (1.3.114). And she maintains her disguise when she could easily get rid of it upon arriving in Arden where her father is. I would argue that it is Ganymede – even more than Rosalind – who embodies the quintessential spirit of Shakespearean freedom. He is a naked, onstage revelation of that other, emancipated life all actors achieve in becoming somebody else. It's true that in order to follow through on her original, cisgender desire for Orlando, and secure a more conventional life in the world, Rosalind has to banish Ganymede and go back to being Rosalind. But it is also true that, as a result of this reversion, Ganymede dies, circumventing the prohibition on death in comedy by dint of the fact that he never was a real person anyway. But of course there are no real persons on Shakespeare's stage. I suggest that Ganymede's inimitably 'soft' death lingers beyond the curtain of *As You Like It* as a wistful and bitter crystallisation of what is lost when we give up on freedom. I further suggest that we *should* mourn Ganymede, and that in mourning him we should be moved to do what we can to prevent the freedom he embodies from dying again.

* * *

The shift from considerations of character to wider analyses of group dynamics that took place in the Shakespeare criticism in the 1980s and 1990s was sometimes accompanied by a more intense inspection of genre.[41] After a lecture I gave a couple of years ago at the University of Queensland, Brandon Chua intelligently objected that Shakespeare's ideological choices as expressed at the level of genre are not progressive. In particular, Chua suggested that *Twelfth Night* renders a relationship between an aristocratic woman and her steward 'unthinkable' via the mechanisms of comedy, whereas Webster, in *The Duchess of Malfi*, elevated a similar relationship by making it the subject of a high tragedy.[42] It is an interesting challenge, though not, I think, uncontestable in relation to Shakespeare's plays in general. In *All's Well that Ends Well*, for instance, Shakespeare does sympathetically dramatise the difficulties of cross-class love. And to the extent that he does so from the point of view of his lower-class female wooer, Helena, he goes further than Webster's *Duchess*. That said, my starting point in this book is not that Shakespeare's plotting is always progressive; instead, I wish to make the case that the extraordinary energy and richness with which he endows his characters tend to exceed his plots, gesturing towards a more perfect scenario in which their potential really could be consummated.

The life that Shakespeare wants for his characters exceeds the life of genre. We see this in *All's Well* when Helena loses the deep, significant and elusive Shakespearean subjectivity she expresses at the beginning of the play as she becomes more and more identified with the plot. When, as a result, she does indeed get her man, this self-loss plays a major part in rendering that triumph so hollow and unsatisfying.[43] As we see so much more positively when Rosalind cuts loose into her new, transgendered life as Ganymede, Shakespeare is not only interested in freedom of doing. He is even more concerned with the emancipation of being.

Still, as I said in the first chapter, if we focus too much on self, then we leave too much out. Shakespearean character is always made in interaction, as well as before an audience. I have suggested that Ganymede is a sort of pure emanation of Shakespearean freedom, but his semi-magical genesis in fact is the result of the complex interaction of Rosalind's mother-wit with the social and interpersonal circumstances of her banishment and desire for Orlando. Antony, we have seen, blossoms ultimately in Cleopatra's mourning for him. As for the Egyptian Queen herself, I have praised her suppleness of spirit in reconceiving her own identity as a series of 'becomings' (*Antony and Cleopatra*, 1.3.97); but even this achievement is not a wholly individual one. Cleopatra in fact speaks of her 'becomings' when she says 'my becomings kill me, *when they do not / Eye well to you*' (1.3.97–8; my emphasis). Even her inimitable, progressive freedom requires validation from her lover. And Antony and Cleopatra, and Rosalind and Orlando, are only two among many more characters in their respective plays. So though it is true that we are always centrally concerned with character in Shakespeare, we are never just concerned with one character. Shakespeare's seekers after their own freedom are obliged to seek this via the business of more-or-less successfully integrating with a whole range of other, more-or-less successfully realised, self-integrating selves. My argument in this book is that this absorbingly complex affair straightaway, in itself, and as it were *prior to the specific details of the plot* makes Shakespeare political.

I have mentioned Hegel's claim that Greek drama is not really interested in human individuality except insofar as it expresses 'the battle between the essential powers that rule human life'; it is in Shakespeare, the philosopher insisted, that the modern individual emerges, and emerges as free.[44] Bradley, following Hegel, added that 'Shakespeare's dramatic representations are the fullest reconciliation of the fate of the individual and the collective (or universal) that we have.'[45] Greenblatt's and Holbrook's books give the impression Shakespeare is ultimately interested in individual freedom, though in his later book on the range of English Renaissance tragedy, Holbrook broadens out his idea of freedom in the direction of human equality, citing the English socialist historian R. H. Tawney's view that 'society is free' insofar as it enables 'all its members to grow to their full stature'.[46] I will argue here that Shakespeare's plays convey the encompassing largeness of freedom in both its individual and political aspects. They are able to dramatise the interplay between personal and political freedom because of (1) their uncontested breakthrough into richer, more realised characterisation, which is (2) nevertheless always forged in relation to other characters and their freedoms. This dialectic between the individual and collective is fundamental to drama as interaction and has significant ramifications. It resonates for instance with Andrew Hadfield's argument for a strong Republican strain in Shakespeare.[47] But if Hegel is right and Shakespeare's characters are defined by a new, specifically individual freedom, this, as Bradley intimates, considerably ramps up the dialectical ante between the personal and the political in the plays. I will suggest that the Shakespearean struggle for freedom foretells the great political passion of modernity, amounting to a serial and probing experiment in liberal democracy *avant la lettre*. That is why it appealed to the Chartists and to other freedom fighters, in England and abroad, after Shakespeare's death.

The artistic desirability of a complete integration of elements is politicised by Shakespeare's portrayal of the individual's potential for freedom. We have seen in the reading of Antony earlier that the Shakespearean self is intensified, elaborated and problematised – richer than any single figure or identity can express. The political integration of such selves is correspondingly harder to accomplish. But then, and precisely because it *is* harder, it would be a greater and more beautiful achievement: a mode of collective life as varied, brilliant and fulfilling as Shakespearean character is! Shakespeare, I believe, was pointing towards this when, in Act Four, scene one of *A Midsummer Night's Dream*, Theseus and Hippolyta discourse, at some length, of the 'musical confusion of the hounds' within which all the world seems joined in 'one mutual cry'(106–23). Of course this 'musical confusion' works as an oblique reflection on the strange order to be discerned amid the amorous misadventures of the play in general. But it goes beyond this, insinuating a larger truth or principle. In the end, I suggest, this 'musical confusion' is an acoustic image of the politics of freedom that all Shakespeare's plays enact. 'I never heard / So musical a discord, such sweet thunder,' says Hippolita, and her awed admiration can help us recognise the complex beauty of Shakespeare's politics of freedom as a volatile, never-ending and open-ended process.

But at this point I want to try out my own formula – even definition – for Shakespearean drama:

Any Shakespeare play presents selves seeking self and society.

The wished-for outcome is therefore, as the young Shakespeare has it at the end of *The Two Gentlemen of Verona*: 'One feast, one house, one mutual happiness' (5.4.170). In that phrase, self and society are fulfilled in each other, which suggests that perhaps a slightly longer-form definition is needed:

Any Shakespeare play presents selves seeking self and a society which validates and enables self.

There are certainly real obstacles in the way of this achievement. 'One feast, one house, one mutual happiness': these words actually conclude a comedy in which one of the male principals (Proteus) has tried to rape the other's fiancée, who in his turn, and perhaps even more shockingly, has just offered to give her up to his now repentant friend. There is no encompassing political solution here. It's all about the two gentlemen of Verona, and them alone – violent and violently casual misogyny undercuts the 'mutual happiness' which the play itself suggests it is labouring to exemplify. What also undercuts this effort is the fact that one of these male leads is (still) called Proteus – a name which looks forward to Antony's protean transformations, and which neatly encapsulates the challenge to any social order of Shakespeare's model of personality as fundamentally changing and unfixed.

And yet – '*One feast, one house, one mutual happiness*'. It is true that this seems ironised by what actually happens in the play, but the poetry of the idea lingers, even and perhaps especially because the play in actual fact falls so lamentably short of it. It lingers as an *ideal*, and not just in *Two Gents*.

The phrase suggests not something cold, contractual and merely legalistic; its most immediate referent is the double marriage in the offing for Valentine and Silvia, and Proteus and Julia. But in relation to the whole play which it closes, it suggests a larger 'mutual' marriage in which all the separate energies and personalities involved would be reciprocally fulfilled. That such a 'mutual' marriage need not be construed in restrictively heteronormative terms is suggested by the brilliant contrivance I have already noted in *As You Like It* whereby Rosalind's and Orlando's eventual marriage is simultaneously achieved and queered *by means of a homosexual flirtation*. This intimates at least the possibility of a larger, all-involving 'marriage' in which everyone is fulfilled beyond the exclusivity and division of marriage as we have so far known it. And this possibility is not at all destroyed by the fact that it doesn't come true in *The Two Gentlemen of Verona*, or even *As You Like It*. Naturally it doesn't, but it remains in play as the means by which we see and understand the limits of these dramas; it remains in play to provoke us into thinking what the play and what life would be like if it actually did incarnate such mutual happiness at the end.

I am suggesting that Shakespeare's plays automatically function as an ethical and political solicitation, inviting us to imagine a world where, for instance, Ganymede not only survives but is happy and satisfied. Given that they evoke character as a splendidly interpersonal achievement potentially obtainable by all, they cannot but project, and be haunted by, at least the idea of a free society of mutually fulfilled individuals. *Two Gents* and *As You Like It* are comedies, and of course tragedy dramatises this in a different way. The splendid self-manifestation of its heroes indicates what would and indeed should be possible for them but is not. Antony cannot find freedom in the political world of *Antony and Cleopatra*, though he increasingly desperately looks for it there. He finds it after death, in his lover's imagination. And yet, *Antony and Cleopatra* remains political. When Antony is dying, he doesn't yearn for refuge in some sequestered metaphysical love nest. What he imagines is a new social ordering of the world of the dead:

> Eros! – I come, my queen: – Eros! – Stay for me:
> Where souls do couch on flowers, we'll hand in hand,
> And with our sprightly port make the ghosts gaze:
> Dido and her Aeneas shall want troops,
> And all the haunt be ours.
>
> (4.15.50–54)

This suggests something between a royal court and the party after the Oscars, and of course Antony's expectation of death is too self-centred. 'One feast, one house, one mutual happiness' would involve starring roles for everybody. And yet, Antony's fantasy nonetheless suggests the sort of comic resolution which is perhaps always projected by tragedy as the political solution of the problem it actually dramatises. More to the egalitarian point would be Lear's desire to 'shake the superflux' to the wretched and dispossessed and 'show the heavens more just' (*King Lear*, Conflated Text, 3.4.34–7). But in any case the political pathos of tragedy is twofold. It rests partly in the fact that the hero's superb self-realisation is unsustainable in the conditions presented by the world of the play. At the same time, it derives from the sad and ironic fact that those who retain the world, and their self-security within it, are unable to realise themselves as fully as the hero is in forsaking these things. In Shakespeare's tragedies, the subjectivity of the hero is surpassingly vividly 'switched on'. But the unrealised potential of less developed characters is affectingly set off by this brightness, particularly in the theatre, where such relatively shadowy figures are actually physically present and exposed to the gaze of an audience. In admiring the hero's existential victory, we are therefore simultaneously mourning the existential victory each loser has failed to attain. Even in tragedy, I suggest, the prospect of a more universal freedom remains in play, sometimes as the memory (or fantasy) of a possibility of life which the tragic action has destroyed, sometimes as a possibility renewed now that – at last – the crisis is over and 'the time is free' (*Macbeth*, 5.11.21), but always as an irresistible implication of the collective life that would obtain if all characters were able to achieve the state of rich, ambivalent freedom which Shakespeare's heroes enjoy and suffer.

Nobody wins in tragedy. And yet, paradoxically, tragedy is where Shakespearean character is most richly expressed. This is because in moving out towards death, the tragic hero also moves liberatingly beyond merely provisional social arrangements. Tragedy affords an opportunity to pursue the Shakespearean vocation for being someone else. The challenge is to convert this deadly liberation into a productive politics. But the intensity of freedom in tragedy also points to an inherent darkness which we will often confront in these pages – a darkness which, incidentally, I see as not necessarily politically regressive but rather as something for which, as Jonathan Dollimore says, the radical political project needs to take responsibility.[48] Freedom is an irreducibly ambivalent as well as an important thing, and because it's important we need to face up to and perhaps embrace its ambivalence. Comedy is more positive and affirmative, which is why it can't match the honest intensity of tragic freedom. Moreover, what freedom in mutual happiness does achieve is compromised by exclusion. Take Shylock, for instance. He is so painfully excluded in *The Merchant of Venice* that most readers and theatre goers find it derails the comic resolution, resenting its moonlit beauty as the trussing up of tragedy as comedy. The intensely negative pathos which such excluded characters attract is the comedies' inverted testimony to the Shakespearean politics of freedom. Having said that, for all the differences between the genres, Ganymede tastes and represents, albeit in a more symbolic form, something that is very like tragic freedom. Though comedy and tragedy offer different takes on the politics of freedom, both remain deeply concerned with it.

I have been writing as if Shakespearean drama presents contending egos seeking self-realisation and their own satisfaction and a society which will enable and protect these things. To an extent, that is true. But of course, in Shakespeare as in life, the forms of self-realisation and satisfaction are many and various. We saw in the previous chapter that Oliver first tastes the sweetness of freedom when he gives up asserting himself. And some of Shakespeare's greatest figures apparently give away their freedom, relinquishing self for duty or society – think of Henry V, Hamlet or Prospero – but then such is the greatness of these characters *as characters* that this self-sacrifice can't but appear as an alternative, further or higher form of freedom or self-realisation. Philosophers have tended to call liberation into pure potentiality 'negative freedom'.[49] Sartre writes, 'The being which is what is can not be free. Freedom is precisely the nothingness which is *made-to-be* at the heart of man and which forces human-reality *to make itself* instead of *to be*.'[50] But according to Erich Fromm, such negativity can only be resolved in the concreteness and continuing vocation of specific sexual relationship(s) and ethical and political activity in the wider world.[51] That is what negative freedom is *for*. He or she who gives it away gets something for nothing: an easy bargain. But Shakespeare suggests that the situation in fact is somewhat more complex. In giving life to Ganymede, he demonstrates that 'negative freedom' can be a substantive form of being in its own right, with a corresponding ethical value. And yet, it is still true that an alternative commitment to life in the world is not necessarily a diminution. Spiritual identification with the variety of life that exists beyond selfhood might access the plenitude of possibilities vouchsafed in a moment of subjective liberation on the more widely dispersed plane of the social. Maybe Ganymede dissolves into the conventional conclusion of *As You Like It* in a way that is meant to suggest that his distinctively expanded form of subjective life can be differently realised by means of an engaged commitment to the variety of lives we live together.

I believe that what I have described is indeed part of what is going on at the end of *As You Like It*, but if the end of that play still seems vaguely disquieting and unsatisfactory that might be because recent, postmodern thought has been famously suspicious of 'organic form' and any totalising ambition in thought, art or politics. Important questions need to be asked about the limits of 'mutual happiness', and whether these don't in fact set limits on individual freedom. For instance, can 'mutual happiness' cater to Proteus's desire for Silvia, as well as for Julia? Can it make room – and if so, in what way – for Shylock's honest hunger for revenge? Can it accommodate the specifically 'peerless' love of Antony and Cleopatra (*Antony and Cleopatra*, 1.1.42)? And if not, then is it really worth the sacrifice? Doesn't Antony just matter *more* than Octavia? After his death, remember, 'there is nothing left remarkable / Beneath the visiting moon' (4.16.69–70). Sartre privileged an explosively personal kind of freedom above all moral and political kinds when he brought his existentialist philosophy together with Shakespearean freedom in a play about the rakehell Shakespearean actor

Edmund Kean (1787?–1833). 'I want to create disorder! To whip a great lady
and betray her to a royal prince,' crows Sartre's Kean. 'And if that isn't
enough, I shall set fire to the theatre. Order in a desert, that's what I want.
Set fire to the theatre and Kean shall perish in the flames.'[52] Maybe we
should just go all out for such blazing individual freedom and let the
chimera of 'mutual happiness' go hang?

These are awkward questions, leading into treacherous territory. It would
be easier to rest in morally uncontroversial positions, condemning Proteus
the would-be rapist, or the way in which Christians in the play first abuse
then wantonly punish and, indeed, destroy Shylock in *Merchant*.
Alternatively, we might want to make a blind commitment to society that
overrides any restrictively particular interest. But since the self is the most
remarkably realised and lavishly endowed feature in Shakespeare, and since
Shakespearean plays present selves seeking self-fulfilment in society, where
society curtails or prevents such fulfilment the self indeed has a reasonable
claim against it. And nor will this just be a matter of championing the self
against society; instead, it is intrinsic to a political vision whereby society's
own proper functioning must all the time be measured against, and even
recalibrated, according to the needs and desires of the selves that make it up.

The politics of Shakespearean form which I am gesturing towards here
resonates powerfully with the classical statement of liberalism: John Stuart
Mill's *On Liberty* (1859). Mill takes his epigraph and moral bearings from
Wilhelm von Humboldt's 'leading principle' of 'the absolute and essential
importance of human development in its richest diversity'.[53] This political
and cultural aspiration, according to Mill, entails a fierce commitment to
the individual. 'If all mankind minus one, were of one opinion, and only
one person were of the contrary opinion,' he writes, 'mankind would be no
more justified in silencing that one person, than he, if he had the power,
would be justified in silencing mankind.'[54] But we need to hold on here to
the fact that such opposition to 'the tyranny of the majority' is always
undertaken not just for the sake of the dissenting individual but even more
for the sake of the majority itself.[55] Mill argues that where heresy is
suppressed '[t]he greatest harm done is to those who are not heretics',
and that where there aren't any devil's advocates, a good society should
invent them.[56]

Comparably, even while Shakespeare elicits the hope for 'mutual happiness', he remains sufficiently true to the restless integrity of freedom to

admit and dramatise the fact that any such arrangement will be too safe, conventional and domesticated for some. The most flamboyant Shakespearean villains naturally come to mind here, but perhaps they are exceptions who prove the rule. Richard III with his deformity, Edmund with his illegitimacy: both of them want to punish a society which excludes and devalues them, remaking it in their own image. And such inversions of the social order leave it structurally unchanged. By contrast, Ganymede's passing in *As You Like It* stands for a more fundamental kind of opposition to the society which the play reverts to. We have seen that because of the richness of Shakespearean polysemy, Ganymede's vanishing simultaneously represents the suffering of his exclusion from society and the possibility that he is subtly transmuted into a redeeming spirit of freedom within it. Still, as a form of death, Ganymede's disappearance most powerfully and directly speaks for a fundamental, ontological opposition to the reconfigured social order, one which intimates that at the end of the play, Ganymede would just walk if he could – as, for that matter, Jacques does in throwing his lot in with an anchorite's religious opposition to the world which 'kills' Ganymede. And I should say at this point that Ganymede and Jacques aren't just sops for sexual dissidents and refuseniks; Ganymede isn't just a name for a kink which eventually gets straightened out in Rosalind's sexuality. As *On Liberty* encourages us to see, Ganymede's death turns out a light in the play as a whole, giving us the measure of its political and existential failure. That's why, as I have suggested earlier, we all should mourn Ganymede, and even as we mourn him be moved to do what we can to prevent the freedom he embodies from dying again.

Such Shakespearean freedom as Ganymede represents is *politically* important. It opens Shakespearean form, demonstrating that any resolution, however positive, needs to open up to new freedoms. Shakespeare is aware of how readily freedom degenerates into a violent free for all: a 'universal wolf' that will devour everything, including itself (*Troilus and Cressida*, 1.3.121 ff.). But Ulysses's recommendation that we should shut it out with an unassailable hierarchy is unlikely to appeal to modern subjects, and it sacrifices all the positive potential for freedom Shakespeare also dramatises. It might still seem desirable to ban what infringes on the freedoms or desires of others. But this isn't so straightforward, even in apparently the most cut and dried of cases. Clearly Shylock has to be stopped from extracting a pound of Antonio's flesh. But stopping him is nevertheless a cunning infringement of his freedom within the law, and it allows the corrupt, racist and slave-owning world of Venice to go on as before, and even smugly to celebrate itself in the final act; whereas if Shylock had done his dreadful deed, it might have forced a comprehensive social reckoning. Moreover, such is the complex force field of human life and action, that almost everything one is or does will entail at least some infringement on the rights of others. Valentine's perfectly innocent engagement to Silvia infringes upon Proteus's freedom to pursue her. One measure of freedom might paradoxically be the freedom to act against the freedom of others; in this connection, we might think of Macbeth's murder of Duncan. And that returns us to the related and important question of whether freedom is quantitative or qualitative. Is Sartre's Kean right after all? Is the great man's freedom more superb, fuller and more realised, and therefore worth more than the little freedoms of others? Shakespearean drama doesn't give us a smug and sentimental liberalism; it gives us a dramatic competition between freedoms. The broader hope of freedom for all is constantly being tested against other, fiercely particular antisocial freedoms. I have insisted that we should mourn Ganymede in terms of the loss of freedom that his 'death' represents, but the free fruition of Rosalind and Orlando's love *requires* the extinguishing of Ganymede. Freedom is a thing divided against itself in Shakespeare; it is political process and struggle. There is no innocence or external position, only the poetry of freedom and the shared endeavour to make the most of it.

Shakespeare can help us recognise that freedom is not a fixed principle or idea but instead is an ongoing drama. William Hazlitt's faith that 'the spirit of poetry' is 'favourable to liberty and humanity' was severely disturbed by the shock of recognising while reading *Coriolanus* that 'the language of poetry naturally falls in with the language of power.'[57] And this led the most progressive of English Romantic critics to transfer his investment of political hope from the faculty of poetry to the faculty of the understanding: 'The one is a monopolising faculty, which seeks the greatest quantity of present excitement by inequality and disproportion; the other is a distributive faculty, which seeks the greatest quantity of ultimate good, by justice and proportion.'[58] Reflecting on this move, Bate proposes, in *Shakespearean Constitutions*, that 'a similar argument might be played out in slightly different terms: the language of poetry may fall in with the language of power, but poetry, and still more drama, also has the capacity to anatomize power.'[59] I agree but would venture that Bate neglects a more fundamental truth: the fact that drama is plainly itself a 'distributive faculty', since it is divided into parts. In drama, poetry can only achieve a monopolising power in the context of this essential pluralism. And what follows is that the splendid self-realisation of the Shakespearean hero (or heroine) cannot but stand for the potential self-realisation of the other characters, and even of all characters collectively. Hazlitt didn't fully appreciate this dialectical doubleness of Shakespearean freedom, but he did implicitly recognise it when he said that anyone who studies *Coriolanus* 'may save himself the trouble of reading Burke's *Reflections*, or Paine's *Rights of Man*, or the Debates in both Houses of Parliament since the French Revolution or our own'.[60] This Janus-faced aspect of Shakespearean freedom was key to David Thacker's production of *Coriolanus* at the RSC in 1994 when he cast and costumed the young Toby Stephens as an expressly Napoleonic hero in front of an enormous but torn blow-up of Delacroix's famous painting of 'Liberty Leading the People' (which features on the cover of this book). Thacker's production knew that, contra Hazlitt, freedom is Napoleon, but it is also the Revolution. It boldly posed the question of the relation between Shakespeare and revolutionary politics, which brings Kossuth back to mind. In the London Tavern in 1853, Douglas Jerrold and company recognised that the two opposite sorts of freedom – individual and heroic, general and political – came together in Shakespeare and the Hungarian hero alike. And yet, their union in the plays remains dialectical, unstable, dramatic, as it also did in the interplay between Kossuth's personal heroism and the cause he championed, if truth be told.

* * *

This book argues that, politically speaking, there is no settled or final solution in Shakespeare. Instead, play after play wages an unresolved, ongoing fight for freedom. This makes sense because any formal resolution of the fight would not only put a stop to drama; it would also delimit and deny freedom itself, since freedom is ever-new, inherently dramatic. Acknowledging Shakespeare's politics of freedom beyond resolution allows us to move beyond the thought-killing cliché that he has no identifiable politics, and to begin to see and understand the real contribution he has made in the past and can still make in the future to personal and political life. In *Spectres of Marx* (first published in French in 1993), Jacques Derrida discerned in Hamlet's responsibility towards the Ghost an intimation of a democracy that is always 'to come'.[61] Unlike Marx's utopia, Derrida's Shakespeare-derived dream is not the communist fruition of teleological history but the 'messianic promise' of a state of perfect responsibility to all that will never be realised. And yet, far from being hopeless, this unrealisable dream – 'life beyond life, life against life, but always in life and for life' – elevates human beings above mere biology, supplying the ecstatic, aspirational energy of human history.[62] We have seen earlier that some such aspiration towards perfect freedom in 'states unborn and accents yet unknown' does genuinely haunt Shakespeare's plays (*Julius Caesar*, 3.1.114). But the real, sublunary struggle for freedom in them is much more down and dirty. Post-Marxist thinkers such as Slavoj Žižek have argued against Derrida that politics and even religion need to be more engaged in real-world struggle.[63] But the Shakespearean struggle for freedom seems to me to resonate less with Marxist conviction than with the late philosopher Gillian Rose's concept of 'the broken middle'.[64] To be in the broken middle, according to Rose, is to be ethically and politically responsible, endlessly negotiating between conflicting interests; and is that not where, as a supreme dramatist, Shakespeare always and necessarily is?

The critic and theorist Jacqueline Rose, Gillian Rose's sister, has more recently pointed to a feminist tradition of political thought and action which can help us understand Shakespearean freedom because it already conceives of politics as itself dramatic. Rose singles out Rosa Luxemburg's 'famous theory of spontaneity', which profoundly influenced Hannah Arendt.[65] She proposes that Luxemburg's theory resonates with what the British psychoanalyst Marion Miller wrote with regard to the Freudian technique of free association: 'the idea is revolutionary that creativeness is not the result of an omnipotent fiat from above, but is something which comes from the free reciprocal interplay of differences that are confronting each other with equal rights to be different, with equal rights to their own identity.'[66] Now this ringing formulation could clearly also do double duty as a description of dramatic form – and, given his particular genius for fully realised, autonomous characters, of Shakespearean drama in particular. For Adrienne Rich, Rose observes, the point is 'to think *along with* the human forces newly pushing forth, in ever-changing forms and with ever different faces'.[67] And Shakespearean drama, where character and politics are both made and remade in action, might teach us to do exactly this. As Luxemburg wrote in 'The Russian Revolution', 'Only unobstructed, effervescent life falls into a thousand new forms and improvisations, brings to life creative force, itself corrects all mistaken attempts.'[68] To my mind, this feminist tradition which Rose brings to light suggests an unusually significant role for Shakespeare criticism: a vocation for creatively unfixing politics as we usually conceive of it in the name of a more real and more open dramatic politics of freedom.

Shakespeare is sometimes seen as comfortably transcending politics, but I am suggesting that this couldn't be more wrong. Shakespeare's politics of freedom does not make for an easy life. It offers no ready assurance. Instead, it pitches us into a moral muddle where important decisions can only be made provisionally, in the heat of the moment, as (to borrow Rich's phrase) human forces newly push forth, in ever-changing forms and with ever-different faces. We might think here of how support for the wave of revolutions known as the Arab Spring seemed morally right before those revolutions gave way to further injustice and chaos. Luxemburg's idea that such an open process will itself correct all mistaken attempts is an appealing one; but it all gets considerably more daunting when we recognise that among those mistakes might be a moral and political catastrophe such as the Holocaust or what (as I write) is happening in Syria.

To hazard another definition, freedom is the virtue that entails at least the possibility of evil. One of the scandals of recent Shakespeare studies has been the vogue for the thought of that 'documented anti-Semite' and 'crown jurist of the Third Reich', Carl Schmitt.[69] Schmitt's work is about freedom, though certainly not democratic freedom. Instead, it is concerned with the untrammelled, post-Machiavellian freedom of the 'sovereign'. Only he has the freedom to abrogate the rule of law and step into a nameless, unprecedented beyond: as Schmitt memorably phrases it, 'Sovereign is he who decides the exception' [*Ausnahmezustand*].[70] Subtitled 'The Intrusion of Time into the Play', Schmitt's reading of *Hamlet* argues for a fundamental connection between real political history and Shakespeare. This is disturbing because, given Schmitt's own place in history, it encourages the suspicion that the partly Shakespeare-derived figure of the sovereign in Schmitt's thought functions as a kind of John the Baptist to the Führer. But then it is true that fascist Germany directly appropriated Shakespeare, with the Nazi paper *Der Stürmer*, for instance, comparing 'the crime that ... deprived Hamlet of his inheritance' to the Treaty of Versailles and 'Gertrude's betrayal [to] that of the spineless Weimar politicians'.[71] It's tempting just to turn away in disgust – and this sort of wicked real-world appropriation certainly makes more transcendental readings of Shakespeare's ethics and politics look more appealing. But as Nietzsche insisted, some of Shakespeare's characters really do exercise a sort of sovereign freedom 'beyond good and evil', whether we like it or not.[72] This, as we have seen, was what troubled Hazlitt about Coriolanus.

Howard Barker writes powerfully on the subject:

This is a society of the timid which, even whilst it licenses every violent act and every shape of fornication in the name of liberty, still has a horror of autonomy. Populist democracy can tolerate very little of the active self, for self is no respecter of rights, and tragedy is the supreme moment of self and the worst enemy of rights, it tramples rights, it is after all is said and done, *the illegal form of things*. Is there a single tragic protagonist who could not be described prima facie, as one who murders rights? Tragedy is not humanist and intends no good to man. But intending no good to him, it enhances him. That is its mystery and precisely its power to threaten the soul.[73]

Barker defines a tragic kind of freedom which does not hesitate to violate the freedom of the many *on purpose*. This is the sort of freedom that appealed to Dostoevsky's Raskolnikov in *Crime and Punishment*.[74] Certainly freedom – in Shakespeare, Dostoevsky and life – can be a deeply disturbing thing, which leads to murder and other outrages; I have mentioned the terrible freedom which Macbeth expresses in killing Duncan. It is freedom – as we've known since Adam and Eve ate the apple – which brings evil into the world. But Barker is suggesting something darker still; he is suggesting that evil is the ultimate form of freedom.

I think Barker is right to say that individual freedom at its most extreme violates and challenges a more general political freedom in Shakespearean tragedy; but I think he's wrong to imply that's all there is to it. Tragedy is not humanist and intends no good to man, he snarls, suggesting that in the name of individual freedom, tragedy acts against freedom for all. It does – as we saw in the previous chapter, in my brief reading of Edmund; and as we see in Sartre's *Kean* – but we might equally say that it intensifies the need for freedom for all by so vividly exemplifying individual freedom and its value. The political challenge is to make this general. We saw earlier that Thacker understood what Hazlitt also struggled with: freedom in Shakespeare is Napoleon *and* the Revolution. Barker retreats from this complexity by effectively saying that freedom is Napoleon rather than the Revolution.

The struggle for freedom for all is always the struggle against the 'supreme' freedom of self to which Barker gives such memorable expression, and this renders freedom morally complex and unstable – as well as vividly dramatic. But Barker, though himself a dramatist, gives us only one side of the story. Because he doesn't dramatise freedom so richly and variously as Shakespeare does, he is not so truthful and sophisticated a politician of freedom. Philosophers have struggled to reconcile personal freedom and social flourishing, but Shakespeare stages that struggle in action. He encourages a kind of vigilant, open-minded engagement with human life in its variety which adds up to a politics of freedom. We need to recognise that Shakespeare's politics of freedom does not rule out violent extremity, which might, at any given time, constitute an important enactment or recovery of freedom, but might equally entail terror and mayhem. If freedom in order to be freedom needs to incorporate evil, the awkward but necessary question arises of how much evil is enough? And what's still more awkward and troubling is that perhaps we cannot know in the abstract; perhaps we can only answer the question dramatically, in practice, with, say, Macbeth or those who oppose him, trusting to Luxemburg's assurance that the process itself will correct all mistaken attempts – but without any guarantee that it will prove in the end to have been worth the risk.

3

'Freetown!' (*Romeo and Juliet*)

❧

1   Freetown!

On the 5th of September, 1607, *Hamlet* was played on board ship 'at the mouth of the Mitombo River, in what has since become Freetown harbour in Sierra Leone'.[1] Or so we have long been told; Bernice Kliman has cast some doubt on whether this performance actually occurred.[2] If it did, it was certainly an important occasion: the first-ever recorded performance of *Hamlet*, 'the first-ever recorded production of a Shakespeare play outside Europe', 'the beginning not only of Shakespeare in Africa but of the recorded history of Shakespeare in non-professional performance'.[3] But even if it didn't, the mere idea of a Shakespeare performance presaging the eventual establishment of a society of liberated slaves called Freetown is a remarkable thing, as well as one which chimes powerfully with the case this book is making for an association between Shakespeare and freedom. In this chapter, I want to pick up on the fact that in *Romeo and Juliet* Shakespeare named and imagined Freetown for himself. It's a hint, I suggest, that his masterwork of free love is at the same time a serious exploration of the possibilities of social and political freedom. But it is one which imagines such freedom as a dark and dangerous as well as a promising thing.

When the Prince intervenes to quell the riot between the Montagues and Capulets in the first scene, he concludes his speech as follows:

> You, Capulet, shall go along with me,
> And Montague, come you this afternoon,
> To know our farther pleasure in this case,
> To old Freetown, our common judgement-place.
>
> (1.1.97–100)[4]

Freetown!

Shakespeare got it from Arthur Brooke, where Capulet's castle is called Freetown; Brooke Englished it from William Painter, where Capulet's place is Villafranca.[5] But, by first transferring 'Freetown' to the Prince, and then transposing it beyond the story's scene and making it 'our common judgement-place', Shakespeare endued it with an authority that's surprisingly otherworldly and egalitarian. By rendering it '*old* Freetown', he lent it a further, immemorial quality, as though it were somehow always there, positively shadowing the imperfections of our civic life. The Prince is – of course he is – a prince of this world, but a breath of equality nevertheless moves through his peremptory 'You, Capulet, shall go *along with me*.' 'To know our farther pleasure' certainly has its regal high-handedness; but with the introduction of Freetown, which explicitly broadens out this princely pleasure into common judgement, it anticipates something of the sex and mutuality of Romeo and Juliet as opposed to the violence the Prince interrupts.

Freetown!

It's an idea beautiful enough to exceed the Prince's princeliness, particularly in this the greatest canonical work of adventurously free love. But the fact that it is the Prince who speaks for Freetown helps emphasise that it is not to be thought of as a fantasy land of libertarian licence. It is Free**TOWN**, placeholder for a real civil society: **FREE**town, one defined above all by liberty and freedom. In fact, 'Villafranca' to this day is a town or commune outside the walls of Verona, deriving its name from its tax-free status from 1185, but also associated with freedom via the 1859 Treaty of Villafranca in the Italian Wars of Independence that were contemporaneous with Kossuth's rebellion in Hungary. In Shakespeare's play, in contrast with the wearyingly destructive feud which stands for all such blights on our lives, Freetown is 'our common judgement place', its freedom sourced in and guaranteed by inclusive conversation and agreement.

In this small but significant moment of literary history, then, Shakespeare turned Freetown from the mere, meaningless name of a posh villa into a precious, unexpected glimpse of a real place and prospect: serious grounds for hope, albeit ones that remain just off stage. Verona may be fair ('In fair Verona, where we lay our scene' (Prologue, 2)), but Freetown is fairer, and this activates a significant pun where Freetown *is* fairer because it is *fairer*: more just.[6]

* * *

Freetown! It flashes on the mind's eye, and then it is gone: 'like the lightning, which doth cease to be / Ere one can say "it lightens"' (2.2.119–20). But, for me at least, it also appears in another fleeting epiphany in *Romeo and Juliet*. Capulet has somehow tasked an illiterate servant with inviting a list of people over to his momentous masked ball, where of course Romeo and Juliet are destined to meet and initiate the most exemplary love affair in Western culture. When this nonplussed man asks for help reading the relevant names, Romeo sympathetically obliges:

> *Signor Martino and his wife and daughters;*
> *County Anselm and his beauteous sisters;*
> *The lady widow of Vitruvio;*
> *Signor Placentio and his lovely nieces;*
> *Mercutio and his brother Valentine;*
> *Mine uncle Capulet, his wife and daughters;*
> *My fair niece Rosaline, and Livia;*
> *Signor Valentio and his cousin Tybalt;*
> *Lucio and the lively Helena.*
>
> (1.2.63–71)

I'm interested in the way that Mercutio and Tybalt appear in this list. This coupling with 'his brother Valentine' is the first we've heard of Mercutio. Later in the play, Tybalt sneers, 'Mercutio, thou consortest with Romeo', to which Mercutio snorts, '"Consort"? What, dost thou make us minstrels?' (3.1.44–5). The implication seems to be that Mercutio is gay, though if he is, he's unfulfilled – it being something of a downer to be a gay man in love with the most famous heterosexual in history.[7] But then the list for Capulet's party actually intimates that Tybalt's gay as well. It's in verse, with each line – economically, deftly, rather emblematically – *placing* those to whom Capulet is extending his invitation. Some are presented in terms of the patriarchal family – Signor Martino and his wife and daughters; the lady widow of Vitruvio (a rather nice line of blank verse); Mine Uncle Capulet, his wife and daughters. Other lines pair men with attractive women: County Anselm and his *beauteous* sisters, Lucio and the *lively* Helena – and I feel compelled to say here that Signor Placentio with his trophy nieces sounds particularly disagreeably pleased with himself. Anyway, it is in this overwhelming context of patriarchal families and lovely girls that Mercutio and Tybalt are accompanied by male valentines – which in this the greatest and most famous drama of sexual love in Western culture is highly suggestive to say the least.[8] The continuing conversation between Romeo and Capulet's unlettered retainer infuses this prospect of sexual liberty with a transcendent, even a heavenly aura:

> ROMEO A fair assembly. Whither should
> they come?
>
> SERVINGMAN Up.
>
> ROMEO Whither? To supper?
>
> SERVINGMAN To our house.
>
> ROMEO Whose house?
>
> SERVINGMAN My master's.
>
> (1.2.72–77)

Of course the richest, most vivid icon of freedom in *Romeo and Juliet* is the superbly realised forbidden conjunction of Romeo and Juliet themselves, but this exchange between Romeo and Capulet's uneducated servant fleetingly extends the privileges of their love. 'A fair assembly': the pun on 'fair' – just as well as beautiful – comes together with the political connotations of 'assembly' and 'house' to suggest this metaphysical fantasy might be achieved politically. After all, the pleasures proffered by the Capulet ball are very much this-worldly ones: good company, good food, romance, the possibility of sex. That the benighted patriarch of Shakespeare's play is momentarily invested with a more celestial authority sustains the possibility that sexual freedom for more than Romeo and Juliet might actually be realised here.

But then of course brother Valentine and Signor Valentio don't actually 'consort' with Mercutio and Tybalt at the Capulet ball; the play doesn't indicate they make it to the party at all. And yet, Capulet's bash as much as any other scene in the play dramatises the possibility of

Freetown – because it is masked. Given identities, privileges, prejudices and names are suspended, and (as we shall see) the dialogue hints that the disguises worn are actually truer to the undetermined potential of human freedom than the socially recognisable, socially corrupted faces they cover. None of us is innocent: even the most beautifully unstained of souls shares in the guilt, violence and oppression of the system that sustains us all. But when they escape their faces, Shakespeare's revellers, for so long as that free time lasts, also erase the system – showing that we really could live otherwise, that it doesn't have to be this way. It is this which enables Romeo and Juliet to meet, converse, dance and fall in love. The ball truly is a fair assembly; to that extent, it can be thought of as really taking place in Freetown, not Verona.

2   This Is Not Romeo, He's Some Other Where

Because of the feud and the violence it permits and is most characterised by, Verona really isn't so fair. A place where 'women, being the weaker vessels, are ever thrust to the wall' (1.1.14–15), it is also disfigured by 'neighbour-stained steel' (1.1.80). Shakespeare's three main characters aren't just alienated there; they're *aliens*. Capulet says explicitly of Juliet, 'My child is yet a stranger in the world' (1.2.8); the same can be said of Romeo and Mercutio. But aliens testify to the existence of a world elsewhere. Introduced deliberately, separately and in series, after the idea of Freetown has been seeded – Romeo first, then Juliet, then Mercutio – these three substantiate the Freetown life which the play has briefly indicated is not so much impossible as it is tantalisingly out of reach. Alas, they can bear witness to Freetown only tragically, in circumstances that prevent its full, collective realisation; in that sense, it isn't an accident that all three of them die in the end.

Shakespeare keeps them out of the mindless brawl that kicks off the action, making Benvolio the mediator between the brawl and Romeo. You can see why he spares the lovers; but this would have been an obvious place to introduce and employ Romeo's most fascinating and attractive friend, except that (as we'll see) Shakespeare wanted to save Mercutio for Freetown too.

The first thing we learn about Romeo is that he 'was not at this fray'. Simon Palfrey writes of his fundamental 'un-at-homeness', and Benvolio reveals that this hero-to-be has been 'underneath the grove of sycamore / That westward rooteth from this city side'.[9] 'Underneath' is odd, particularly in combination with 'rooteth'. It suggests that Romeo is not just a westbound fugitive from the day rising in the east; it imagines him 'walking' in a sort of underworld. When Benvolio approaches and Romeo withdraws, as Benvolio puts it, 'ware of me', 'into the covert of a wood', there are intimations of a *Hamlet*-like ghastliness. And yet, Benvolio does not recoil from the Romeo-ghost; instead, he recognises in his friend's shrinking disappearance a revelation of his own deepest feelings: 'measuring his affections by my own, / Which then most sought, where most might not be found, / Being one too many by my weary self' (1.1.16–28).

Romeo's dad confirms he didn't just get out of the wrong side of bed this morning but is habitually opposed to the workaday world: 'Many a morning hath he there been seen, / With tears augmenting the fresh morning's dew.' As soon as sunrise starts to unveil the day, Romeo steals 'away from light . . . / And private in his chamber pens himself, / Shuts up his windows, locks fair daylight out / And makes himself an artificial night' (1.1.29–39). The young man in his bedroom: but Benvolio's sympathy makes it impossible to keep Romeo at a condescending arm's length, and the image of Romeo's desperate fight against the day is painfully concrete and vivid, suggesting that he actively wants not just to be a stranger in this world, but to negate and leave it altogether.

That, soon enough, will be associated with love-sickness. But it precedes love-sickness; love-sickness comes as an acceptable diagnosis and post-rationalisation for what at this point is a more inchoate, primal and mysterious alienation. 'Black and portentous,' as his father says (1.1.139). Such darker depths help explain the element of bad faith involved in Romeo's soon-to-be-avowed love of Rosaline. He's cheering himself up; it's a much needed distraction. But it needn't taint Romeo's second love for Juliet to say that this affection, too, meets his preceding need for another life. When he says, 'Tut, I have lost myself, I am not here. / This is not Romeo, he's some other where' (1.1.195–6), Romeo speaks what remains unchangeably true for him. And though of course he does arrive – here, in himself – when he falls for Juliet, their love consummates Romeo's tragic opposition to daylight Verona rather than resolving it.

For now, before it is labelled and understood as love melancholy, Romeo's 'artificial night' – his refusal of this appearing world – recalls that off-stage, non-appearing and yet oh so near world of 'Freetown', where no doubt he'd be more at home.

3   How Stands Your Dispositions to Be Married?

If Romeo's otherworldly melancholy is associated with Freetown, so too, I submit, is Juliet's virginity. This is underlined by the fact that 'Shakespeare makes Juliet so early a teenager, only just, we must suppose, pubertal.'[10] Juliet's virginity is presented at the beginning of the play less in terms of patriarchal ownership than as radically other to established culture. The fact that this otherness is subsequently developed in the characterisation of Mercutio, instead of Juliet – hardly, in the end, a sex denier – underlines that what we're dealing with isn't so much ordinary male possessiveness as it is a potentially hopeful as well as devastating rejection of sexuality as we know it. And in fact, she always will be radically other, though not by refusing sex. Capulet says, 'She is the hopeful lady of my earth' (1.2.14). But, actually, she's more than that. She is the hopeful lady of *the earth in general*, refusing to be just the obedient daughter and keeping open the possibility of something better. And this great creative refusal is foreshadowed when she is introduced in the play by the sheer negative pathos of virginity.

Shakespeare gives us Juliet on the very cusp of sexual eligibility, but the nurse's jolly worldliness about her getting married is shadowed by a half-confessed sadness for the spiritualised autonomy she stands to lose. What most speaks to this is the holy alter ego the nurse produces for Juliet in the form of memories of her own dead and therefore ever-virgin child: 'Susan is with God; / She was too good for me' (1.3.24 ff.). But Juliet's weaning also has a flavour, in the nurse's memory, of apocalyptical trauma. The earthquake which shakes the wall she's leaning against (1.3.24 ff.) becomes all the more portentous when the nurse recalls smearing 'wormwood on the nipple' as there's a star called Wormwood in Revelation (1.3.31, Revelation 8.10–11). And such ill-omened signs resonate disturbingly with the way that the nurse's recollection weirdly accelerates Juliet's weaning into sexual knowledge:

And then my husband – God be with his soul,
'A was a merry man – took up the child:
'Yea,' quoth he, 'dost thou fall upon thy face?
Thou wilt fall backward when thou hast more wit,
Wilt thou not, Jule?' And by my holidam,
The pretty wretch left crying and said 'Ay'.
To see now how a jest shall come about!
I warrant, and I should live a thousand years,
I never should forget it. 'Wilt thou not, Jule?' quoth he,
And, pretty fool, it stinted, and said 'Ay'.

(1.3.40–49)

This vignette does just what the play does at this point, utterly collapsing the time between Juliet's infancy and her marriageable sexuality. Of course, the nurse's husband is perfectly well meaning; indeed, in this flashback he is comforting Juliet. Still, if anything could make virginity seem an excessively brief freehold prior to the gigglingly compliant worldliness with which the nurse now recalls it, it's this earnest toddler's instant recognition of what feminist critics used to call 'compulsory heterosexuality'.[11] That the nurse's husband compares the infant Juliet's upsetting fall to sexual congress lends a whimsical grief to his joke, but the adult couple's laughter is nevertheless partly at the expense of a hurt child, and it somewhat sinisterly foreshadows her initiation into the sex and marriage they chucklingly embody. In their own admittedly cuddly way, the nurse and her dead husband are the agents of coercive ideology here – and the cuddliness doesn't, to me at least, make the coercion any less troubling. What does complicate it, though, is the nurse swearing at the beginning of the scene by her own 'maidenhead at twelve year old': she also has been in Juliet's position (1.3.2).

She concludes by again leaping from Juliet's infancy to her marriage:

Thou wast the prettiest babe that e'er I nursed.
An I might live to see thee married once,
I have my wish.

(1.3.60–3)

I have *my* wish: Juliet's marriage is not her own. And what Lady Capulet says in response encourages further sympathy for the girl:

> Marry, that 'marry' is the very theme
> I came to talk of. Tell me, daughter Juliet,
> How stands your dispositions to be married?

Marry, marry, married: no wonder Juliet returns coldly, 'It is an honour that I dream not of.' But resistance, it would seem, is vain. The nurse hugs herself with proud, uncomprehending satisfaction:

> An honour. Were I not thine only nurse
> I would say thou hadst suck'd wisdom from my teat.

And Mummy says simply: 'Well, think of marriage now' (1.3.63–70). This passage of dialogue menacingly suggests the world has no ears for the virgin's disinclination, fear or revolt while re-emphasising that Juliet has been raised all her life to fulfil the sexual imperative in marriage; it's been mother's milk – or at least wetnurse's milk – to her. And what makes the unavoidable prospect even more horrible is what Mummy now says of the bridegroom:

> This night you shall behold him at our feast;
> Read o'er the volume of young Paris' face
> And find delight there writ with beauty's pen.
> Examine *every married lineament*.
>
>   (1.3.81–4; my emphasis)

Every bit of him, too, has been made for their wedding. It clearly is, as Othello says, 'destiny unshunnable, like death' (*Othello*, 3.3.279).[12] And by now every instinct for freedom is surely screaming in protest.

4   Cold-hand Man

Romeo and Juliet rescue each other, but Mercutio's happiness hangs pathetically on a name in a list of invitees with no further reality in the play. Aside from that teasing reference, there isn't any 'brother Valentine' for him, and he's at odds with prevailing sexual arrangements. It might, then, be best to think of him as not so much gay as queer. His emphatic, repeated, dying curse on 'both your houses' locates him, ultimately, beyond normal domesticity. He mocks heterosexual custom –

> Romeo, humours, madman, passion, lover,
> Appear thou in the likeness of a sigh,
> Speak but one rhyme and I am satisfied.
>
> (2.1.7–9)

– and, in general, is opposed to sex. He has an odd, sad little speech on Romeo which casts it as humiliation:

> This cannot anger him. 'Twould anger him
> To raise a spirit in his mistress' circle
> Of some strange nature, letting it there stand
> Till she had laid it and conjur'd it down –
> That were some spite.
>
> (2.2.23–7)

And in 1973 at Stratford, Mercutio 'constantly carried a grotesque, coarse-featured life-size female doll, upon which he vented a sado-masochistic sexual loathing'.[13] At a somewhat later point in the play, he says more heartily to his friend in terms which define a proper blokeish personality as the transcendence of male sexuality as such:

Why, is not this better now than groaning for love? Now thou art sociable, now art thou Romeo, now art thou what thou art, by art as well as by nature, for this drivelling love is like a great natural that runs lolling up and down to hide his bauble in a hole. (2.4.85–89)

That final image has a characteristic brilliance, but a typically negative brilliance. The surreal intensity evokes a pained fastidiousness masked as male sociability, and the intriguing suggestion of being 'by art' intimates that Mercutio seeks a form of life and friendship that is something more than merely natural.

The play hints in various ways at the homosexual origins of Mercutio's distaste for heterosexual love. Joseph A. Porter has argued that the Valentine who is coupled with Mercutio in the list of invitees for Capulet's party is a secret cipher for Romeo, whereas I am suggesting we should think of him as a ghost from Freetown; but it is true that, as Roger Allam argues and many actors and directors have realised, there is an ambivalent sexuality about Mercutio's relations with Romeo, and that even his puns 'show a particular interest in Romeo's "prick"'.[14] Given that

Tybalt, like Mercutio, is associated with a male Valentine, Mercutio's comment on Tybalt's hyper-masculinity might be worth quoting here: 'By Jesu, a very good blade, a very tall man, a very good whore!' (2.4.29–30). This suggests homosexual ambivalence. Masculinity tips over into sodomy; Tybalt is too good to resist. Yet at the same time as the line expresses Mercutio's attraction to Tybalt, it recoils from his imagined promiscuity.

It's interesting that both Tybalt and Mercutio threaten to unmask each other in the course of the play. It's as if Mercutio looks Tybalt up and down and says, 'By Jesu, a very good blade, a very tall man, a very good whore', only for Tybalt to answer him coldly, 'Mercutio, thou consortest with Romeo', which now seems to express a certain jealousy. Of course, I am taking the lines out of context but between these two, there is a certain painful solidarity – a hateful kinship – and perhaps it brings out the pathos of this to consider that they might have been friends or even lovers in Freetown.

The play begins with Romeo's alienation and Juliet's virginity; but Romeo and Juliet ultimately find new freedom in each other, as Paul Kottman argues.[15] Mercutio's wild freedom prepares the way for this. But Mercutio opens up the room from which Romeo makes an artificial night – he opens up Juliet's virginity – into a whole and permanent form of being. He does not leap into completely new being, as the lovers do. His freedom remains purely negative, involving him in an agonised and angry complicity with the very reality he rejects. Romeo and Juliet bring a little bit of Freetown blazingly to life here. Mercutio just longs for it, and the longing turns bitter and corrosive, as we see, for instance, in his great Queen Mab speech:

> ROMEO   I dreamt a dream tonight.
>
> MERCUTIO   And so did I.
>
> ROMEO   Well what was yours?
>
> MERCUTIO   That dreamers often lie.
>
> ROMEO   In bed asleep while they do dream things true.
>
> MERCUTIO   O then I see Queen Mab hath been with you.
>   She is the fairies' midwife, and she comes

In shape no bigger than an agate stone
On the forefinger of an alderman,
Drawn with a team of little atomi
Over men's noses as they lie asleep.
Her chariot is an empty hazelnut
Made by the joiner squirrel or old grub,
Time out o'mind the fairies' coachmakers;
Her waggon-spokes made of long spinners' legs,
The cover of the wings of grasshoppers,
Her traces of the smallest spider web,
Her collars of the moonshine's watery beams,
Her whip of cricket's bone, the lash of film,
Her waggoner a small grey-coated gnat,
Not half so big as a round little worm
Prick'd from the lazy finger of a maid.
And in this state she gallops night by night
Through lovers' brains, and then they dream of love;
O'er courtiers' knees, that dream on curtsies straight;
O'er lawyers' fingers, who straight dream on fees;
O'er ladies' lips, who straight on kisses dream,
Which oft the angry Mab with blisters plagues
Because their breaths with sweetmeats tainted are.
Sometime she gallops o'er a courtier's nose
And then dreams he of smelling out a suit;
And sometime comes she with a tithe-pig's tail,
Tickling a parson's nose as 'a lies asleep;
Then dreams he of another benefice.
Sometime she driveth o'er a soldier's neck
And then dreams he of cutting foreign throats,
Of breaches, ambuscados, Spanish blades,
Of healths five fathoms deep; and then anon
Drums in his ear, at which he starts and wakes,
And being thus frighted swears a prayer or two
And sleeps again. This is that very Mab
That plaits the manes of horses in the night
And bakes the elf-locks in foul sluttish hairs,
Which once untangled much misfortune bodes.

> This is the hag, when maids lie on their backs,
> That presses them and learns them first to bear,
> Making them women of good carriage.
> This is she –

ROMEO   Peace, peace, Mercutio, peace.
> Thou talk'st of nothing.

MERCUTIO   True, I talk of dreams,
> Which are the children of an idle brain,
> Begot of nothing but vain fantasy.

(1.4.50–98)

In an otherwise sage account, Stanley Wells suggests that the 'imaginative and poetic delicacy' in this speech is 'totally at odds' with Mercutio's 'coarse attitude to sex' as well as that it is hard 'to integrate this fantasy into a concept of Mercutio's role or into the overall design of the play'.[16] I disagree. I have tried to show that his attitude to sex is one of troubled repugnance not coarseness, and I suggest that his Queen Mab speech deepens rather than contradicts this.

The first thing to notice is the sheer vigour of Mercutio's imaginative relation to the world. He sees things 'not half so big as a round little worm prick'd from the lazy finger of a maid'! What is equally evident is his fancifulness: the whole extraordinarily vivid and fertile vision of the tiny Mab's nocturnal mischief. Vigour and fancifulness are hallmarks of Mercutio as Shakespeare renders him throughout the play. But what is particularly established in this speech is that Mercutio's fancifulness works in and is limited by the fully felt and known physical world we all live in – in all its grainy shittiness, of round little worms, emptied hazelnuts, cricket bones, foul sluttish hairs, and so on – and equally by the substantial, almost indeed inviolable cultural world with which it combines to constitute human reality, and which here ensures that maids dream of men, soldiers of slaying, and parsons of tithes, ineluctably. Mab stands before Freud for the fact that even our most intimate fantasies and dreams are thoroughly determined, but this female fairy provides no hope of male valentines. That Mercutio is ultimately opposed to the reality his wit conjures in this speech is evident in his 'angry' Mab's sheer fury of blistering, disfiguring and disturbing, in a crescendo of humiliation that climaxes in rehearsals for heterosexual coitus. When he said 'making them women of good carriage', Adrian Schiller, Mercutio in Michael Boyd's 2000 Royal Shakespeare Company (RSC) production, 'sat astride the prostrate Romeo and moved his pelvis over his friend's', explicitly linking this unromantic vision of heterosexual sex with his own homosexual frustration.[17]

But Mab, in spite of herself, *serves* the world she is angrily opposed to – teaching maids to bear, making them women of good carriage; helping soldiers be soldiers; lawyers lawyers – and this furious conformism gives us a key to her author: Mercutio. Romeo interrupts him, telling him he talks of nothing. But in fact his fantasy is limited to angry, scornful reflections of what is. Or to put it another way: it is not fantastical, not nothing, enough. When he lies in his death throes, Mercutio says of Tybalt, 'Is he gone, and hath nothing?' (3.1.93). He means, presumably, didn't I hurt him at all? But, in the wider context of the play, where Freetown is the not and never land that is just off stage, *Is he gone, and hath nothing?*, also has a positive wistfulness, as if Mercutio were imagining that his more violent alter ego has left this unsatisfactory world and somehow seized that more fulfilled, alternative life that wasn't available to either of them here. And if I was right to say that, in the midst of their enmity, Tybalt and Mercutio recognise each other, it's also possible that now, in the moments before his death, Mercutio feels bereaved of the man who, as well as being his murderer, was also – even more than Romeo – his secret companion and fellow sufferer.

It will be clear by now that I am offering a reading of Mercutio that has something in common with but at the same time substantially differs from Baz Luhrmann's characterisation of Romeo's friend as a compulsively watchable and implicitly gay drag queen in his 1996 smash hit *William Shakespeare's Romeo + Juliet*. But the Mercutio I find in the play is a less camp, more energetically negative figure.

In creating his Mercutio, Shakespeare expanded brilliantly on a hint in Arthur Brooke's *The Tragical History of Romeus and Juliet*, where we read that Mercutio has cold hands. During a break between dances at the Capulet ball, Mercutio takes Juliet's hand: 'The frozen mountayne yse was never halfe so cold / As were his handes, though neer the fire he dyd him holde' (2.61–2). But Romeus takes Juliet's other hand, and the heroine responds gratefully: 'Mercutio's ysy hande had all to frosen myne / And of thy goodness thou agayne hast warmed it with thine' (2.89–90).[18] You can see what happened when Shakespeare read this. The detail of his cold hands in the sources disclosed to Shakespeare Mercutio's wholly negative form of being. Poor Mercutio, as Shakespeare himself perhaps thought; he cannot warm himself at the world's fires, but he has nowhere else to go.

When Benvolio tells Romeo 'brave Mercutio is dead', he goes on to say, 'That gallant spirit hath aspir'd the clouds / Which too untimely here did scorn the earth' (3.1.118–20). It's an excellent epitaph, reminding us that there's more to Benvolio than we might presume and associating Mercutio with that glimpse of Freetown afforded when Capulet's servant indicated that 'the fair assembly' was 'up' above. Here Mercutio could only 'scorn the earth', which could not accommodate him. His *untimeliness* was the predicate of a spirit of Freetown caught in the toils of unfreedom.

5   But You Shall Go to the Ball!

Romeo and Juliet *have* to meet at the misfits masked ball where normal social roles and identities are suspended; but then if it really were 'a *fair assembly*' Mercutio would meet 'brother Valentine' there too, as we have seen Shakespeare takes pains to suggest.

Mercutio hints he is always masked when he says, 'Give me a case to put my visage in: / A visor for a visor' (1.4.29–30). And Juliet even more directly expresses the point that what others think of as our faces may in fact conceal what we are. When she modestly remarks on her own unlovely face, her (as he thinks) husband-to-be Paris says with an unconscious possessiveness that couldn't be better calculated to steel his intended's resolve for freedom: 'Thy face is mine, and thou hast slandered it.' Juliet responds, 'It may be so, for it is not mine own' (4.1.35–6). The dancers at the ball may doff such faces. The masks they wear are Freetown faces; they are the faces of their freedom.[19]

The ball, like Freetown, is a 'common judgement place'; like the Forest of Arden in *As You Like It*, it is a common judgement place in the sphere of sexual selection. Sexual selection has its cruelties, but cruelty isn't the focus here. The ball enables a more liberated choice, though that the male Valentines aren't apparently there indicates that there are limits to this.

And it's true that adverse forces threaten. Tybalt's feline eyes glint green and narrow when he identifies Romeo and calls for his rapier. But, for now, this is the best approximation of Freetown Verona can afford; Capulet has heard fair things of Romeo, and he answers with a good grace: 'I would not for the wealth of all this town / Here in my house do him disparagement' (1.5.68–9). When Tybalt continues to rage, Capulet loses his own temper, reverting in the process to the Italian patriarch who will tyrannise over his own daughter and her 'scope of choice' (1.2.17). He ends in confusion:

> Be quiet, or – More light, more light! – For shame,
> I'll make you quiet. – What, cheerly, my hearts!
>
> (1.5.86–7)

Here Freetown and Verona are contending *within* Capulet, who, incidentally, sounds rather like Claudius after The Mousetrap. Freetown is fading like a guttering candle, threatening to subside into the customary darkness and violence of Verona. 'For shame, I'll make you quiet,' the patriarchal bully growls. But his only just credible call for peace and good cheer is what sufficiently enables Romeo's and Juliet's meeting.

'More light, more light': the love of that peerless pair is typically thought of as an extraordinary illumination, and as much for its rare intensity as its tragic brevity.[20] Their first meeting is a glimpse in benighted Verona of the possibilities of Freetown at its most ravishing, and it transfigures the occasion that makes it possible. Signor Martino and his wife and daughters; the lady widow of Utruvio; County Anselm and his beauteous sisters, and so on: we can imagine their faces touched with such a light as perhaps could also soften and reveal Mercutio and Tybalt redeemed from bitterness. Given the encouragement we get from the list of invitees, we might at least *imagine* the presence of Brother Valentine and Signor Valentio: lineaments of gratified desire. After all, Shakespeare goes further in that direction when he releases into *As You Like It* the dancing projection of sexual freedom that is Ganymede.

Otherwise, we have seen *Romeo and Juliet* condemns Mercutio to wild, hilarious and melancholy opposition to a world which can't accommodate him; in Tybalt, Mercutio's surreal irony becomes sheer fury. The male

Valentines Shakespeare so briefly conjures for them express the tantalising possibility that their amazing energy could be redeemed into a love which expresses the same degree of force in more positive form. But such fulfilment isn't available in the play. The following piece of dialogue makes explicit what we will probably have guessed: for sex, Mercutio has to fall back on masturbation.

> MERCUTIO   . . . the bawdy hand of the dial is now upon the
>   prick of noon.
>
> NURSE   Out upon you. What a man are you?
>
> ROMEO   One, gentlewoman, that God hath made, himself
>   to mar.
>
>   (2.4.108–12)

And we should note that masturbation here shades into self-harm. He is not a happy masturbator. When he offers his most memorable obscenity in the play, 'O Romeo, that she were, O, that she were / An open-arse, thou a poperin pear!', immediately after he says, 'Romeo, good night. I'll to my truckle-bed; / This field-bed is too cold for me to sleep' (2.1.37–40).[21] A truckle bed, Arden editor René Weis explains, is 'a low bed on castors, usually reserved for children, and pulled out for use from an adult high or standing-bed'. He goes on to say, 'Mercutio is jesting when he evokes an image of himself cosily tucked in a child's bed at home while Romeo is out in the field.'[22] Maybe, but this is to ignore the fact that Mercutio's are the very last memorable words before Romeo and Juliet's famous balcony scene. In that context, the image of a grown man trying to sleep on a sexless bed while his beloved friend, warmed with desire, pursues a love destined to light up the world is hardly a humorous one. And the fact that it comes straight after Mercutio's ambivalent evocation of 'an open arse' sharpens the sense of sexual frustration. What Mercutio says about the cold recalls his icy hands in Brooke; we can imagine him, perhaps, trying to warm them between his thighs, as he tosses and turns on his 'truckle bed'; it is not a night, apparently, for solitary self-harming. His simple conclusion, 'Come, shall we go?', is unutterably sad (2.1.41). Mercutio has to retire from the field. There is no conceivable balcony scene for him.

Romeo and Juliet lose their bliss in the process of attaining it: that is their tragedy. But at least Romeo and Juliet attain their tragedy. We pity them but they make it that far. Mercutio and Tybalt stand for the many more who don't.

6   Love's Charter

As Palfrey observes, Mercutio dies to make way for Juliet.[23] *Romeo and Juliet* transcends coldness, irony and scorn to give us the miracle which as long ago as 1797 August Wilhelm Schlegel designated the 'self-created existence of the lovers' [*selbstgeschaffne[s] Dasein der Liebenden*].[24] This is a great touchstone of freedom. If Mercutio and Valentine are dancing 'up' in Freetown, Romeo and Juliet come blissfully together *here*. They abolish the distance between Freetown and reality. Thanks to them, Shakespeare is able to bring freedom home. That said, they don't altogether transcend Mercutio's negativity. Their love retains a destructive aspect; it must, because it must negate the present world, and this brings us up against *Romeo and Juliet*'s dramatisation of the destructive abstraction of freedom *even in its positive forms*.

In *Romeo and Juliet*, Shakespeare worries that the free love of his principals might be a further iteration of the violence it seems to defy.[25] 'My only love sprung from my only hate,' as Juliet puts it (1.5.137). The play infamously begins with expressions of casually violent misogyny: 'I will be civil with the maids, I will cut off their heads' (1.1.21–2). But if this sexualises civic strife, Romeo has an early speech – from before he even meets Juliet – which makes the disturbing suggestion that love and strife are one:

> O me, what fray was here?
> Yet tell me not, for I have heard it all.
> Here's much to do with hate, but more with love.
> Why then, O brawling love, O loving hate,
> O anything of nothing first create,
> O heavy lightness, serious vanity,
> Misshapen chaos of well-seeming forms,
> Feather of lead, bright smoke, cold fire, sick health,
> Still-waking sleep that is not what it is.
> This love feel I that feel no love in this.

The Arden editor suggests 'Romeo is keeping Benvolio at bay with a parody of lovers' discourse in order to forestall his question about the identity of his beloved at line 197.'[26] But when Romeo invites Benvolio's scorn, saying, 'Dost thou not laugh?', Benvolio answers, 'No, coz, I rather weep ... /At thy good heart's oppression': none of which sounds insincere. Romeo goes on startlingly to nominate such sympathy as Benvolio has just shown him 'love's transgression', a sin which doubles the grief of the world (1.1.171–87). And this seems to confirm his scepticism about love's capacity to heal, rather than worsen, the social breach.[27] Moreover, when Juliet later speaks of 'wreak[ing] the love I bore my cousin / Upon his body that hath slaughter'd him', it hints that love's recompense for civil war might darken into sadomasochism (3.5.100–102).

Palfrey acknowledges that Romeo and Juliet 'oppose the world they are born into: but the nature of their love is also born profoundly from it'.[28] And Julia Kristeva insists that when Romeo kills Tybalt, far from betraying his commitment to love, it actually releases 'the fury that underlies his love'.[29] But it is still true that the balcony scene effects an enlightenment in the sense not just of illumination but equally of a transcendent refinement – a *lightening* – that at first seems to float beyond the miasma of violence:

> ROMEO   Two of the fairest stars in all the heaven,
>   Having some business, do entreat her eyes
>   To twinkle in their spheres till they return.
>   What if her eyes were there, they in her head?
>   The brightness of her cheek would shame those stars
>   As daylight doth a lamp. Her eyes in heaven
>   Would through the airy region stream so bright
>   That birds would sing and think it were not night.
>   See how she leans her cheek upon her hand.
>   O that I were a glove upon that hand,
>   That I might touch that cheek!
>
> JULIET   Ay me.

ROMEO   She speaks.

ROMEO

    O speak again bright angel, for thou art
    As glorious to this night, being o'er my head,
    As is a winged messenger of heaven
    Unto the white-upturned wondering eyes
    Of mortals that fall back to gaze on him
    When he bestrides the lazy-puffing clouds
    And sails upon the bosom of the air.

                              (2.2.15–32)

Romeo is ready to float up to Juliet 'aloft' on her balcony; he's about to rise
to her 'up' in Freetown. Of course there's a phallic implication, but what's
imagined here is a rarer erection: one which entails ecstatic existential
change. And though Romeo perhaps does not lift physically off from his
tip-toes – though it'd be fun to see in a theatre – nor does he 'fall back' into
everyday Verona. Juliet is calling his soul home to Freetown before our
eyes, murmuring, 'Deny thy father' (2.2.34); 'I'll no longer be a Capulet'
(2.2.36); 'doff thy name' (2.2.47). It's thrilling and edifying, but it does also
involve its own kind of violence: the refined violence of a transcendent
erasure of ordinary identity.

    Advancing in the shadows, 'the mask of night' likewise on his face
(cf. 2.2.85), her love takes the heroine at her word. And he looms in view
not as any customary kind of Italian man, but as a nameless visitor from
beyond, and she is suitably frightened:

What man art thou . . . (2.2.52; my emphasis)

                    * * *

In her essay on *Romeo and Juliet*, Catherine Belsey quotes Jacques
Derrida's meditation on love to bear out that desire – not just desire
in this play, but desire in general – involves a specifically metaphysical
hunger for fulfilment: 'You have always been "my" metaphysics, the
metaphysics of my life, the "verso" of everything I write (my desire,
speech, presence, proximity, law, my heart and soul, everything that
I love and that you know before me).'[30] The French philosopher offers
his own reflections on *Romeo and Juliet* in 'Aphorism, Countertime',
which takes the form of a series of numbered maxims. The gaps

between these disjointed reflections brilliantly manifest the impossible, metaphysical union Romeo and Juliet long for. They can't simply 'have' each other because, as Derrida's eleventh maxim puts it: 'I love because the other is the other, because its time will never be mine.'[31] It is this which launches Shakespeare's lovers beyond merely having into their yearning freedom.

'Aphorism, Countertime' casts a particularly penetrating light on the way in which the conundrum of names and naming in the play relates to freedom, suggesting that though, on the one hand, Romeo and Juliet want to 'doff' their names in favour of the transcendence that is figured by Derrida's gaps, names at the same time actually stand for and participate in just this sort of metaphysical freedom. Ideally, my name liberates me to be myself, and others to love me as such; it's in this spirit that Juliet wants Echo to make herself hoarse 'with repetition of my "Romeo"'(2.2.163). She wants 'Romeo' but not 'Romeo Montague'; yet without the social and familial specification which a surname confers, Juliet's Romeo could be any of a thousand Romeos. Moreover, Derrida brings out a transcendental aspect to naming. My name, he notes, is destined to *survive me*. And as part of aphorism 24, he observes: 'A proper name does not name anything which is human ... And yet this relation to the inhuman only befalls man, for him, to him, in the name of man. He alone gives himself this inhuman name.'[32] If then, as Palfrey says, names 'brand us as mortal and confined; they also confer immortality'.[33] To put it in terms most pertinent to my argument, names name that social identity which Romeo and Juliet want to go beyond but they equally speak to and for transcendence. We can now hear the wonder as well as the frustration that has helped to make the following the play's most famous line: 'O Romeo, Romeo, wherefore art thou Romeo?' (2.2.33). And we can understand the paradox whereby the lovers actually cherish and repossess at the same time as they wish to do away with their names.[34]

And what goes for names goes equally for the basic building blocks of social life and language: they are, all of them, original, originating and transcendent. It's just that we've forgotten. We've forgotten because we take them for granted. But the civic, *Romeo and Juliet* suggests, is not so much the obstacle to transcendence as it is itself already transcendental. And this means that the freedom which Romeo and Juliet attempt really could be attempted on a wider scale. The lovers don't only discover the 'vertiginous substance' of their own freedom, as Kottman argues; they discover the vertiginous substance of freedom *as such*, and this, potentially, is a charter for much more than private passion.[35]

7   Boundless as the Sea

Romeo and Juliet are sacrificed to Verona, but their civic importance to that Freetown which the play asks us to envisage actually depends on their private fulfilment. So let's, for heaven's sake, give them back their balcony scene, and then draw the political moral.

Of the two of them, Juliet is particularly intelligent about what they're getting into, knowing – immediately – that they are moving past established social forms and (almost) language:

> ROMEO Lady, by yonder blessed moon I vow,
>   That tips with silver all these fruit-tree
>   tops –
>
> JULIET O swear not by the moon.
>   . . .
>
> ROMEO What shall I swear by?
>
> JULIET   Do not swear at all.
>   Or if thou wilt, swear by thy gracious self,
>   Which is the god of my idolatry,
>   And I'll believe thee.
>
> ROMEO   If my heart's dear love –
>
> JULIET
>   Well, do not swear.
>
>   (2.2.107–16)

Her use of the word 'idolatry' to express her feelings betrays some unease and, at the same time, she worries about their breakneck venturesomeness, and in terms which recall and intensify Romeo's earlier misgivings about the violence of love:

> Although I joy in thee,

> I have no joy of this contract tonight;
> It is too rash, too unadvis'd, too sudden,
> Too like the lightning which doth cease to be
> Ere one can say 'It lightens'.
>
> (2.2.116–20)

Juliet grabs back at the thought that their love could come to an honest, organic fruition here:

> Sweet, good night.
> This bud of love, by summer's ripening breath
> May prove a beauteous flower when next we meet.
>
> (2.2.120–22)

But, in truth, there is no returning, and she speaks from gloriously beyond the ordinary world of limitation and identity when she says:

> My bounty is as boundless as the sea,
> My love as deep; the more I give to thee,
> The more I have, for both are infinite.
>
> (2.2.133–5)[36]

Of course it's very beautiful, but what does it mean for life and love? What does it mean for Shakespeare's politics of freedom? I've suggested that the unfulfilled Mercutio relates to the unredeemed world of Verona which can't positively accommodate him by means of energetic irony, but of course such irony ultimately feeds off and so negatively preserves the status quo. Juliet's speech is actually *more* negative, going beyond all bounded forms of life as we know it. It goes beyond the negative name-lessness that we have seen the pair partly struggle to attain, because that is readily imaginable as a different, albeit mysterious kind of single identity. We can almost picture the nameless Juliet, the nameless Romeo. Whereas if what Juliet says blows your mind, it should, because identity is softly exploding into the infinite here. Indeed, it is worth remarking that one of the most cherishable things about Shakespeare's play is the way in which the utterly particular – a teenaged girl's amorous enthusiasm – becomes infinite. And yet, where does this leave Juliet? It leaves her hungering for two things with a fair chance of accessing the infinite: sex and marriage. Inasmuch as both aim at absolute union, these perhaps are one. But sex and marriage are forms of this life; they communicate with the infinite only inasmuch as they become hospitable and even transparent to death. And that is why *Romeo and Juliet*, and its implicit politics of freedom, has to be radically darkened and changed. Identity politics isn't enough. Certainly the play asks us to imagine how Mercutio's negativity might be more positively fulfilled by the negation of negative conditions that gay liberation would entail. It insists Freetown has to be able to accommodate Mercutio and Valentine as well as Romeo and Juliet. For Mercutio and Valentine are entitled to their basic liberties, to sex and (why not?) marriage, just as Romeo and Juliet require theirs. Nevertheless, it won't do to imagine a smug and sated Mercutio; it wouldn't even be Mercutio. Nor will it satisfy to imagine Romeo and Juliet in a better world where they get married, have kids and get fat.

8   Come, Civil Night

'The poem brings us back to ourselves' [*Die Dichtung führt uns in uns selbst zurück*], says Schlegel.[37] But most of us don't expect to go out in a blaze of glory. What would become of Romeo and Juliet if they *didn't die*? Julia Kristeva reports on the prospects for their marriage as follows:

Either time's alchemy transforms the criminal, secret passion of the outlaw lovers into the banal, humdrum, lacklustre lassitude of a tired and cynical collusion ... Or else the married couple continues to be a passionate couple, but covering the entire gamut of sadomasochism that the two partners already heralded in the yet relatively quiet version of the Shakespearean text. Each acting out both sexes in turn they thus create a foursome that feeds on itself through repeated aggression and merging, castration and gratification, resurrection and death. And who, at passionate moments, have recourse to stimulants – temporary partners, sincerely loved but victims still, whom the monstrous couple grinds in its passion of faithfulness to itself, supporting itself by means of unfaithfulness to others.[38]

Monstrous couple indeed! It's true that there's no Mercutio without his restless energy, no Romeo and Juliet without their more positive negation of ordinary life; but is this really how the Romeo and Juliet marriage would turn out if they remained faithful to a passion that was not cut so tragically short? Is this obscene epiphany really a revelation of what goes on behind closed doors in Freetown?

Maybe, maybe not. Certainly the mind quails to imagine a happy social life for the lovers. According to Kottman, this is because Romeo and Juliet are fulfilled absolutely apart from the social, even ultimately from each other. Shakespeare, he argues, dramatises the pair's 'coming to grips with their freedom with another as their capacity for active separation, with the fact that *claiming* this separateness, even in its sorrowful effects, is the essential happiness of their individual lives'.[39] This is an intriguing point, and we'll return to it later. Kottman suggests Romeo and Juliet manage this trick of growing together apart at two particular junctures in the play. The first is when Juliet allows Romeo to leave without her when, Kottman insists, she really could have just followed Romeo to Mantua. He writes imaginatively about their protracted goodbyes: '*You* say good night; no, *you* say good night . . . *You* hang up; no, *you*, hang up.'[40] But if it's the case that the lovers are typical in 'coming to grips with their freedom with one another', it's equally true that Juliet doesn't want just to elope with Romeo. She wants to be *married*. The personal, she insists, is political, and she insists on keeping the political in play. But if Kristeva is right about the marital prospects for Romeo and Juliet – if 'everything is thus malevolent, perverse, foul' – then she's probably also right that it means 'the end of the immaculate home, of aseptic marriage – the pillar of the State'; Freetown accordingly becomes a hell to contemplate, and to be avoided at all costs.[41] We might remember in this connection that Juliet says, 'Come, *civil* night':

> Thou sober-suited matron all in black,
> And learn me how to lose a winning match,
> Played for a pair of stainless maidenhoods.
> Hood my unmann'd blood, bating in my cheeks,
> With thy black mantle, till strange love grown bold,
> Think true love acted, simple modesty.
>
> (3.2.10–16)

Her sexual frankness may not be as dismaying as it was to commentators of earlier, more fastidious epochs, but we deceive ourselves if we do not hear the note of sublime and disturbing boldness.[42] Nevertheless, what Juliet says doesn't altogether back Kristeva up, for its shamelessness is mixed with a 'simple' and covering 'modesty' not at all compatible with the cynical sex games Kristeva imagines. Indeed, it is striking in this play of free love that Juliet imagines the dark sponsor of her love as 'a sober-suited matron'. But then this sober-suited matron is veiling 'strange love grown bold', which is to say enabling the most extreme impudence, of which Kristeva's obscene fantasy perhaps does catch the flavour; this particular sober-suited matron is simultaneously a bawd. But virginity is in the mix too. Juliet assumes Romeo is also a virgin, speaking of a '*a pair* of stainless maidenheads' to be lost in the 'winning match' that she is somehow playing from beyond her own maidenhead in wild fantasies that involve an inalienable poetic darkness which may after all be the secret content of her modesty. She goes on:

> Come night, come Romeo, come, thou day in night,
> For thou wilt lie upon the wings of night
> Whiter than snow upon a raven's back.
> Come, gentle night, come, loving black-brow'd night,
> Give me my Romeo, and when I shall die
> Take him and cut him out in little stars,
> And he will make the face of heaven so fine
> That all the world will be in love with night
> And pay no worship to the garish sun.
> O, I have bought the mansion of a love
> But not possess'd it, and though I am sold,
> Not yet enjoy'd. So tedious is this day
> As is the night before some festival
> To an impatient child that hath new robes
> And may not wear them.
>
> (3.2.17–31)

Of course this is all *ravishing*: 'gentle', 'loving', alluringly 'black-browed'. But it's also verse which turns explicitly away from light, just as Romeo was said to have done in the first scene, favouring, instead, night, death and darkness, albeit in expectation of further, wholly new illumination. For night reveals its own alternative light source in the son it gives birth to: Romeo. At the same time, Juliet tastes her own death in the darkness: *and when I shall die*. And bypassing the death of her living lover with what can only be described as breathtaking insouciance, she asks night to dismember him in lights so 'fine' as will persuade the world of the superior beauty and delicacy of night. It all adds up to nothing less than aesthetic and spiritual revolution – as Novalis did not fail to appreciate when he turned *Romeo and Juliet*'s poetry into his own mystical offering to darkness at the onset of German Romanticism.[43] It's chilling but instructive to remark that Shakespeare opened this vein once more, in his most demonic play: 'Come, thick night, / And pall thee in the dunnest smoke of hell' and so on (*Macbeth*, 1.5.48–9, 3.2.47–51). Even the raven who croaks himself hoarse at Duncan's fatal entrance makes its prophetic appearance in Juliet's speech, carrying her snow-skinned lover on its back.

9   O Happy Dagger

'Universal freedom,' wrote Hegel in *The Phenomenology of Spirit*, 'can produce neither a positive work nor a deed; there is left for it only *negative* action; it is merely the *fury* of destruction.' He went on to say a page later, 'The sole work and deed of universal freedom is therefore *death*.'[44] These are strange and disturbing words, but they resonate with the vision of *Romeo and Juliet*.

A brilliantly riddling speech of Juliet's helps bring out what 'civil night' really entails. She is asking her distracted nurse if Romeo really has committed suicide, as the nurse would seem to have implied:

> Hath Romeo slain himself? Say thou but 'Ay'
> And that bare vowel 'I' shall poison more
> Than the death-darting eye of cockatrice.
> I am not I if there be such an 'I',
> Or those eyes shut that makes thee answer 'Ay'.
> If he be slain say 'Ay', or if not, 'No'.
> Brief sounds determine of my weal or woe.
>
> (3.2.45–51)[45]

Juliet's reaction to Romeo's supposed death is overlaid with a meditation on the killing effects of conventional identity; social thought emerges from passionate experience. The first line links the active 'no' of suicide with the 'ay' of affirmation and seemingly longs for the death it goes on to lament.

The second line, at the same time as it starts to suggest that confirmation of Romeo's death will be the death of Juliet, also hints that the public, objective 'I' of given identity is poisonous. The next complete thought, in the fourth line, presents this superb formulation:

I am not I if there be such an 'I'.

Juliet's identity depends on Romeo's life, but what comes to the fore here is that a given, social identity denoted by 'I' is fatal to the more real, more negative identity which Juliet now cherishes. The line that follows imagines eyes expiring at the 'ay' of affirmation. And in the penultimate line of the speech, life is associated not with 'ay' but with 'no'. All of it, in sum, nudges us towards imagining and accepting an I beyond 'I': a Freetown subjectivity that is death to this present world but which might just constitute a new one.[46]

Shakespeare knows the risk he is taking here. 'I am not I if there be such an "I"': it is very close to Iago's, 'I am not what I am' (*Othello*, 1.1.66).[47] And that negation of the name of God or Yahweh – *I am that I am* – defines a specifically demonic deviation from what is in favour of self-creating negativity (Exodus 3.14). Juliet, quick as she is, realises this, calling Romeo, 'Beautiful tyrant, fiend angelical' (3.2.75). And indeed her great 'Come, civil night' speech just analysed acknowledges its demonic character not just retroactively after *Macbeth* has been written but also when the key word 'possessed' sounds in the following lines:

> O, I have bought the mansion of a love
> But not possess'd it, and though I am sold,
> Not yet enjoy'd.

In the context of her paean to night, the thought of being bought but not enjoyed unavoidably suggests whoredom, and that of possession confirms that the civil night *Romeo and Juliet* entails risks what revolution always risks: demonic terror.[48]

That terror is inseparable from the hope of fulfilment; it is what makes the death-loving aspiration of the play's principals so painful and distressing. It obliges us to confront the truly deadly quality that abides in freedom. The second part of the tragedy is marked by a great crescendo of the poetry of death. Juliet says, 'Come, cords, come, Nurse, I'll to my wedding bed / And death, not Romeo, take my maidenhead' (3.2.136–7). Romeo falls

upon the ground, 'Taking the measure of an unmade grave' (3.3.70).
The nurse begs him to stand for Juliet's sake, asking, 'Why should you
fall into so deep an O?' (3.3.89–90). Romeo moans:

> O, tell me, Friar, tell me,
> In what vile part of this anatomy
> Doth my name lodge? Tell me that I may sack
> The hateful mansion.
>
> (3.3.104–7)

Capulet says, 'Well, we were born to die' (3.4.4). And Romeo also says,
'Come, death, and welcome! Juliet wills it so' (3.5.24). Juliet whispers: 'O
God, I have an ill-divining soul! / Methinks I see thee, now thou art so
low, / As one dead in the bottom of a tomb' (3.5.54–6). And even: 'Indeed,
I never shall be satisfied / With Romeo till I behold him – dead' (3.5.93–4).[49]
She ends Act Three by saying, 'If all else fail, myself have power to die'
(3.5.243). And she speaks these remarkable words:

> Chain me with roaring bears,
> Or hide me nightly in a charnel-house,
> O'ercovered quite with dead men's rattling bones,
> With reeky shanks and yellow chapless skulls.
> Or bid me go into a new-made grave,
> And hide me with a dead man in his shroud.
>
> (4.1.80–5)

What makes the speech the more riveting and haunting is that it so
vividly expresses the internal necessity of what the Prologue established
straightaway as a 'death-marked love', one which already has launched
itself beyond life in night-inspired reverie (Prologue, 9). This is also the
reason why if, on the one hand, it will be a hideous torment for Juliet to
pre-experience her own death as the friar asks her to, on the other it
merely insists on the really experienced reality of what she has, so to
speak, already spiritually experienced (4.2.93–103). Capulet moans,
'Death is my son-in-law, death is my heir', not knowing that what he
says of death actually applies to Romeo (4.5.38). But this also intimates
the truth that Romeo's secret and more profound name is Death: 'O be
some other name!' (2.2.43). And, of course, it is equally true that Juliet is
Death to Romeo.

It remains easiest and most comfortable to read this powerful death wish in *Romeo and Juliet* as intimating private freedom from social life; but as so often in this play, the civic is at stake within private feeling, with Capulet's patriarchal lamentation going on to hint that death might actually liberate the present, moribund culture which is characterised above all by the feud: 'Death is my son-in-law, death is my heir. / My daughter he hath wedded. I will die, / And leave him all.' His melancholy conclusion – 'life, living, all is death's' – unwittingly resonates with his daughter Juliet's more ecstatic invocation, 'Come, civil night' (4.5.38–40).

I have mentioned that Kottman builds his case for the play's investment in freedom by arguing the lovers are paradoxically (but also wonderfully) fulfilled as separate individuals in each other. They ultimately attain this autonomy together because at its end the play makes such elaborate and remarkable provision for each of them to experience the other's death before taking their own lives. Derrida recognises this as a profound transgression: 'the theater of the impossible: two people each outlive the other'.[50] 'These lovers of the night,' Kristeva confirms, 'remain solitary beings.'[51] And that they claim their freedom *in the family vault* expresses their defiance of all ancestral and family claims on their identities.

Kottman therefore crows with them:

Let Verona in Adige melt! A plague on both houses![52]

Kottman suggests that for Juliet the vault has ceased to be the sort of 'sacred storehouse' of remembered identity that can make a historic unity of the living and the dead (*Macbeth*, 2.4.35). Because she has gone beyond family, the dead simply have 'lost their dignity for her': that is the specific source of her painfully grotesque fantasies of madly playing with her ancestors' bones (cf. 4.3.51). In this Kottman recognises that 'the cost of her freedom is high indeed.' 'Not only,' he suggests, 'must she outlive the claims of her living family members on her life, she must forsake the community of the living and the dead that bind her to others as human.'[53] This is a powerful reading, but the tragic climax of *Romeo and Juliet* can be read otherwise. Instead, I suggest that the tragic freedom the lovers achieve in the family vault presents *a profound challenge to society from within*. The simple fact that Romeo dies in the Capulet vault intimates this.

Kottman is also author of a thoughtful book called *A Politics of the Scene*, and this climactic scene of *Romeo and Juliet* surely asks us to imagine what would happen to the family vault if Tybalt and the others lying about had claimed their freedom-in-death as Romeo and Juliet have?[54] Well, for one thing, it'd be more than a family vault: the dead Montague Romeo's presence there is just the start of this. Kottman insists 'there is no ritual' by which 'the community can respond to the free, separate actions of individuals';[55] but the fact that Shakespeare's lovers seize their freedom at the symbolic heart of tradition which they thereby subvert is a challenge to conceive of an alternative tradition. I suggest that it in fact is a challenge to conceive of a wholly voluntary union of free and separate selves, whose individual freedom is constituted by (1) embracing death as a liberation from merely given identity and (2) mutual recognition. *Strange love grown bold*: it offers an image of a wholly new social formation. We're still in the Capulet tomb, but with intimations of what it will be to live and die in Freetown.[56]

This, I think, marks an important ethical and political advance on Sophocles' *Antigone*, which Hegel, at the end of his *Aesthetics*, famously calls 'the most magnificent, most satisfying, work of art'.[57] Hegel admired Antigone's challenge to Creon and the law in burying her criminal brother Polynices. This, in the play, ultimately ruins Creon and kills Antigone, who hangs herself after Creon has buried her alive, but not for nothing; for, according to Hegel, the law is civilised by its traumatic exposure to the claims of family feeling, while family feeling is disciplined by its exposure to the law. *Romeo and Juliet* clearly resonates with the issues, action and atmosphere of the Sophocles play; but whereas Antigone fights against the law in the name of the family, Shakespeare's lovers, as Kottman has shown, fight against the family for the sake of the individual. This represents a further refinement of freedom. I suggest that where *Antigone* foreshadows and calls for a society which can accommodate the integrity of family, *Romeo and Juliet* demands nothing less than Freetown: a politics of really liberated individualism.[58] I have insisted already that such a liberation would extend beyond Romeo and Juliet to the frustrated Mercutio, and even Tybalt. When Romeo is forced to procure his poison from the wretched, reluctant apothecary, we see that the making of a free society where Romeo and Juliet could thrive would also require a massive redistribution of wealth in order to bring the general population to a point where they could even think of freedom. 'In the midst of sublime ecstasy,' as Chris Fitter insists, 'Romeo and Juliet are simultaneously in the midst of the frictions of class.'[59] The better life will require the undoing not just of individual identity but of the social system itself.

Before the physical crisis, Romeo's unconscious has already instructed him that he has died and revived:

> I dreamt my lady came and found me dead –
> Strange dream that gives a dead man leave to think! –
> And breath'd such life with kisses in my lips
> That I reviv'd and was an emperor.
>
> (5.1.6–9)

It is a disarming undoing of tragic destiny in terms of what might have happened, but we should note that it doesn't dodge death. Romeo awakens to enjoy imperial fulfilment from somehow *within* death. He is lord of his own joys. It's a beautiful moment, and even more beautiful to reflect that everyone is such an emperor in Freetown.

When the end really is upon us, Romeo says, 'Why I descend into this bed of death / Is partly to behold my lady's face' (5.3.28–9): a stirring reminiscence of the more real, blank and masked face with which he first fell in love at the Capulet ball.[60] It is chilling to think back to that at this point and imagine Romeo and Juliet falling in love in their death masks. But in *Romeo and Juliet*, the grave is at the same time the wedding chamber. As much as it spells the end of love, it also is 'a feasting presence full of light' (5.3.86); echoes here of the Resurrection animate something more secular and entirely new. Romeo muses on what is called 'a lightening before death' whereby doomed men often are made merry (5.3.90). He wrings his hands to think of any such 'lightening' while (as he thinks) he looks upon his wife's dead face. And yet, Juliet's beauty is not defeated by death. It is consummated there. And death *is* a feasting chamber full of light, and 'unsubstantial death *is* amorous', inasmuch as it is there if anywhere that infinite, as yet unsubstantiated love and self flourish (5.3.103).

So it is accident, and it is not accident, that Romeo kills himself. And when Juliet revives, it is accident and it is not accident that shortly afterwards: *She stabs herself, falls [and dies]*. As she sheathes the blade in her breast, she cries, 'O happy dagger!' (5.3.169). She is leaving a world that is dead to her now her lover is no longer in it, but the blade of her knife at the same time glints with all the dark poetry of death that she and Romeo have thrilled to. In Verona, after Romeo and Juliet have perished in their feasting chamber full of light, the next day will bring but a 'glooming peace' (5.3.305). But the sun is rising on Freetown.

4

Freetown-upon-Avon

§

1 Freeman!

This chapter returns to the real-world inspiration and effects of Shakespearean freedom. In September 1769, the great Shakespearean actor David Garrick made Freetown a bit more real; he did so in the then obscure provincial English town that happens to be Shakespeare's birthplace – and now houses the Shakespeare Birthplace Trust and the Royal Shakespeare Company, not to mention the Shakespeare Institute, where I work. Garrick's Stratford Jubilee wasn't just the first major Shakespeare celebration; it seeded all others. More than anything barring Shakespeare's birth itself, it put Stratford on the map: indeed, for the first time it provided decent access to the town by road. Whenever there's cause to celebrate Shakespeare, the Jubilee comes to mind, and it's no accident that the three authoritative book-length studies of the Jubilee were published in the previous anniversary year of 1964.[1] Now that we've experienced 2014 and the 450th anniversary of Shakespeare's birth, as well as 2016's 400th anniversary of Shakespeare's death, the Jubilee's interest has freshened again. But it's worth stressing that in 1769 it was all freshness. Cosy, ironic or weary familiarity with what literary festivities have become can prevent us from grasping how novel and surprising it was, perhaps even to Garrick himself. I suggest that the Jubilee moved through Garrick. It was a *happening*, mocked and marvelled at, ideologically disorganised, susceptible to different interpretations; yet, if only we have eyes to see it, it was instrumental to the association of Shakespeare with freedom that proved important to Western modernity and might still provide us with a credible, substantial and interesting reason for celebrating Shakespeare today.

Stratford Town Council precipitated the Jubilee by making Garrick its first ever Freeman, successfully flattering him into donating a statue for the gaping niche in the Sheep-Street–facing facade of the recently rebuilt Town Hall. But, practical considerations apart, transforming Garrick into the Freeman was a decisive step towards the creative conjunction of Shakespeare and freedom. The actor had already done much to link his name and fortunes with Shakespeare's, both on stage at Drury Lane and by erecting a 'Shakespeare Temple' in his garden at Hampton, whose fine statue by Roubiliac (now in the British Library) was said to look as much like Garrick as it did the Bard. And yet, Garrick's encroachment on the great man's identity and reputation was justified inasmuch as he really did possess an actor's gift that was supremely well matched to Shakespeare's talent for characterisation. With his darting glance and mobile face, he alone could live up to the chameleon poet.[2] Now Richard III, now Romeo, now Macbeth, he seemingly could become anyone: Freeman indeed!

Garrick was only 5'3", framed perhaps to be a character comedian, but certainly not a leading man. He recognised this himself, wryly observing, 'Mr. G – k, could he *Speak* the *Part*, is well form'd for *Fleance*, or one of the *Infant Shadows* in the Cauldron Scene.'[3] And yet, Garrick utterly super-seded more heroically proportioned rivals such as James Quin, reinventing acting as a more realistic art in the process. He brought dramatic characters into fully realised and convincing life. 'That young man never had his equal and never will have a rival,' proclaimed Alexander Pope: hardly a pushover.[4] Praise for Garrick tended to recognise the special freedom of his performances. Charles Churchill attacked actors in his satirical poem *The Rosciad*, but he singled out Garrick's 'powers' as 'vast and unconfined'.[5] Perhaps the most exhilarating tribute comes in Fanny Burney's epistolary novel *Evelina*:

O my dear Sir, in what raptures am I returned! Well may Mr Garrick be so celebrated, so universally admired – I had not any idea of so great a performer.

Such ease! such vivacity in his manner! such grace in his motions! such fire and meaning in his eyes! – I could hardly believe that he had studied a written part, for every word seemed spoke from the impulse of the moment.

His action – at once so graceful and so free! – his voice – so clear, so melodious, yet so wonderfully various in its tones – such animation! – every look *speaks!*

The actor's sheer liveliness, according to Evelina, transcends its scripted origin. His combination of ease and vivacity sets forth the very image of liberty. Paradoxically, by dint of being so inimitably, irreducibly itself, Garrick's performance also realises the 'idea' of performance as such. Nor is it just a matter of what's going on behind the fourth wall, on stage; so inspired is Evelina that she is all but irresistibly moved to muscle in on the leading lady and claim a dance with Garrick for herself: 'And when he danced – O how I envied Clarinda. I almost wished to have jumped on the stage and joined them.' Garrick's acting has revealed to her a whole existential condition of dancing freedom! Something similar inspires fans to get up on stage at rock concerts; we too, such border-crossings proclaim, share in the star's flamboyant freedom. Of course, it's true that Burney, rather than presenting Garrick's acting *en soi*, is depicting the impression it makes on an impressionable country girl; but impressionable country girls may be better barometers for receiving and understanding impressions than more sophisticated and jaded people. And Evelina doesn't just *fancy* Garrick, or not in some easily dismissable way; she fancies Garrick because the freedom his performance incarnates is utterly desirable in our world, beyond the theatre. 'I am afraid you will think me mad,' she concludes, 'so I won't say any more; yet I really believe Mr Garrick would make you mad too, if you could see him.'[6]

Further evidence that Garrick's performances expressed the maddening freedom to which Evelina testifies is given in his own short 1744 essay on acting. This commences with a brilliant prose sketch of how to render Able Drugger from *The Alchemist*. Here, as in Evelina's description, we again witness Garrick's capacity for achieving general significance via the most particular detail: 'and by declining the right Part of the Head *towards the Urinal*, it casts the most *comic Terror and Shame* over all the *upper* Part of the Body ... and to make the *lower* Part equally ridiculous, his *Toes* must be *inverted* from the *Heel*, and by *holding* his *Breath*, he will unavoidably give himself a *Tremor* in the *Knees*', and so on. Drugger comes to inimitable life as 'the compleatest low Picture of *Grotesque Terror* that can be imagin'd by a Dutch Painter'. But having made this essayistic exhibition of his chosen comic turn, Garrick smartly announces: 'Now to *Macbeth*'.

The contrast he makes between Drugger's terror and shame and Macbeth's is a brilliant one. Garrick notes that where Drugger is unheroically preoccupied with a broken urinal, Macbeth's attention is 'intensely riveted' to the murder he has committed. A basic similarity of culpable terror ends in the tremendous difference in moral seriousness between these two situations, and Garrick goes on to show in detail how this difference can be brought into embodied life by an actor playing Macbeth. After the murder, he writes, Macbeth should be 'a *moving Statue*, or indeed a *petrify'd Man*': and the way one of his clauses gives way to the other evocatively suggests both Macbeth and his actor shuffling uneasily between opposed states of being. Garrick also contends that Macbeth's inward convulsion should involve a sensory derangement: 'his Eyes must *Speak*, and his *Tongue* be *metaphorically Silent*.' The writing here calls for special attention. It is not enough for the actor's tongue just to be actually silent; Garrick wishes him to evoke something like tongues in his eyes. Macbeth's ears, meanwhile, should open to unreal, perhaps metaphysical mutterings and rumbles, even while they are '*deaf* to the *present* and *audible* Voice of his Wife'.

Again and again Garrick is obliged to reach beyond ordinary language to convey what the actor must do. One of his most striking recommendations is that Macbeth's attitudes should be 'quick and permanent' – which means, presumably, part of the rushing, quickly passing present even while they are resolving into that hideous posture of moral derangement whereby Macbeth will always be remembered. When Garrick goes on to suggest that the Macbeth actor's voice should be '*articulately trembling*, and *confusedly intelligible*', his shifting again between related but non-identical paradoxes underscores that Macbeth is lost to simple description in the gaps that fissure it. Description is always normative; by means of Duncan's murder, Macbeth has gone beyond norms, as well as his own dictum: 'I dare do all that may become a man; / Who dares do more is none' (*Macbeth*, 1.7.46–7).[7] He cannot be categorised or named – and, if only for that technical reason, cannot finally be understood.

What I hope is evident here is that Garrick's description of acting Macbeth is operating as the profoundest kind of criticism. In addition to venturing beyond ordinary, comprehensible humanity, Garrick also demands of the actor playing Macbeth both the most horrible reduction of man into murderer and at the same time, and in complete contrast to this process of brutal integration, the most shattering breakdown: 'the Murderer should be seen in *every Limb*, and yet every *Member*, at that Instant should seem *separated* from his *Body*, and his *Body* from his *Soul*.'

Macbeth is both a monster *and* a man in pieces. As a further paradox, Garrick suggests that this disintegrated creature should present a picture of an expressly 'compleat *Regicide*'. What Garrick perceives, and presumably sought to convey upon the stage, is that from this murderous point in the plot, Macbeth is not so much a man as he is a naked, screaming contradiction, compelled to embody his own terrible thought that 'nothing is but what is not' (1.3.140–1). From the inside, that is his torment; from the outside – to spectators both off and on the stage – it is one of the secrets of his terrible but also magnetic obscenity. Garrick ends on an urbanely whimsical note:

> And as at that Time the Orb below should be hush as death; I hope I shall not be thought minutely circumstantial, if I should advise a real Genius to wear Cork Heels to his Shoes, as in this Scene he should seem to tread on Air, and I promise him he will soon discover the great Benefit of this (however seeming trifling) Piece of Advice.[8]

Though attractively dressed up as the modesty of a merely practical man of the theatre, Garrick's tip actually conveys the further, poetic truths that by means of Duncan's murder Macbeth has, one, walked into what Macduff will shortly call 'death itself' (2.3.74) and, two, in a fuller sense than usual, demoralised his world, by gutting not just its confidence and self-possession but also its moral character. As a result, it's now as if he were walking on the moon, in a specifically moral version of zero gravity, soundless and floating. His nightmare from before the murder that the very earth he treads is going to 'prate' his guilt abroad proves in the event to have been a sentimental delusion of an irrevocably vanished world (2.1.56–9).

What we are seeing here is a major shift from a conception of acting as imitation towards a new conception of action as expressive freedom. How much of this even Garrick could realise in the theatre is of course open to question, but it is also true that these are just traces of what he could do on stage, and they go some way towards showing why his contemporaries experienced his newly realistic impersonations of people not himself as a sudden and thrilling revelation of human freedom and possibility. The time was ripe for this, and across the channel Denis Diderot's *The Paradox of Acting* (written in 1773, though not published till 1830) would shortly marvel at the fact that the actor was strangely able to will a new reality into being.[9] Of course, Hamlet had wondered at the same phenomenon when he asked how an actor could not just simulate but seemingly feel a grief not his own: 'What's Hecuba to him, or he to Hecuba, / That he should weep for her?' (*Hamlet*, 2.2.536–7).

But now a series of comic anecdotes about the difficulty of painting him suggest that Garrick had gone decidedly beyond the aesthetics of imitation. *The London Chronicle* of November 1786 advertised a lithograph showing an increasingly furious Hogarth's frustrated attempts to paint the actor.[10] The novelty of this was that the print was backed with a wheel depicting thirty likenesses of Garrick from pictures by Reynolds, Gainsborough and others; turning the wheel revealed the confounding mobility of Garrick's face and the impossibility of a definitive portrait. Meanwhile the inscription on the front recorded how 'Hogarth eventually got into a violent passion and would have thrown his pallet and brushes at Garrick's head if the wag had not made his escape from the storm of variegated colours.' Gainsborough's obituary in *The Morning Chronicle*, August 1788, reveals that he had suffered similarly in trying to capture the chameleon player on canvas.[11] Though he certainly studied human nature and behaviour from life, Garrick is something more than a mimic; and he cannot himself be mimicked. He can only finally be identified with the ineffable quickness of creativity itself.

It was suitable, then, that the Corporation of Stratford had chosen such a person to be its first and representative Freeman. Stratford formally honoured Garrick's freedom in an exquisite box carved from the mulberry tree it maintained was 'undoubtedly planted by Shakespear's own hand'.[12] This artefact is now in the British Museum. It is a finely carved piece, detailed with beguiling Shakespeareana, and a frieze on its back of Garrick as Lear on the heath. In return for the rich gift of the Freedom of Stratford which this lovely box contained, Garrick furnished the Town Hall with its Shakespeare statue – which (have a look next time you're there) still stands proud, if somewhat blackened by age, over Sheep Street – along with a portrait of Shakespeare to hang inside, though this was lost in the same fire as the rather better and better-known portrait of Garrick with Shakespeare's bust that the Corporation acquired at its own expense. Most important, Stratford's first Freeman gave the town its Jubilee in honour of its most famous son. And with that the idea of Freetown really shimmers into life again.

Of course Garrick saw the Jubilee as a wonderful opportunity to enhance his own interests, celebrity and identification with Shakespeare – and you've got to say, why not? But it seems equally clear he was moved to extend and share the Shakespearean freedom which the Corporation had conferred on him, and with which he no doubt felt already blessed by the dramatist in the form of his vocation for the Shakespearean stage. With the Jubilee, Garrick took Shakespeare to the people; he took Shakespeare out of the institutions of the theatre and scholarship and, quite literally, to the streets. And in doing so, he took the political potential of Shakespearean drama into the political world as such.

A contemporary watercolour from the collection of the Shakespeare Birthplace Trust shows Garrick presiding over the Jubilee in gorgeous style, sporting his long staff, with his large mulberry-wood medallion hanging round his neck, trimmed in multicoloured ribbon: the Freeman as the rainbow man.[13] But Garrick wasn't just arrogating the Bard's many-splendoured freedom to himself. On the contrary: he really did give Shakespeare's freedom away. To the schedule of the day's entertainments, he added this: 'The Steward hopes that the Admirers of Shakespeare, will, upon this Occasion, wear the Favors which are called the Shakespeare Favors.' Note the Freeman is happy to turn Steward in order to celebrate Shakespeare's freedom. The sashes, rosettes and badges he commends to the crowd were made of a rich silk ribbon, three inches wide, with a picot edge. The ribbon maker, one Mr Jackson of Coventry, explained in the flyers that were handed about:

A Ribband has been made on purpose at Coventry call'd The Shakespeare Ribband; it is in imitation of the Rainbow, which, uniting the Colours of all Parties, is likewise an emblem of the great Variety of his Genius. 'Each change of many colour'd Life he drew.' Johnson.[14]

Thus did every lapel in Stratford gorgeously proclaim that Shakespeare's inclusive genius really was for each and all. And as we look at the admittedly black-and-white reproduction of the ribbon (Figure 4.1), it may be worth recalling that 'storm of variegated colours' the frustrated Hogarth supposedly threw at the actor, not just because – had Hogarth only thrown the storm down on canvas – he might have come as close as you could get to capturing the shifting creativity that was the actor's real essence, but also because it was this variegated storm in Shakespeare and himself which

FIGURE 4.1   The Shakespeare Ribband 1769, SBT 1910–27, reproduced by permission of Shakespeare Birthplace Trust

prompted Garrick in Shakespeare's name to preach and celebrate a rainbow coalition in 1769 in Stratford.

At the most ceremonious banquet, the Freeman served up turtle: a hell of a turtle in fact – it weighed, when living, no less than 327 pounds. Why turtle? 'Let the type and shadow of the master grace his board', Garrick's great correspondent Edmund Burke had written, explaining that it was the consummation of all meats and therefore most fitting for a dinner in honour of one who 'can represent all the solidity of flesh, the volatility of fowl, and the oddity of fish'.[15] 'The lad of all lads was a Warwickshire lad,' sang Stratford, and thus was Shakespeare's freedom at once celebrated and brought home.[16] (See Figure 4.2.)

And if the keynote was of bright festivity, it wasn't exclusive of more serious, even quasi-religious feelings, as became clear when, after Garrick had edified everyone with his Shakespeare Ode, they all passed round and

FIGURE 4.2 The Stratford 1769 Jubilee, SBT, 1993-31/210, reproduced by permission of Shakespeare Birthplace Trust

eagerly drank from a mulberry goblet that was ornamented with silver. 'Garrick was a worshipper himself', as Cowper wrote in *The Task*:

> He drew the liturgy, and form'd the rites
> And solemn ceremonial of the day,
> And call'd the world to worship on the banks
> Of Avon, fam'd in song.[17]

Note here that he called *the world* to worship. 'It is scarce credible the Number of Persons of all Ranks that came to see it', marvelled *The Public Advertiser*.[18] The costs may have been prohibitive, and Garrick may have ridiculed the Stratford locals when he reprised the Jubilee for his Drury Lane audiences, but the original intention and atmosphere of his first ever Shakespeare Jubilee were unprecedentedly liberal and inviting.[19]

And if this at least symbolically involved everyone, it also extended a new spirit of tolerant inclusiveness to all aspects of human personality. 'Wenches! never was any paradise so plentifully and beautifully inhabited as here at this time', according to the excited correspondent of *Lloyd's Evening Post*.[20] And if you didn't like wenches, there was a horse race.

As a man who had understood and played Macbeth so powerfully, we would not expect Garrick to dodge the darker aspects of freedom which, as we saw in the last chapter, Shakespeare also recognised in *Romeo and Juliet*. His Bard is the more god-like for his daemonic inscrutability. Consider lines such as these for instance:

> The subject passions round him wait;
> Who tho' unchained, and raging there,
> He checks, inflames, or turns their mad career.[21]

This presents Shakespeare as a sorcerer possessed of a hectic and rather frightening power in tension with the civilising mission that the *Ode* otherwise invests him with. And when Garrick tries to phase away from such daemonic passions into an overwhelming joy, that joy quickly darkens into a wildly permissive sensuality which seems to remember and reprise them. 'With kindling cheeks, and sparkling eyes ... the Bard in transport dies': this makes us very intimate with Shakespeare indeed.[22] The *Ode* goes on to envision in intricate detail his ecstatic mental impregnation, the huge fruit of which is testimony, of course, to his amazing fertility, but also suggests an exceptionally painful birth. For what springs fully formed from Shakespeare's head isn't a paragon of conventional virtue – nor even some sylph-like goddess, nor even Hamlet – but rather the enormous libertine Falstaff, his superabundant largeness very explicitly expressing a vitality that exceeds all limits. Or, as Garrick puts it: '*a world where all pleasures abound*'. For, we're told, '*the world too is wicked and round.*'

> So FALSTAFF *will never decline,*
> . . .
> *And his rain and his rivers are wine;*
> . . .
> *And away with all sorrow and care.*[23]

Thus the rainbow man presents the fat man as the happy avatar of all the freedom and fullness of Shakespearean being. And he does so without blanding out the darker shades of the spectrum such freedom entails. That he does so in public and in relation to rebuilding a town hall and, by implication, a real community is striking, and perhaps should put us on our mettle as we celebrate Shakespeare in our own time. At its heart, Garrick's civic Shakespeare Ode offers an undiscriminating celebration of life. *Banish plump Jack, and banish all the world*; but Falstaff returns from banishment to Stratford in 1769 to become the unexpected type of civic flourishing, a flourishing based not as it usually is on sacrifice and repression but on emancipating all we desire and are.[24] The *Ode* invokes Euphrosyne as goddess of liberty, and its ideal of freedom even creeps into Edward Thompson's satirical send-up of Garrick in the following lines of his dedication (to John Hall): 'Now Bird of Freedom strain your throat, / Give LIBERTY your highest note.'[25]

The first ever Shakespeare Jubilee has been especially mocked for not, in fact, including any Shakespeare – and it is difficult to imagine that a Shakespeare festival today could get away without including any plays or poems. But I've been trying to bring out a neglected radical stripe to what Garrick did. As we have seen from his essay on acting, Garrick could be as minutely responsive to Shakespeare's text and its implications as anyone. Still, at Stratford he celebrated Shakespeare not so much as literary heritage to be preserved against the depredations of time and change, but instead as example and inspiration. He celebrated Shakespeare as the very quintessence of freedom, as the proof and promise of *new life*.

2   Wilkes and Liberty!

Garrick certainly had friends in high places, and he was not at all averse to hobnobbing in glamorous circles. He may not have been tall, but Johan Zoffany's 1762 portrait of him presiding in a relaxed state on the riverbank at Hampton presents him as every inch the gentleman. This scene takes in his decorous foreign wife; his noble, gigantic and well-groomed mastiff, pleasantly christened Dragon by Garrick; a frolicsome child, probably Garrick's nephew, Carrington (the Garricks themselves remained child-less); his own attractively proportioned Shakespeare Temple, affording through its dark doorway a tantalising glimpse of that commanding

Roubiliac statue of the Bard; and sweeping views of the Thames, to which Garrick, with a cane and his actor's authoritative grace, directs Mrs Garrick's gaze, to say nothing of the discreetly approaching servant with tea service.[26] The year before the Jubilee, Garrick performed in his Temple to Shakespeare for King Christian VII of Denmark. In 1777, he entertained a royal audience at Windsor, and it was rumoured a knighthood was in the offing. When he died in 1779, Garrick became the first commoner ever to be given a state funeral – an exceptionally grand affair, at which Johnson wept openly, and even the King and Queen paid their respects. His monument in the Abbey proclaims that 'till eternity with power sublime, shall mark the mortal hour of hoary time, Shakspeare & Garrick like twin stars shall shine, and earth irradiate with a beam divine': not bad for a boy from Lichfield! And yet, Garrick didn't get his knighthood. 'I do most sincerely rejoice to find,' his old friend Mrs Pye had written to him from Paris, 'that you are not sunk into *Sir David*'. Carola Oman, Garrick's biographer, goes on to reflect: 'some characters who were anathema to Windsor were his closest friends. Wilkes ("Jack Cade") had been to dine at Hampton. He supplied Burke with funds.'[27]

Ultimately, Garrick's connections were too progressive for the peerage. And if such friends didn't want him 'sunk into *Sir David*', that perhaps partly explains why the peerage didn't want him at all. It resonates with the neglected, unexpectedly radical complexion of the Stratford Jubilee explored earlier. We mustn't, I suggest, just think of David Garrick as a self-interested toady and social climber, who also happened to be one of the best Shakespearean actors ever. It's not fair to Garrick; and it also obscures important features of the more significant and powerful Shakespeare he gave to England and the world.

If anyone was the political muse of the Jubilee, it was the maverick demagogue John Wilkes. Champion of electoral reform, freedom of religion, freedom of the press, and even a free America, Wilkes was the foremost figurehead for liberty in British politics. But he was just as much a *libertine*: author of the pornographic poem 'An Essay on Woman' and leading light of the Hellfire Club, who dressed in Franciscan robes to enact mad, drunken debauchery with courtesans attired as nuns – and on one infamous occasion, a baboon. The inspiring attractions of political liberalism, and the darker freedoms it entails, come together in Wilkes, and in a way that strikes lights with Falstaff's centrality in Garrick's Shakespeare Ode. When he was imprisoned for seditious libel for his attack on George III in number 45 of his radical paper, *The North Briton*, the cry of 'Wilkes and Liberty!' rang through British politics. The protest was serious and sustained, with seven protestors dying as they chanted 'No liberty, no King' at the St George's Field Massacre in 1768. Coverage of events in Stratford in *Lloyd's Evening Post* on the 8th of September, 1769 made the connection between Garrick and Wilkes, but Garrick also alluded to it himself in a cryptic announcement placed in *The Public Advertiser* of the 8th of July that year:

A CARD

The Mulberry Box presents Compliments to the Standish of the same Materials, hoping they shall meet very soon at the London Tavern, and that an uninterrupted Friendship may thenceforward succeed to their late Separation, as they are appointed to Joint Shares in the same Office, viz. Grooms of the *Stool* to the Supporters of the *Bill of Rights*.[28]

Well, I say cryptic but you will recognise the mulberry box as the exquisite artefact we've met already within which Garrick received his Freedom of Stratford. The 'standish of the same materials' was a gift given by the town to George Keate for delivering Garrick this freedom. The Society of the Supporters of the Bill of Rights was founded in 1769 to aid Wilkes and press for parliamentary reform; it is the first major extra-parliamentary political association in Britain. Garrick, therefore, in the *Evening Post*, is making a connection between the Freedom of Stratford and the serious campaign for political freedom that is getting underway in this period; indeed, he subordinates Shakespeare and Stratford to that real-world campaign by casting himself and Keate as '*Grooms of the Stool* to the Supporters of the Bill of Rights'. The careful reader of this book will note that, in his cryptic advert, Garrick is looking forward to a political meeting at the *London Tavern* – the very place where Kossuth was presented with a model of the Shakespeare's birthplace nearly a hundred years later. It is doubly a landmark in the history of Shakespeare and freedom.

But though it's true that Wilkes influenced Garrick's Shakespeare Jubilee, the Jubilee much more evidently influenced the cause of Wilkes and liberty. Oman in the passage previously cited suggests that Wilkes not only went to dinner at Garrick's temple to Shakespeare but was also associated with Jack Cade, the leader of the peasants' revolt against the crown which was dramatised by Shakespeare in *2 Henry VI*. After Stratford, jubilees very much based on what Garrick had done for Shakespeare were held in Wilkes's honour. Wilkes's forty-fifth birthday on October the 28th, 1769 – a special one, since it resonated with and recalled that consequential number 45 of *The North Briton* – was duly celebrated in King's Bench Prison, with songs adapted from the Jubilee song book, *Shakespeare's Garland*, and another three-hundred-pound turtle.[29] It was done all over again on the 18th of April, 1770: the day of Wilkes's release. The published text on this occasion is dedicated to 'the spirited and noble freeholders of Middlesex', who had repeatedly voted for Wilkes each time his election was declared void by the government on questionable grounds.[30] These celebrations recognise that 'Mr. Garrick may brag / Of his Warwickshire wag', but they re-appropriate the greatest hit of the Jubilee as follows:

> No threats, no persuasions can move him,
> Still true to a people who love him;
> Their laws and their rights he will ever defend,
> For the friend of all friends is a Middlesex friend:
> > Middlesex friend,
> > Freedom defend,
> And the friend of all friends is a Middlesex friend.[31]

They also include a ninth song, 'To Liberty', to be sung, delightfully, 'to any tune the reader pleases'.[32]

3   The Shakespearean General

I have written this book partly to challenge the diminished political importance of Shakespeare in contemporary life. Whereas the 1769 Jubilee directly derived a culture and a politics of freedom from the vitality of Shakespeare as such, present-day scholarship struggles to find circumstantial and thematic reasons for Shakespeare's political significance. The likelihood that Shakespeare's *Richard II* was performed before the Essex rebellion, eliciting Queen Elizabeth's furious rejoinder 'I am Richard the II. Know you not that?' is now much cited.[33] Andrew Hadfield's *Shakespeare and Republicanism* builds a solid contextual case for a radical Shakespeare, pointing, for instance, to the 1582 publication, in

Latin, of George Buchanan's republican history of Scotland,[34] or to the 1599 publication of Lewis Lewkenor's translation of Gaspar Contarini's paean to *The Commonwealth and Government of Venice* as a beacon for a more enlightened politics.[35] It proves that Republicanism was an available idea to the Bard. Moreover, Hadfield reminds us, he 'was the only English dramatist who staged the complete story of the end of the Roman republic from the triumph of Julius Caesar to the victory of Augustus, the first proper Roman emperor'.[36] But if that really were all there was to it, Milton – with his much better attested Republicanism, which resonates so powerfully with Satan's rebellion in *Paradise Lost* – would be a much better source for political progressives.[37] At this point, we might care to recall Kossuth's testimony in the London Tavern that he had learned his politics from Shakespeare: 'What else are politics than philosophy applied to the social condition of men? and what is philosophy but knowledge of nature and of the human heart? and who ever penetrated deeper into the recesses of those mysteries than Shakspeare did?'[38] It was Garrick who opened up the heart of Shakespeare's politics. As the greatest character actor of his age, he chan-nelled the sheer liveliness and charisma of Shakespeare's characters to produce something more than mere bardolatry: hero-worship of a lonely genius. In 1769, he performed on the banks of the Avon not so much an exclusive cult of personality as what we might call a *culture of personality*, encouraging others to find themselves in Shakespeare as he definitively demonstrated he had done. If the Shakespeare of the Jubilee was, on the one hand, the by now perhaps over-familiar transcendent genius, at the same time he was a figure unprecedently thrown open to identification, participation and creative re-invention. Garrick offered Shakespeare to the people as the prospect of their own transcendence. And this, I suggest, released a great political force.

Of course, the idea of Shakespeare as an oppositional, progressive play-wright predates Garrick, and it's not just that *Richard II* seems to have been played as a warm-up for the Essex rebellion. Maximilian E. Novak argues that by 1715, Shakespeare had been invested with the status of national poet in the form of a specifically Whiggish, progressive energy.[39] And Michael Dobson has shown that at 'the first monument to the playwright to celebrate him in a national context' – the Temple of British Worthies at Stowe – Shakespeare is invoked as father to a variety of cultural national-ism 'specifically opposed to the government of the day'.[40] After Garrick,

one indication that theatre could be politically combustible is provided
when the actor and theatre manager James Winston records in his diary
entry for the 8th of January, 1820 that 'the Birmingham Theatre had been
set on fire the night before by the radicals in consequence of Bunn, the
manager, forcing the song of "God Save the King" to be repeatedly sung.'[41]
But it is in Chartism that we really see how an appreciation of
Shakespeare's genius for characterisation could combine with the development of a more democratic politics (albeit one that stopped short of
women's suffrage) to produce a lively idea of fulfilment for all. And
whereas Garrick derived his politics of freedom from the expressive individualism he found in Shakespeare, Chartism brought together the politics
of freedom with the remarkably Shakespearean vision and appeal of
Thomas Cooper.

Cooper wasn't the only Chartist to link the movement to Shakespearean
drama. The Chartist paper *The Northern Star* ran a column titled 'Chartism
from Shakespeare' from the 25th of April (just after Shakespeare's birthday),
1840.[42] Anne Janowitz has suggested that in seeking a past as well as a future,
Chartist writers were obliged to reshape a tradition they were simultaneously defining themselves against; thus, for instance, 'the dramatic
sequence which culminates in the presentation of Henry V as the embodiment of absolutist coherence' is 'appropriated by the working class to
describe its own will to national power'.[43] And yet, I suggest that
Shakespeare's creation, across the plays, of a plurality of vividly realised
dramatic characters ultimately did prove a good source for what Janowitz
has called 'that civic subjectivity' of the more comprehensive franchise they
were seeking.[44] Shakespeare puts flesh on the bones of Chartism's crucial
demands for a fairer politics: the vote for all men, a secret ballot, no property
qualification for MPs. By invoking the plays, the Chartists were able to look
beyond their shopping list of conditions into the more realised, fulfilled and
developed common life such conditions intended to facilitate.

And this is where Cooper comes in. Born in Leicester in 1805, he was the
illegitimate son of a dyer, who had died when Thomas was just a child.[45]
Cooper found in Shakespeare a man who had been 'humbly born . . . (yet
who had) climb(ed) up into the realms of truest grandeur'.[46] And from this
he drew a general lesson: clearly 'that region is open to all humanity.'[47] But
Shakespeare is not only an example of a boy made good for Cooper. His
engagement with the plays was as deep and intense as Kossuth's. In his

autobiography, Cooper writes: 'The wondrous knowledge of the heart unfolded by Shakspere, made me shrink into insignificance; while the sweetness, the marvellous power of expression and grandeur of his poetry seemed to transport me, at times, out of the vulgar world of circumstances in which I lived bodily.'[48] This strongly echoes Kossuth's testimony to Shakespeare's deep, politically significant knowledge. In what Cooper says, Shakespeare's politics opens up again, becoming something much more intimate and revealed than mere citation or circumstantial resonance. Cooper's testimony to Shakespeare's power combines a cognitive insight into human being ('wondrous knowledge of the heart') with a creative prospect of sheer and heightened possibility ('out of the vulgar world of circumstances'). It recalls the inventive as well as expressive power of Garrick's acting, which in turn is reflective of that double truth whereby Shakespearean character is both splendidly itself and at the same time the power to become somebody different. 'Wondrous knowledge' calls for worshipful humility; but Shakespeare's knowledge, according to Cooper, isn't knowledge of what will be out of reach for all but the rarest and most brilliant spirits, it is knowledge of what is most deeply held in common: knowledge of the *heart*. Reading Shakespeare is not in the end just an abasing experience. It ravishes Cooper, at least on occasion, into a new reality of sweetness, power of expression, grandeur; and Cooper is a *Chartist*, so he experiences this Shakespearean vision as more than just a sublime enhancement of his own ego – it opens into his vision of social freedom as such. What this will mean in terms of actual political life is imagined in William Whitmore's lines which Cooper published in *Cooper's Journal: or, Unfettered Thinker and Plain Speaker for Truth, Freedom, and Progress*:

> The young spring morn breaks brightly on a scene
>   Of festival outstretching far and wide:
> Toil is respited, mute the town's huge din,
>   And throngs of freemen, consciously allied
> To England's Shakspere, hail with soul-felt pride
>   This glorious natal day![49]

Thus did Chartism make of Garrick's original Shakespeare celebration a much more explicitly radical thing. 'Throngs of freemen consciously allied to England's Shakspere' presents a vision of Shakespeare's Freetown made actual. As for Kossuth, so for Cooper: the heart of Shakespeare's work finally belongs to more than just one person. 'The great recommendation of this knowledge', Cooper felt sure was, 'its immense utility'.[50] In learning *Hamlet* 'entirely and perfectly *by heart*', by committing to memory 'thousands of lines' of other poetry, he did not consider himself to be turning away from politics;[51] on the contrary, he believed he was going deeper into it. Making Shakespeare's language his own in this way seemed to him perfectly consistent with storming around Nottingham with Chartist comrades, singing, 'The lion of freedom is come from his den.'[52] Whitmore's poem about the united throng of Shakespearean freemen was called 'Shakspere's Birthday – in the Future'. There was a job to be done, a new world to be wrestled into being.

It was fundamentally because Cooper construed Shakespeare to be part of this revolution that, in 1841, the year following the appearance of the 'Chartism from Shakespeare' series in *The Northern Star*, he broke away from the main Leicester Chartist association, setting up a rival branch which he styled 'The Shaksperean Association of Leicester Chartists'.[53] They held their meetings in the 'Shaksperean Room'.[54] They also compiled and sang from their 'Shaksperean Chartist Hymn Book'.[55] Here is a representative inclusion:

> Britannia's sons, though slaves ye be,
> God, your Creator, made you free;
> He life and thought and being gave,
> But never, never made a slave!
>
> . . .
>
> All men are equal in His sight,
> The bond, the free, the black, the white:
> He made them all, – them freedom gave;
> God made the man – Man made the slave![56]

Now it has to be said that this doesn't any more than Whitmore's 'Shakespeare's Birthday' attempt to imitate the quality and sophistication of Shakespeare's verse. There is more of the Chapel than the Bard to such texts; and never mind Shakespeare, they are vastly inferior to, say, the hymns of Charles Wesley. And yet, I would contend they're still significant. The association with Shakespeare pushes their conventional spirituality into a more secular, political sphere, mobilising in and as its background all the individuated complexity of Shakespearean drama, to which, as we've seen, Cooper's commitment wasn't at all casual. 'Britannia's sons', Cooper tells us, was composed by one John Bramwich: a stocking weaver. 'He was a grave, serious man', we are further informed, 'the very heart of truth and sincerity'. And then Cooper plainly states, 'He died of sheer exhaustion, from hard labour and want, in the year 1846.'[57] This cruelly premature death is a reminder that the stakes were high in Chartism. It is a reminder that Cooper and Bramwich were right to fight as they did. Not enough has been made of the fact that they did so expressly in Shakespeare's name, in obedience to what Cooper regarded as his 'wondrous knowledge of the heart', in the hope of bringing into being a sweeter, grander, more expressive world of freemen consciously allied to England's Shakespeare. In such a world Bramwich would flourish and not die. But the campaign for now needed something other than sophisticated poetry; it needed marching songs, militant anthems, cruder and more serviceable than Shakespeare but testifying to the politically relevant transcendent truth that Cooper and his Shaksperean Association of Leicester Chartists nevertheless found in the Bard.

What Cooper's Shaksperean Association actually did speaks to a more powerful confidence than we are used to in the political efficacy of high art for the people in general. In 1842, Cooper recalls, they held one or two meetings in the Shaksperean Room during the week, and one on a Sunday. 'Unless there was some stirring local or political topic,' he goes on, 'I lectured on Milton, and repeated portions of the *Paradise Lost*, or on Shakspeare, and repeated portions of *Hamlet*.'[58] There was clearly no divide between literature and politics for Cooper, and thus when he later lectured in Belfast, his topics were as follows: Shakspere, Milton, Burns, Byron, Shelley, French Revolution, Civilization, Cromwell.[59]

He called himself the 'Shaksperean General'.[60] It is a suggestive moniker first because it associates Shakespeare with an explicitly militant politics. Beyond that, 'general' suggests the Chartist stand Cooper was making for Shakespearean character as exemplifying the sort of splendid self-realisation he wanted for all. Cooper demonstrates more explicitly and forcefully than Garrick had that Shakespearean singularity – the sheer, irreducible life of his characters – can facilitate a politics of freedom.

He was liable to sign routine memoranda about branch activities as follows: 'Given at Head Quarters . . . COOPER, General to the Shakspere Brigade'. Considering this from a different historical juncture, though one full of its own comparable political turmoil and possibility, the literary scholar Philip Collins observes, 'Here, as in other respects, Chartism reminds one of the Black Panthers; and one is thus reminded, too, that Chartism looks much less alarming in 1969 than it did to solid citizens like us in 1839.'[61] Garrick, Cooper, Kossuth: we can now pick out a pattern in their distinctively activist responses to the Bard. All three make Shakespeare their touchstone, invested with the self-realising charisma of his characters. This they channel through their own charisma as an achievable and desirable existential goal. It redoubles and dignifies their own personalities, but they don't just glory in this. Instead, they offer up this heightened charisma as a Shakespearean benison for everybody. The Shakespearean general stands for the fuller, more realised life that will obtain in a transfigured political reality.

When Cooper was arrested for rioting in the Potteries in 1842 (a charge he disputed), he raised money for his legal expenses by mounting a production of *Hamlet* in which he took the title role – after all, he still 'knew the play by heart'.[62] He performed it twice in a crowded amphitheatre which could comfortably seat 3,000; but despite this box office success, the actors and their costumes had cost him so much that 'the income hardly covered expenses.'[63] In prison, Cooper, like Kossuth, yearned for Shakespeare; and when the plays arrived, though he was confined in his cell, he 'revelled' in him.[64] Also in prison, Cooper wrote his epic poem 'The Purgatory of Suicides', which he had originally intended to write in blank verse but ultimately cast into Spenserian stanzas. The 'Dedicatory Sonnet to Thomas Carlyle' avowed that the 'free / Of soul with quench less zeal must ever glow / To spread the freedom which their own minds know'.[65] We have seen that normally for Cooper there was no division between politics and poetry but (in spite of the recalcitrantly political spirit of his dedicatory poem to Carlyle) Cooper's period of forced retirement presented the purely personal freedom of scholarly detachment to him as something like a demonic temptation. In one of the most Dostoevskian scenes in his memoir, Cooper's prison chaplain, impressed with his autodidactic accomplishments, offers him the chance to go to Cambridge University. It is worth quoting their dialogue as Cooper recalls it in full:

'Go to Cambridge, from this gaol!' I repeated in wonder.

'Yes: all your wants will be provided for. You will have no
    trouble about anything – only – ' and he stopped and
    smiled.

'Only I must give up politics?' said I; 'I see what you mean.'

'That's it,' said he; 'that's all.'

'I would not degrade or falsify myself by making such a promise,'
    I replied, 'if you could ensure all the honours the University could
    bestow, although it has been one of the great yearnings of my
    heart – from a boy, I might say – to go to a University.'[66]

It is a moving, indeed heroic moment. Cooper is offered what he has so
much wanted, and what has been barred to him by birth; but the price – in
effect, to give up his fight for equal rights for others – is too high. He will
not degrade or falsify himself by making such a promise. He is the
Shaksperean *General*. The intense and generous humanism expressed by
the panoply of Shakespearean character is not a private property, and it
would be self-hoarding corruption to make it just his own. And so, Cooper
didn't get on the stage coach to Cambridge on the 4th of May, 1845; instead,
he left prison in rags.

He rededicated himself to the struggle. His message was, to quote from
his journal, 'Look up, ye toiling millions! There are better days in store.'[67]
In his third letter in the same organ written 'To the Young Men of the
Working Classes', he urged, with an echo of Heminge and Condell, 'Read
him, working men, – read England's – the world's – *your* Shakspere.'[68]

As with Kossuth and Mandela, so too with Cooper's struggle, and his prison
sentence: these men weren't just paying lip-service to Shakespearean freedom.
But if Cooper's commitment to the cause was ardent, his view wasn't rose
tinted or self-deceiving, as we see from his subsequent recollections of
a conversation with a by now reactionary Wordsworth in 1846, just four
years before that greater poet's death. In a conversation both men seem to
have enjoyed, Cooper and Wordsworth still disagreed politically about events
in France, and about Byron's epic poem, which Wordsworth judged immoral.
'I ventured the plea,' recalls Cooper, 'that *Don Juan* was descriptive, and that
Shakspere had also described bad passions in anatomising the human heart,
which was one of the great vocations of the poet.'[69] Cooper did not shy away
from the darker aspect of Shakespearean freedom we discerned in *Romeo and*

Juliet. His accommodation of expressly and unequivocally 'bad passions' goes beyond his onetime advocacy of violence in the struggle. The Shakespearean element in his Chartism involves a subtle openness to that human complexity which is inalienable from freedom, and this for the time being leavens and enriches even as it contributed to a fervent nature that would later narrow into evangelical commitment when Cooper converted to the Baptist Church in 1856.

Cooper welcomed the 'wonders' and 'political earthquake' of 1848, which he called 'the most remarkable year of the nineteenth century'.[70] His own career confirms Kossuth's avowal that an enthusiasm for Shakespeare really isn't incompatible with a passion for political freedom. In the pages of his journal, the same William Whitmore who had conjured visions of 'Shakespere's Birthday – in the Future' also offered encouraging verses to Kossuth and the Italian freedom fighter Mazzini: 'Kossuth, droop not, the Magyar's strength matures: / Mazzini, to thy life's Idea still cleave! . . . / The phoenix, Freedom, aye will spring replete / With fresh life-vigour from the ashes of defeat!'[71] For his part, John Alfred Langford wrote from Birmingham, also for *Cooper's Journal*, these lines 'To Kossuth': 'The annals of the world contain no name, / At which we freely with more reverence bow, / Than thine, immortal Kossuth!'[72] Cooper renewed his own commitment to a specifically Shakespeare-inflected freedom in the fresh campaign for the extension of the franchise he launched in 1849. Instead of another mass Chartist petition, Cooper now argued in favour of individual petitions, to be sent to Parliament in batches of a hundred. The day he fixed upon for dispatching these was of course Shakespeare's birthday. 'You could not, unenfranchised, honour the birthday of our greatest Englishman more worthily,' he declared, 'than by joining to claim your rights as freemen that day.'[73] In 1849, Cooper wanted to make what Whitmore foresaw of 'Shakespere's Birthday – in the Future' come true today. He argued that Shakespeare's anniversary should be declared a national holiday, like Burn's night, and that 'our order ought to see to this; for the unequalled woolstapler's son belongs to us.'[74] Two years later still, in 1851, Cooper fulfilled one of the great desires of his life, making a pilgrimage to Stratford and kneeling on Shakespeare's grave.

It should be admitted that Cooper's confidence in Shakespeare's revolutionary potential wasn't absolutely consistent. After the 'political earthquake' of 1848, for instance, and in the very first issue of *Cooper's Journal*, he looked enviously towards the revolutionary upheavals on the continent, feeling that 'Shakspere', by comparison, was not progressive.[75] In a later number of the paper, he expressed the 'rapture' he felt 'in conversing with the mind of Shakspere' but admitted he could get even more excited by reading philosophy.[76] In another article, he opined that Bacon's wisdom was 'more profound than Shakspere's'.[77] Nor was he above reading instrumentally. We have seen that he praised Shakespeare's 'immense utility', and he wrote, for example, that 'if a man wants a rich English vocabulary, he can find it in Milton and Shakspere.'[78] Crucially for Cooper, and just as he had been for Garrick, Shakespeare wasn't so much a model as a stimulus. 'Sooner or later,' he wrote, 'imitation brings a man into derision, or into neglect. Remember that *all* truly great men were *themselves . . .* Who was Shakspere's model?'[79]

Part of what I'm doing here is attempting to recover – and, indeed, to *recreate* – the lost tradition of Shakespearean freedom that extends from Garrick, through Cooper, to Kossuth, all of whom tap into Shakespeare's characterisation as both a lively inspiration and an existential mandate for a pluralist politics even as they exemplify the promise of such a politics in their own vividly Shakespearean self-realisation. There are, as it were, genetic links between these charismatic Shakespeareans. The line between Garrick's and Cooper's Shakespearean efforts to extend the franchise can be traced via the association between Garrick and Wilkes, as well as in the evident indebtedness of Whitmore's and Cooper's ambitions for Shakespeare's birthday to the original Garrick Jubilee. And there are subsequent connections between Cooper and Kossuth as well. Douglas Jerrold – the prime mover behind the Kossuth Shakespeare tribute – was also instrumental in publishing *The Purgatory of Suicides*, which he recommended and lent to Charles Dickens. And while Kossuth was fighting the emperor in his Hungarian homeland, Ernest Jones, a Chartist leader somewhat to the left of Cooper, was unwittingly following Kossuth in asking to read Shakespeare in prison – though, unlike Kossuth's, Jones's request was refused. Jones was another radical in whom literary and theatrical pretensions and emancipatory politics came together. A friend of Charles Kean (son of Edmund) as well of Charles Kemble, he had written several plays and dreamed of becoming a playwright, before turning to poetry.[80] And in case we are still inclined to think that Kossuth's beautiful Shakespeare tribute is just a winsome one-off, we should also

note that Jones's comrade on the left of Chartism, George Julian Harney –
who was imprisoned around the same time as Cooper for his part in the
Lancashire Plug Plot riots in 1843 – was also presented with a complete
Shakespeare in 'an artistically carved oaken box'. 'Old Chartists,' the
National Reformer's correspondent avers, 'can remember the *Red
Republican* [which Harney edited], and new strugglers for freedom
ought to recognise that the political liberty we use was by the persistent
efforts of those who, like George Julian Harney, had to answer in the
felon's dock for the cause'.[81]

Garrick did not answer for the cause in the felon's dock, but Cooper,
Jones, Harney and Kossuth did, and all of them were associated with
Shakespeare: ample confirmation that, for some at least, the expressive
freedom of Shakespeare's characters opens naturally into democratic activism. This association lasted. Harney did not receive his Shakespeare
tribute till the 1870s. In the same decade, the Warwickshire radical Tom
Mann set up a Shakespeare Mutual Improvement Society when he moved
to London. And later, when he was imprisoned on the other side of the
world for inciting miners to strike in New South Wales in 1906, he too
sought solace in Shakespeare.[82]

4   Shakespeare and Garibaldi

We have seen that in 1769 at Stratford, Garrick drew the liturgy and
formed the rites for a popular celebration of Shakespeare with significant egalitarian overtones. Antony Taylor has written that this 'established the tradition of looking beyond the regional and metropolitan
elite and actively encouraging a plebeian involvement in the management and fundraising for the Jubilees'. 'In Stratford,' he observes,
'Garrick's direct legacy' was the construction in 1879 of that forerunner
of the Royal Shakespeare Company, the Shakespeare Memorial
Theatre, 'by the Flowers brewing dynasty, sons of the strongly
Owenite Richard Flower, who took it upon himself to continue
Garrick's work of bringing Shakespeare to the people'.[83] But before
that milestone came the Shakespeare Tercentary of 1864. When the
well-to-do of Shakespeare's hometown arranged a more exclusive commemoration, the following text was printed:

TIME! SHAKESPEARE THE POET OF THE PEOPLE

People of Stratford! Where are the seats reserved for you at the forthcoming festival? What part or lot have you who originated it, in the coming celebration? None! But you will be permitted to see the Fireworks, because they cannot be let off in the Pavilion; and you are promised something for yourself *after the swells have dined.* Only wait till the next week, and see the dainty mess that shall be BREWED for you out of the cold 'wittles'. PEOPLE OF STRATFORD, who would not see your town disgraced on such an occasion, your streets empty, or blocked up by the carriages of *profitless swells*, take counsel together at once!

> Call a meeting without delay!
> Form your own Committee!!
> Hold your own Festival!!!
> Look to your own business. Lay out your own money.
> Get up your own out-door sports and in-door pastimes, and
>   let your watchword be
>   SHAKESPEARE the POET OF THE PEOPLE
>   AND HURRAH FOR THE PAGEANT[84]

And the people not only got their pageant, they got a whole week of popular celebrations, and some thirty thousand of them came on the first day.

Meanwhile the National Shakespeare Committee in London was struggling. It tried, as Taylor writes, 'to broaden its base by soliciting the support of trade union and reformist organizations that might endorse the objective of keeping Shakespeare's name before the public as an emblem of the unsung genius of the people'.[85] To achieve these objectives, it employed Mrs G. Linnaeus Banks, wife of the radical journalist George Linnaeus Banks, as a go-between with the working-class committee that had been formed to perpetuate Shakespeare's memory.[86] And here was another link with Kossuth; for George Banks, who himself was known as the Poet of the People, had popularised the wearing of soft broad-brimmed hats such as were favoured by the Hungarian hero during his stay in London.[87] Moreover, Banks's own association with Shakespeare was in no way temporary or casual; he had rebuked Stratford for not properly celebrating Shakespeare in 1853.[88] In the event, it was the workmen who made most of the London tercentenary. 'In the name of the workmen of England I plant this tree,' announced the actor-manager Samuel Phelps as he sank an oak

FIGURE 4.3 Shakespeare and Garibaldi, P. D. Gordon Pugh, *Staffordshire Portrait Figures and Allied Subjects of the Victorian Era Including the Definitive Catalogue* (London: Barrie & Jenkins Ltd, 1981), Plate 96

in homage to Shakespeare in the soil of Primrose Hill.[89] As Taylor suggests, the choice of this site was significant. It 'located the festivities within the cycle of popular recreations and revel that were traditionally performed on the site at Whitsuntide and in the early spring'; it represented 'the restoration of traditional Anglo-Saxon liberties', reaffirming 'the right of the people to the soil of their native land'.[90] Primrose Hill moreover, as Richard Foulkes points out, adjoined the working-class district of Chalk Farm, which it segregated from the more exclusive Regent's Park.[91] And

the emancipatory charge of this Shakespearean tercentenary was confirmed, in a more international key, when it exploded into a political
protest in favour of General Garibaldi, a demonstration that had to be
broken up by police.

The concreteness and sheer popularity of the historical association of
Shakespeare and liberty is materially evinced by the matching ceramic
figures of Garibaldi and Shakespeare that were produced at this time
(Figure 4.3).

They really look like twins, and theirs, presumably, is the shared face of
freedom. The association of Shakespeare and Garibaldi at Primrose Hill in
1864 speaks to what Taylor describes as 'a strong sense of Shakespeare as
a universal beacon of liberty'.[92] And Taylor further observes, as does
Andrew Murphy, that these events indirectly stimulated the foundation
of the Reform League. On Whit Monday in 1866, the Shakespeare
Tercentenary was cited as an important moment in the history of
English Liberties during Reform League demonstrations that again were
held at Primrose Hill.[93] In 1867, the government finally extended the
franchise to the significant effect that the working-class population
became the largest body of voters in the nation. This led, two years later,
to the inception of the Labour Representation League and, eventually, to
the foundation of Labour as a formal political party and an elected
government.[94] What I am suggesting is that in the background of this
important history we can make out the figures of Cooper, Jones, Harney,
Kossuth, Garrick and Shakespeare.

5   Shakespearean Suffragettes

The conjunctions between Shakespeare and freedom in the crucible of
modern life are many and various. On April the 27th, 1864, the
Birmingham Freethinkers met 'to add their contribution of praise to
the bulk of that so fulsomely bestowed on him of late in every quarter of the
globe'.[95] And if Shakespeare was associated with secular freedom,
the secularist leader Charles Bradlaugh also saw him as a trailblazer for
the specifically sexual freedom that secularism bequeathed to the free love
and contraception campaigns of the early twentieth century. According to
Bradlaugh, Shakespeare really should have been called 'Shagspere'.[96]
Moreover, the inclusive, free society which the Jubilee first presented as

Shakespeare's gift to the world takes further ritual form in the pageants with casts of thousands which were a feature of English cultural life in the regions especially in the first part of the twentieth century. As Dobson observes, 'this was a form committed, like the civic amateur dramatic societies founded at the same time, to the participation of all classes in the national culture, and like them it was profoundly engaged with Shakespeare as both a symbol and an expression of that culture'.[97]

It even included women, which is a relief given that the story of Shakespeare and the politics of freedom I have told so far has been so overwhelmingly male. In fact, there were strong connections between Shakespeare and women's suffrage. This comes across very clearly in the ecstatic review in *The Suffragette* of Harley Granville Barker's elegantly minimalist 1912 production of *The Winter's Tale* which especially praised:

> the dauntless, potent, unflinching Paulina – the eternal Suffragette whom all the greatest geniuses of all ages have loved to portray. Paulina, penetrating to forbidden chambers and telling tyrannts to their faces of the wronged woman and the helpless child; Paulina turning full on the unjust king the flood of her fierce eloquence, while his attendants fawn and cower for fear of his insane wrath.

'The real heroine of *The Winter's Tale*', this report goes on, 'is the woman who makes things happen – the militant Paulina, just as the real heroines of the twentieth century are the women who make things happen – the militant Suffragettes.'[98]

When the Actresses' Franchise League (AFL) was formed in 1908, it established a significant link between the professional theatre and the campaign for women's suffrage.[99] And during Stratford's three-week Shakespeare festival in 1909, the campaigning Suffragists powerfully claimed Shakespeare as their own. You stepped off the train at Stratford, as Susan Carlson observes, to be greeted with messages chalked on the pavement such as 'Women's Suffrage: Rother Market, Tonight at 7'.[100] And outside the NUWSS (National Union of Women's Suffrage Societies) in the town was hung a yellow and black 'to be or not to be' banner, referring of course to the female vote.[101] On most days while festivities lasted, rallies were held explaining 'What we Want and Why we Want it'.[102] And appearing on the stage of the Memorial Theatre itself were the president of the AFL Gertrude Elliott and her husband Johnston Forbes-Robertson, also famously active in the cause. The annual Shakespeare parade – a legacy

FIGURE 4.4   Shakespearean Suffragettes, Rother Street, Stratford, 16 July 1913,
PH350/2227, Warwickshire County Record Office

of Garrick's 1769 Jubilee, and one which continues to this day – was
commandeered by the Suffragettes. As one pro–women's-suffrage newspaper reported, 'the most conspicuous figures in the picturesque procession were undoubtedly the band of Suffragettes, recognised on all sides by
the purple, white, and green. They carried bouquets in the colours, and
when, in the Shakespearean address, Mr. Whitelaw Reid quoted Milton,
"We *must* be free or die", I saw that it was with difficulty the women
restrained themselves from cheering.'[103] In 1911, Ellen Terry argued in
London that Shakespeare was 'one of the pioneers of women's emancipation' and that 'Portia, Beatrice, Rosalind, Volumnia have more in common
with our modern revolutionaries than the fragile ornaments of the early
Victorian period.'[104] And as the photograph (Figure 4.4) shows, the
Suffragettes took to the streets of Stratford again in 1913.

     As campaigning was intensified in 1914, *The Suffragette* put out a call for
women to raise their banners at the Shakespeare Festival once more.[105]
Given everything we have learned about Shakespeare and freedom to this
point, this forging of a link between Shakespeare and the suffragettes was
really only natural. After all, the life in the plays isn't exclusively male.

If you had to choose, Juliet is a more important trailblazer for Shakespeare's politics of freedom than Romeo. Even if all his characters were originally played by men, Shakespeare's dramatic franchise clearly extends to women.

Political Shakespeare did not begin in 1985 with the publication of the landmark Jonathan Dollimore and Alan Sinfield volume of that title.[106] Indeed, even that important intervention had much less immediate and concrete political effect than did the older tradition of bringing together Shakespeare and progressive politics I have been investigating here. Writing in 1964, the Communist critic Arnold Kettle insisted that the popular nature of Shakespeare's achievement 'can scarcely be exaggerated', and that 'no great writer has had more impact' and that 'in circles which are not normally thought of when cultural matters are discussed'.[107] But such impact has been largely forgotten. 'Current left-political criticism, so often rather disaffected with the high literary canon', writes Peter Holbrook, 'should know more about radical mobilizations of Shakespeare.'[108] Indeed it should, and it particularly needs to know about the vital and important tradition associating Shakespeare and freedom.

5   Viva la Libertá!

We have seen from the parts played by Kossuth and Garibaldi that the tradition of associating Shakespeare and freedom in English culture had a European dimension. Dobson has pointed to a major apparent contradiction in the original Jubilee: its celebration of Shakespeare both as a universal genius and as specifically English.[109] *The lad of all lads is a Warwickshire lad.* But the centrality of the idea of freedom to the festival can perhaps help resolve this tension. After the Jubilee, Shakespeare's freedom frees the English to be themselves, throwing off the yoke of more established cultures: Greece, Rome and France. Free Shakespearean England then, in turn, sets other cultures free. It is wrong, I think, to consider even the native tradition of Shakespearean freedom as simply and exclusively English. With its crowds ambling through squares and galleries festooned with groups of marble statuary, before resorting to free and distinctly engagé theatres, the urban scene of Whitmore's 'Shakspere's Birthday – in the Future' is more evocative of some ideal continental city than it is of modern Leicester, and I speak as a Leicester schoolboy. This romance of freedom explains why news of the first Shakespeare Jubilee was enthusiastically received even in France, despite Garrick's mocking subversion of French pretensions to cultural superiority: during the festivities Garrick shooed off a planted and hyperbolically foppish actor (Tom King) pretending to be a French Shakespeare detractor. But Germany is the most striking example in Western culture of how Shakespearean freedom fuelled nascent nationalism; as we shall see in the next chapter, this initiated an extended effort in Germany to think through Shakespearean freedom, which contributed greatly to its development and importance beyond the German-speaking lands, in Western culture as such.

But before that, it's important to remark that the international potential of Shakespeare's freedom was in fact already evident at the Jubilee itself. 'It was not confined to the English only,' reported *The Public Advertiser*, 'for the Scotch and the Irish were as eager in paying their devotion.'[110] We have seen that Garrick's subsequent account of the festival to Drury Lane mockingly excluded Stratford residents; it also excluded the Irish. Perhaps Garrick was finally overwhelmed by the relentless attacks of those theatre folk such as Samuel Foote, and scholars such as George Steevens, who were horrified by the threat which his great Shakespeare giveaway represented to their own Shakespearean interests. But it is likely Garrick was also influenced by resuming his own institutional role back in the capital of discrimination in London as its leading actor-manager. In any case, he partially retreated from the radical inclusivity of what he attempted in Stratford. And yet, the part played there by the Scot James Boswell sufficiently demonstrates that the first Shakespeare Jubilee really wasn't just for the English. Boswell came to Stratford resplendent in the costume of a Corsican chief (Figure 4.5).

As the latter-day editors of his journals suggest, Boswell saw in Corsica's fight for independence – first from the Genoese, then from the French – his own private struggles for liberty externalised.[111] Boswell visited Corsica, went native with the rebels there and launched himself when he returned into an elaborate newspaper campaign intended ultimately to persuade the British government to intervene and support them. He personally raised money to send arms to Corsica, and he edited a volume of essays 'in favour of the brave Corsicans'. But his 'little monument to liberty' was his own book: *An Account of Corsica; The Journal of a Tour to That Island, and*

FIGURE 4.5 James Boswell Esqr from *The London Magazine*, September 1769, print made by Johann Sebastian Müller after Samuel Wale, British Museum Reg. No. Ee,4.130; PRN. PPA176530, ©The Trustees of the British Museum

Memoirs of Pascal Paoli (the Corsican rebel leader). It was a great success in Britain and in Europe, and it had a real impact on European politics. The French government commissioned a translation, and the British sent secret supplies to the rebels. But, in spite of Boswell's efforts, Britain wasn't about to declare war on France on behalf of a small island of apparently little strategic interest, and the rebellion had been decisively routed by the time of the Stratford Jubilee.[112]

But that didn't stop Boswell from hitching his one-man international liberation movement to Garrick's Shakespeare festival. His diary entry for the 2nd of September, 1769 tells how, in preparation for Stratford, he sought out 'an embroiderer in Bow Street, Covent Garden; gave him, cut out in paper as well as I could, the form of a Corsican cap, and ordered *Viva la Libertà* to be embroidered on the front of it in letters of gold'.[113] Two days later he was tramping all over London searching for other Corsican necessaries, then happily observing that he could get it all in his 'travelling-bag, except my musket and staff'. The staff he describes as 'a very handsome vine with the root uppermost, and upon it a bird, very well carved'. 'I paid six shillings for it,' he records. 'I told the master of the shop, "Why, Sir, this vine is worth any money. It is a Jubilee staff. That bird is the bird of Avon."'[114] Only a deep and natural association of Shakespeare and freedom will make of Boswell's Corsican kit and a staff that might have been carved in Arden such a miraculously coherent ensemble. It confirms that the time was ripe for Garrick to turn Stratford into Freetown.

In the course of his trip there, Boswell attempted to keep his Shakespearean-cum-Corsican thirst for liberty pure, by marshalling the image of his fiancé or, as he prefers to call her, 'my valuable spouse' against any spectres of sexual temptation. He took to the road in high excitement, travelling part of the way in the company of an agreeable and familiar female escort. 'I allowed myself no other liberty than once drawing my hand gently along her yellow locks', he insists.[115] When he found himself at the Jubilee chatting up Captain Sheldon's wife, and with the image of his 'valuable spouse' fading alarmingly, he improvised: 'I rose and went near the orchestra, and looked steadfastly at that beautiful, insinuating creature, Mrs. Baddelely of Drury Lane, and in an instant Mrs. Sheldon was effaced.'[116] As no doubt goes without saying, Mrs Baddelely's Shakespearean sex appeal is an ambivalent defender of Boswell's purer impulses. Here is that same tension between liberty and libertinism we saw in Wilkes brought into a much more explicit association with Shakespearean freedom.

But Boswell also lived it up in the sense of being seriously edified by the Jubilee. He believed for a moment he could live a better life if he lived it in Stratford. His Corsican contribution was a hit, and he wrote his 'Verses in the Character of a Corsican at Shakespeare's Jubilee' in the very midst of festivities. They tell the story of a proud and noble exile come 'to soothe my soul on Avon's sacred stream', offering a piteous glimpse of the Corsican river Golo 'o'er which dejected, injured freedom bends'. They suggest that if Shakespeare had lived 'our story to relate,' and Garrick had deigned to act it, then 'from his eyes had flashed the Corsic fire, / Men had less gazed to pity – than admire'! 'O happy Britons!', the peroration swells, 'on whose favoured isle, / Propitious freedom ever deigns to smile/ . . . let me plead for liberty distressed, /With generous ardour make us also free; / And give to Corsica a noble jubilee!'[117]

A word on Boswell's timing. In one sense, it was vanity to have continued the campaign for Corsican liberty when that had clearly become impossible. But as we have seen, Walter Benjamin's 'Theses on the Philosophy of History' suggest that to save the future, we have first to save the past, redeeming its lost potential in the interest of a better tomorrow.[118] And perhaps it was in that spirit that Boswell took it upon himself to embody and plead for Corsican liberty just as it was sliding into the dustbin of history. Though he excluded the Irish, Garrick included the Corsican Boswell in his stage play about the Jubilee, and Boswell seems to have lent Garrick his costume so the impersonation might be more apt. And that fantastical figure of Boswell in full Corsican costume embodies the flamboyant freedom of the Jubilee at its best as well as its hope that Shakespeare's freedom might come to be the glory of a free people who felicitate in the freedom of others.

5

Freetown-am-Main

❦

1   Zum Schäkespears Tag

The previous chapter focused on the role of Shakespeare in English political culture, and we have seen that it was by no means a purely insular one. This chapter demonstrates the part played by Shakespeare in Europe after the Garrick Jubilee. In August 1771, the twenty-two-year-old Johann Wolfgang Goethe returned to the family home in Frankfurt-am-Main.[1] At his urging, a festival was held there in Shakespeare's honour on the 14th of October: the Protestant name day for 'William'. Goethe presided over the party, and gave the oration; he also arranged that, under his direction, the actor Friedrich Rudolf Salzmann should act as master of ceremonies for a similar celebration in Strasbourg.[2]

This double whammy was the *first ever Shakespeare festival in Germany*, and evidently in part inspired by Garrick's Stratford Jubilee: the first Shakespeare celebration anywhere.[3] Like the Jubilee, Goethe's *Schäkespears Tag* represents a break for freedom – freedom from the overwhelming cultural authority of France, but also from eighteenth-century decorum more broadly. In Shakespeare's name, the young Goethe threw away everything that limits the free expression of a free spirit. And while this had its political aspect, Goethe's immediate point is that Shakespearean freedom represents a thrilling enlargement of experience.

News of the Jubilee arrived at the right time in Germany, providing a major stimulus to already nascent enthusiasm for the Bard. In 1759, Gotthold Ephraim Lessing suggested, 'the drama of Shakespeare was akin to the German *Volksdrama*'.[4] The year 1762 had seen the publication of the first volume of Wieland's path-breaking translation of Shakespeare; now Goethe faithfully copied 'Fête de Shakespeare' – the report of the

Jubilee in the *Mercure de France* of December 1769 – in eight pages of manuscript which he bound into his copy of Wieland's translation.[5] Another eighteenth-century German, Johann Wilhelm von Archenholz, saw Garrick's Drury Lane dramatisation of the Jubilee no less than twenty-eight times. More than any other book, Archenholz's *England und Italien* is said to have furnished the German idea of England.[6] And for Archenholz, *The Jubilee* was a central phenomenon of English culture, remarkable for the direct commerce it established between art and life.[7] It is worth noting Archenholz was editor of the German journal *Minerva*, which passionately advocated the French Revolution; Hegel was one of its avid readers, and Hegel is the great philosophical proponent of Shakespearean freedom.[8] Again we find separate pieces in the story coalescing in a coherent tradition of Shakespeare and freedom that recent years have somehow mislaid.

In 1776, another German, Georg Christoph Lichtenberg, asserted that Shakespeare, Hogarth and Garrick are 'of kindred mind', excelling in 'knowledge of mankind made perceptible'.[9] Germany was delighted to discover in Shakespeare, and English culture more broadly, an inspiring power of realisation, of bringing being into experience. By 1796, August Wilhelm Schlegel was in a position to declare Shakespeare 'ganz unser': a naturally German genius, annoyingly displaced in the West Midlands.[10] I jest, but in due course we shall see that this German repatriation of Shakespeare in fact amounts to much more than a crudely nationalistic appropriation.

Martha Winburn England has brought out the impact of Stratford's Shakespeare Jubilee in Europe in general and Germany in particular. Of Goethe's *Schäkespears Tag* celebrations, she writes:

One could wish to have seen Garrick at Stratford wring praise from his enemies and reduce his friends to maudlin unintelligibility with his ode and oration in one of the greatest performances of his life. The vision of Goethe on the evening of Shakespeare Day equally fires the imagination. Genius paid tribute to genius in the brightly-lit rooms on the first floor of the Goethe home. With music and dancing, toasts and festive garments, the Great Pagan hailed Shakespeare as the Great Pagan and in impassioned words acknowledged him master.[11]

Indeed! Such fervent yet touchingly formal homage paid from genius to genius across national barriers explains much of the exceptional appeal of what Goethe contrived for Shakespeare's Day; and yet it is very much less well known than it should be, and England's account leaves out the remarkable liberation of self and species which the younger genius (Goethe) found and trumpeted in the elder (Shakespeare), and which he had intimated already in letters describing his ambitions for the occasion to another great German writer: Johann Gottfried Herder.

Goethe wrote twice from Frankfurt to his slightly older friend and mentor in 1771. The two had met in Strasbourg, with Herder introducing Goethe to *Ossian* and 'Volkpoesie' as well as to Shakespeare. Now Goethe confided his plans for *Schäkespears Tag* and hoped to tempt Herder to come to the party. Hereafter I quote in English translation, but at this point I give Goethe's German to express at least something of the transition through which Shakespeare moves into other European languages and cultures. He wrote to Herder, 'Die erste Gesundheit, nach dem "Will of all Wills" soll auch Ihnen getrunken warden' [The first toast after the 'Will of all Wills' shall be drunk to you!]. His tone is characterised by a playfully liturgical emphasis, one which echoes the spiritualised quality we observed in the Garrick Jubilee; and he adverts for a second time to 'the Warwickshire lad' of its major hit song:[12] 'Ich habe schon dem Warwickshirer ein schön Publikum zusammengepredigt.' This charming sentence means, approximately – by preaching up the Warwickshirer I have gathered up a lovely congregation for him. It conjures a beguiling image of the young Goethe as an apple-cheeked evangelical selflessly converting Germans to the national poet of another country on soap boxes and in market squares. In the earlier letter he had written, Goethe had urged his friend to bear 'einen Teil unsrer Liturgie' [a part of our liturgy]. And though, in the end, Herder didn't submit to Goethe's blandishments and turn up in Frankfurt, we will see that he certainly didn't let Shakespeare down.[13]

But for now my point is that on Shakespeare's Day, Goethe was concerned to hail the Bard with something like religious awe; it recalls the lines quoted in the previous chapter from Cowper's *The Task* – 'He drew the liturgy, and form'd the rites ' – lines which saluted Garrick's Jubilee for calling the world to worship on the banks of the Avon.[14] Some two hundred years after his birth, Shakespeare struck Germany as a revelation. And what Shakespeare revealed to Goethe too were the possibilities of freedom.

What Goethe said to the lovely congregation he had gathered around himself on Shakespeare's Day in 1771 testified to the blissful new life he had found in the English author, and in terms which anticipate the famous Protestant hymn 'Amazing Grace' (published in 1779), though of course, for the 'Great Pagan', grace is aesthetic rather than Calvinist:[15] 'I sensed my own existence multiplied in a prism, everything was new to me, unfamiliar, and the unwonted light hurt my eyes. After a while I learned to see, and thanks to my ever-grateful spirit, I still sense vividly what I have won.'[16] Reading Shakespeare is a kind of secular salvation for Goethe, described here as a dazzling multiplication and intensification of being. It equally enables a great jump into vividly real new freedom: 'I leapt into the open air, and only then felt that I had hands and feet.'[17] Since this strikingly new body is a specifically *Shakespearean* endowment, it naturally entails a new voice, and it is with this that Goethe is impatient to speak out:

> I have had all I can take.
> I need air, let me speak![18]

And yet, the revolutionary new life Goethe derives from Shakespeare is not for him alone; it portends a more general liberation. 'Today', Goethe proclaims, 'we honour the memory of the greatest wanderer, and with him *ourselves*' – *we* already share in the wanderer's wayward freedom.'[19] Garrick had instructed his Jubileeites to look to Shakespeare as their own 'bosoms' lord'; we have seen that his first ever Shakespeare festival celebrated the Bard less as literary heritage than as an example and inspiration for new creative work.[20] Two years later, while extolling Shakespeare's merits in this first German tribute, Goethe is equally concerned to embody and proclaim the human freedom that is revealed in him.

Shakespeare's Day doesn't perhaps suggest the wildest of parties, but Goethe offers to the Bard a tribute that defies conservative respectability. He warns his auditors: 'Do not look to me please for extensive and orderly writing, equanimity is no one's Sunday best.'[21] The 'Sunday best' here is of course a joke, because in rejecting orderliness and equanimity, Goethe is, like Lear, undressing himself of just such conventional coverings: 'Off, off you lendings!'[22] Goethe wants to divest himself of eighteenth-century finery to get back to that great Romantic value, Nature, which Garrick had also tried to recover in returning to 'hallow the turf' that had pillowed Shakespeare's head in Stratford.[23]

On *Schäkespears Tag*, the young German genius cries out in frustration, 'What does our century know about Nature!' 'From *where* would
we know it,' he continues, 'we who from boyhood up see and feel only
in strait-laces and under powdered wigs?' And yet, there is one among
the great dead who brings us back to Nature. No prizes for guessing.
'Often,' Goethe admits, 'I feel *ashamed* before Shakespeare.'[24]

The pleasing prospect on this first *Schäkespears Tag* of an inspired
young man threatening to get naked in a gesture of creative rebellion
also constitutes and phases into a vivid appeal for wider political
change.[25] 'So gentlemen, let's be off!' crows the young Goethe – 'The
contemplation of one such prodigy makes our spirit firier and more
exalted than gazing at *the shuffling millipede of some royal procession.*'[26]
Again he seems to echo Shakespeare: 'O for a muse of fire!'[27] His
contemptuously anti-monarchical sentiment is an expressly incendiary
one, and some years before revolution in France. In beckoning his auditors
to follow in the footsteps of Shakespeare's great ascent, Goethe is also
implicitly remembering the procession of Shakespearean characters which
Garrick had planned for Stratford, contrasting both with the tired millipede shuffle of royal pomp and circumstance.[28]

Goethe's Shakespeare's Day represents an extraordinary access of
energy, one which confers a new self, a new voice and a new culture, and
in doing so it heralds real political change. Ernst Beutler was right to have
hailed it as a beautiful new dawn or 'Morgenrote', and one feels that the
Corsican Boswell would have enjoyed the occasion.[29] And if we still feel
inclined to take a young man itching to take his clothes off and make grand
political gestures less than wholly seriously – even if he *is* Goethe – his
serious philosophical contemplation of the conditions of human action
should convince us:

Shakespeare's theatre is a beautiful curiosity cabinet in which the world's history is
drawn past our eyes on invisible threads of time. His plots are not plots after the
common fashion, but his plays all turn on the hidden point (yet to be seen or defined
in any philosophy) where the distinctiveness of Self, the alleged freedom of Will,
encounters the necessary path of the whole. Our corrupt tastes, however, befog our
eyes so that we need a new Creation almost to free us from this darkness.[30]

In this rich passage, 'the alleged freedom of Will' becomes expressly the
point at issue. It is flamboyantly confirmed in Will Shakespeare, whom

Goethe presents here as a sort of massive male version of his own Queen Mab, easily drawing on invisible threads of time no less a thing than the cabinet-chariot of world history itself. A similarly powerful freedom is also implicitly confirmed in the young Goethe, and indeed in this very rhapsody to which Shakespeare's free spirit has stirred him. At the same time, Goethe is intellectually honest enough to admit that just such *alleged* freedom is thrown into question by the plays themselves.

2   Herder's New Historicism

On *Schäkespears Tag*, Goethe recognised in the plays what we might fairly describe as a new historicism: a revelation not of the antique pastness of the past, but instead of the ongoing historicity of culture as it is driven by and at the same time bears down upon our own selves and lives. The paradoxical consummation of Shakespeare's freedom, in other words, is an epoch-making vision of the limits of freedom.

Herder had shown Goethe his own great Shakespeare essay in draft form prior to Shakespeare's Day; it was eventually published in 1773. Goethe had perhaps wanted Herder to send it as 'einen Teil unsrer Liturgie';[31] and he probably meant to honour it when he promised the first toast to Herder after the 'Will of all Wills'. That imagined toast brings Herder and Garrick together, and indeed Herder's essay mentions the man 'who has revived Shakespeare and been the guardian angel of his grave', while regretting that he 'has had to change, cut and mutilate his works so much'.[32] In their explosive new proclamation of Shakespeare, Garrick, Goethe and Herder meet. But only Herder has the theoretical distance needed to see and formulate a truth implicitly central to all three of them: that Shakespeare is a great advent in human history, and not just in his own time but also now, again, in the late eighteenth century, on the threshold of Romanticism.

Herder kicks off his essay with a 'tremendous image' of Shakespeare's self-realisation, which he derives from Mark Akenside's *The Pleasures of the Imagination*: an image of a titanic figure 'seated high on the craggy hilltop, storm, tempest, and the roaring sea at his feet, but with the radiance of the heavens about his head'.[33] He then repudiates ordinary criticism, in a vein which will appeal to any weary Shakespearean:

What a library of books has already been written about him, for him, against him! And I have no wish to add to it. I would rather that no one in the small circle of my readers would ever again dream of writing about him, for him, against him, excusing him or slandering him; but would rather explain him, feel him as he is, use him, and – if possible – make him alive for us in Germany. May this essay help in the task.[34]

Make him *alive* for us in Germany! Like Garrick, who took Shakespeare to the streets – like Goethe, for whom he was the way back to Nature – Herder, too, wants to break out of the Shakespeare industry, even though, by contemporary standards, it had scarcely begun. Herder, like Garrick and Goethe, is interested in Shakespeare's life potential *for us*. He admires England as a nation which 'had no desire to ape ancient drama and run off with the walnut shell, but rather wanted to create its own drama'; and his cheeky turn of phrase suggests that, just as Shakespeare had unloosed the tongue of Herder's protégé Goethe, he had liberated the tongue of his master as well.[35] Certainly, for both Goethe and Herder, there's an element of anti-French feeling, of looking to Shakespeare to consolidate German in contradistinction to French culture; we have seen that this is perfectly consistent with the jingoistic drift of the Jubilee. And yet, as also at the Jubilee, Shakespeare more emphatically heralds a positive new freedom. Goethe doesn't blench to invoke 'the Warwickshirer', but at the same time his 'spelling of the name *Schäkespear* and even his father's abbreviation *Schacksp.* [in his household account] lay claim to a German genius'.[36] I have said that by 1796 the Germans will think of Shakespeare as 'ganz unser'; but I've also intimated that we mustn't misunderstand this as just a cynically political thing. At its best, the German vocation for Shakespeare is based on the non-possessive ease with which non-English enthusiasts can access and speak for the Bard's more transcendent significance. After all, as Herder puts it, 'it was the very freshness, innovation and difference that demonstrated the primal power of his vocation'; Shakespeare was and will always be a foreigner at home.[37] Roger Paulin therefore suggests Herder has 'the excursions of 1769' very much in mind and is arguing that 'while it is the preserve of the English to dwell on their particular notions of fame and significance, the Germans may penetrate to the very nature of creative genius, and to history, itself.'[38]

The German response to Shakespeare entails a revolutionary reconceptualisation of history. Herder explicitly admires Shakespeare as 'not a poet, but a *creator*', one who actually gives us 'the history of the world!'[39] He doesn't of course mean that Shakespeare scripted world history. Instead, like Goethe, he intuits that Shakespeare represents a freedom not *from* being but *of* being: a freedom of being fully and comprehensively what we are; and for Herder, we are ultimately historical creatures.[40] 'In the last resort,' he maintains, 'each play remains and cannot but remain – what it is: "History!"'[41] But then art and dream encroach into history. Indeed, Herder recognises art and history as the very motors of historical change. In this context, it will not surprise us to learn that, by the time he died in 1803, Herder had become, like Archenholz, another controversial advocate of the French Revolution. In contemplating Shakespeare, Herder concludes, 'the soul creates its own space, world and tempo as and where it will.'[42] The Corsican Boswell would agree, and the letters spelling out *Viva la Libertà* on the front of his hat might glow more gold as he did so. The soul certainly creates its own space and tempo when the Leicester Chartist William Whitmore imagines 'Shakspere's Birthday – in the Future' in an ideal city where Shakespeare and culture are the lifeblood of a spiritually as well as politically liberated people. What the Shakespeare-inspired Herder thrills to is the thought of his own still emergent German nation grasping the ever-new possibility of the world. And if this (as we shall see) resonates with Hegel, it also nods in the direction of Goethe's own beautiful vision of 'the Mothers', surrounded by floating images of creation, in the second part of *Faust*.[43]

And yet, such inspiring creative freedom as Goethe and Herder find in Shakespeare is not altogether undetermined; it retains a certain resistant thickness of life. We have seen that, for Goethe, freedom is limited in Shakespeare by 'the necessary path' of the play as a whole; and both of these German thinkers recognise that Shakespearean freedom is limited as well as animated by deeper energies than have yet been expressed in the history of politics. We are now in a position to recognise this as ultimately a positive thing; these thinkers welcome and embrace Shakespeare as an opportunity to *come home* to this deep history. Indeed, what may have excited Goethe and Herder above all about Garrick's Stratford Jubilee was the thought that it had begun to lay claim to this more profound and fuller life. Certainly, both of them assert that Shakespeare brings us to the brink of an epoch of richer and more fascinating being; their writings on the subject are fired by a shared conviction that as Germans – and thus fundamentally free from a narrow, proprietary interest in Shakespeare – they have a special responsibility for bringing it on.

This enthusiasm is not naïve; it doesn't exclude the darker life of freedom. Both Goethe and Herder recognise that the Shakespeare revolution they envisage entails risk. They conceive of Shakespeare as an existential earthquake. One of the most powerful and celebrated passages in Herder envisions a kind of mystical tsunami:

> Step then before his stage, as before an ocean of events, where wave thunders upon wave. Scenes from nature come and go before our eyes, however disparate they seem, they are dynamically related, they create and destroy one another so that the intention of their creator, who seems to have put them together according to a crazy and disorderly plan, may be fulfilled.[44]

Life, as conveyed to us in Shakespeare's art, is more turbid and engulfing than we typically admit, and entirely to be distinguished from the neo-classical tidiness of French models such as Racine and Corneille. Shakespeare's great waves, Herder goes on to say, are 'dark little symbols that form the silhouette of a divine theodicy'. They outline a sublime but ungraspable justification of life's intrinsic evil and pain.[45]

In this respect, Herder's essay resonates with a profound but largely forgotten tradition of German Shakespeare criticism, one which extends from Johann Georg Hamann (1730–88) to Georg Gottfried Gervinus (1805–71) and which regards Shakespeare as specifically Christian, and more specifically Protestant, because of his freedom from the moral law.[46] The ethical danger of this is its tendency to tip into antinomianism, which permits what would otherwise be rejected as evil in the name of Shakespeare's religio-aesthetic complexity or mystery; but what's refreshing about being reminded of such work is that it's indisputably Shakespeare criticism oriented towards the deepest, most controversial and disturbing things in life.

But in fact, Herder goes beyond Protestant antinomianism; like Goethe the Great Pagan, he goes beyond Christianity as such. What he ultimately descries in Shakespeare's corpus is the figure of 'Spinoza's giant god: *Pan! Universum!*'[47] And here we may again return to Garrick, for this esoteric figure from Herder was given a more familiar Shakespearean name at the Stratford Jubilee, when he was recognised as Falstaff. Falstaff in Garrick's Shakespeare Ode is, as we have seen, the avatar of '*a world where all pleasures abound*'; and even as he says so, Garrick acknowledges with a wink that '*the world too is wicked and round.*'[48] And since this wicked fullness of life outlasts the lives of all ordinary mortals, the libertine king of the Boar's Head has effectively become an immortal god such as Herder also envisions.

In Frankfurt, Goethe warmed to the same theme when he insisted that 'what we term evil' in the plays 'is only the obverse of good, and forms a necessary part of it'. Shakespeare, he went on, 'conducts us through the whole world but we refined and inexperienced people shriek at the sight of a common or garden grasshopper: Help, here's a monster that will gobble us up!'[49] From such timidity, Herder, Goethe and Garrick all saw, the Bard can liberate us into a life that is richer, darker and more real.

Thus, at the climax of his oration, Goethe calls in Shakespeare's name for nothing less than a cultural revolution. This means – it has to mean – obliterating what culture we already have:

Now, gentlemen! Kindly blow all noble souls out of the Elysium of so-called good taste, where they drowsily half-exist, half-not, in twilit boredom, hearts stuffed with feeling and no marrow in their bones, and, because they are not tired enough to rest, and too lazy to do anything, dawdle and yawn their shadow lives away between the laurel bush and the bay.[50]

Such words, such imperatives, echo down the years. It is an admonition that, in Shakespeare's name, we should fire the professors and the high priests of culture; we should change our perspective, and our lives.

To Herder and Goethe alike, Shakespeare is a shot in the arm: the transfusion and advent of a richer and deeper sense of history and historical possibility *within history*. Herder ends his great Shakespeare essay with the hope that his younger friend will 'raise a monument to [Shakespeare] here in our degenerate country'.[51] This is the German equivalent of Garrick's original desire to 'erect the statue and devote the pile'.[52]

But for Garrick, the point of the statue – indeed, the whole point of *Shakespeare* – was to inspire life, and the monument was only complete when the statue was surrounded with living characters and impassioned devotees. Even then it was only a monument. The real fulfilment of Shakespeare's legacy would be the coming into being of a real Freetown, which Garrick had attempted to herald or foreshadow at the Stratford Jubilee. Goethe contended on *Schäkespears Tag* that, though Freetown

might come into being in Stratford, it might equally come to life in
Frankfurt. Or Strasbourg.

3   A Wider European Legacy

The German adoption of Shakespearean freedom gave it significant further
momentum and cultural credibility on the continent. The Jubilee did have
an impact in France, but Shakespeare for the Germans represented a more
revolutionary upheaval. The revolt was partly against French taste and
decorums; thus, Friedrich Schlegel snarled, 'Out of superficial abstractions
and rationalizations, out of misunderstood antiquity and mediocre talent,
there arose in France a comprehensive and coherent system of false poetry
that rested on an equally false theory of literature; and from this a sick
mental malady of so-called good taste spread over all the countries of
Europe.'[53] Despite being the seat of this sickness, it was France of course
that actually had the Revolution. This great political earthquake of
European modernity came to be linked with the Bard in, for example,
Victor Hugo's *William Shakespeare*.[54] Writing in 1875, the Irish critic
Edward Dowden read *The Tempest* in the light of the Revolution, calling
Stephano's song an 'impassioned hymn of liberty, the *Marseillaise* of the
enchanted island' and crowing that Caliban is 'possessed' by 'a fanaticism
for liberty!'[55] And if upon reading Shakespeare, Goethe saw his own
existence multiplied in a prism, feeling he had leapt into the air and
discovered he had hands and feet, Hector Berlioz in 1827 experienced
a similar transfusion of energy and intensity, one which recast a more
recognisably Christian experience of salvation in new terms: 'I felt . . . that
I was alive and that I must arise and walk.'[56] Specifically Shakespearean
emancipation played its part in revolutionary France as well.

   And if Shakespeare caused Berlioz to take up his bed and walk, he had
a similar effect on Pushkin. The great Russian author said, having read
Shakespeare, 'I feel that my soul has expanded suddenly, and I can create.'[57]
Indeed, for a year or so, Shakespeare looked likely to recreate Russian
culture in general. In 1786, Catherine the Great, no less – who in fact was of
Prussian origin – adapted *The Merry Wives of Windsor*, using her Falstaff
to mock the cultural pretensions of the French. During the same year, she
wrote two new Russian plays, *From the Life of Rurik* and *The Beginning of
the Rule of Oleg*, both of which she described as an 'imitation of

Shakespeare, without observing the usual rules of the theatre'.[58] In 1787, the young Nikolay Karamzin, who would ultimately become a highly celebrated chronicler of Russian history, published a groundbreaking translation of *Julius Caesar*: the first Russian translation substantially based on Shakespeare's original. In his influential preface to the play, Karamzin said of the English dramatist:

He did not want to conform to the so-called *unities* which are so rigidly kept by our present dramatic authors; he did not want to impose narrow limits on his imagination; he looked only at Nature and did not care about anything else. He knew that man's mind could fly instantly from the furthest reaches of the Moguls to the bounds of England. His genius, like the genius of Nature, embraced both the sun and the atoms within its vision. He portrayed with equal art a hero and a jester, the wise and the foolish, Brutus and the Cobbler.[59]

Here the revolutionary German Shakespeare goes East. Karamzin's bold restatement of Shakespeare's freedom testifies to the freedom of untrammeled imagination in general ('man's mind'), which is nonetheless identified with Nature. Shakespeare, for Karamzin, takes us from pole to pole, from the farthest reaches of the Moguls to the bounds of England. He gives us both microscopic detail and sublime grandeur, both the sun and the atoms. And he extends the category of Nature into culture, at the same time as he enacts an ethos as inclusive as is Karamzin's syntax when it yokes together 'a hero and a jester, the wise and the foolish, Brutus and the Cobbler'. Here, as in Garrick and the Germans, existential and political emancipation are one. Shakespeare vibrates with the great events and imperatives of the day but only because there is a real material basis in his work for the revolutionary climate it has partly stimulated. Written just before the Revolution in France, Karamzin's preface anticipates Hugo's much later suggestion that Shakespeare, the Revolution and nineteenth-century literature all converge; that no doubt was why when the Revolution reached its height in 1794, a now frightened Tsarina had Karamzin's *Caesar* and its polemical preface burned. And yet, mere flames could not extinguish the fire of Shakespearean freedom in Russia, which Catherine herself had helped kindle. Following Goethe and the Germans, Belinsky also saw Shakespeare as 'the king of nature', enjoying a sovereign freedom; and Turgenev just saw Shakespeare *as* Nature – 'simple yet infinitely varied, harmonious, wise and free'.[60] Russian authority continued to set its face against this freedom, with a group of official critics campaigning against Shakespeare in 1850s Petersburg, and the ban on *Julius Caesar* effectively lasted into the twentieth century till the Moscow Art Theatre (MAT) production of 1903.

Meanwhile, as we know from Kossuth's enthusiastic and high-profile association with the Bard, Shakespeare was involved in the European revolutions of 1848. Dezső Keresztury suggests that throughout Central and Eastern Europe in the early nineteenth century, *Hamlet* was 'soul stirring reading for restless spirits yearning for revolution'.[61] In Prussia, the uprising of the Silesian weavers in 1844 was the first proletarian rising in central Europe – and, later, the subject of an important play by Gerhart Hauptmann as well as an extraordinary and harrowing series of works of art by Käthe Kollwitz. During the revolt, 'the poet and radical literary scholar Karl Grün toured from town to town holding popular lectures on Shakespeare, the proceeds from which were sent via the provincial government to help the weavers of the Liegnitz district.'[62] South of the Carpathians, in Wallachia, *Julius Caesar* was published in Bucharest in 1844 as the first complete Romanian translation; Shakespeare and his republican hero Brutus were embraced by the forerunners and leaders of another ill-fated anti-Habsburg revolution.[63]

In Hungary, Kossuth was only one of several Shakespeare-inspired revolutionaries. An alternative version of *Hamlet* provided almost unbelievably direct motivation and soul food for revolution. The first Shakespeare translation had been *Romeo and Juliet*; this was published in Pozsony (now Bratislava) in 1786. But *Hamlet*, brought out in Kassa (Košice) in 1790, was much more important. Both plays were free adaptations of German prose versions, but *Hamlet* was significantly Magyarised by its author the poet, critic, translator and nationalist Ferenc Kazinczy. Kazinczy's Hamlet fought a Habsburg Claudius in the name of the venerable past of Hungary as this was embodied by the Ghost, and he did so successfully, avenging his father and nation, and royally ascending the throne. This more positive, liberationist *Hamlet* was a great success. As Kazinczy asked in his preface:

Who would not cry with joy when our destroyed, trampled-on Nation raises its head from the dust once again, and returning to its language, dress and mores, it will once again be what our Ancestors were, it will be what half a year ago the faint hope would not have believed; a free nation?[64]

As Zdeněk Stříbrný notes, 'the victorious Prince prevailed in Hungary until 1839, when he was allowed to die for the first time in the new translation of Péter Vajda.'[65]

Meanwhile the political temperature in Hungary was rising. In his *World*, Count István Széchenyi had identified 'Shakespeare's giant soul' as the moving spirit of his will for reforms.[66] Kossuth went further than Széchenyi, both in politics and in his identification with Shakespeare, but there were more Shakespeareans in radical circles in Hungary than just these two. To his revolutionary cabinet in 1849, Kossuth appointed József Eötvös: one of the most important Hungarian novelists, and one who had been influenced by Shakespeare in his early work *Revenge*.[67]

But the major Hungarian challenger to Kossuth for the mantle of Shakespearean freedom has to be the radical poet Sándor Petőfi, who wrote in his essay on Shakespeare:

Shakespeare. Change his name into a mountain, and it will surpass the Himalayas; turn it into a sea, and you will find it broader and deeper than the Atlantic; convert it into a star, and it will outshine the sun itself . . . Before his appearance the world was incomplete, and when creating him God said: 'And behold him, oh, men, from now on you shall never doubt of my existence and greatness, if ever you dared to doubt!'[68]

This presents Shakespeare as a sort of existential supernova, and as a Nietzschean substitute for an elided Christ. By 1848, Petőfi was the undisputed leader of the Young Hungary movement for a free, democratic and thoroughly Magyarised nation which would live in perfect harmony with the other progressive nations of the world.[69] For Petőfi, energetic bardolatry was not at all inconsistent with the politics of freedom he expressed in the simple and effective refrain of his highly influential 'National Song':

> We swear by the God of Hungarians
> We swear, we shall be slaves no more.[70]

Petőfi's mix of Romantic Shakespeare worship with popular militancy very much chimes with what the 'Shaksperean General' Thomas Cooper was doing in England to extend his campaign for male suffrage at the same sort of time, and it is clear that Shakespeare played an important part in the development and motivation of modern liberalism both in England and in Europe.

While Cooper faded rather quickly into undeserved obscurity, Petőfi and Kossuth retained their force beyond the grave. Just before the Nazi takeover in Hungary, the Budapest daily *Esti Ujság* (18 March 1944) published a long article on 'The Triumphant Entry of Lajos Kossuth into New York, December 6, 1851', reverting very strikingly to the proposition that Kossuth 'owed his immense success pre-eminently to Shakespeare'. During the war, left-wing demonstrators met under the statue of the Shakespearean Petőfi in Budapest, reciting his 'National Song' in defiance of the Reich. Even within the Reich, it is worth observing, Stauffenberg attempted to assassinate Hitler after an evening of reading the English dramatist.[71] And later, with the Cold War at its height, Hungarian Americans promulgated Kossuth as a champion of Western liberty by once again recalling his Shakespearean associations and command of English.[72] After the German catastrophe, George Steiner is right to make us face up to the disturbing fact that a man might listen to Schubert and read Shakespeare before flicking the switch of the gas chamber; but the tradition of associating Shakespeare with freedom can accommodate the fact that freedom is always dangerously unstable and difficult to maintain at the same time as it affirms a mutually reinforcing conjunction between Shakespeare and positive political freedom which such a volatile context only makes the more precious.[73]

Naturally enough, the most moving passages of Stříbrný's important, to my mind insufficiently read book on *Shakespeare and Eastern Europe* concern the influence of Shakespeare in his native Czechoslovakia. Stříbrný traces the Prague Spring of 1968, which Gorbachev recognised as the precursor of his Russian perestroika, back to a grass-roots cultural change that included dissident productions of Shakespeare. 'Perhaps the most innovative', he writes, 'was *Romeo and Juliet* at the National Theatre in Prague'. He goes on:

The whole production voiced an impatient and impassioned protest against the futile grudge and cold-hearted cruelty of the old generation who had turned the world into a battlefield, where 'civil blood makes civil hands unclean'. Above the hatred and the slanging matches of the old world, free love, free speech, but also human tolerance and mutual understanding were stressed as the highest values.[74]

Stříbrný also details the part played by Shakespeare at the Balustrade theatre in Prague before recalling, with expressively terse eloquence, the career of Václav Havel, 'who started as a stage-hand at the Balustrade to become its most prominent playwright, then a dissident, and finally our President'.[75] Thus did Shakespeare's Freetown transpire again – this time on the continent, and very much in living memory.

6

Free Artists of Their Own Selves!

§

1 Shakespeare Criticism as the Struggle for Freedom

At this point in the book, I want to home in on the great German philosopher Georg Wilhelm Friedrich Hegel's philosophical discovery of Shakespearean freedom. I have invoked this several times already but, as one of the great intellectual events in the history which brings freedom and Shakespeare together, it now deserves more extended attention. Hegel inherited the German tradition of Shakespearean freedom discussed in the previous chapter. Born in Stuttgart in 1770 – the year after Garrick first feted Shakespeare in Stratford – he was introduced to the Bard, via Johann Joachim Eschenburg's first complete German (prose) translation, at the tender age of eight. One of his teachers, a Herr Löffler, presented him with Eschenburg's Shakespeare, correctly predicting that though he would not understand it now, it would benefit him in the end.[1] Before his death in Berlin in 1831, Hegel had the chance to see Shakespeare acted in the original by the English and Irish actors Charles Kemble and Henrietta Smithson at the newly opened English theatre in Paris.[2] Hegel was indisputably the most famous and influential thinker of his day. Freedom was central to his project, and it was in this context that he described Shakespeare's characters as 'free artists of their own selves'.[3]

Free artists of their own selves!

It's hard to imagine a more exciting critical proposition than this, and there is certainly no critical dictum in history more apt to this enquiry into the relationship between Shakespeare and freedom.

According to Harold Bloom, Hegel's dictum is simply the best thing on 'Shakespearean representation *yet written*'.[4] It is 'the insight into

163

Shakespearean representation of character that still needs to be developed by us'. Bloom elaborates as follows:

Iago and Edmund and Hamlet contemplate themselves objectively in images wrought by their own intelligences and are enabled to see themselves as dramatic characters, aesthetic artifices. They thus become free artists of themselves, which means they are free to write themselves, to will changes in the self. Overhearing their own speeches and pondering those expressions, they change and go on to contemplate an otherness in the self, or the possibility of such an otherness.[5]

He is onto something important here: the reflexive richness of Shakespearean consciousness as it is illuminated by Hegel; the process by which it stands back from itself, therefore gaining the objective distance needed to alter itself. This standing back from itself opens a mysterious otherness – a gap – within the self. Any achieved change fills in this gap and is folded back into the substantial self reflected upon. But the reflecting self then stands back from and changes itself again! It is a model of self-consciousness that entails perpetually dawning new life. In the intimate inwardness of Shakespearean character, the German philosopher found a promising power of human self-renovation. Shakespeare's characters' free artistry of themselves mirrors what is true of us too; Shakespeare can help us see that we are free artists of our own selves as well.

Now this is clearly wonderfully inspiring and motivating, a thought with real potential to inspire creativity and change; but in our time, it has to be tested against the power of culture to delimit and determine any individual human life. This is because so much contemporary thought has sharpened our knowledge of the power of culture over the individual. Bernard Williams, for example, observes that every human agent's history 'is a web in which anything that is the product of the will is surrounded and held up and partly formed by things that are not'.[6] Though we might cherish above all things our own private individuality, a moment's reflection is all it takes to recognise that general conventions of race, nation, profession, class, gender, sexuality and so on constitute much of what we are and do. No-one is simply free, no-one simply his or her own. Nor, I hasten to say, does Hegel think they are. More than any philosopher before or since, he describes how free individuality is achieved in the most detailed relationship to the whole history of culture, including the central institutions of family, the state, art and religion. We'll return to this.

After Hegel, modern thought has tended to emphasise ways in which freedom is subordinated and threatened by larger forces – of class society for Marx, 'ideology' for Althusser and 'power' for Foucault; of the unconscious for Freud; of *différance* for Derrida. These big guns of contemporary theory are the so-called masters of suspicion, but it's important to say immediately that they aren't opposed to human freedom. On the contrary: they tend to advocate emancipation. Terry Eagleton admits that Marx is typically seen as 'all about faceless collectives which ride roughshod over personal life' but proposes that in fact 'the free flourishing of individuals is the whole aim of his politics, as long as we remember that these individuals must find some way of flourishing in common.' In support of this, he quotes Marx's avowal in *The Holy Family* that free expression is 'the vital manifestation of one's own being', which suggests that Marxist individuals are, just as much as Shakespeare's or Hegel's, 'free artists of their own selves'.[7] Except that Marx is centrally occupied with identifying, analysing and changing the historical conditions which prevent such freedom. That's what the suspicion (of which he and other great moderns are master) is *for*.

In reflecting on his own career-long project as a philosopher and Shakespearean, Jonathan Dollimore has offered a helpfully lucid reaffirmation of this 'commitment to emancipation inseparable from painful and difficult historical analysis'. Dollimore elaborates as follows:

Marx had said, famously, that hitherto philosophers had sought only to understand the world; now they were to change it too. But, if anything, this effort to change the world itself required an even greater effort of understanding. To change in the direction of emancipation meant above all that one had to understand the ideological conditions that prevented change.[8]

As Antonio Gramsci puts it: 'pessimism of the intelligence, optimism of the will'.[9] Or as I prefer to say in these pages: *get real but do not give up*. If we want to preserve any credibility for Hegel's attractive proposition that Shakespeare's characters are free artists of their own selves, we will have to re-examine it in relation to the manifest power that culture and ideology exert over the individual.

Free artists of themselves! It's too good an idea – in both senses of the word 'good' – to give up, but keeping it alive entails the hard work of making it real. The good news is that Dollimore and many other contemporary thinkers share in this effort – rather than just fantasising about change in ways which, by unrealistically compensating for an adverse reality, actually preserve the status quo. And yet, you can feel the strain involved in Pierre Bordieu's tortuous formulation of the individual's '*intentionless invention* of regulated improvisation'.[10] Michel de Certeau recovers a bit more freedom from the overbearing power of culture when he writes of 'the clandestine forms taken by the dispersed, tactical, and make-shift creativity of groups or individuals already caught in the nets of "discipline"', but not much.[11]

The sheer difficulty of finding freedom in modern life has encouraged some thinkers to idealise violence. Derrida's later work, *The Gift of Death*, marks a break here, rehabilitating Søren Kierkegaard's meditation on the sacrifice of Isaac as paradigmatic for a recklessly self-authorising kind of action which bursts beyond conventional ethics.[12] And Jacques Lacan follows Hegel in exploring specifically Shakespearean drama as a proving ground for freedom when he writes, 'Why on the threshold of the modern period would *Hamlet* bear witness to the special weakness of future man as far as action is concerned? I am not so gloomy, and nothing apart from a cliché of decadent thought requires that we should be.'[13] Slavoj Žižek derives his explosive conception of action directly from Lacan's response to theatre: 'an act does not occur *within* the given horizon of what appears to be "possible" – it redefines the very contours of what is possible'; 'an act accomplishes what, within the given symbolic universe, appears to be "impossible", yet it changes its conditions so that it creates retroactively the conditions of its own possibility.'[14] Both the social situation and the revolutionary subject are thereby transfigured by the deed; as the tragic drama of the English Renaissance knew, 'You are the deed's creature' (*The Changeling*, 3.4.137).[15] From within this sector of contemporary thought, frustrated freedom erupts into creative violence. And it is impossible not to notice the disturbing resonance with the 'real-world' outbreak of terrorism which is the most horrifying face of contemporary politics; intellectual life may not be as abstracted from the real life of politics as, perhaps self-protectingly, we tend to think it is.

I began this book with John Carey's question: what good are the arts? Now I want to ask a similar question: what's the point of Shakespeare criticism – what is it *for*? Given the vast amount of intellectual and pedagogical energy (let alone funding) that has been and continues to be lavished on the subject, it is a question that is surely worth asking. And to my mind it isn't, in contemporary Shakespeare studies, asked anything like enough. One possible answer to it – the one I wish to offer here – is that Shakespeare criticism, whether knowingly or not, has been an intellectual struggle for freedom; that many of the critics who have contributed most to the historical development of Shakespeare studies have sought to affirm freedom intellectually by reading, promoting and interpreting Shakespeare.

It is well known that Jacob Burkhardt's *The Civilization of the Renaissance in Italy* established the Renaissance as the cradle and crucible of individual freedom.[16] But Hegel's proposition that Shakespeare's characters are 'free artists of their own selves' puts Shakespeare right at the heart of this before Burkhardt. And I want to suggest that after Hegel, the struggle to affirm freedom has been a central feature of the tradition of Shakespeare criticism; I want, indeed, to suggest that something like a Hegelian subconscious animates Shakespeare scholarship to this day.

For the founding father of Shakespeare studies, there was nothing subconscious about it. A. C. Bradley's brother F. H. Bradley was a real-life Hegelian philosopher; A. C. himself was glad to acknowledge his debt to Hegel's ideas about both tragedy and the Bard, in an important but too little known essay on Shakespeare and Hegel.[17] Indeed, it is a major irony of English literary studies that Bradleyan character criticism has come to be the antithesis of 'theory' when in fact it is based in what is arguably the most ambitious philosophical system the West has ever seen. To jump from Bradley's *Shakespearean Tragedy* to the defining work of Shakespeare scholarship in our own time, and one which is taken to mark a decisive break from Bradley, is to find that it bears the almost unbelievably Hegelian title *Renaissance Self-Fashioning*. This book, which established the new-historicist phase of criticism that has since dominated literary scholarship, bears witness to both its inheritance and its difference from Hegel and Bradley. While planning it, Stephen Greenblatt 'intended to explore the ways in which major English writers of the sixteenth century created their own performances' in order 'to understand the role of human autonomy in the construction of identity': in other words, he wanted to analyse his subjects as what Hegel calls 'free artists of themselves'. But contemporary intellectual conditions prevented this; and as he thought things through, this most influential of contemporary critics found himself unable to deliver any 'moments of pure, unfettered subjectivity'. What he found instead was that 'the human subject … began to seem remarkably unfree, the ideological product of the relations of power in a particular society.' Nevertheless, his epilogue confides an 'overwhelming need to sustain the illusion that I am the principal maker of my own identity', a need whose urgency and power stem from acknowledging that 'to abandon self-fashioning is to abandon the craving for freedom' – which, according to Greenblatt, is 'to die'.[18]

It's a familiar but still outstandingly powerful moment in contemporary criticism; and yet its relation to Hegel's pioneering proposition is less recognised. Sometimes the stakes of literary criticism are justifiably said to be too low. Not here. We need Shakespeare's 'free artists of their own selves' as icons and proof of what makes a really human life possible and worthwhile. Greenblatt's is like a grimly serious version of the Tinkerbell story. You don't believe, but you've got to: because, as Greenblatt indicates, not believing will entail nothing less than your own death.[19]

Greenblatt's book was first published in 1980 in America; its struggle to affirm freedom was echoed across the Atlantic by the British cultural materialist movement of the same period. Dollimore's *Radical Tragedy* was the most important book to emerge under that banner and, like *Renaissance Self-Fashioning*, it too has a resonantly revealing title, with the very terms 'radical' and 'tragedy' already pitting the hope for change against a grim and grievous fatedness. In the book, Dollimore points to a section of Gramsci's *Prison Notebooks* originally entitled 'Marx and Machiavelli'. Gramsci observes that, in Dollimore's words, 'the most original contribution of the philosophy of praxis is its anti-essentialism'.[20] Drawing back the bolt of an unchanging 'human condition', this opens the gates of change. Gramsci ushers in 'the concrete *action* of man, who, impelled by historical necessity, works and transforms reality'.[21]

But other cultural materialists rather lamed this militant subject at the gate of change.[22] In a much more decided fashion than Greenblatt, Catherine Belsey and Francis Barker treat personal agency as a bourgeois illusion: a manipulative fiction by which the state 'persuades people they are free in the very act of harnessing them to its own economic and political needs'.[23] But, as Herbert Marcuse observes, 'thereby, a major prerequisite of revolution is minimised, namely, the fact that the need for radical change must be rooted in individuals themselves, in their intelligence and their passions, their drives and their goals.' When subjectivity becomes 'an atom of objectivity', Marxist theory has ironically 'succumbed to that very reification which it had exposed and combated in society as a whole'.[24]

In this context, *Radical Tragedy* offers a double critique. First it attacks otherworldly notions of redemption and transcendence which remove the tragic subject from its historical predicament. Then it undermines feel-good, illusionary notions of freedom, both in the Renaissance and in the present. The aim of this double critique is to capture the scope for real freedom in difficult circumstances. *Radical Tragedy* describes the movement between feeling we can't change things and feeling that maybe we can; between seeing the amazing contingency of the social order – that which isn't natural *can* be changed! – and realising that the social order, contingent though it is, may be harder to refashion than nature itself. The resultant gains may be limited, but they are the only gains we can truly work for. Looking back some thirty years later, Dollimore proposes that the book unfolded not as 'a vision of political freedom so much as a subversive knowledge of political domination, a knowledge that interrogated prevailing beliefs, submitted them to a kind of intellectual vandalism, radical in the sense of going to their roots and even pulling them up'.[25] No other contemporary critic spells it out more clearly: *get real but do not give up*. None is clearer about the sheer energy, vigilance and commitment needed.

For some, Greenblatt, Dollimore and others conceded too much freedom. And two tendencies in subsequent criticism that are apparently unaware of Hegel nevertheless effectively attempt to recover some of the inspirational energy of his affirmation of freedom in Shakespeare. Both are promising inasmuch as they mine real and salient features of Shakespeare's art: first, its flamboyant self-consciousness about the way it creates identity and society in performance – this is what contemporary critics call 'performativity'; and, second, its process of elaborate self-realisation, as, for instance, expressed in soliloquy. Criticism that champions performativity is often energised by political commitment to women's and gay liberation. According to Lisa Jardine, 'to retrieve agency for the female subject in history' is the aim and end of feminism.[26] After *Radical Tragedy*, Dollimore offered a whole history of homosexuality which found scope for 'sexual dissidence' in spite of its violent repression.[27] Beyond Shakespeare studies, Judith Butler's theoretical intervention *Gender Trouble* argued for a new ontology of performance, thereby giving creative control of their own identities back to those routinely stigmatised and oppressed under patriarchy.[28] No-one, to my knowledge, remarked that this rendered female and queer subjects 'free artists of their own selves' in the tradition that goes back to Hegel on Shakespeare; but Butler's notion of 'performativity' offered a way of self-making which worked simultaneously within and against ideology and, after Butler, the Shakespearean transvestite in particular became a lit-crit icon of queer freedom.[29] This was certainly an advance, tapping the neglected transsexual energy in Shakespeare as an important source of Shakespearean freedom. But in a more recent development, 'queer' has become effectively disjoined from actual homosexuality or any other concrete kind of gender trouble, to the effect that it has come to mean anything non-normative.[30] *Radical Tragedy* made some of the same moves in an effort at going beyond given conventions and oppositions but in a later book, *Sex, Literature and Censorship*, Dollimore cautioned that such epiphanies can engender a delirious, wishful and compensating kind of freedom not to be confused with the real thing:

The result of such theoretical work-overs is not so much a demonstration of the intrinsic instability of the social order, or its effective subversion by marginal forces ... but an abstract, highly wrought re-presentation of it – a theoretical narrative whose plausibility is often in inverse proportion to the degree to which it makes its proponents feel better.[31]

Thus, the real power and recalcitrance of, say, heterosexuality is vaporised and its imminent collapse envisaged. 'Dream on,' says Dollimore. And he notes that where such claims are made, 'the very concept of subversion has become a kind of disavowal.'[32] It's not that performativity in itself isn't a promising notion, but freedom is concrete, hard won. Dollimore insists we have to engage critically and energetically with historical reality to carve out real freedom within it.

Taking a different tack from the emphasis on performativity, and taking his bearings less from Butler than from Marxist critics especially of the Frankfurt school, Hugh Grady has attempted to recover Shakespearean freedom in a way that also recalls Hegel. Grady opposes Shakespearean subjectivity to the 'instrumentality' typical of late capitalism – that process whereby the self becomes the mere means to an end, be it of profit, professional productivity or whatever.[33] He aligns Foucauldian and

Althusserian influences on new historicism and cultural materialism with Niccoló Machiavelli's early modern theories of power and subjectivity. And he demonstrates that both Machiavelli and Shakespeare anticipate the ways in which the systems of modernity – pre-eminently, the capitalist economy, the state bureaucracy and the legal system – dominate individuals. In a particularly interesting move, Grady proposes that in Shakespeare deliberate action is a reflex of Machiavellian ideology through which the self turns itself into a means to an end, breaking with the full and vital complexity of its subjective experience in the social world. This is seen, for instance, in the ways that Iago, Henry V and Hamlet become cruel automata of their own wills, only apparently independent of a process of rampant reification that signals the onset of capitalist modernity and which, according to Grady, Shakespeare brilliantly emblematised as a 'universal wolf' (*Troilus and Cressida*, 1.3.121). Grady opposes to this an alternative conjuncture whereby the late Foucault, Lacan, the Frankfurt School and Žižek are combined with Michel de Montaigne to illuminate the Shakespearean self's subversive, uncontainable pluralism and excess. It is a telling argument, but it is also telling that Grady has to mobilise so much heavy theoretical artillery. It indicates just how hard it has become to make a case for Shakespearean freedom, and indeed for freedom as such.

The rich selfhood which unfurls in Shakespeare, according to Grady, isn't a natural bloom: instead, it is always formed in dialectical reaction to Machiavellian power. The playful Hal and the ineffably complex Hamlet (so long as they're able to resist inevitable interpellation into required princely roles) are its best exemplars. Their self-experience, according to Grady, is 'unfettered, aimless, disconnected and alienated – but also suffused with libido and creative of some of the most remarkable insights, poetry and dramatic moments'.[34] This shelters and sustains the flame of freedom within Shakespearean subjectivity, which, as we shall see, is also where Hegel originally locates it.

The potted history of Shakespearean freedom I am offering here is the story of the extended fortunes of Hegel's proposition that Shakespeare's characters are 'free artists of their own selves', but it is also a story of diminishing returns. Richard Wilson's *Free Will: Art and Power on Shakespeare's Stage* represents a courageous and sustained effort to maintain the historical association of Shakespeare and freedom in spite of the scepticism which threatens it.[35] But to rehabilitate freedom, Wilson's book conscientiously excludes the more assertive, even morally dangerous aspect of freedom until what we are left with is more politically palatable and promising but less existentially convincing and rich.

Free Will wrestles admirably with the difficulties of freedom. Unlike other critics committed to emancipation, Wilson is to be commended for confronting awkward and unappealing facts of Shakespeare's biography. As Charles Nicholl has shown, the Bard cut a poor figure when called to a London courtroom in 1612 to testify in the Mountjoy affair, siding with his London landlord – a selfish patriarch who refused to make good on his debt to his own daughter – before leaving the courtroom in such a hurry that he had time only to sign his deposition 'Willm Shaks'.[36] Back in Stratford in 1615, Shakespeare declined to take the part of local people when they were threatened with eviction from the Welcombe fields: an episode which so scandalised the dramatist Edward Bond that, in his play *Bingo*, he imagines the Bard sitting in his garden while over the wall the authorities open fire on protestors.[37] This compromised Shakespeare was certainly no freedom fighter, and Wilson acknowledges that 'recent studies like [James] Shapiro's *1599* have returned us to the old idea of Shakespeare as a veritable *gentleman in waiting*.'[38]

But Wilson attempts to rescue Shakespearean freedom by remaking it. To this end, he offers his brilliant interpretation of Shakespeare's portrait of himself as 'our bending author' (*Henry V*, Epilogue, 2): one who 'bows to the power he bends'.[39] According to Wilson's most ebullient reading, Shakespeare portrays himself doing just this in that cameo in *The Merry Wives of Windsor* when Will the cheeky schoolboy's queer punning subverts his Latin lesson. In thickly historicised and often genuinely revelatory readings of *Hamlet* and *Macbeth* in relation to the nascent absolutism of James I and of Denmark's King Christian IV, Wilson goes on to argue that Shakespeare positively declines to oppose the sovereignty of the human subject or the sovereignty of art to sovereignty as such, to the effect that he is able to short circuit 'the sovereignty that always begins by coming back in the idea that the essence of human freedom lies in mastery and appropriation'.[40] Instead, and taking his theoretical cue from Judith Halberstam's *The Queer Art of Failure*, Wilson suggests that Shakespeare's central themes are '*the power of weakness*' and '*the escape from his own sovereignty*'.[41] His reflections on the Sonnets and *Antony and Cleopatra* resonate powerfully with these thoughts, and never more so than when he quotes 'Cleopatra's intuition that "My desolation does begin to make / A better life"'(5.2.1–2).[42] In favour of this more edifying understanding of freedom, Wilson also quotes Arendt and Heidegger writing in a way that notably recalls the resignation of the fifth-act Hamlet: 'If men wish to be free, it is precisely sovereignty they must renounce'; 'Freedom reveals itself as the "letting be" of what is.'[43]

Free Will is one of the most intellectually engaged investigations of Shakespearean freedom in recent years, and I am sympathetic to its ethically ambitious attempt to broker a deal between individual and political freedom; but I think in the process it gives away too much individual freedom. It's worth recalling here John Stuart Mill's insistence that 'the work of a state, in the long run, is the worth of the individuals composing it.'[44] Mill speaks to a *necessary* tension between individual freedom and social flourishing, one which has to allow for the sort of shabby behaviour Shakespeare and the rest of us at least sometimes go in for. In fact, it has to allow for worse. Relevant again here is Howard Barker's provocative question: 'Is there a single tragic protagonist who could not be described prima facie, as *one who murders rights?*'[45] Much to the agony of theologians, true freedom permits evil. It is irreducibly ambivalent, unstable and complicating. It is good in itself, but at the same time may be wicked. Wilson can't accommodate what, as we will see shortly, Bradley, after Hegel, called 'the good in Macbeth'.[46] Nor can he quite accommodate that more delightfully self-sovereign freedom which, liberated from the ideological constraints of the ordinary, workaday world, Rosalind suddenly enjoys in Arden.

Peter Holbrook speaks powerfully in favour of such freedom in *Shakespeare's Individualism*, insisting, as noted already, that personal freedom is nothing less than the core value of Shakespeare's art.[47] Moreover, according to Holbrook, Shakespeare's 'commitment to liberty and individuality is the main reason we should read him today'.[48] This is especially the case because, Holbrook argues, freedom in our time really is threatened, even in the supposedly free West. Holbrook serves up a killer quote from Max Weber:

The forward progress of bureaucratic mechanization is irresistible ... When a purely technical and faultless administration ... is taken as the highest and the only goal, then on this basis one can only say: away with everything but an official hierarchy which does these things as objectively, precisely, and 'soullessly' as any machine … [By rational calculation] the performance of each individual worker is mathematically measured, each man becomes a little cog in the machine and, aware of this, his one preoccupation is whether he can become a bigger cog.[49]

What is especially killing about this is that Weber spoke these words in a lecture of 1909 – more than a hundred years ago – of a world that is not nearly so bureaucratic and mechanised as ours is. And it is worth highlighting that little cog's preoccupation with becoming a bigger one, since it intimates that freedom in our time isn't just a simple matter of the individual against society. Rather and paradoxically, the individual tends to co-operate with the society that denies him his freedom; ideology operates by masking and naturalising the sacrifice it asks for: the central lesson of Belsey's intervention in the debate about Shakespearean subjectivity. But since freedom is a terrible burden as well as a great gift, it is equally the case, as Jean Paul Sartre and Erich Fromm have shown, that people can be deliberately moved to give away the very thing which arguably makes their lives worth living.[50]

The upwelling of a genuine hunger for Shakespearean freedom in Holbrook's book constitutes an important affirmation of what has increasingly been repressed in Shakespeare studies. To neglect this, Holbrook suggests, 'deprives us of a powerful resource – the imagination of a great writer – through which to resist encroachments on personal freedom (which, sadly, are set to become even more oppressive)'.[51] To tap into that resource, Holbrook suggests, we first need to recognise how readily contemporary scepticism tips into compliance. The 'cynicism about freedom' of the 'radical university-based Left' in particular, he proposes, 'meshes with the needs of an increasingly bureaucratized, surveyed and managed world'.[52] And it is in an effort to fight such compliance that Holbrook attempts to recover something of the motivating poetry of freedom. He highlights a wonderful moment in George Orwell's 1984 when Winston wakes from a dream of erotic freedom with the word 'Shakespeare' on his lips. Orwell represents Shakespearean freedom not as an academic concept but as a felt and precious reality – a reality like a kiss on the mouth – one which matters just as much and as urgently as our own most vivid and valued experiences.[53]

2 Edmund, Iago, Hamlet

If we can demonstrate that Shakespeare's characters achieve an aesthetic approximation of freedom within history, then they may continue to step out of their plays and inspire real-world political action, and even change. I say *continue* because we've seen in this book that they have done so before – in the 1769 Jubilee in Stratford, and its aftermath; in the revolutions of 1848, and the political career in exile of Louis Kossuth; in the Shakespeare celebrations which morphed into the pro-Garibaldi demonstration of 1864; in the campaigns and lives of Cooper, Harney and others; in nascent Germany; in the struggle for independence in the Caribbean, and on Robben Island. But before we liberate Shakespeare's 'free artists of their own selves' back into the world, we need to rescue them from Bloom's anti-political reverie. In *The Western Canon*, Bloom singles out Iago, Edmund, Hamlet as exemplary 'free artists of themselves'. Certainly, Edmund is a good example of the psychological 'self-overhearing' and consequent change that Bloom finds from Hegel. His famous first soliloquy, 'Thou, nature, art my goddess', is his psychological primal scene; you can almost hear the gears shift, deep in his psyche, as he contemplates his own illegitimacy, and the social prejudice against it, before energetically resolving to turn it from a humiliating disadvantage into the very foundation of his being and a charter for outrageous moral freedom (*King Lear*, Conflated Text, 1.2.1–22).[54] We have seen already that he concludes this speech with a cheeky knob-gag which expresses his self-delighting liberty perfectly: 'I grow; I prosper. / Now, gods, stand up for bastards!' Edmund *is* a 'free artist of himself' here, cutting loose from a life of shameful stigmatisation. When he mocks his father's superstitious astrological determinism – 'Fut! I should have been that I am, had the maidenliest star in the firmament twinkled on my bastardizing' (1.2.120–22) – he is simultaneously claiming his own proud autonomy. But we also need to recognise that for all his powerful psychological and existential victory, the freedom Edmund wins is actually very limited; he's still a bastard. He shows wit and spirit in deriving his liberty from this, in turning the stigma round, but he doesn't otherwise alter the distinction between legitimacy and illegitimacy that prevails in his culture. And it's important to recognise, too, that only his own powerful but solitary will sustains the transvaluation of values he does achieve. It's true this disturbs others, and that Goneril's and Regan's dissident desire for him derives from it. But this trouble is becalmed with Goneril's and Regan's deaths. Bloom writes, 'Edmund is a free artist of himself: *he feels nothing.*'[55] And again, he's onto something, especially when the author of *The Western Canon* links Edmund's affectless freedom to Dostoevsky's portrayal in *Demons* of his supremely demonic villain Stravrogin. As we shall soon see, it links up powerfully with Hegel's specifically negative model of subjectivity and metaphysics. Edmund feels *nothing*: and pure, undetermined negation is indeed a kind of terrible freedom.

But Edmund's unfeelingness in *King Lear* hardly spells complete freedom from ideology, because it is fundamentally a refusal to feel the ideological shame which would otherwise cripple him, and therefore an inverted admission of the power ideology exerts over his life. He patently admits this after being vanquished by his brother. Edgar says:

> My name is Edgar, and thy father's son.
> The gods are just, and of our pleasant vices
> Make instruments to plague us.
> The dark and vicious place where thee he got
> Cost him his eyes.

To which Edmund answers simply:

> Thou has spoken right, 'tis true. (5.3.168–72)

But Edmund finally betrays his illegitimacy. 'I pant for life. Some good I mean to do, / Despite of mine own nature' (5.3.242–3). Once more Bloom isn't wholly wrong to see 'free artistry' here. *Despite of mine own nature!* That really is exciting, intimating a fundamental freedom from one's own established self. But it also is another simple inversion, flipping evil into good without really disturbing the distinction between them, and a capitulation to conventional moral priorities to boot. I have suggested that Edmund represents the freedom to enter evil, and he does. But looked at with the cold eye of ideology critique, that looks, in his case, to be rather less of an impressive achievement. Arguably, when Edgar becomes Poor Tom, and as a result brings elements of the abject and obscene into respectable legitimacy, he gets one step further from ideology – one step further into free artistry of himself – than his shameless brother does.[56]

Get real but do not give up. It clearly won't do to see Edmund as simply free from ideology. And if Bloom's Hegelian reading of him gets us only so far, the same is true of what he says of his second example of Shakespearean freedom: Iago. Where even a cursory examination of Edmund makes it plain that really to get to grips with Shakespearean freedom, we have to look at it at least partly from a political angle, an engaged consideration of Iago demonstrates that we need to take on board Hegel's philosophical challenge as well. Iago says, 'I am not what I am', probably the most Hegelian utterance in all of Shakespeare (*Othello*, 1.1.66). But to understand why, we have, at least briefly, to look at Hegel's philosophy of identity.

Back at the beginnings of professional Shakespeare criticism, Bradley had the integrity to recognise that since Hegel's aesthetics are irreducibly 'connected with his view of the function of negation in the universe', no response to what he says about Shakespeare or tragedy can hope to be accurate which doesn't take account of this highly distinctive and, indeed, disturbing philosophy.[57] But Bloom doesn't relate Hegel's proposal that Shakespeare's characters are 'free artists of themselves' to his overall philosophy of radical negation. In *The Phenomenology of Spirit*, Hegel insists on the fundamental importance of self-realisation.[58] Yet the sort of *spiritual* self-realisation Hegel has in mind is at once much stranger and even more fundamental than the sort of watershed moments of coming into one's being which we associate with the term: a baby's self-recognition in a mirror, an adolescent's sexual awakening and so on. What Hegel is after is almost the opposite: those moments when I recognise myself as intrinsically other to my very identity and life in the world: 'I am not what I am.' We can illustrate this by what we might call 'the biographical fallacy': even the most exhaustive description of the facts and circumstances of my life – as in, for instance, an obituary – will almost certainly be unrecognisable to me as my true self. In fact, we can go further, because the biographical record is actually the very thing liable to make me exclaim, 'That's exactly *not* what I am!' The *auto*biographical fallacy appears because the same thing holds even if the description is my own. We are, it would seem, confusingly and fundamentally different from ourselves. Novalis, one of Hegel's more poetic German contemporaries, was on to it. As he puts it in an aphorism: 'Mankind: metaphor'.[59] Another way of expressing this is Rimbaud's, 'J'est un autre.'[60] Iago says essentially the same.

As with Edmund, it's not possible to say he gets entirely free of ideology. Iago's most peculiar and most stirring as well as most Hegelian utterance of course goes deeper than *I'm just pretending*, but it does also mean that, and Iago *is* pretending because he wants to dupe and punish his superior in return for the professional injury which Othello has served him in appointing a more cultivated and connected kind of a man (Cassio) to the position he, Iago, had been counting on. It's true his subsequent behaviour goes well beyond any justifiable response to that professional slur – hence, the popularity of what Coleridge nominates his 'motiveless malignity'.[61] It's also true that Iago has a memorable speech which suggests you can design your life just as you might your garden, in the process curtailing and harvesting especially bodily passions (1.3.317 ff.). But Iago's 'motiveless malignity' exceeds self-interest so far as to suggest that something bigger and more malign than self-restraint or an impulse towards creative self-improvement is blowing through him. And this seems confirmed in his ecstatic praise for and identification with his 'divinity of hell' (2.3.324).

What Iago *does* is destroy; a very particular grudge opens the floodgates to utter negation. Maybe the man who says 'I am not what I am' in Shakespeare *is* an exemplar of Hegelian free artistry of himself; but if he is, this admits that such freedom is a much darker and more dangerous force than the triumphant humanism which Bloom finds in the Bard. I observed earlier that Lacan and Žižek conceptualise a more violent form of freedom, but Iago goes beyond these thinkers' ultimate commitment to progressive politics. A Hegelian reading of this Shakespearean villain brings us face to face with the sheer negativity of freedom, striking lights with Howard Barker's definition of tragedy as '*the illegal form of things*', with the Nazis' appropriation of Shakespeare, and indeed with the renewal of terrorism in contemporary history.[62] It's a far cry from Wilson's self-sacrificing, ethically repristinated version of Shakespearean freedom. And it challenges any straightforwardly positive, ethical account of Shakespearean freedom.

Holbrook tells us that the tragedy of *Hamlet* 'is committed to individual freedom', and it is perhaps unsurprising that Bloom proposes that 'it is Hamlet, more than anyone else in Shakespeare, who is the free artist of himself.'[63] Once again, he may be right, but only if we admit complexities he is at pains to exclude. And as before, ideology has to be acknowledged.

I mean, let's be honest: it's difficult to imagine a subject more interpellated than Hamlet is! He says himself, 'The time is out of joint. O cursed spite / That ever I was born to put it right' (1.5.189–90). He is Hamlet son of

Hamlet, required to avenge Old Hamlet's death; and in the end he does avenge it. So clearly he can't be simply seen as any kind of counter-cultural hero.

Nor does he really score so highly in terms of 'self-overhearing' and resulting change. After all, most of his soliloquies confirm his abject depression: 'O that this too too solid flesh would melt' (1.2.129); 'O what a rogue and peasant slave am I' (2.2.527); 'How all occasions do inform against me' (4.4.22). As even just these first quoted lines reveal, Hamlet gets stuck deeper and deeper in the mire each time he fails to change and rescue himself from it. He is dutifully obedient, thoroughly constrained by ideology; at no point does he step outside of it to the extent of clearly thinking or saying that revenge is wrong or even questionable.

And if ideology goes deep in him, he is even more constrained by deeper forces. Take his most famous – indeed, *the* most famous – speech: 'To be, or not to be' (3.1.58 ff.). Here our tormented prince presents life in such entirely and exhaustingly negative terms as to make death very plainly 'a consummation devoutly to be wished'. He stops short of that consummation only because of 'the dread of something after death': the fear it will not, after all, be the end, that it will inaugurate some other, further form of being. In other words, Hamlet chooses to go on living *only by rejecting life twice*: first he rejects this life; then he rejects the merest whiff or prospect of another.

So, imagine you had to choose. It's a no-brainer! Surely Marlowe's world-defeating Scythian shepherd boy Tamburlaine is a much more obvious candidate for the palm of literary self-making? How can Bloom see Hamlet as the paragon of free artistry of his own self?

To understand this, I think we need to go back to Hegel. In the same section of the *Aesthetics* where he calls Shakespeare's characters 'free artists of themselves', the German philosopher also suggests that though, when we look at it from the outside, 'Hamlet's death seems to be brought about accidentally, owing to the fight with Laertes and the exchange of rapiers', in fact, this accident fulfils his deepest longing and thereby acquires the inner justification that facilitates a strange joy, release and resolution at the play's end. Dying isn't just a calamity for Hamlet because, as Hegel says, 'death lay from the beginning in the background of Hamlet's mind.' He also says, rather wonderfully, I think: '*The sands of time do not content him.*' And he suggests that Hamlet's 'melancholy and weakness, his worry, his disgust at all the affairs of life' render him 'from the start ... a lost man, almost consumed already by inner disgust before death comes to him from outside'.[64] Hegel perceives that Hamlet is, in short, an alien.[65]

This is expressed dramatically in his withdrawal from society and the social pecking order – he shows a marked lack of positive interest in the succession – and also from sexual relations and marriage. Hamlet says, 'I say we will have no more marriages!' (3.1.146–7): an amazing thing to say in a play. Kenneth Branagh's gorgeous flashbacks of himself as Hamlet making love to Kate Winslet's Ophelia may be a cop out; Hamlet may in fact die a virgin, and a thirty-year-old virgin at that. And, strange though it is to say, it may be exactly this sympathy for death, this shrinking from life, which constitutes his quintessential Shakespearean freedom, his iconic status as the paradigm of Western subjectivity. When, in his later book on *Hamlet*, Bloom writes of 'the negative power of Hamlet's conscious-ness', suggesting, 'Unsponsored and free, Hamlet longs for a mighty oppo-site, and discovers he has to be his own', he is exploring this same peculiarly negative quality of the most famous character in all dramatic literature.[66]

I am not what I am: unlike Iago, Hamlet achieves this radically alienated, Hegelian subjectivity in the process of doing *exactly what's expected of him*. By the end of the play, after all his agonies of failure and indecision, he is successfully interpellated as the revenging son, as the Hamlet who avenges Hamlet. And yet, he fulfils that role in so belated, light-hearted and impersonal a way as to subvert it in its very fulfilment. Though he avenges his father, he nevertheless secures his absolute difference from him. Indeed, the play marks the fundamental difference between Hamlet and his own deed by staging that deed's reductive enactment in dumb show. It is clearly everything other than what he does which makes Hamlet Hamlet in the end.

I am not what I am: if, as Bloom contends, 'it is Hamlet, more than anyone else in Shakespeare, who is the free artist of himself', then he must remind us of Kierkegaard's Knight of Faith: 'The moment I set eyes on him I instantly push him from me, I myself leap backwards, I clasp my hands and say half aloud, "Good Lord, is this the man? Is it really he? Why, he looks like a tax-collector!"'[67] And this, in a sense, makes him all the more fascinating; but it remains strange that such an agonized conformist should, in the Western tradition, have become our crowned prince of freedom. Unless what Shakespeare is telling us, contra Bloom, is that we can't have freedom without ideology, that the best we can ever hope for is to undermine ideology from the inside, and at the cost of ruining what identity ideology confers upon us, which is all the substantial self we have. Such freedom is radical, even heroic. It would be so much easier just to fall in line.

3   Hegel's Fuller Account

We have now briefly analysed Edmund, Iago and Hamlet – all three of the characters Bloom holds up as exemplary of that free artistry of themselves which he regards as the central achievement not just of Shakespeare but of the entire Western canon. These characters actually achieve freedom only fitfully and ambivalently; even when they do achieve it, it is as complex, difficult and disturbing as we also found it to be in Chapter 3's more comprehensive examination of *Romeo and Juliet*. It is certainly not the pure act of self-creation Bloom claims to find in Shakespeare. But it is no less important for that. In fact, it is *more* important because it is more real and credible, truer to the adverse conditions of our lives, and as a result more likely to help us think through and achieve real, genuinely valuable personal and political freedom and change.

But if Hegel's idea that Shakespeare's characters are 'free artists of their own selves' really is so important, then it's time we looked at it more closely. Here, in English translation, is the main passage in which the philosopher formulates the notion, and which, remember, Bloom considers 'the best critical passage on Shakespearean representation yet written' (not that he quotes it in full):

In the portrayal of concretely human individuals and characters it is especially the English who are distinguished masters and above them all Shakespeare stands at an almost unapproachable height. For even if some purely single passion, like ambition in Macbeth or jealousy in Othello, becomes the 'pathos' of his tragic heroes, still such an abstraction does not devour their more far-reaching individuality at all, because despite this determinant they still always remain complete men. Indeed the more Shakespeare proceeds to portray on the infinite breadth of his world-stage the extremes of evil and folly, all the more, as I have remarked earlier, does he precisely plunge his figures who dwell on these extremes into their restrictedness; of course he equips them with a wealth of poetry but he actually

gives them spirit and imagination, and, by the picture in which they can contemplate and see themselves objectively like a work of art, he makes them free
artists of their own selves, and thereby with his strongly marked and faithful
characterization, can interest us not only in criminals but even in the most downright and vulgar clouts and fools. The way that his tragic characters reveal
themselves is of a similar kind: individual, real, directly living, extremely varied,
and yet, where this emerges necessarily, of a sublimity and striking power of
expression, of a depth of feeling and gift for invention in images and similes
produced on the spur of the moment, of a rhetoric, not pedantic but issuing
from the actual feeling and outpouring of the character – take all this into account,
this combination of directly present life and inner greatness of soul, and you will
scarcely find any other modern dramatist who can be compared with Shakespeare.
Goethe in his youth did try to achieve a similar truth to nature and an individuality
of personality but without achieving the inner force and height of passion [of
Shakespeare's characters], and Schiller has fallen into a violence which has no
really solid kernel in its expansive storming.[68]

The first thing to notice, perhaps, is just how subordinated – almost
buried – Hegel's most striking and inspiring formulation is.
The emphasis is not on Shakespeare's characters' free self-creation of
themselves but, rather, on how convincingly they are crafted as 'concretely
human' by their author. It's true that what sets the seal on this artistry is the
life Shakespeare confers on his creatures. According to Hegel, he 'actually
gives them spirit and imagination'; his tragic characters seem to 'reveal
themselves'. But this combination of 'directly present life and inner greatness of soul' is what sets Shakespeare apart from the German pretenders,
Goethe and Schiller; it is *his* genius, not that of his characters, which
remains Hegel's ultimate concern here.

But of course the devil is in the detail. Hegel implicitly distinguishes
Shakespearean theatre from the 'humoral' drama of his contemporaries
such as Ben Jonson where characters are dominated and driven by 'some
purely single passion'. He insists that even where Shakespeare does endow
his characters with some outstandingly grand passion – such as Othello's
jealousy or Macbeth's ambition – 'still such an abstraction does not devour
their more far-reaching individuality at all, because despite this determinant they still always remain complete men.' As a result, as Hegel says at
another point in his *Aesthetics*, Shakespearean drama makes greater and
more fulfilling demands of those charged with bringing it to life in

performance: 'we require of the actor that he shall for his part bring them before our eyes in this entire completeness.'[69]

Hegel finds that in Shakespeare an allegorical power 'to portray on the infinite breadth of his world-stage the extremes of evil and folly' developed in unique and paradoxical tandem with a seemingly opposite facility for realistic detail: thus 'does he precisely plunge his figures who dwell on these extremes into their restrictedness'. *Restrictedness* is an interesting word, suggesting the obdurate facticity of the delimited self. But the Shakespearean self is not just limited and obdurate, because the dramatist also endows his characters with the 'spirit and imagination' to reflect on a mental picture 'in which they can contemplate and see themselves objectively like a work of art'. This cool distancing of the self from the self within itself is the mysterious otherness which Bloom observes in Shakespearean selfhood. It suggests that no-one simply coincides with what he or she is, which is how Shakespeare 'can interest us not only in criminals but even in the most downright and vulgar clouts and fools'. It is this internal difference from what we are which makes all of us – kings, criminals and vulgar clouts and fools alike – potentially free artists of our own selves.

It is interesting, and not at all remarked by Bloom, that such free artistry is associated in this passage with comedy alone. The way that Shakespeare's tragic characters reveal themselves, according to Hegel, 'is of a similar kind: individual, real, directly living, extremely varied, and yet, where this emerges necessarily, of a sublimity and striking power of expression, of a depth of feeling and gift for invention in images and similes produced on the spur of the moment, of a rhetoric, not pedantic but issuing from the actual feeling and outpouring of the character': the philosopher's impressions run together in this approximation of the rich experience he is describing. He does not, as a lesser thinker might have done, just fasten on and elaborate the impressive idea just crystallised that Shakespeare's characters are 'free artists of themselves'. He leaves that for us to do! But that Hegel doesn't do it himself should serve as a useful reminder that his insight into Shakespearean freedom emerges as part of a complex intellectual experience of that self-realising power Shakespeare's characters derive from being richly themselves ('individual, real, directly living', speaking 'a rhetoric, not pedantic but issuing from the actual feeling and outpouring of the character') and from an opposite 'inventive power' released by their reflective distance from that rich restrictedness. Hegel recognises that Shakespeare's characters' freedom includes both *the freedom to be yourself* and *the freedom to be something different*, and that these are not abstract, separable powers but instead are inherent in 'concrete' personality and freedom. All this is summed up under his rubric of 'directly present life and inner greatness of soul'.

Of course Hegel's philosophical discovery of Shakespearean freedom didn't come out of nowhere. We have seen that the Garrick Jubilee prepared for it, as well as that Goethe's leap into his own creative destiny was inspired by Herder, the Jubilee and Shakespeare. In letters to Goethe, Schiller contrasted his and Shakespeare's realistic characterisation with the flatter, allegorical figures of antique drama.[70] And back in England, Hazlitt wrote, in a lecture of 1818, that 'each of [Shakespeare's] characters is as much itself, and as absolutely independent of the rest . . . as if they were living persons.'[71] But Hegel more than any other writer before him brings out the texture and meaning of Shakespearean freedom. In his essay on Hegel and Shakespeare, A.C. Bradley writes:

> A part at least of Hegel's meaning may be illustrated thus. We are interested in the personality of Orestes or Antigone, but chiefly as it shows itself in one aspect, as identifying itself with a certain ethical relation; and our interest in the personality is inseparable and indistinguishable from our interest in the power it represents. This is not so with Hamlet, whose position so closely resembles that of Orestes. What engrosses our attention is the whole personality of Hamlet in his conflict, not with an opposing spiritual power, but with circumstances and, still more, with difficulties of his own nature. No one could think of describing Othello as the representative of an ethical family relation. His passion, however much nobility he may show in it, is personal. So is Romeo's love. It is not pursued, like Posa's freedom of thought, as something universal, a right of man. Its right, if it could occur to us to use the term at all, is Romeo's right.[72]

In other words, in their 'directly present life and inner greatness of soul' Shakespeare's characters are above all themselves. Elsewhere in his lectures on aesthetics, Hegel emphasises their *Partikularität* or sheer individuality.[73] This helps crystallise what will be evident from what I have quoted already: that Hegel is as much concerned with freedom of being and expression as he is with freedom of action. He finds in Shakespeare the sort of self-cultivating, self-realising power that is at the same time co-extensive with and revelatory of the German ideal of *Bildung*. It's true that he recognises the resoluteness and defiance which characters such as Macbeth 'accomplish only from the necessity of maintaining themselves against others or because they *have* reached once and for all the point that they have reached'. But even here what is achieved in action is the 'progress and history of a *great soul*, its inner development, the picture of its self-destructive struggle against circumstances, events, and their consequences'.[74]

Bradley also brings out the fact that Hegel's affirmation of Shakespearean freedom involves a significant moral challenge. He comments: 'The passion of Richard or Macbeth is not only personal, like that of Othello; it is egoistic and anarchic, and leads to crimes done with a full knowledge of their wickedness; but to the modern mind the greatness of the personality justifies its appearance in the position of hero.'[75] And this is where he goes on to say:

Is there not such good in Macbeth? It is not a question merely of moral goodness, but of good. It is not a question of the use made of good, but of its presence. And such bravery and skill in war as win the enthusiasm of everyone about him; such an imagination as few but poets possess; a conscience so vivid that his deed is to him beforehand a thing of terror, and, once done, condemns him to that torture of the mind on which he lies in restless ecstasy; a determination so tremendous and a courage so appalling that, for all this torment, he never dreams of turning back, but, even when he has found that life is a tale full of sound and fury, signifying nothing, will tell it out to the end though earth and heaven and hell are leagued against him; are not these things, in themselves, good, and gloriously good?[76]

This brave and powerful passage fingers a really major problem. It is the one Howard Barker approaches when he says tragedy is '*the illegal form of things*'; it is the one Wilson somewhat glosses over in offering his conscientiously refurbished construction of freedom in Shakespeare.[77] Macbeth's freedom, his power of realising his own 'directly present life and inner greatness of soul', is so good in itself that it threatens our more general idea of what goodness is. Bradley portrays this in more or less Hegelian terms of 'self-division and self-waste of spirit, or a division of spirit involving both conflict and waste'. In *Macbeth*, the good of individual freedom becomes so great that it violates the greater good of which it is part, which in turn reasserts itself and eviscerates it. But Bradley insists that 'on *both* sides in the conflict there is a spiritual value' and that 'the

tragic conflict is not merely of good with evil, but also, and more essentially, of good with good.' 'Only in saying this,' he cautions, 'we must be
careful to observe that "good" here means anything that has spiritual value,
not moral goodness alone, and that "evil" has a similarly wide sense.'[78]

Hegel's Shakespeare, then, administers a moral shock, but an educative
one: a sharp reminder of what any fully sentient person knows already –
our lives are fatally divided against themselves; our goals of individual
freedom and social flourishing are always liable to come into conflict. It is
an issue that is as central to Hegel's intellectual project as it is to
Shakespearean drama, and is the main focus of the next chapter.

Perhaps surprisingly then, Hegel leads us back from abstraction.
According to him, the most intellectually interesting thing – the very
fullest fulfilment of personal freedom – is the concrete self-realisation of
Shakespeare's characters. Still, he perceives a hard, philosophical core to
this, one 'connected,' in Bradley's phrase, 'with his view of the function of
negation in the universe'. Bloom does well, I think, to emphasise that
Hegel's Shakespearean creatures come strangely to share in their own
creation, recognising that they are 'dramatic characters, aesthetic artifices'.
And it's not just that they suddenly see themselves as if in a picture; for by
dint of that self-recognition they simultaneously render themselves
pictures *in process*, which henceforward they themselves will be able to
reshape and change.

The X-ray of Shakespearean character which Hegel offers is deeply
impressive. He demonstrates that Shakespearean freedom is a strange
combination of being what you are and at the same time not being, and
that this is evinced not just in what Shakespeare's characters say but,
equally, in the way that they say it. He points, on the one hand, to the
fire of thought that flows from the inwardness of characters such as Juliet
as though from some inexhaustible inner resource. Hegel sees Juliet at the
beginning of the play as not much more than a little girl who 'in all
naïveté . . . has peeped into her surroundings in the world, as into a magic-
lantern show'. But then suddenly, he suggests:

We see the development of the whole strength of this heart, of intrigue, circum-
spection, power to sacrifice everything and to submit to the harshest treatment; so
that now the whole thing looks like the first blossoming of the whole rose at once in
all its petals and folds, like an infinite outpouring of the inmost genuine basis of the

soul in which previously there was no inner differentiation, formation, and development, but which now comes on the scene as an immediate product of an awakened single interest, unbeknown to itself, in its beautiful fullness and force, out of a hitherto self-enclosed spirit. It is a torch lit by a spark, a bud, only now just touched by love, which stands there unexpectedly in full bloom, but the quicker it unfolds, the quicker too does it droop, its petals gone.[79]

This is a beautiful evocation of Juliet's instantaneous as well as tragically brief flourishing. There can scarcely have been a better description of the heroine of *Romeo and Juliet*'s sudden efflorescence; but in the third chapter of this book we saw that it is very much rooted in the soil of night and not being, which brings me on to Hegel's brilliant demonstration of how Shakespearean metaphor is always dividing self from self, and thereby accomplishing 'the liberation of the inner life from a purely practical interest'.[80]

Roger Paulin admits that here 'Hegel is, of course, repeating traditional insights of rhetoric, especially as applied to classical drama', but he observes that nevertheless 'it is different from the Romantic emphasis on the wealth and variety of Shakespeare's language.' It is different from the Romantic emphasis because it derives from Hegel's hard philosophical model of human personality. Paulin goes on to say that Hegel's view of Shakespearean metaphor is 'not undifferentiated':

A character may hold back the anguish of his soul and preserve his freedom by choosing an image related, but not in all points similar, to his situation. Thus Northumberland in *2Henry IV* (1.1.67ff.) seizes on the metaphorical analogy with Priam, or Richard II (4.1.173ff.) the comparison with crown and well. The character, too, while fully accepting his fate and pain, may nevertheless wish to break out of its hold. When Macbeth utters, 'Out, out, brief candle', he is lifted out of the cycle of crime and base passion by the power of his own imagination, and enters into some higher sphere of mind. The metaphor, too, may display inner calm and acceptance in the face of adversity, as when Cleopatra likens the asp to a sucking child. (5.2.300ff.)[81]

This is nicely expressed. But Hegel's analyses of Shakespearean metaphor and character are in fact even more 'differentiated' and particularised than Paulin suggests and a closer inspection of what Hegel says shows his theory is able to cope with and indeed derives its strength from a most engaged and responsive reading of Shakespeare. Hegel says of Richard II, for

instance, that he 'has a heart that however much it secludes itself in its grief
yet retains the force to set it steadily before itself in new comparisons'. 'And
this,' he goes on, 'is precisely the touching and childlike aspect in Richard's
grief, that he constantly expresses it to himself in felicitous images and
retains his suffering all the more profoundly in the play of his self-
expression.'[82] These are critical remarks which very much illuminate and
renew the famous lines the philosopher subsequently goes on to quote:

> Here, cousin, seize the crown.
> Here, cousin. On this side my hand, on that side thine.
> Now is this golden crown like a deep well
> That owes two buckets filling one another,
> The emptier ever dancing in the air,
> The other down, unseen, and full of water.
> That bucket down and full of tears am I,
> Drinking my griefs, whilst you mount up on high.
>
> (4.1.172–9)

There is a resoluteness in the sheer lucidity and completeness of the image,
which bears out the compliment Hegel has already paid to Richard as
a suffering consciousness who nonetheless 'retains the force to set it
steadily before itself in new comparisons'. But force is indeed, as Hegel
suggests, at the same time combined with – and leavened by – the 'touching and childlike' quality of imagery of one bucket dancing in the air while
the other drinks its own grief in the well. In sum, potency and childlike
charm come together in something like the self-authorising 'felicity' of
a still innocent imagination not altogether subdued by the great grief it
plays with.

And yet, for all of this flexible responsiveness to the detail of individual
character, the essential similarity Hegel perceives between unlike
Shakespearean *personae* enables him to cap his reflections on metaphor
in the plays with a generalisation. He suggests that Cleopatra's comparison
of the poisonous snake which is biting her breast to a sweetly sucking baby
can stand for 'the gentle and tranquilizing nature' of the distance from self
and grief which metaphor always opens up. Hegel's reflections on
Shakespeare's figurative language show in the richest detail that in his
drama 'it is the *dramatis personae* who appear as themselves the poets and
artists, since they make their inner life an object to themselves, an object

which they remain powerful enough to shape and form and thus to manifest to us the nobility of their disposition and the might of their mind.'[83] This is a negative power to be other than what they are which can help us contextualise and understand how Hamlet's curious, convoluted freedom can nevertheless be positively exemplary. It is also a power expressed, as it were in another dramatic plane, in the salient Shakespearean motif of disguise.

4   Falstaff Resurrexit

Hegel's more detailed and illuminating model of Shakespearean freedom does, I think, bring out something that is really there in the plays, and not just in his noble heroes. We should pay attention when Hegel writes that 'Shakespeare's vulgar characters, Stephano, Trinculo, Pistol, and the absolute hero of them all, Falstaff, remain sunk in their vulgarity, but at the same time they are shown to be men of intelligence with a genius fit for anything, enabling them to have an entirely free existence, and, in short, to be what great men are.' Falstaff is 'the absolute hero of them all' because of his vulgarity, because he demonstrates the sheer availability of Shakespearean heroism to us all.[84]

The fat knight sees through ideology while ignorant armies clash on Shrewsbury field:

Honour pricks me on. Yea, but how if honour prick me off when I come on? How then? Can honour set-to a leg? No. Or an arm. No. Or take away the grief of a wound? No. Honour hath no skill in surgery, then? No. What is honour? A word. What is in that word 'honour'? What is that 'honour'? Air. A trim reckoning! Who hath it? He that died o'Wednesday. Doth he feel it? No. Doth he hear it? No. 'Tis insensible then? Yea, to the dead. But will it not live with the living? No. Why? Detraction will not suffer it. Therefore I'll none of it. Honour is a mere scutcheon. And so ends my catechism. (5.1.127–39)

But of course this is only part of the story that 1 *Henry IV* dramatises. The opposite truth is embodied in Hotspur, for whom honour is more real than mere life. This too has the Hegelian aspect of fashioning oneself as something other than one actually is, and Falstaff proves in the end to be something more than just the fat nemesis of ideology. When he seemingly rises from the dead at Shrewsbury, it secures the point that, just as much as

Hotspur, Falstaff stands for a vitality – '*Give me life*' – that cannot be reduced to mortal conditions (5.3.58). The fact that even such excessive life is painfully contradicted by death is the tragic burden that, in this generically promiscuous history play, Hotspur is forced to bear; Falstaff gets to walk off with the comic palm of inextinguishable freedom.

Any character who stands up in his own death and emphatically proclaims, 'I am not what I am' demonstrates his invincible superabundance. The rather delicious and complicating irony is that in doing so, Falstaff expressly frustrates Hal's much more deliberate and politically serious effort to become a 'free artist of his own self' in *1 Henry IV*. This is the crucial passage:

PRINCE HENRY
What, old acquaintance, could not all this flesh
Keep in a little life? Poor Jack, farewell!
I could have spared a better man.
O, I should have a heavy miss of thee
If I were much in love with vanity.
Death hath not struck so fat a deer today,
Though many dearer, in this bloody fray.
Embowelled, will I see thee by and by.
Till then, in blood by noble Percy lie.　　*Exit.*
　　Falstaff riseth up.
FALSTAFF Embowelled! If thou embowel me today, I'll give
you leave to powder me and eat me too tomorrow.
'Sblood, 'twas time to counterfeit, or that hot termagant
Scot had paid me, scot and lot too. Counterfeit? I lie, I am
no counterfeit. To die is to be a counterfeit, for he is but
the counterfeit of a man who hath not the life of a man;
but to counterfeit dying, when a man thereby liveth, is to
be no counterfeit, but the true and perfect image of life
indeed. The better part of valour is discretion, in the
which better part I have saved my life. Zounds, I am afraid
of this gunpowder Percy, though he be dead. How if he
should counterfeit too and rise? By my faith, I am afraid
he would prove the better counterfeit. Therefore I'll make
him sure; yea, and I'll swear I killed him. Why may not

he rise as well as I? Nothing confutes me but eyes,
and nobody sees me. Therefore, sirrah (*stabbing him*), with a
new wound in your thigh, come you along with me.
                            He takes up Hotspur on his back (5.4.101–26)

When Hal vanquishes Hotspur and sees Falstaff, too, laid out on the field of battle, it's like a dream come true. At a stroke – and just in time for the play's end! – it fulfils his two dearest wishes: to supersede his great rival for warlike honour and his father's affection and to slough off his dissolute ways and companions now he's ready to assume his princely destiny and bearing. The apparently perfect correspondence of this dream to the very reality he finds himself facing explains why his speech above the fat knight's corpse is so shockingly detached. Hal is speaking in the strange conditions of a hyper-real vision of the consummation of his personality. He *is* partly looking at a dead man, of course – and at a dead man with whom he has been most intimate at that – but this bald fact of death is leavened and ameliorated by the fact that he is equally looking upon his own existential triumph.

Yet, for now at least, Falstaff has the last laugh. *Falstaff riseth up*! If Hal tentatively assumes a new and transformed identity, Falstaff trumps this identity by rising from his assumed death. He frustrates and even seems to mock the prince's transcendence. Having outrageously stabbed Hotspur's corpse, he steals Hal's triumph and his demonstration to Henry IV and the world that he is a better man than Hotspur is. Hal even declares himself a willing accessory to this: 'For my part, if a lie may do thee grace, / I'll gild it with the happiest terms I have' (5.5.152–3). So the play doesn't even end with the prince having overcome Hotspur but not the fat knight. It ends in the appearance that the prince has accomplished nothing at all. This extraordinary reversal, which we might compare to, say, the postponement of marriage in *Twelfth Night*, suggests that Hal is still a long way from making himself Henry V. And it further sharpens our sense of what it will cost to do so.

But this same moment is also a stunning, and intellectually stimulating, *coup de théâtre*, one which seems to convert Hal's promised and predictable metamorphosis into the respectable Prince of Wales into the much more interesting and outrageous as well as self-chosen and generally available kind of freedom such as Falstaff exemplifies. There is a kind of dramatic insouciance involved on Shakespeare's part because we know that all who are slain on stage in the end will rise, if only to take their bows; thus, Shakespeare is making a virtue of necessity here. It is a daring moment of theatre 'going naked', revealing and revelling in its own technology. When Falstaff says 'he is but the counterfeit of a man who hath not the life of a man', he is partly blowing the gaff on the condition of the actor. But Falstaff proceeds to pay a compliment to the acting life when he says, 'but to counterfeit dying, when a man thereby liveth, is to be no counterfeit, but *the true and perfect image of life indeed.*' This applauds the fact that actors make their living out of counterfeiting death (as well as life) as a sort of humane victory over mortality. That said, the revelatory overtones of 'the true and perfect image of life indeed' beg a more religious reading.

Staging resurrection in Shakespeare's culture inevitably recalls the resurrection of Christ. That Shakespeare chooses to recall that most central and admired episode of Christianity in such a peculiarly comic key is strange and striking. But what sails particularly close to the wind from a theological point of view is that the scene explicitly brings the Easter story into dangerous contact with the thought of '*counterfeit* dying'. To speak this phrase while dramatising resurrection is subversively to whisper that God didn't *really* die on Golgotha and therefore wasn't really sacrificed, because – let's face it – He was always going to resurrect Himself. This insinuation that God, like Falstaff, was just 'playing dead' on Calvary is shocking. Of course, it is only expressed by implication in the scene, but Falstaff's incidental language – 'Sblood' (God's blood), 'Zounds' (God's wounds), 'by my faith' – insistently brings his resurrection together with *the* resurrection. And when Falstaff's counterfeit resurrection phases into the counterfeit glory of his subsequent claim to be Hotspur's conqueror, the threat to Christian piety becomes worse; the extra wound he dishes out to the dead Hotspur, comparable to the wound made in Christ's side, is especially hard to stomach. But of course Falstaff is at this point, as so often, scandalously funny, which is presumably what irresistibly wins back the prince's affection.

And this element of joyousness, I think, offers a more positive way to read Falstaff's rising than as simply a bitter satire on Christian faith. If counterfeiting emerges here as 'the true and perfect image of life indeed', then perhaps it doesn't really matter if Christ was counterfeiting! Art, acting and religion come together in this strange Shakespearean scene. For art such as Shakespeare's clearly *is* counterfeit life. *Why may not he rise as well as I?* Indeed, he might well, because his death too is counterfeit. In fact, *Hotspur* is counterfeit; and so is Hal. As Jennifer Ann Bates writes, 'Only the *counterfeiting* man is real.'[85] It's all counterfeit!

It is life in excess of life; it is life energetically remade, and Falstaff is allowed to participate in his own counterfeiting. And such excessiveness, this scene of comic resurrection suggests, is what Christianity is and calls for. Death is a real and terrible truth; Hotspur's in fact very obdurate mortality expresses this. But the essence of both art and religion is the life that exceeds (merely mortal) life. Death is all around him, but Falstaff's too big to die; like Barnardine in *Measure for Measure*, he refuses! And even when he *does* die, in *Henry V*, he lives on, returning in *Merry Wives* and beyond, in Verdi's *Falstaff*, and in the cultural imagination more broadly.

Falstaff was the first example of Shakespearean freedom in this book. He was a touchstone for Garrick's first civic Shakespeare festival. Now we have seen that he is a paragon of Shakespearean freedom for Hegel as well. Since that makes an 'absolute hero' of one of 'Shakespeare's vulgar characters', it speaks to the sort of political emancipation for which Cooper and Kossuth campaigned in Shakespeare's name. You just can't put Falstaff down. 'I saw him dead, / Breathless and bleeding on the ground,' says Hal, rubbing his eyes. And then to the spectre of Falstaff he mutters, 'Art thou alive? / Or is it fantasy that plays upon our eyesight?' (5.4.130–2). But it is not fantasy; it's no spectre – it's Falstaff, irreducible to his own death! His very fatness symbolises that free condition of Shakespearean superabundance which Hegel calls 'the principle of subjectivity'.[86] Bradley rejoices in Falstaff as 'the enemy of … everything respectable and moral' and an image of 'freedom'.[87] We have seen time and again in this book that freedom can lead to terrible wickedness and crime, that this adverse potential cannot be extirpated from it; especially when he violates Hotspur's corpse, Falstaff enacts some of that badness. Shakespeare owns up to the dirty element in freedom. At the same time he insists on the irreducible creativity and liveliness it expresses. Falstaff's resurrection on Shrewsbury field stands for the ambivalent and yet irresistible promise of Shakespearean freedom. It also stands for the almost religious force that freedom acquires within the context of secular modernity.

7

Freetown Philosopher

The earliest writing of Hegel's we have is a free adaptation of Act Four, scene one from *Julius Caesar*, which the philosopher wrote as a fifteen-year-old schoolboy.[1] Shakespeare's original is a grim, gangster-like little scene, in which Antony, Octavius and Lepidus are making a hit list of victims in the way of their efforts to take the Roman Empire. At first it seems surprising that this – of all the scenes in Shakespeare! – should have interested an earnest young philosopher in the hey-day of German Romanticism. But in reworking the dialogue, Hegel brings out the contrast between the unedifying egotism of Shakespeare's lines and the idea of freedom that inheres in *Julius Caesar* as a whole. From the first, Hegel was interested in the 'knot intrinsicate' of human freedom (*Antony and Cleopatra*, 5.2.295).[2] And if the mature philosopher into whom he develops will describe Shakespeare's characters as 'free artists of their own selves', this glimpse into his earliest, most primal interests establishes that Hegel was always concerned with the question of what such splendid self-manifestation might mean or portend *politically*. Drawing on both Shakespeare and the later Hegel, this chapter attempts to answer that question.[3]

Hegel marvelled at – indeed, he luxuriated in – the self-creating freedom he found in Shakespeare, but he also felt it wasn't enough. As Jennifer Ann Bates writes in *Hegel and Shakespeare on Moral Imagination*, 'the philosopher is concerned with more than individual freedom.' Bates goes on to explain, 'the universal good is understood in Hegel in the way that existentialists like Sartre and De Beauvoir would later view it, i.e., as the commitment to freedom that is the commitment to the freedom of others.'[4] The great world-historical attempt at political freedom made in Hegel's own lifetime of course was the French Revolution, and till the end of his life the philosopher drank a toast on the anniversary of the storming of the Bastille.[5] Terry Pinkard, his biographer, relays the anecdote that Hegel, along with his soon-to-be-famous friends Hölderlin and Schelling, 'erected a "freedom tree" – a kind of revolutionary Maypole – on the fourteenth of July, 1793 (a year into the Terror, during which the guillotines were working full time) on a field near the town of Tübingen and danced the revolutionary French dance, the Carmognole, around it, while singing the words to the *Marseillaise* (which Schelling had translated into German)'.[6] This alluring story, Pinkard admits, is 'almost certainly false'; but 'its believability for those who later told it lay in its adequately capturing the spirit that was undoubtedly animating the three friends'.[7] There is a connection to the English history of Shakespearean freedom, for Pinkard further observes that Hölderlin, Schelling and Hegel were all avid readers of the enthusiastically pro–French Revolution German journal *Minerva*, edited by Johann Wilhelm von Archenholz: it was also Archenholz, you may recall, who saw Garrick's Drury Lane dramatisation of his freedom-inflected Shakespeare Jubilee no less than twenty-eight times, and whose views of English culture were crucial to establishing the German idea of England. As Pinkard shows, Hegel's 'sympathy for the French Revolution' came together with his admiration for what he saw as the liberal 'English life of freedom'.[8] He recoiled from the 'freedom frenzy' of the Terror, which he believed tore down the very structures that made freedom possible.[9] Many commentators have followed Karl Popper who, in *The Open Society* (Volume II), denounced Hegel as a craven apologist for the Prussian state; but in fact, Hegel conceives of the state as 'the highest expression of the ethical substance of a people, the unfolding of a transcendent and rational order, the "actualization of freedom"'.[10] He wanted to protect and develop the revolutionary impulse for freedom by means of a secure political order.

* * *

So, how does Shakespeare fit into this? Well, for Hegel, Shakespearean personal freedom is at once a step towards that new and better political order and an obstacle in the way of achieving it. On the one hand, its sheer seductive flamboyance exemplifies the existential condition of richly realised personal freedom which politics should aim at. On the other, it entails political chaos. I mean, imagine if we brought *all* of Shakespeare's free

artists of themselves out of their individual plays and put them together at
some sort of free artists of themselves convention, starting, say, with
Antony, Cleopatra, Falstaff, Rosalind, Macbeth; Hegel sees it'd be like
herding cats. The German philosopher holds art to a very high standard
indeed, suggesting it should be considered not as any kind of 'agreeable or
useful child's play' but rather as 'an unfolding of the truth which is not
exhausted in natural history but revealed in world-history' and at the same
time 'the presence and reconciliation of the Absolute in what is apparent
and visible'.[11] As postmodern readers, we have a terminological problem
here in that the Absolute sounds like some obdurate bedrock of being and
has uncomfortably totalitarian connotations, but for Hegel the Absolute is
pure freedom and therefore an open-ended, dynamic process. Hegel wants
art to reveal the ideal social set-up for promoting such freedom, and I will
argue in this chapter that Shakespeare's plays actually do reveal something
like this. That is the source of their political importance, and their power to
motivate advocates of freedom from Garrick to Cooper, from Kossuth to
Mandela.

But – though you wouldn't know it from Bloom's bardolatrous
response, or indeed any other Shakespeare criticism – Hegel sees
Shakespeare as immature, not quite 'child's play' but certainly
a cultural dead end. Although in its own terms, the sort of personal
freedom which Shakespeare specialises in may be infinite, inasmuch as
it fails to open up to everything else, it is at the same time severely
constrained.

Hegel wasn't the first thinker in the German tradition to suggest that
Shakespeare's work is unpromisingly subjective. In the comparative study
of Greek poetry he wrote in 1795–7, Friedrich Schlegel unfavourably
compared modern art as exemplified by Shakespeare's *Hamlet* with classical objectivity. Greek art, according to Schlegel, attains the wide view of *das
Objective*, from which *Hamlet* falls off into *das Interessante*: excessive,
unharmonious singularity. This fall at best precipitates a crisis in modern
culture, revealing our need for a new objectivity and disinterestedness.[12]
For Schlegel, Shakespearean personality is grotesque and wayward,
whereas for Hegel, as we have seen, it is much more impressive; but
Hegel concurs with Schlegel in seeing Shakespeare's achievement as tend-
ing towards 'the right of personality', 'a purely subjective end', 'the principle of subjectivity'. This distortion of *das Objective*, he suggests, has to be

corrected by our own subsequent recognition that 'the individual is only the one life.'[13]

The German identification of this degenerate solipsism in Shakespearean character resonates with Søren Kierkegaard's definition of the demonic as the 'shut up', and it strikes lights with Hamlet, whom Kierkegaard, Schlegel and Hegel all saw in such restrictively subjective terms.[14] Hamlet says that even if he were bounded in a nutshell, he could count himself a king of infinite space (2.2.248–50); but Hegel encourages us to turn this round. Since the nutshell is Hamlet's own individuality – we might say his own skull – we can imagine him saying something like, 'Though I count myself a king of infinite space, I remain imprisoned in a nutshell. Though I am king of an infinite kingdom, of fantasy, desire, possibility, still I remain in prison, cut off from other life by this horrible wall of bone!'[15] On the one hand, Shakespeare wallows in Hamlet's unbounded subjectivity. On the other, he insists you've got to get out – beyond nutshell skulduggery – into the wider world.

Hamlet seems to admit this when he answers Rosencrantz and Guildenstern's stupidly sententious response to his nutshell shtick. They pompously identify his bad dreams as ambitious reveries which, they go on to say, wise men know are just insubstantial shadows. 'Then are our beggars bodies,' retorts Hamlet, 'and our monarchs and out-stretched heroes the beggars' shadows' (2.2.256–8). Such impossibly fast-moving wit is of course completely typical of the Prince of Denmark, and it is not surprising that R and G are utterly defeated by it. But once you've got your head round what Hamlet is saying here, it is possible to see that it both anticipates Hegel and brilliantly renews his dull friends' purely conventional wisdom. Hamlet helps us see that aspiring men stretch beyond themselves in ambitious fantasy, and that such fantasy is not at all limited to coveting the crown, as Hamlet's friends wrongly imply he does. But if ambition stretches men into the shadows beyond mere bodily life, other, irresistibly real and suffering bodies nevertheless remain behind, beseeching them to return to a world they can't in any case transcend – for 'outstretched heroes' can't completely disjoin themselves from the reality we share in common. Hamlet's witty rejoin-der therefore effectively admits that he has – that we all have – got to return from a limitless fantasy life to the real historical world of suffer-ing beggars.

And what Hamlet admits here is what Hegel believed about Shakespeare in general. Hegel admits that personal freedom is more realised and defined in the English dramatist than ever before, but he also observes that, however luxuriously extensive such purely personal freedom may feel, it is still bounded by human individuality itself; it is still a dead end.[16]

Or, rather, it would be a dead end, except that Hegel himself takes over where, according to him, Shakespeare leaves off, carrying the Shakespearean 'principle of subjectivity' like a torch into what we might think of as more objective life, the larger life of the world, only to discover that subjectivity isn't so much expunged as it is actually consummated there.

Hegel is Freetown's philosopher; he is Freetown's *town planner*. He wants to *think* Freetown into being, and the philosophical blueprint he offers for this makes the enhanced freedom he found in Shakespeare the basis of nothing less than a new politics. Hegel is able to move from individual freedom to the establishment of Freetown as a real social system because social ethics are hard wired into his ontology. We have seen, in the previous chapter, that he conceives of the self as radically other to itself, not to be identified by its mere givenness – as, for instance, Western, white, middle-class, male; such predicates, according to Hegel, are accidents, non-essential. Instead, Hegel recognises personality in its radical freedom to be otherwise, a way of being beyond being which he finds superbly pioneered by Shakespeare's self-creating characters. According to Hegel, Shakespearean individuality is fulfilled in otherness: *I am not what I am* (*Othello*, 1.1.66). But Hegel sees himself as stepping beyond Shakespeare in recognising that self seeks itself in otherness. Or, as he puts it in the *Phenomenology*: '*Self-consciousness achieves its satisfaction only in another self-consciousness.*'[17] Hegel perceives a connection between the personal freedom to be other (than you are: white, middle-class or whatever) and the otherness of other people. And this is a point that tends to be supported by two of the most irreducible truths of our lives: one, we require others for our own flourishing; and, two, we somehow ultimately recognise ourselves *in others*, in relationship. We will naturally think of love here; but Hegel, rather beautifully, favours a phenomenon that is more basic to a range of human interactions: mutual recognition. Mutual recognition, Hegel suggests, enables reciprocal flourishing, and he wants it to happen between all people all the time; he also wants cultural institutions and practices to facilitate, protect, participate in and maximise it, to the effect that it doesn't just enhance our ethical and political life so much as it becomes the very basis of that life.

In the introduction to his sweeping *Philosophy of History*, Hegel suggests that world history is nothing but the progress of the consciousness of freedom. Shakespeare plays an important part in this, but Hegel starts before Shakespeare, at the beginning of recorded time, and he wants to go well beyond Shakespeare at the other end. He does not find much self-conscious freedom in the earliest forms of human civilisation, which he calls 'The Oriental World': ancient China, India and Persia. These cultures, he suggests, are defined by rigid, patriarchal order and unquestioned tradition. That said, he does detect a first flickering of freedom in the worship of transcendent light in Persian Zoroastrianism; this, for him, is the beginning of 'true history'. But it is the Greeks' decisive victory over the Persians in the epic battle of Salamis that marks the emergence of 'free individuality' from Oriental despotism. And yet, Greek freedom is in turn limited by two factors. The first is slavery: only *some* Greeks are free. And the second is the fact that, according to Hegel, the Greeks as it were *automatically* identified their own interests with the interests of the state.[18] They didn't yet have the idea of perfectly individual and therefore always potentially dissident conscience. To this point in world history, freedom has been on the rise, but with the advent of the Roman Empire, according to Hegel, it slips back again. The joyous possibilities of the free spirit that come through in Greece are crushed by the power and bureaucracy of Rome. Roman thinkers have no choice but to retreat into the unworldliness of such creeds as Stoicism, Epicureanism and Scepticism. But what alters this regressive situation is the advent of Christianity. In Christianity, 'each [individual] has to accomplish the work of reconciliation on his own self': in Christianity, each soul is infinitely valuable, infinitely self-responsible.[19] And this advent of infinite subjectivity makes freedom fully possible for the first time.[20] It is the great watershed moment, but, according to Hegel, it admits of one energetic further refinement which proves crucial to the development of modernity. Luther's 'Reformation breakthrough' sweeps away everything – all the clutter and corruption of the church – that stands between the individual and the Absolute. 'With this,' Hegel resonantly concludes, 'is unfurled the new, the last standard around which the peoples rally – the banner of *free spirit* . . . This is the banner under which we serve, and which we bear'. According to him, 'the essential content of the Reformation' is 'man is destined through himself to be free.' And 'time since has had, and has now, no other work to do than the imbuing of the world with this principle.'[21]

This is exactly the point at which Shakespeare slots in. The story Hegel tells in the *Philosophy of History* is the German religious version; what Hegel says about Shakespeare in the *Aesthetics* (as discussed in the previous chapter) enables us to see that Shakespeare represents the supreme secular version of the same thing. Margreta de Grazia has acknowledged this, recording that, for Hegel, 'Hamlet's "inwardness" is the dramatic counterpart to the historical Luther's "introversion of the soul upon itself."' De Grazia is understandably dismissive of Shakespearean freedom compared to Luther's which, as she observes, 'was "actualized" through nothing less than the historical movement of the Reformation'.[22] But my argument in this book is that in the contribution it makes to an evolving secular modernity, Shakespearean freedom might in fact be considered equally historically important, and more progressive.

To put Hegel's remarks on Shakespeare in the context of his wider philosophical project is to see that, rather wonderfully, what he wants to achieve is infinite Shakespearean subjectivity *for all*; but to bring this to pass, he needs to think his way beyond not just Shakespeare but the whole ethos of individualism in modernity which, he contends, Shakespeare's plays exemplify. He accomplishes this partly by thinking through (in both senses) the threat of evil that freedom entails. Peter Singer notes that just after announcing that the history of the world is the progress towards freedom, Hegel adds that 'freedom' is 'an indefinite, and incalculably ambiguous term . . . liable to an infinity of misunderstandings, confusions and errors'.[23] And this matters because freedom can be really dangerous. We saw in the previous chapter that Bradley's Hegel-inspired criticism registered the moral ambivalence and challenge of Shakespearean freedom, and Hegel's wider philosophy encourages us to see that the Shakespearean achievement of 'absolute subjective personality' moving 'free in itself and in the spiritual world' could have dire real-world effects.[24] When, in 1789, the news of the fall of the Bastille electrified Europe, the eighteen-year-old Hegel was not alone in proclaiming a 'glorious dawn'. 'All thinking beings,' he insisted, 'shared in the jubilation of this epoch.'[25] But also like other intellectuals of the day, Hegel recoiled

from the Terror which succeeded the Revolution. And it radically transformed his concept of the nature of freedom. 'Universal freedom,' he wrote
in *The Phenomenology*, 'can produce neither a positive work nor a deed;
there is left for it only *negative* action; it is merely the *fury* of destruction';
I noted this in relation to the death-longing of Romeo and Juliet. Hegel
observes a page later, 'The sole work and deed of universal freedom is
therefore *death*.'[26] The challenge he faced was how to divert the tremendous energy of freedom to a more creative fruition.

Napoleon personified the problem. Hegel was living in Jena when
Bonaparte crushed Prussia there in 1806. You might expect the German
philosopher to have sympathised with the German state but instead – and,
again, he wasn't alone among European intellectuals in this – he fell utterly
for Bonaparte, writing the day after Jena was occupied: 'The Emperor –
this world soul – I saw riding through the city to review his troops; it is
indeed a wonderful feeling to see such an individual who, here concentrated to a single point, sitting on a horse, reaches out over the world and
dominates it.'[27] Napoleon seemed to Hegel an actual manifestation of the
sort of 'absolute subjective personality' moving 'free in itself and in the
spiritual world' which he also found in Shakespeare. For Hegel and many
others in the nineteenth century, Bonaparte was a living hero, and 'when in
1814 Napoleon was defeated, Hegel referred to this as a tragic thing, the
spectacle of an immense genius destroyed by mediocrity.'[28] Thus, in spite
of all the destruction he caused, Hegel doesn't just reject the Shakespearean
energy he found embodied in Napoleon. He wants to bring such immense
geniuses and their energies *home*, so that they can work productively for
and with rather than against society. His aim is to marry personal freedom
at its most realised and powerful with a more comprehensive and shareable
politics of freedom.

But how to accomplish this? Well, the first major step is the philosopher's development of his notion of *Sittlichkeit*. This is to be understood,
in the words of one of his most lucid contemporary commentators as
'the ethos of the most strongly coherent sort of moral communities;
those that are held together, not by material self-interest or coercion, but
by a deep, genuine respect for particular moral authority figures, and an
intensely felt, conservative rootedness in a particular historic tradition'.[29]
Sittlichkeit is, you would think, pretty much opposite to freedom. In the
face of Terror, freedom is 'thrown back to its starting-point, to the

ethical and real world of culture'; 'individuals who have felt the fear of death' will then 'again submit to negations and distinctions, arrang[ing] themselves in the various spheres, and return[ing] to an apportioned and limited task, but thereby to their substantial reality.' And yet, this substantial reality has irrevocably changed. Exposed to the awful challenge of revolutionary freedom, the order of the world has been 'refreshed and rejuvenated'.[30] It has been refreshed and rejuvenated because it has been denaturalised, in the sense of being exposed as provisional and unnecessary, not just the way that things are. It has been opened up to the whole point and aim of human history as the progress towards the most consciously cultivated freedom.[31] And if Hegel wants to convert powerfully realised, Shakespearean personalities to this aim, at the same time he wants them to see this not so much as a self-disposing sacrifice but, instead, as their greatest possible fulfilment. Ultimately Hegel explicitly rejects the common-sense understanding of freedom as 'being able to do what one wants'.[32] Hegel wants us to enlarge ourselves till we are able to identify our egos with a new, free society. He foresees a happy resolution between the really free choices of individuals and the needs of society in general according to a principle that can be formulated as follows: *the free will of each is the free will of all.*[33]

It is a powerful vision: one in which the personal freedom that Hegel finds revealed in Shakespeare supplies the energy for a transforming re-engagement with the world. But it is time to admit that while Hegel's portrait of Shakespeare as an out-and-out individualist (not to mention its continued critical currency in Bloom, the later Greenblatt and others) no doubt points to something important in the plays, it can hardly be said to speak their whole truth – as I have argued in previous chapters. Hegel presents Shakespeare as trading in the sort of atomised freedom which stands in the way of bringing Freetown into being. In fact, the plays prefigure and more concretely model just the sort of irreducible and endless creative contention that constitutes Hegel's vision of freedom. Drama, after all, is more inter-subjective than it's subjective. And if we have seen that Hegel says, '*Self-consciousness achieves its satisfaction only in another self-consciousness,*' drama brings this to life on stage. Authorship is dispersed in characterisation; character is made and changed in interaction; and because drama has an audience, within a further inter-subjective milieu that is also physically present in the theatre.

There are precedents for seeing such political possibilities in German aesthetics more broadly. The Germans conceptualised the symphony, for instance, as philosophy by other means: 'no longer a vehicle of entertainment, but a vehicle of truth'.[34] And this was a truth that had political resonance given the harmony into which symphonic form works its heterogeneous elements. That said, with its fully realised characters and plots, drama is clearly much better adapted to the concrete reality of our erotic and political lives than the symphony. For all his strictures on Shakespearean subjectivity, elsewhere Schlegel found in Shakespearean drama just the kind of 'indirect mythology' he believed was needed in the modern age. He wrote of the 'artfully ordered confusion', 'charming symmetry of contradictions', 'wonderfully perennial alternation of enthusiasm and irony' that derive from a dramatic plurality of characters and viewpoints, tracing this back to its source in 'the motley throng of the ancient gods'.[35] Nietzsche argued that tragedy breaks 'the spell of individuation'.[36] And as G. K. Hunter observes, Shakespeare in German criticism is substantially the poet of the *Volksgeist*: which is why Herder, writing in 1777, is able to claim that *all* his plays are history plays; and how Ulrici writing in 1847 could claim that 'historical drama, dealing with the life of nations, acquires a greater and more significant beauty than comedy or tragedy.' Hunter further notes that, via Georg Brandes, 'these ideas became important in the work of the most notable modern writer of history plays – August Strindberg – who admired, and sought to reproduce, precisely this "polyphonic" effect of court and tavern, the "realism" of the people in their greatness and triviality.'[37] Hugo von Hofmannsthal saw drama as a much needed 'ceremony of the whole' in an increasingly riven world without inclusive communal rituals.[38] And Hans Georg Gadamer, who died only in 2002, developed a related case for art as 'a space in which both the world, and our own place in the world, is brought to light as a single but inexhaustibly rich totality', one where we can 'dwell' out of ordinary time and open 'to the true possibility of community'; but this, too, is clearly most plausibly true of plays.[39] In *Free Will*, Richard Wilson quotes Gadamer's assertion that it was Shakespeare who saved him from German jingoism:

I am perfectly willing to admit that my generation grew up under authoritarian conditions; but in my case it was very clear what I had to do. I really wanted to go to the theatre and read Shakespeare ... The liberation came in 1918, and the fact that I was reading Shakespeare was already a sign of new things. I am trying to tell you how in spite of everything I escaped the prevailing militarism.[40]

In a pregnant passage of *Radical Tragedy*, Jonathan Dollimore suggests that after Bradley the English critical tradition emphasised those elements in Hegel's legacy – character rather than history, reconciliation rather than dialectical process – which wrenched an idealist inheritance from this more social and materialist context.[41]

But the German tradition of responding to the inherent sociality of Shakespearean drama suggests strongly that it is the art form best adapted to Hegel's broader vision of freedom. It can even be said to make manifest the sort of subjective enlargement I've suggested Hegel is calling for, where the individual identifies not so much with his or her own subjectivity as with *subjectivity as such*. This is a hard idea to grasp but drama makes grasping it possible, because subjectivity as such is palpably present in the theatre in the form of *the overarching subjectivity of a whole play*: Hamlet's subjectivity is part of, but also something different from, the subjectivity of *Hamlet*, to which he nonetheless sacrifices himself in the end. We'll come back to this.

Meanwhile, with due respect to Hegel, Shakespeare is perhaps not best seen as a wall of merely individual subjectivity into which modernity crashes; instead, the dramatist who named and evoked Freetown in *Romeo and Juliet* is perfectly qualified to partner Freetown's philosopher as Freetown's own laureate, assaying its civic possibilities by means of his dramatic experiments. The plays in fact anticipate quite precisely the inter-subjective possibilities of modernity which Hegel defines in the *Phenomenology*, as can be seen if we take them one by one, moving from least to most socially constructive phenomena, starting with total chaos.

Hegel writes of a consciousness 'which sets up the law of *its* heart' and 'therefore meets with resistance from others, because it contradicts the equally individual laws of their hearts', leading to a 'universal state of war'.[42] This destructive 'freedom frenzy' is just the sort of thing Hegel feared that Shakespeare's 'purely subjective ends' pointed to, and it is true that at any moment the inter-subjective artifice of a play might dissolve into atomised disorder. Indeed, dramatic interest and tension at least partly depend on this. *King Lear* speaks the fear that humanity will prey upon itself like monsters of the deep (*King Lear*, Conflated Text, 4.2.50–1). In *Troilus and Cressida*, something like that actually comes to pass. Graham Bradshaw writes, 'Hector is then butchered, put down with no more chivalry or honour than would be sensible to show a rabid dog – *and why not?*'[43] This shocking question points to the absolute collapse of the play's values. In *Troilus*, as well as in intimations that 'chaos is come again' from elsewhere in the canon (*Othello*, 3.3.93), Shakespeare presents as concrete actuality what Hegel only describes. At another point in the *Aesthetics*, Hegel finds that, in Shakespeare's tragedies especially, 'inner motives of passion, and characters who want their own way and have regard to nothing else, lead to war and collisions.'[44] This is the world of the 'universal wolf' (*Troilus and Cressida*, 1.3.121): an image which Hugh Grady suggests offers a brilliantly prescient critique of what the Frankfurt School theorists would later designate 'instrumental reason' – the process of alienation deeply inherent in capitalism whereby the self turns itself into a means to an end (for profit, financial security etc.), thereby breaking with the immanent complexity of its subjective experience in the social world.[45]

But the 'universal wolf' hardly represents the sum of social possibilities in Shakespeare. And perhaps the most famous thing in the *Phenomenology* is the next step away from the chaos of each against all: the philosophically significant drama which Hegel discerns in the relations between master and slave. Common sense would dictate that a master secures his substantial and superior identity in lordship over his slave. But given Hegel's negative conception of personality (*I am not what I am*), where true selfhood is attained in self-transcendence, the reverse is in fact true: paradoxically, it is the slave who comes closer to the real, ecstatic nature of freedom. It is he, not the master, who realises himself in relation to another. By contrast, the master is spiritually lost, marooned in inactivity – because the slave does everything for him – and also marooned in his own purely self-relating and therefore, according to Hegel, ultimately illusory personality. The master never gets to the deep subjective truth that is the Hegelian *I am not what I am*; instead, he is lost in desperately trying to shore up a more positive identity. The master is a weak and doomed tyrant in denial. He uses the slave to prop up his own sense of self and therefore doesn't recognise him as anything other than a facet of his own will, a sort of inferior, outsourced limb. As Hegel says, 'servitude has the lord for its essential reality', whereas nothing at all for the master is really real.[46] The master cannot discover himself in otherness, because he recognises nothing other than himself. He cannot realise himself in 'another self-consciousness' because he does not recognise the free consciousness of the slave.

But the slave's dread of the lord is on the way to real enlightenment. It is a sort of negative epiphany of the reality of the Other, but one which also brings him close to the truth of his own alienated being. According to Hegel, the slave's dread of the lord is most deeply a dread of 'the simple, essential nature of self-consciousness, absolute negativity, *pure being-for-self*'.[47] He contemplates the lord with a shiver of terror, perhaps because his master beats him, but also because for the slave the master models as a real external reality his own consciousness's recognition of its strange alienation from itself: *I am not what I am*. Moreover, the slave 'in his service ... rids himself of his attachment to natural existence in every single detail': his alienated labour instead of working against real identity rather tends to confirm it because identity is ultimately alienated from itself. Now admittedly if you were living in irons or under the lash such philosophical speculations might be more or less comforting, but they nevertheless tell us something provocatively brilliant about Hegelian freedom and how paradoxically it might be most fully realised within the apparent alienation of social life.[48] Hegel begins here, I feel, to shock us into the recognition that individual freedom might be not so much opposite to as actually consummated in subjection. And this, too, resonates with Shakespeare. Richard II, for instance, really unfurls as himself in his usurpation by and subjection to Bolingbroke, who for his part progressively loses himself in becoming king. We have heard Juliet imploring Night to teach her 'how to lose a winning match' (3.2.12).[49] And if, for much of his play, Hamlet cavils with subjection, he finally, almost mystically discovers himself within it. At first, he can't identify with his ordained role of revenger; but by the end of the play he is mysteriously fulfilled in the otherness of a 'divinity that shapes our ends', a 'providence' that has to remain fundamentally obscure to him, and even opposite to his own purposes, or it wouldn't be truly other (5.2.10 and 158).

Still, mercifully, slavery isn't Hegel's highest evocation of the life of freedom. As I have indicated already, mutual recognition is. Hegel extols the ethical and existential merits of that ordinary magic through which the self finds itself in the other who reciprocally finds itself in the self. This readily transcends the alienation of master-slave relations and is most vividly and richly exemplified by Shakespearean lovers such as Romeo and Juliet. But it is not a purely private achievement. It instantiates a general truth, and one with radical political potential. As Hegel puts it, 'I am only truly free when the other is also free and is recognized by me as free.'[50] If self is consummated in otherness, then it must relate to what is other as truly and independently so. One plus one may make two, but it also makes infinitely more than two, because it discovers – in experience, on the pulses – the proper and fertile creative relationship of self to otherness as such. As Hegel puts it, 'For the surrender of its own will is only from one aspect negative; in principle, however, or in itself, it is at the same time positive, viz. the positing of will as the will of an "other", and specifically of will, not as a particular, but as a universal will.'[51] Later in the *Phenomenology* he allows himself to frame this in more positively religious terms:

The reconciling *Yea*, in which the two 'I's let go their antithetical *existence*, is the *existence* of the 'I' which has expanded into a duality, and therein remains identical with itself, and in its complete externalization and opposite, possesses the certainty of itself: it is God manifested in the midst of those who know themselves in the form of pure knowledge.[52]

In recent years, there has been considerable, sometimes heated speculation about whether Shakespeare was a Protestant or Catholic; but it is possible that what Hegel says here brings us closer to Shakespeare's God than any such confessional speculation can take us, for the God that Hegel evokes here is the God of drama. In his *Dialogue on Poetry*, Schlegel maintains that 'the highest and only life' is 'the life of man among men'.[53] But what Hegel teaches is that this is the proper, political locus for all the poetry and motivational power of religion. It is an insight which appears again in Martin Buber's essentially dramatic model of ethics and spirituality: *I and Thou*.[54]

In what Hegel writes, God is brought into being – *manufactured* even – in the specifically dramatic process of erotic or ethical human exchange. He (Hegel says 'it') is the third person, neither self nor other, in whom both of those pre-existing persons are consummated. Nothing supernatural is involved. The face of God can be glimpsed in, say, the reciprocal flourishing of *Romeo and Juliet* and, equally, in the drama of suffering and compassion that is presented by *King Lear*. This is a sort of spirituality arising out of human life and not to be opposed to it. Indeed, one great attraction and achievement of Hegel's thought is its recognition that the ordinary world – the inter-subjective world of strife and contention, conversation and creativity – already is metaphysical. *This* world is the spirit world. Hegel's metaphysics give us the something more which inheres in ordinary experience. What he calls 'absolute substance' is just 'the unity of the different independent consciousnesses which, in their opposition, enjoy perfect freedom and independence'.[55] Hegel combines personal and social freedom by recognising and teaching that each of our lives is at the same time only part of a larger life or mind. This is a far cry from feel-good mysticism, because the Hegelian one life or mind is the opposite of a transcendent God beyond the complexities of real-life existence. Instead, it is the myriad-minded world. And here's the rub: it is harder to think of a better working model of this than a Shakespearean play. For by dint of its very structure, the ethos of such a play is always there, waiting to be discovered by each and potentially all the protagonists as the most fundamental truth of their own individual and shared 'lives': the truth, as Hegel describes it, of '"I" that is "We" and "We": that is "I"'.[56] Or, as the 1980s charity pop song has it: *We Are the World*. As a corollary, the world is what we make it. It could be – it always could be – otherwise.

That crucial creative recognition can only be realised from within the conventional cultural life which Hegel calls *Sittlichkeit*. In a very real sense, there is nothing beyond *Sittlichkeit*. Paul Kottman is right to say that Hegel like Shakespeare is 'concerned with drama', 'with the stakes of actions . . . how individual words and deeds cohere and form a shared practical world'. Regarding the 'subjective inner life of Shakespeare's characters', he suggests that 'what must strike us is how their words and deeds imply and inflect a network of inheritable practices (kinship ties, civic relations, economic bonds, military duties).'[57] This, again, is why Bloom is wrong to strike a Hegelian wedge between Shakespearean freedom and ideology. But *Sittlichkeit* isn't quite ideology, and it is not simply opposed to freedom in the way that ideology typically is by contemporary critics. Indeed, Hegel recognises that, as a particular configuration of human culture and possibility, *Sittlichkeit* itself is a work of freedom, and it is one which enables freedom: it is the whole culture of royal masculinity in medieval Denmark, for instance, which enables Hamlet to be Hamlet, Prince of Denmark. And yet, these cultural conditions of his being at the same time limit Hamlet's freedom to be the more singular and inimitable Hamlet he also obscurely yet crucially is, and could be. In a similar way, any historical or cultural configuration of *Sittlichkeit* will simultaneously enable and impede freedom. Moreover, the shared, practical world of *Sittlichkeit* is at once the enabling condition of all ethical and political life, and that which has permanently to be opened up to that more ideal condition where the free will of each is the free will of all. Shakespeare's characters struggle to realise their freedom in various *sittlich* forms: Athenian, Roman, Christian, capitalist, medieval, and (to Shakespeare) contemporary and so on. None of them takes place in the conditions of our own contemporary *Sittlichkeit*, though each reflects upon and contributes to our cultural inheritance. Taken together, they give us Hegelian spirituality not just in action but in the image of something like our own fraught, fretful and thrilling lives as those lives are shaped by and changed in history. By so lavishly endowing the myriad minds he creates with separate, autonomous energy, Shakespeare opens up (1) the individual's struggle with other individuals to realise his or her freedom, (2) the individual's struggle to realise his or her freedom through and against *Sittlichkeit*, and (3) the individual and collective struggle to realise *political* freedom through and against *Sittlichkeit*.

Above all, I suggest, Shakespeare can help us understand Hegel's portrayal of freedom as a positive and absolute commitment to the endless contradictions and compromises of life and responsibility. Which means Hegel was wrong! Far from being 'mere child's play', Shakespeare's plays *are* Hegelian *Geist* or Spirit *avant la lettre*, subject to all the stresses and travails to which such Spirit is always subject in the ordinary world, labouring and yearning through the given traditions and institutions of historical life towards its consummation as perfect, universal freedom where the free will of each is the free will of all. According to the philosopher, recognising this could lead us out of 'the colourful show of the sensuous here-and-now': by which Hegel means mere experience. It could lead us beyond 'the nightlike void of the supersensible beyond': by which he means metaphysical religion. What it could lead us *into* is

what Hegel very beautifully calls 'the spiritual daylight of the present', the
spiritual daylight of a new day in Freetown.[58]

But that new day in Freetown, it's worth emphasising, shouldn't be
thought of in utopian terms of simple, untroubled peace. We mustn't
imagine a kind of Diet Coke* advert – full of impossibly shiny happy
young people appallingly contented with their own perfect bodies, lives
and world. We have seen that Hegel criticises Shakespeare's intense
subjectivity, but his philosophy recognises just such restlessly rebellious
freedom as necessary for an energetic social transformation. Intensely
subjective subjects such as Shakespeare fashioned and prepared the way
for might lead to the Terror, but they are at the same time best
equipped to (1) recognise the subjectivity of society itself and (2)
bring their own subjective energy to the service of society's transforming self-realisation. And it is not even completely wishful thinking to
suppose that they actually will do so, if only it can be demonstrated to
them that their own subjectivity is actually vested in society's larger
life. Meanwhile, their revolt in the cause of individual freedom tests,
tempers and promotes the wider social commitment to liberty.
Maverick, dissident and subversive elements are best for social renovation. 'Spirit' sinks, in Hegel's words, 'into mere edification, and even
insipidity, if it lacks the seriousness, the suffering, the patience, and the
labour of the negative.'[59]

Hegel wants to incorporate the negative energy of subjective freedom
into the wider world. As Slavoj Žižek writes,

One should adopt the authentically Hegelian *absolute* position which ... involves
a kind of speculative 'surrender' of the Self to the Absolute, albeit in a Hegelian-
dialectical way: not the immersion of the subject in the higher unity of an all-
encompassing Absolute, but the inscription of the 'critical' gap separating the
subject from the (social) substance into this substance itself, as its own antagonism,
or self-distance.[60]

We have seen that there is more to Shakespeare than 'absolute subjective
personality' moving 'free in itself and in the spiritual world'. We are now in
a position to see that such 'absolute subjective personality' does not in the
end impede social progress; it can actually *be* social progress, as the gap
which constitutes an opening for freedom within *Sittlichkeit* or the given
system. As the detachment of personality from the settled state of the world

and its own selfhood – from what we would now call cultural conditioning or ideology – it also is a kind of miracle. Hegel writes:

That an accident as such, detached from what circumscribes it, what is bound and is actual only in context with others, should attain an existence of its own and a separate freedom – this is the tremendous power of the negative; it is the energy of thought, of the pure 'I'.[61]

We have already acknowledged this in the realm of 'Shakespearean absolute personality' in, for example, the case of Hamlet. As I remarked in the previous chapter, although Hamlet's name underlines he is his father Hamlet's son – a royal Prince of Denmark – he is nonetheless thoroughly unable to avenge Old Hamlet's murder. At the same time, he is removed from politics and the succession. And, equally, he's taken out of sexuality and marriage. In other words, his paradigmatic individuality is entirely forged in refusal and negation. The real possibility that he dies a virgin is not irrelevant to this. For just such reasons, Hegel perceives that though dissociated subjectivity may very well be a kind of miracle, it is at the same time a terror, indistinguishable from non-being, death and the demonic, hence Hamlet's pain, frustration and humiliation. He really *wants* 'to be' in a more conventional sense, as no doubt at some level we all do. He wants to make a success of his life; he wants to please daddy if not to become entirely one with him, to fulfil himself according to conventional sexual canons and so on. That Branagh flashback to picturesque lovemaking with Ophelia is as much as anything a desperate attempt to *rescue* the Prince of Denmark from the sheer terror and weirdness of his blankly virginal non-being, though at the same time this makes him precisely what he is.

Still, Hegel insists on 'tarrying' with Shakespeare and such negative experience, for 'the life of Spirit is not the life that shrinks from death and keeps itself untouched by devastation, but rather the life that endures it and maintains itself in it.' In fact, Hegel goes further. The life of Spirit doesn't just suffer the individual's break into alienated and deadly freedom: 'It [actually] wins its truth *only* when, in utter dismemberment, it finds itself.'[62] This is for two reasons. The first is that the abstract freedom of individuals such as Hamlet epitomises abstract freedom as such, instructing, even *inducting* society into its own subjective freedom to be whatever it wills. Second, the very nature and destiny of the social world as the freedom of all of its members is expressed in the separated life of those who are part of it. In other words, the world is made to be broken; it even is made in *being broken*. Elsewhere, Hegel writes of a 'speculative Good Friday', suggesting that, like the life of Christ, the life of Spirit is to be found in mortification and death.[63] In the *Phenomenology*, he writes of the 'bacchanalian revel' of Spirit, communicating not just the joy of liberated freedom but also that such joy is actually achieved in energetic dismemberment: for Bacchus is not only the god of wine but equally *Dionysus Zagreus*, who is torn in pieces.[64] What this means is that the purity of a new day in Freetown – the very purity of 'the spiritual daylight of the present' – actually depends not on settled quiet but rather on a constant state of creative separation, contention, even strife. According to the philosopher, ultimate reality is 'a fragmented being, self-sacrificing and benevolent, in which each accomplishes his own work, rends asunder the universal being, and takes from it his own share'. And this tearing particularity is not to be opposed to but actually constitutes its universal substance, with the interplay between them making it '*actual* and *alive*'.[65]

Like so much we have encountered already in Hegel, this sounds exciting but hard to get a grip on. Or, rather, it's hard to get a grip on until you realise that this description of ultimate reality in fact does *double duty* as a revelatory description of dramatic form. For we could clearly describe *a play* as 'a fragmented being, self-sacrificing and benevolent, in which each *character* accomplishes his own work, rends asunder the universal being, and takes from it his own share'. To bear this out, let's return again to *Hamlet*. Hamlet clearly derives his life from the play *Hamlet*, tearing away from the tragedy as such into his own gloriously separated being, and yet at the same time, and in the very act of doing so, clearly accomplishing so much of the play's own work. Rosalind and Henry V arguably give too much up to the larger design of their respective plays, but Hamlet ultimately manages to do exactly what is expected of him in such a curiously extended, over-determined and indifferent way as effectively to subvert *sittlich* convention even in the act of fulfilling it. In the previous chapter, I offered a reading of *Hamlet* in terms of ideological coercion and resistance. Now that we have seen how Hegelian *Sittlichkeit* itself is a work of freedom, and one which enables as well as limits freedom, it is possible to acknowledge that Hamlet really is fulfilled in his fulfilment of conventional expectations even while he creatively opens them up. This simultaneous affirmation and subversion of self and society may be one reason why Hamlet has proved so magnetic to generations of critics and theatre goers. He may be an icon of individualism, but he also reveals the need for and actually makes a change within the real ideological world.

The more you look at Hegel, the more his philosophical thought and Shakespearean drama seem to grow together, intimating a profound and illuminating perspective on Shakespeare's plays as a struggle for freedom. This distinctively worldly advocate of Spirit insists that Spirit's 'complete reality' is beheld in the concrete political 'life of a people or nation'. And he offers a beautiful image of this as the explosion of 'universal Substance ... into stars as countless self-luminous points' which are 'explicitly for themselves' and yet remain together 'through the sacrifice of their particularity'. These constellate the universal which they at the same time enjoy for their own soul.[66] It's an image almost worthy of Dante, but again it equally serves as a striking epitome of the existential and ethical conditions of a Shakespeare play as a constellation of characters; again, a play of Shakespeare's actually gives us a more living, concrete and mobile idea of the interplay between separated individuality and communal identity than Hegel's metaphor does. We have been contemplating Hamlet, and in this book in general I am naturally concentrating on the big lights: those Shakespearean heroes whose freedom is realised most richly and spectacularly – Hamlet, Iago, Cleopatra, Juliet. But there are little lights as well, such as the Gravediggers in *Hamlet*; such as Barnardine in *Measure for Measure*, who refuses to die for the plot; and such as the eunuch Mardian who in *Antony and Cleopatra* says, 'Yet have I fierce affections and do think what Venus did with Mars' (1.5.17–18). Shakespeare's constellation of characters is as capacious and at the same time more vividly differentiated and realised than Hegel's metaphor for ethical life.

Hegel places the 'principle of subjectivity' he finds in Shakespeare at the heart of modern politics. In *Philosophy of Right*, he suggests, the modern state turns 'the principle of subjectivity' into a real political reality.[67] But this interplay between self, others and society as such is also what a Shakespeare play gives, and it does so in a vividly concentrated embodied form which we can readily entertain and ponder. In other words, Shakespeare's plays accessibly *model* Hegel's philosophy of modern life to the modern political world which Hegel is writing for. Shakespeare's artistic achievement constitutes a living emblem of the politics of freedom, whose poetic force corresponds to the spiritual intensity of Hegel's philosophical programme.

Any of Shakespeare's plays is both itself and a part of a great sequence of other such plays. If this great sequence represents, on one hand, one of the pinnacles of human art, at the same time it stages, in different ways and different ideological circumstances, a specifically endless and ongoing struggle for freedom. 'Shakespeare and no end,' said Goethe. If Popper considered democracy the only viable possibility for a positive politics, because it was the only form of government that embodied the scientific, trial-and-error method and thus enabled society to modify itself in light of experience, this in fact was very much the kind of social life that, one, Popper's *bête noire* Hegel envisioned and, two, is found in Shakespeare's processual, changing drama, where play succeeds play without contributing to some overarching system.[68] Shakespeare's drama as a whole gives us many individuals who are as thrillingly and agonisingly liberated and alive as Hamlet, or Antony, or Rosalind or Falstaff. What a world, what an incoherent world! But in many ways it is our own, modern world of differentiated and heightened individuality. It is hardly surprising that Hegel despaired of corralling such independent characters into a shared political project; yet, that is just what he imagined in more abstract form in works of philosophy which constitute a call to modern freedom where the free will of each becomes the free will of all – a vision of freedom that is taken up by Marx, that other Shakespeare fan and Hegel's more materialist and revolutionary successor.[69]

Even supposing we could achieve it, the delicate balance between personal and social freedom would have to be continuously renegotiated in a complexly changing world; but it is probably impossible to arrive at. Certainly more typical in Shakespeare, at least in the tragedies, is tearing tension between what *King Lear* refers to as 'the gored state' and the equally wounded and deformed subject (5.3.319).[70] And yet, Shakespeare's characters seek their freedom together, in conflict but also in collaboration with one another, within a system which operates as a kind of engine for freedom in that its most splendid effect is, as Hegel recognised, characters who are free artists of their own selves.

That in their very pursuit of freedom they are liable, even likely, to hurt each other perhaps remains a price worth paying. It is certainly a necessary condition of their freedom. And to read Shakespearean drama through Hegel's philosophy is to begin to see that vulnerability positively, as an opportunity for self-enlargement and identification with the larger life of the world. Lear is one character who seems to travel that road. Here as elsewhere Hegel asks us to see something that Shakespeare intimates, and that intimation helps us see what Hegel means.

* * *

Hegel is the sort of philosopher who aims at much more than edification: Marx develops his legacy in that direction; he does not break away from it. And reading Hegel encourages us to read Shakespeare in such a way as could ultimately transform not only our experience of Shakespeare but the world. One major obstacle in the way of such impact is the temptation to be what Hegel calls a 'beautiful soul'.[71] 'The beautiful soul', Gillian Rose writes, 'repulses the world and retreats from it'. Rose goes on to observe: 'She is a *beautiful* not a holy soul (as Schiller wanted her to be called) because she does not sanctify life . . . but both denies it and sublimates the denial into an ethos that is ethereal to the point of unreality.'[72] The 'beautiful soul' line on Shakespeare is that his excellence is unshareable. It isn't an uncommon view. It is widely exemplified by reactionary commentators for whom *any* Shakespearean interpretation or production is essentially unworthy. They see Shakespeare as a humiliating rebuke to life; he is to be worshipped as a transcendent genius cut off from other human activity. But that wasn't the case in his own time, and it wasn't how Garrick or Goethe saw him. From a Hegelian point of view, Shakespearean creativity may differ in *degree*, but it doesn't differ in *kind* from human creativity in general; it is just one expression of that wider 'life of the Spirit' which we all share, which has many manifestations, and which must always be renewed.

And this enables an unexpected connection between Hegel and Garrick. Both the German philosopher and the pioneer of the Stratford Jubilee suggest that Shakespeare shouldn't be cordoned away in the theatre or education. He shouldn't be cordoned off *at all* because, as the most revealed form of human creativity, art such as his has special potential to teach humanity its own, analogous freedom, but only insofar as it is made publicly available as something in which we may all join. Shakespeare has to be removed from the grip of vested interests and freshly presented as an avatar and revelation of our shared potential, beyond the institutions of heritage, theatre, education. Genius has to be understood not as the private property of a superhuman elite but rather as a festive summons to share in a spirit of creative hope. Garrick heard in Shakespeare what Hegel calls 'the Spirit that calls to *every* consciousness'.[73] He was criticised and laughed at for offering a Shakespeare celebration without any Shakespeare, but when the greatest actor of his day chose to celebrate Shakespeare in Stratford for the first time by not putting on a single play but instead by devising entirely new work that transcended its original Shakespearean inspiration in non-dramatic, audience-involving forms – an Ode, an oration, songs – he was refusing to hypostasize the Bard as a fetish in favour of honouring him as a free spirit with vital potential for engendering new life.

Because of the British weather, Garrick failed to effect the Shakespearean procession he wanted to lead through Stratford, in which, for instance, Shakespeare's Juliet and Falstaff would have come among the people, elbow to elbow, incarnate, in the street, partly to honour the refurbishment of a town hall. Instead, he staged this procession in his theatrical reprisal of the Stratford festival back at Drury Lane. His actors wound their way through and drew in some of the audience before ritually assembling on stage around Shakespeare's statue. The Jubilee's most splenetic detractor, Samuel Foote, spoke a prologue at the rival Haymarket theatre on the 16th of January, 1770 which ended as follows:

> To solemn sounds see sordid scene-men stalk
> And the great Shakespeare's vast creation – walk![74]

But for all its spleen, this couplet self-defeatingly concedes that such a mass mobilisation of Shakespeare's characters really is rather wonderful. Péter Dávidházi writes, 'Celebrated as the greatest theatrical spectacle of its age, *The Jubilee* most probably owed its great appeal to the unprecedented extent to which it involved the audience and encouraged everyone to take an active part in the ceremony.'[75] And as Martha Winburn England elaborates, 'The participation of the spectators was carefully plotted.

By the time the final curtain fell, the audience stood on common ground with Falstaff and Lear, singing the familiar songs from the *Garland* [the Jubilee songbook], all ... together, all together doing obeisance to the statue.'[76] And yet, what Garrick had originally envisaged was an even more radical and Hegelian thing.

Of course walking alongside, rubbing shoulders and even conversing with Shakespeare's characters in the ordinary public streets of Stratford would have been great fun; but, as such a thing had never happened before, it could equally have administered a significant, even a revolutionary shock, inducting actual human selves and society into the same self-creating freedom that Shakespeare and his characters themselves enjoy and ultimately insisting that there is no difference between us and them. 'Spirit thus comes before us as *absolute freedom*', in Hegel's words, and the world is simply an effect of its will.[77] The incarnate Shakespearean creation cut loose within the workaday world would have signified the creative possibilities of human life in general. We are the world; O brave *new* world ... (cf. *The Tempest*, 5.1.186). In Hegel, it is just this sort of excessive, unnecessary, even 'fictional' life that proves to be most real, and in fact it is real life that turns out to be inauthentic, inessential. We saw this demonstrated dramatically in the previous chapter when Falstaff rose from the dead on Shrewsbury field in *1 Henry IV*. Hegel helps us see that if the weather had held in 1769 in Stratford and you had been able to look into Cleopatra's eyes, you would, in a Hegelian perspective, have been looking into the heart of being. Equally, you would have been looking deep into your own eyes and heart: seeing, perhaps for the first time, into the richness of your own potential.

Hegel aimed at a revelation of human creativity of religious intensity and depth. The stated objective of the *Phenomenology* is to help 'the joy of beholding itself in absolute Being enter self-consciousness and seize the whole world'.[78] At its most ambitious, Garrick's far more frolicsome festival aimed at something not altogether different. For both Garrick and Hegel, 'Being' is ultimately revealed and achieved in creative freedom. By smashing the established order and installing a new one, the French Revolution had demonstrated to the German philosopher that society itself is a made thing, and one that therefore can always be made again. As Žižek writes, 'Hegel is as unforgiving here as Marx: every retreat from politics ... culminates in a self-serving misery in which can be discerned a secret collusion with the existent.'[79] What Hegel wants instead is for us to know that we're free. He recognised that Shakespeare's characters are 'free artists of their own selves'; he tried to turn this 'principle of subjectivity' into a social system, 'one that is supremely open to the free play of the free spirit'.[80] But we have seen in this chapter that it is Shakespeare who really shows us this in action.

Towards the end of the *Phenomenology*, Hegel wistfully acknowledges the melancholy cultural situation of modern life:

> Trust in the eternal laws of the gods has vanished, and the Oracles, which pronounced on particular questions, are dumb ... The works of the Muse now lack the power of the Spirit ... They have become what they are for us now – beautiful fruit already picked from the tree which a friendly fate has offered us, as a girl might set fruit before us.[81]

This is wonderful, direct and affecting writing from a philosopher with a reputation for turgid obscurity. At the same time as the melancholy of a disenchanted world is masterfully expressed, it is prepared for a subtle but complete reversal. Hegel goes on to say that 'the girl who offers us the plucked fruits is *more* than the Nature which directly provides them'; she sums it all up 'in a higher mode, in the gleam of her self-conscious eye and in the gestures'.[82] But what does this mean? Well, the gleam of the girl's self-conscious eye manifests and portends a new and higher realisation of her gifts. It proffers 'the *inwardizing* in us of the Spirit which in them was still *outwardly* manifested'.[83] In other words, the disenchantment of the world actually presents an opportunity for a more real and intense re-enchantment. The rites no longer work, and art seems dead; yet in fact it is only their fetishised objectivity that has died. In Hegel's philosophical poem, all of it comes to life again in that self-conscious gleam of a young girl's eye. And if the combination of fruit with a hint of female sexuality suggests a reworking of Genesis, this is an expressly happy fall, one by means of which previous experience will be transformed for the better. As regards Shakespeare, it's an opportunity to move beyond bardolatry. Shakespeare should no longer be worshipped as a *thing*. That wise girl's wink is an invitation to 'inwardize' his achievement in all its intensified subjectivity, an invitation to recognise Shakespeare's achievement as a power in ourselves in which the world itself might be renewed. To read

Hegel, on Shakespeare and for himself, is to realise a simple but consequential thing:

Everything depends on the spirit's self-awareness; if the spirit knows that it is free,
it is altogether different from what it would be without this knowledge. For if it
does not know that it is free, it is in the position of a slave who is content with his
slavery and does not know that his condition is an improper one. It is the sensation
of freedom alone which makes the spirit free.[84]

Shakespeare can give us this sensation. He can teach us that we're free. And
it is a political as much as a personal revelation.

8

Against Shakespearean Freedom

❦

1   American Catastrophes

While tracing the progress of Shakespearean freedom, I have been concerned not to avoid its darker side, and this chapter admits historical reasons for rejecting it altogether. Shakespearean freedom was very much in the mix in the deadly Astor Place riots which exploded in New York in 1854, and it contributed to John Wilkes Booth's assassination of Abraham Lincoln in 1865. At the turn of the century, the great Russian novelist Leo Tolstoy denounced Shakespeare's shameless worldliness and self-indulgence as a wicked influence in human culture. This book seeks to recover and affirm Shakespearean freedom, but not without taking account of the real crises it has precipitated or the gravity of Tolstoy's judgement, which has typically been neglected and glossed over by Shakespeareans.

If the Stratford Jubilee, the first large-scale Shakespeare celebration, was associated with nationalism, it was also associated with the inception of Empire. In support of this point, Michael Dobson fished out the following anonymous but contemporary *Ode to Shakespeare* from the bowels of the Bodleian:

> While Britons bow at Shakespear's shrine
> Britannia's sons are sons of mine.
> Like him shou'd Britons scorn the Art
> That binds in chains the human heart
> Like him shou'd still be unconfin'd
> And rule the world as he the mind.[1]

But it is notable that the Shakespearean conception of Empire expressed here is explicitly imagined as freedom at its fullest extent. And freedom is also crucial to that more familiar and less Nietzschean rationalisation according to which Empire actually liberates its overseas British subjects.[2] In *The Genius of Shakespeare*, Jonathan Bate quotes the 'Ode on the Tercentenary Commemoration of Shakespeare by Robert Bridges, Poet Laureate'. 'And in thy book Great Britain's rule readeth her right', according to Bridges. But his next stanza informs us: 'her flag was hail'd as the ensign of Liberty', and even, expressly paradoxically, 'Her chains are chains of Freedom.'[3] Yet if Shakespearean freedom helps inaugurate Empire, it also inspires Americans, for instance, to resist English domination before and after the Revolution, just as Kossuth's enthusiasm for Shakespeare featured in his struggle against the Habsburgs. We have seen that the nascent German nation appropriated Shakespearean freedom as its own destiny; the Americans were quicker to mobilise Shakespearean freedom *against* the English.

Instructive here are the rival New York performances of *Macbeth* by the American actor Edwin Forrest, known as 'The Native Tragedian', and the great English Shakespearean of his day Charles Macready: a head-to-head which precipitated one of the worst episodes in the city's history before 9/11.

Forrest, who at his smouldering best looked like an 'ante-bellum Elvis', was the very incarnation of American independence.[4] 'Early in life,' he said, 'I took a great deal of exercise and made myself what I am, a Hercules.'[5] But perhaps even that's too traditional and derived from civilised models since, according to one reviewer, his voice was, 'replete with a rough music befitting one who in his youth had dwelt, a free barbarian, among the mountains'.[6] His acting lent Shakespeare's great male parts an extraordinary physical immediacy and power. He was very much identified with freedom and his favourite roles included Robert Conrad's version of the peasant revolutionary Jack Cade, who was associated (as we have seen) with John Wilkes, and whose last, triumphant utterance is, 'The bondman is avenged, my country free!' and the Native American Metamora, whose piercing battle-cry goes, 'Our lands! Our nation's freedom! Or the grave!'[7] In nineteenth-century New York, Forrest was the hero of the gangs and theatre of the Bowery, the latter being as Walt Whitman recalled, 'no dainty kid-glove business, but electric force and muscle from perhaps 2000 full sinew'd men'.[8]

This presented, to say the least, a different kind of theatre from that in which Macready excelled. But in fact, on the transatlantic Shakespeare circuit, Forrest at first made a friend of the Englishman, before becoming increasingly offended by Macready's more academic and reflective style. Such Shakespearean hauteur smelled to The Native Tragedian of the persistent pretensions of English imperialism, against which Forrest not unlike Kossuth mobilised the potential of Shakespearean freedom to inspire a specifically insurgent national pride. The rivalry of the two men played out on both sides of the pond and when Macready's Edinburgh Hamlet sported distractedly with a handkerchief in a gesture Forrest would contemptuously denominate a '*pas de mouchoir*', the American was there to hiss him; it wasn't long before Forrest was imagining his rival as the very embodiment of the played-out *ancien regime* and referring to him as 'the superannuated driveller'.[9]

It is actually unfair that by the time of the crisis Macready in New York had come to stand for the elite exclusivity of English culture since, unlike his friend Charles Dickens, he was a great admirer of American liberty, and at one time he had wanted to retire to Massachusetts.[10] But Forrest and his supporters were bent on punishing Macready and the English in the name of insurgent Shakespearean freedom, and nothing could stop them now. When Macready's Macbeth was being heckled and pelted in the upscale Astor Place theatre on the evening of the 7th of May, 1854, Forrest roared from one of the city's other stages, 'What rhubarb, senna or what purgative drug would scour these English hence?'[11] As Nigel Cliff's excellent *The Shakespeare Riots* tells the story, 'Four thousand people rose as one, and for several minutes they cheered for America.'[12]

Macready kept his dignity throughout the crisis, but he was ready to go home, and who can blame him? That he didn't was only because what turned out to be a misguided delegation led by Washington Irving and horrified by the fast-developing stain on New York's international reputation as a centre for civilised liberal culture persuaded him to perform again. In the meantime, posters were rushed up all over New York that exactly anticipate the idiom of revolt we have already encountered on the handbills distributed for the 1864 tercentenary celebrations in Stratford-upon-Avon ('Shakespeare the Poet of the People!', 'People of Stratford!' etc.), but in New York the immediate consequences would be graver:

WORKING MEN,
SHALL
AMERICANS
OR
ENGLISH RULE
IN THIS CITY?
The Crew of the British steamer have
Threatened all Americans who shall dare to express their
opinions this night, at the
ENGLISH ARISTOCRATIC OPERA HOUSE!
We advocate no violence, but a free expression of opinion
to all public men.
WORKINGMEN! FREEMEN!
STAND BY YOUR
LAWFUL RIGHTS!
American Committee.[13]

The crew of the British steamer hadn't actually threatened anything of the sort, but when Macready resumed the stage at Astor Place on the 10th of May, a 15,000-strong mob descended and attacked the theatre.

It all ended with soldiers firing at point-blank range on a civilian crowd, at least twenty-six of whom died. In a sense, these dead are casualties of the idea of Shakespearean freedom. The violence which Forrest inspired tapped into a powerful postcolonial fury, whose effects are still being felt today, and in places other than in America, and as much in relation to American as to British imperialism. Macready had to be smuggled out of New York in disguise. I'm not for a moment suggesting there weren't good reasons for a Shakespeare-inspired protest against British culture in America in 1854, but Macready's traumatic reception was fundamentally undeserved, and the deaths to which it led were needless. It is surely one of the darkest days in the history of Shakespeare reception. And it stands as a warning against the seductions of Shakespearean freedom. We have seen that American and British contemporaries saw in Kossuth a fresh revelation of Shakespearean freedom, but the war that Kossuth waged had many casualties, including the 'Thirteen Martyrs of Arad': those rebel generals who were humiliatingly executed after their leader Kossuth had escaped. What happened at Astor Place brings their martyrdom back to mind. Kossuth was a focus for political hope in the West, but his legacy at home was more complex and ambiguous. And to reconsider his Shakespeare-inflected struggle for freedom in conjunction with the Astor Place Riot is to face the fact that the cause of Shakespearean freedom can be dubious as well as dangerous.

But Shakespearean freedom had another major effect on American politics, and in such a way as still further darkens the motif. We have seen that Wilkes, via Garrick, was associated with Shakespeare as a proponent of freedom, and he had a major impact on American revolutionary thought.[14] But in American history Wilkes and Shakespeare are most strikingly reunited in the career of John Wilkes Booth (Figure 8.1), who on the 14th of April, 1865 assassinated Abraham Lincoln. His is a story which perversely conjoins, as Albert Furtwangler puts it, 'the English master of action and the American ideal of human freedom'.[15]

'But who was this Booth?' as Carl Sandburg asks in a famous passage. 'In what kind of green-poison pool of brain and personality had the amazing and hideous crime arisen?'[16] Well, two of the main ingredients of this 'green-poison pool of brain and personality' were undeniably Shakespeare and freedom. Booth was the son of the English Shakespearean actor Junius Brutus Booth, who was Edmund Kean's greatest rival. Junius Brutus was named after the most obvious exemplar of Shakespearean freedom, and the one who, at least in part, inspired Booth to kill the president. As we have seen, Kean was cast by Sartre as an exemplar of Shakespearean freedom at its most unrestrained, but the assassin's alcoholic bigamist and not infrequently deranged dad (aka 'The Mad Tragedian') certainly gives him a run for his money.[17] Booth himself was named after that other avatar of liberty we have met already: John Wilkes, a distant relative. His family home, which is still standing, was called Tudor Hall. He went to the Milton's Boarding School for Boys. He became an actor, making his stage debut at seventeen as the tyrant-killer Richmond in *Richard III*. If he acted in *Julius Caesar* (or excerpted scenes) just six times, he nevertheless knew the play by heart from childhood. He was a notable talent, Whitman (again) suggesting that he had flashes of 'real genius'.[18] In 1863 in Washington, he was billed as 'The Pride of the American People'.[19]

Booth's sister recalled that as the Confederacy's defeat became more and more certain, her brother started to fulminate in 'wild tirades' against Lincoln 'making himself a king'.[20] When Robert E. Lee surrendered at

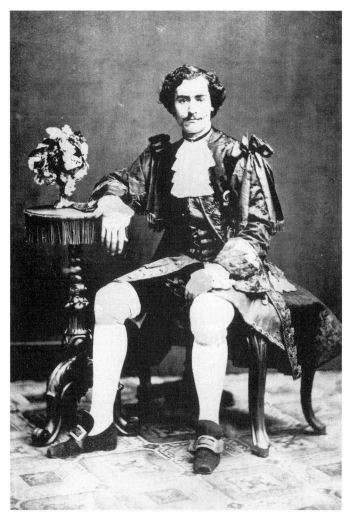

FIGURE 8.1   Photograph of John Wilkes Booth, found in Chicago

Appomattox Court House, Booth said he was done with the stage and that
the only play he wanted to be in now was *Venice Preserv'd*, which is about
assassination. Booth shot President Lincoln in his box at Ford's Theatre in
Washington, subsequently jumping on a stage on which he had frequently
acted.

Whitman takes up the story in a transfixed present tense:

Booth, the murderer, dress'd in plain black broadcloth, bare-headed, with full, glossy, raven hair, and his eyes like some mad animal's flashing with light and resolution, yet with a certain strange calmness, holds aloft in one hand a large knife – walks along not much back from the footlights – turns fully towards the audience his face of statuesque beauty, lit by those basilisk eyes, flashing with desperation, perhaps insanity – launches out in a firm and steady voice the words *Sic semper tyrannis* – and then walks with neither slow nor very rapid pace diagonally across to the back of the stage, and disappears.[21]

'*Sic semper tyrannis*', 'Thus always to tyrants', is attributed to Brutus at Caesar's assassination and is also the state motto of Virginia. Whitman contends that what happened at Ford's Theatre 'illustrates those climax-moments on the stage of universal Time, where the historic Muse at one entrance, and the tragic Muse at the other, suddenly bringing down the curtain, close an immense act in the long drama of creative thought, and give it radiation, tableau, stranger than fiction'.[22]

Certainly there is something ultimate about Booth's act, though it did not quite bring the curtain down on Shakespeare and freedom. Indeed, Booth's own brother Edwin Booth's celebrated and sustained performances of Hamlet after the assassination constitute more than just a strenuous American refutation of what John Wilkes had done; they equally refute the association it implied between Shakespeare and political violence, for Edwin's Hamlet presented 'political murder as a futile act, a hollow victory', 'corrosive and self-destroying'.[23] And yet, it is impossible to deny that mixed up in Booth's assassination of the president were Shakespeare, Brutus, John Wilkes, Milton and the heady modern idea of freedom to which all these authorities contribute. According to Thomas Goodrich, 'All the elements in Booth's nature came together at once – his hatred of tyranny, his love of liberty, his passion for the stage.'[24] The diary of the hunted assassin suggests unstable alternations between self-assertion and self-doubt. 'With every man's hand against me,' Booth writes, 'I am here in despair. And why; For doing what Brutus was honored for . . . And yet I for striking down a greater tyrant than they ever knew am looked upon as a common cutthroat.'[25] *The best o' th' cut-throats*:[26] as his final diary entries betray, and as Stephen Dickey recognises, Booth ultimately havers in Shakespearean terms between 'the valiant tyrannnicide Brutus' and 'the murderous tyrant Macbeth'.[27] Frederick Douglass called the assassination an 'unspeakable calamity' for African Americans, and of course a major irony of all Confederate fighting talk about American freedom is that it was premised on denying the freedom of their slaves.[28] Yet the tyrant Macbeth is also a rebel against all the forces of the universe, including monarch, morality and destiny. The last words of Booth's diary are 'but "I must fight the course" tis all that's left me.'[29] Shakespearean freedom resonates much more hopefully with the emancipation that was Lincoln's most important moral legacy to America and to the world, and it would no doubt be most comfortable just to leave it at that, but John Wilkes Booth – son of a Shakespearean actor, himself a Shakespearean actor, namesake of that radical politician most associated with the first great Shakespeare Jubilee – unavoidably expresses something of the disturbing instability of the phenomenon. And if the association between Shakespeare and insurgent national freedom that Kossuth more positively exemplifies shows an uglier face in Forrest's complicity with the Astor Place Riots, it reveals a still more grotesque aspect in the career of the American assassin. Nationalist passion was the great liberal cause of the second half of the nineteenth century; but Booth's diehard confederate career leads us towards the toxic combination of national pride and racial superiority that had its nadir in twentieth-century Germany, a country and culture which, as we have seen, had earlier been wonderfully enlivened by Shakespearean freedom.

2   Tolstoy contra Shakespeare

If these American instances show, in the most shocking terms, just how wrong Shakespearean freedom could go, one great Russian genius would not have been surprised. In 1906, Leo Tolstoy published a scandalous denunciation of Shakespeare both in Russian (in Moscow) and in English (in London and New York). It wasn't a hasty verdict; Tolstoy had read Shakespeare's tragedies, comedies and histories time and again in English, Russian and German. Nor is Tolstoy Shakespeare's sole great hater. 'The intensity of my impatience with him,' wrote George Bernard Shaw, for instance, 'occasionally reaches such a pitch, that it would positively be a relief to me to dig him up and throw stones at him.'[30] And yet, if Shaw's is the most deliciously enjoyable, Tolstoy's is the most significant and troubling attack on the Bard. According to George Orwell, 'it is unlikely that a heavier indictment will ever be brought against him.'[31]

G. Wilson Knight thought it was based 'on a fundamental misunderstanding of [Shakespeare's] art', but that such a misunderstanding is 'nevertheless extremely significant and valuable'; '[Tolstoy's] conclusions may be
wrong,' we're told, 'but his error is worth more than most critics' truth.'[32]
And George Steiner concurred, pointing out that Tolstoy was himself 'a
supreme creator of animate form and a playwright of considerable power'.
When a critic with such extraordinary credentials as Tolstoy's finds
Shakespearean drama 'puerile in its sentiments, amoral in its fundamental
world-view, rhetorically overblown and often insufferable to adult reason',
we should, Steiner insists, take 'careful notice'.[33] Moreover, according to
Tolstoy, the specifically German promotion of Shakespearean freedom
which has been the main theme of the preceding three chapters of this
book is a wicked error, one which continues to have not just moral but also
spiritual and political consequences.

In *Shakespeare and the Drama*, Tolstoy expressed his opinion of the
plays 'in direct opposition . . . to that established in the whole European
world'.[34] Having looked into the matter conscientiously and over a long
period, he concluded: 'Shakespeare cannot be recognised either as
a great genius, or even as an average author.'[35] Tolstoy does not say
this without a certain hopelessness; he recognises 'that the majority of
people believe so firmly in the greatness of Shakespeare that in reading
this judgment of mine, they will not admit even the possibility of its
justice, and will not give it the slightest attention'.[36] But he feels he has
to speak out because 'the unquestionable glory of a great genius which
Shakespeare enjoys . . . is a great evil, as is every untruth', and one that
is 'causing great injury to men'. 'This injury,' he goes on, 'is twofold:
first, the fall of the drama, and the replacement of this important
weapon of progress by an empty and immoral amusement and
secondly, the direct depravation of men by presenting to them false
models for imitation.'[37]

These are serious charges, lucidly and directly expressed, and striking at the heart of a general consensus about Shakespeare's supreme
value that still persists today. And it surely strengthens his case that in
his effort to make these charges stick, Tolstoy doesn't take the easy way
of finding fault with lesser plays such as, say, *The Merry Wives of
Windsor* or one or another part of *Henry VI*, but instead takes on
King Lear.

To get a full impression of the committed, clear-eyed fury with which Tolstoy critiques Shakespeare's greatest tragedy, it is necessary to quote him at some length:

The fourth scene is again on the heath in front of the hovel. Kent invites Lear into the hovel, but Lear answers that he has no reason to shelter himself from the tempest, that he does not feel it, having in his mind a tempest, called forth by the ingratitude of his daughters, which extinguishes all else. This true feeling, expressed in simple words, might elicit sympathy, but amidst the incessant pompous raving, it escapes one and loses its significance.

The hovel into which Lear is led, turns out to be the same which Edgar has entered, disguised as a madman, *i.e.*, naked. Edgar comes out of the hovel, and although all have known him, no one recognises him – as no one recognises Kent – and Edgar, Lear and the fool begin to say senseless things which continue with interruptions for many pages. In the middle of this scene, enters Gloucester (who also does not recognise either Kent or his son Edgar), and tells them how his son Edgar wanted to kill him.

This scene is again cut short by another in Gloucester's castle, during which Edmund betrays his father and the Duke of Cornwall promises to avenge himself on Gloucester. Then the scene shifts back to Lear. Kent, Edgar, Gloucester, Lear and the fool are at a farm and talking. Edgar says: 'Frateretto calls me: and tells me Nero is an angler in the lake of darkness ... ' The fool says: 'Tell me whether a madman be a gentleman or a yeoman?' Lear, having lost his mind, says that the madman is a king. The fool says no, the madman is the yeoman who has allowed his son to become a gentleman. Lear screams: 'To have a thousand with red burning spits come hissing in upon 'em,' – while Edgar shrieks that the foul fiend bites his back. At this the fool remarks that one cannot believe 'in the tameness of a wolf, a horse's health, a boy's love or a whore's oath'. Then Lear imagines he is judging his daughters. 'Sit thou here, most learned justicier,' says he, addressing the naked Edgar; 'Thou, sapient sir, sit here. Now, you she foxes.' To this Edgar says: 'Look where he stands and glares! Wantest thou eyes at trial, madam? Come o'er the bourn, Bessy, to me.'

The fool sings:

> 'Her boat hath a leak,
> And she must not speak,
> Why she dares not come over to thee.'

Edgar goes on in his own strain. Kent suggests that Lear should lie down, but Lear continues his imaginary trial: 'Bring in their evidence,' he cries. 'Thou robed man of justice, take thy place,' he says to Edgar, 'and thou' (to the fool) 'his yoke-fellow of equity, bench by his side. You are o'the commission, sit you too,' addressing Kent.

'Purr the cat is grey,' shouts Edgar.

'Arraign her first, 'tis Goneril,' cries Lear. 'I here take my oath before this honourable assembly, she kicked the poor King her father.'

'Come hither, mistress. Is your name Goneril?' says the fool, addressing the seat.

'And here's another whose warped looks proclaim what store her heart is made of,' cries Lear. 'Stop her there! arms, arms, sword, fire! Corruption in the place! False justice, why hast thou let her 'scape?'

This raving terminates by Lear falling asleep, and Gloucester persuading Kent, still without recognising him, to carry Lear to Dover, and Kent and the fool carry off the King.[38]

This is in many ways an acceptable account of what happens at this point in the play. And its powerful expression of disturbed, bewildered even disgusted reason in the face of a literary experience that is impossible to organise and comprehend seems, to me at least, to come closer to meeting the challenge of *King Lear* than do many more expert and appreciative views. The sentences are short, the syntax clear and controlled. Tolstoy's account represents the efforts of a writer of arguably comparable genius to catch and be fair to the essential nature and affect of Shakespeare's scenes as written. And yet, Tolstoy is writing in a spirit of heroic restraint, because in fact he hates Shakespeare, hates *King Lear* and hates these scenes for their grotesque irrationality, which he regards as both tedious and immoral, nothing less than a shameless abdication of the most important, for him ultimately religious nature and purpose of drama as an art form. The Russian casts around for a moral compass that will help him find his way through the moral wilderness of Shakespeare's play and almost finds one in the Duke of Albany: 'the only figure with human feelings, who had been already dissatisfied with his wife's treatment of her father [and] now resolutely takes Lear's side'. But Albany, Tolstoy goes on to observe, 'expresses his emotion in such words as to shake one's confidence in his feelings. He says that a bear would lick Lear's reverence'.[39]

Now reverence for Shakespeare can blind us to his strangeness and estrangement effects; but I propose that Tolstoy is right that Albany's strong image is of a piece with the grotesque phantasmagoria of the hovel scenes he has analysed, complicating and disturbing moral judgement. The bear licking Lear's reverence continues a vein of imagery which includes the foul fiend biting Edgar's back; the fool addressing a stool as Goneril; and Poor Tom presenting the naked, self-harming and deranged prospect of 'the thing itself' (*King Lear*, Conflated Text, 3.4.98–100). Tolstoy goes on to contemplate the scene in which the ruined Lear and the blinded Gloucester are brought to contemplate each other face to face, a moment which Frank Kermode regards as the most profound moment in all tragedy, and the philosopher Stanley Cavell calls 'the great image'; but Tolstoy finds that here too Shakespeare errs grotesquely in the same direction:

Hereupon enters Lear, for some reason covered with wild flowers. He has lost his senses and says things wilder than before. He speaks about coining, about the moon, calls for a clothier's yard – then he cries that he sees a mouse, which he wishes to entice by a piece of cheese. Then he suddenly demands the pass word from Edgar, and Edgar immediately answers him with the words, 'Sweet marjoram.' Lear says 'Pass,' and the blind Gloucester, who has not recognised either his son or Kent, recognises the King's voice.[40]

You can see his point. And given the disturbing – more Dostoevskian than Tolstoyan – quality of unhinged sensuousness he points to, it makes sense for Tolstoy to prefer Shakespeare's source, the original *King Leir*, for simplicity, clarity, religious justice.

According to Tolstoy, what Shakespeare lacks is integrity. Tolstoy himself calls it 'sincerity', which he says is 'completely absent in all Shakespeare's works'. In them we meet only 'intentional artifice'; we see 'that he is not *in earnest*', that he is just 'playing with words'.[41] 'The demand for sincerity,' Jonathan Bate has written, 'was Tolstoy's error.' 'The poetry of a teenager in love', Bate goes on, 'is sincere: that is what makes it bad.'[42] This seems patronising, both to Tolstoy and to teenagers in love. But leaving the teenagers aside, Tolstoy isn't in fact asking for Shakespeare to speak in his own person. As Steiner observes, Tolstoy was an able dramatist, and he was also of course the author of some of the most profound and powerfully polyphonic novels there are. What Tolstoy wants from drama isn't romantic self-expression but rather meaning, value, significance; and this he feels is fatally compromised by Shakespeare's compulsive wordplay and restless, for Tolstoy, shameless imagination. To the Russian novelist, Shakespeare's imagination is fundamentally irresponsible, promiscuous, concupiscent. He betrays clear and comprehensible judgement

to weird, often seamily repugnant incoherence. Albany's lines to which he
refers actually support his case better than his own paraphrase:

> A father and a gracious aged man,
> Whose reverence even the head-lugg'd bear would lick.
>
> (King Lear, 4.2.42–3)

The 'head-lugg'd bear' would lick his reverence! What does 'head-lugg'd'
mean? Dragged by the head? It is difficult to see how 'a gracious aged man'
could manage that. Does it perhaps mean dragged, in some way, by its own
head? That is more monstrous, suggesting ferocious, mad propulsion.
'Head-lugg'd' also, onomatopoeically, evokes bulbous deformity. All this
makes the image more gross, taking us away from the disinterested contemplation of 'reverence' its speaker apparently wants to effect in his
hearers. You can see why, for Shakespeare's serious-minded Russian
commentator, this sort of expressive freedom *is* a problem, even
a serious moral fault.

And yet, Shakespeare is not himself responsible for his reputation as the
acme of not just artistic but also moral perfection. That's the Germans'
fault. Wilson Knight tells us, 'Tolstoy's violent attack on Shakespeare is
primarily aroused, not by Shakespeare, but by the Shakespearian commentators'; as well as that, in Tolstoy's account, 'Shakespearian idolatry
was born in Germany, and quickly overspread Europe.'[43] Tolstoy's essay
on Shakespeare isolates this (as he sees it) German infection, choosing as
a particular target the German scholar-critic Georg Gottfried Gervinus
(1805–71) but not before taking a pop at Goethe. Tolstoy also censures
Hegel, who he says justifies the existing order.[44] What Tolstoy sees
valorised and compounded in German Shakespeare worship is above all
the undiscriminating tolerance and inclusiveness that he also finds
betrayed in the 'strange mutations' of human utterance and of plot in
King Lear (4.1.11).

Tolstoy contends that Shakespeare is, in effect, a German invention. Far
from being the national poet in England, he suggests, before the end of the
eighteenth century Shakespeare was valued less than contemporaries such
as Jonson, Fletcher and Beaumont. 'His fame,' according to the Russian,
actually 'originated in Germany, and thence was transferred [back] to
England.'[45] And this happened, Tolstoy proposes, because of Goethe.
Goethe was one of 'a group of educated and talented writers and poets,

who feeling the falsity and coldness of the French drama, endeavoured to find a new and freer dramatic form'. Goethe stood at the head of this group, and he chose Shakespeare as a model, partly because he wanted 'to destroy the fascination of French art', 'partly because he wished to give a greater scope to his own dramatic writing, but chiefly through the agreement of his view of life with Shakespeare's'. When he announced this 'error' to Germany, Tolstoy goes on, 'all those aesthetic critics who did not understand art, threw themselves on it like crows on carrion, and began to discover in Shakespeare beauties which did not exist, and to extol them.'[46] To fit Shakespeare up as the exemplary genius, these critics then had to invent 'aesthetic theories according to which it appeared that no definite religious view of life was necessary for works of art in general, and especially for the drama', 'that ... the representation of human passions and characters was quite sufficient', and that art 'should represent events quite independently of any judgment of good and evil'.[47] We have seen enough in this book to know that Tolstoy's account is a simplification, but we have also seen enough to acknowledge that it isn't completely wrong. Goethe and the Germans really did have much more to do with Shakespeare's surpassing reputation than we now typically realise in Anglo-American culture. And they saw this in terms of emancipation from not just French models but also conventional standards of good and evil. According to Tolstoy, it is this which initiated that perverse Shakespeare worship which has pervaded and perverted the culture of the West ever since.

Tolstoy suggests that Shakespeare worshippers tend to praise one or both of two things in the Bard: his language and his wisdom. He proceeds to demolish both as they emerge from Gervinus's account of Shakespeare. Gervinus's *Shakespeare Commentaries* were an international success, circulating in Tolstoy's time in both German and English. Well aware of the almost unspeakable eccentricity of his position, Tolstoy wants to make his case against the strongest possible opponent, and he pits himself against Gervinus as Shakespeare's 'greatest exponent and admirer'.[48]

Having, in his own mind at least, demolished the aesthetic credibility of *King Lear*, Tolstoy briskly declares that Gervinus's efforts to prove Shakespeare's feeling for beauty (*Schönheits Sinn*) 'prove only that he himself, Gervinus, is completely destitute of it', reminding us that 'in Shakespeare everything is exaggerated.'[49] Still, Tolstoy admits, 'perhaps the height of Shakespeare's conception of life is such that though he does not satisfy the aesthetic demands he discloses to us a view of life so new and important for men that in consideration of its importance, all his failures as an artist become imperceptible.'[50] It is in this connection that Gervinus claims that Shakespeare is 'the very greatest judge of the human soul', 'a teacher of most indisputable ethical authority', 'the most select leader in the world and in life'.[51] And yet, Tolstoy doesn't find the morality which Gervinus culls from Shakespeare at all convincing; he finds it wicked and repugnant. Moreover, he finds it almost unbelievable that a reasonable person could hold up as good the supposedly Shakespearean values Gervinus promulgates. '"Activity is good, inactivity is evil. Activity transforms evil into good," says Shakespeare, according to Gervinus,' observes Tolstoy; and then he comments bitterly, 'In other words, he prefers death and murder through ambition, to abstinence and wisdom.'[52] Tolstoy goes on to show how Gervinus demonstrates that in Shakespeare 'morality, like politics, is a matter in which owing to the complexity of circumstances and motives, one cannot establish any principles', and he finds that the celebrated Danish critic Georg Brandes (1842–1927), 'another of the most modern admirers of Shakespeare', concurs.[53] Gervinus preaches, in Tolstoy's account, a sort of Shakespearean moderation, but one which irrationally and unethically extends to cultivating a position between good and evil, as well as between Christian and heathen precepts. As with the account he gives of *King Lear*, so too with the Shakespearean morality the German promulgates; Tolstoy struggles to restrain his fury at such stupid and pretentious wickedness. He sums it all up as follows:

Action at all costs, the absence of all ideals, moderation in everything, the conservation of the forms of life once established, and the end justifies the means. If you add to this a Chauvinist English patriotism, expressed in all the historical dramas, a patriotism according to which the English throne is something sacred, Englishmen always vanquish the French, killing thousands and losing only scores, Joan of Arc regarded as a witch, and the belief that Hector and all the Trojans, from whom the English descend, are heroes, whilst the Greeks are cowards and traitors, and so forth – such is the view of life of the wisest teacher of life according to his greatest admirers.

This Tolstoy caps with the judgement that 'he who will attentively read Shakespeare's works cannot fail to recognise that the description of this

Shakespearean view of life by his admirers is quite correct.'[54] As Orwell observed, it is unlikely that a heavier indictment will ever be brought against the Bard; but it is clearly equally an indictment of the whole tradition of Shakespeare criticism, and of its German origins.

You wouldn't know it from Tolstoy's account but Gervinus in fact is a card-carrying proponent of Shakespearean freedom, with impeccable liberal credentials. As one of the 'Göttingen Seven', he was publicly expelled from his professorship at the university by King Ernst August of Hanover when he insisted that the king had breached the constitution. He subsequently made a name for himself as a radical polemicist in Heidelberg and was elected to the national parliament in Frankfurt in the revolutionary year of 1848, the year before publishing his major work on Shakespeare. But in 1853, he was found guilty of high treason by the Mannheim Court because of the liberal character of his writings, and he was lucky not to be thrown in prison. He was, by any standards, a brave and engaged person. As for that matter was the other Shakespearean from whom Tolstoy quotes at length. Brandes was, as Tobias Döring writes, both the 'restless campaigner for the modern breakthrough and author of a highly influential biographical study that defined the dominant image of Shakespeare in the early twentieth century'.[55] He fought for sexual freedom and condemned the mistreatment of Alfred Dreyfus and national minorities. He was also a freethinker in religious terms.

In his quarrel with Shakespeare and his advocates, Tolstoy focuses much more on Gervinus than on Brandes. His account of the German Shakespearean's work isn't completely misleading, but it is written without any sympathy or patience for the vision of worldly freedom which the German derived from the Bard, and presumably from his own hard-won political experience. In his *Shakespeare Commentaries*, Gervinus enthu-siastically records that 'Pope has strikingly designated Shakespeare's moral system as one of an entirely worldly character, which the poet places in opposition to the notions obtained from revelation, and which he con-siders sufficient to take the place of these.'[56] For Gervinus, this worldliness is Shakespeare's first, progressive principle, the one from which everything follows; and if Goethe and Herder recognised something similar, it is Gervinus who really develops the thought. He suggests that Shakespeare 'sets aside' transcendent 'religious considerations', and that as a result he 'extolled the love of humanity more than any other writer'.[57] As noted in

Chapter 5, Gervinus is following Johann Georg Hamann in understanding Shakespeare as Christian in the specifically Protestant progressive way in which he 'sets aside rigid law and places free inclination in its stead'.[58] Shakespeare's ethics are, he insists, 'essentially human'. As collateral support for this position, he quotes ambivalently permissive biblical texts such as 'Be ye as wise as serpents, and harmless as doves' and 'He that giveth in marriage doeth well; but he that giveth not in marriage doeth better.'[59] Shakespeare, we are told, sets purity aside in favour of moral engagement. Gervinus's praise for a specifically active ethics corresponds to this overall picture of a worldly and engaged dramatist; it is also of course well adapted to the formal nature of drama as the representation of an action, and it may well have been informed by Gervinus's own activism. Gervinus has no time for emergent forms of German *Innerlichkeit*, where that meant the withdrawal from political responsibility. He writes with unusual vehemence about 'shrivelled forms of private and hothouse life', scorning the Romantic project of bringing 'sentimentality and sensibility into a system', just as Marx does in *The German Ideology*, written around the same time.[60] Gervinus also sets his position squarely against the more metaphysical tradition of reading Shakespeare in Germany that is seen, for example, in Arthur Schopenhauer's description of how Hamlet (among other great literary figures) atones for 'the guilt of existence itself'.[61] In writing against such unworldliness, he is echoing Marx's onetime friend Ferdinand Freiligrath's famous poem 'Deutschland ist Hamlet' (1844), whose exact comparison of Hamlet's ineffectual inwardness with Germany's Gervinus elaborates in his extended critical exegesis of the play in the *Shakespeare Commentaries*; but with this difference: Gervinus makes an explicit case for Shakespeare's ethics and aesthetics of action as a useful resource for future moral, national and political reformation and renewal.[62]

In this context, it is easy to see that the 'principle of wise moderation' which Gervinus discerns in the Bard is not a prescription for bourgeois laissez-faire complacency, as it appears to be in Tolstoy's account, but rather a commitment to charting a course through the complexities and ambivalences of personal and political life. Gervinus regards Shakespeare's opposition (as he sees it) to a religious 'overstraining of human nature' not as capitulation to corruption but as properly responsive to human nature as it is. Religious absolutism is, for Gervinus, an evasive escape into fake and sentimental assurance, and it is in a more charitable spirit of realism that he suggests that Shakespeare taught 'the wise and human medium between the Christian and the heathen precepts of love and hatred of our enemies' which Tolstoy so scorned.[63] The German critic points to a range of examples of Shakespeare's 'express doctrine' that 'it is possible to do too much good in things.' Whereas 'excessive liberality ... ruins Timon', he says, 'moderate liberality keeps Antonio in honour.' Moreover, 'genuine ambition which makes Henry V great overthrows Percy, in whom it rises too high.' 'Exaggerated virtue,' Gervinus goes on, 'brings Angelo to ruin'; but 'Hamlet's too great conscientiousness is a not a crime but a fault, and somewhat of the lack of it in Faulconbridge is not a virtue but a praiseworthy quality.'[64]

The Shakespearean ethic which the German ultimately defines is a moral sensitivity beyond dogmatism to the complexity of particular circumstances, and Brandes took much the same line.[65] But Gervinus recognises the danger that this weakening of clear moral rules could liberate a specifically dangerous freedom. That is why he believes Shakespeare is fit only for the wiser sort: those with leisure and education enough to weigh and discern his always complex moral meanings. It is not fair of Tolstoy to present Gervinus as an ivory-tower elitist. The German is utterly committed to the world. And for him, Shakespeare remains very much a this-worldly poet. Gervinus gives us a Shakespeare who has 'interest enough' in 'the great world life of history ... not to grow weary in its contemplation, power enough to raise himself above its evils, perception enough to hear the harmony in its discords'.[66] It is Tolstoy who wants to transcend this.

Far from being a conservative toady, Gervinus is writing in the tradition of the specifically German interpretation of Shakespearean freedom unfolded in the last few chapters. As we have seen, he risked much for liberty, nearly losing his own in the process. In his *Shakespeare Commentaries*, he writes explicitly, 'free self-determination is esteemed by [the Bard] as the most distinguished gift of our race.'[67] But, with an echo of Hegel, Gervinus also observes, 'true freedom is neither to encroach upon one's own, nor still less upon the freedom of others.'[68] He notes David Hume's judgement 'that political freedom was never the question with Shakespeare', but Gervinus goes on explicitly to say:

It certainly was not in the style of modern political cant. But to write a piece so imbued with democratic principles as *Julius Caesar*, to place in the mouth of the tyrant Henry VIII lessons against all undue exercise of power, to question in *Richard II* the right of inviolability, this indeed, at a time when James I called kings earthly gods was to speak of political freedom.[69]

Indeed. But the distaste Gervinus expresses for 'modern political cant' intimates a significant disaffection from the revolutionary movements of his time; and it is true that, like Hegel's, Gervinus's politics of freedom is not, in the end, a politics of total renovation and the destruction of the existing order. Gervinus proposes that Shakespeare's plays prefigured the Civil War in England, understanding and expressing in advance the arguments on both sides.[70] He affirms that the Bard indeed 'holds open the breach of progress'; in fact, so far as Gervinus is concerned, nobody 'has fought more strongly against rank and class prejudice'. But, he nevertheless insists, Shakespeare is not a poet of the revolutionary conflagration; he asks, 'how could his liberal principles have been pleased with the doctrines of those who would have done away with the prejudices of the rich and cultivated only to replace them with the interests and prejudices of the poor and uncultivated?'[71] And he maintains that the Bard did not 'destroy the charming variety of the world by a universal equalisation' like 'the idealists and dreamers of the present day'.[72] To the contrary, it is just such 'charming variety' that the plays most seriously stand for. Gervinus sees Shakespeare's 'portrait' in his own Henry V,

who was equally qualified for enjoyment and activity, for jest and earnest, for war and peace, for vehemence and self-command, for folly and noble effort, adapted for every business and every society at the right time and in the right place, with kings a king, and with beggars their equal, familiar and proud, selfish and humble, in the variety of being evading nothing but monotonous habit.[73]

Now admittedly there aren't many critics today who would happily accept Henry V as Shakespeare's self-portrait, but a commitment to the charming variety of being is still an appealing rubric for Shakespearean freedom, one which helps us see it as above all a prescription for the fullest realisation of both personal and political life. Ultimately, Gervinus finds in Shakespeare precisely what Hegel also wanted: 'respect' for 'existing forms' conjoined with a desire to 'penetrate into their substance with sound criticism'.[74] 'Thus conservative,' Gervinus writes, 'is this free-minded poet in religious and political things'; but, he maintains it is just this sort of *critical* conservatism that points the way to real cultural and political progress, and he insists that it is 'of more value than … empty revolutionary boasting'.[75]

A fault line shows through here. Gervinus advocates a liberal politics he finds in Shakespeare which seeks to cultivate and make the most of 'the charming variety of the world' by opening up our given traditions and institutions. Tolstoy is a Christian communist committed to a new world of equality and brotherhood which, for him, is more important than such 'variety of being', however charming. According to the great Russian novelist, Shakespeare is too free (in his promiscuous commerce with the existing world) and not free enough (lost in the-world-that-is, and so limited by it). Gervinus and Brandes develop and propound a view of Shakespearean freedom *of and within being*, which we have seen goes back to Goethe, as indeed Tolstoy confirms. But according to Tolstoy, Gervinus, Brandes, Goethe and Shakespeare and his advocates are too committed to this life; they lack that critical distance which itself is a form of freedom and is needed to leverage Tolstoy's new world of brotherhood into existence.

It is, I think, an off-stage contention between 'mighty opposites' (*Hamlet*, 5.2.63). But Tolstoy has been proved right to the extent that subsequent culture has been effectively unable to hear his charges against Shakespeare, and Shakespeare's principally German proponents, who for their part have been widely forgotten. This is a shame, not only because really critical critics of Shakespeare are in short supply but also because Tolstoy's argument with Gervinus can help us see what Shakespeare is and is not, functioning as a tempered, a simultaneously negative and positive revelation of his achievement worth more than mere bardolatry.

Critics have tried to explain away Tolstoy's attack on Shakespeare by suggesting he was unable to respond to the plays either because he was too much of a realist novelist or because he was too much 'a Russian aristocrat … steeped in French culture, including the neoclassical ideals of order, naturalness, regularity, preciseness, clarity, verisimilitude, and decorum'.[76] But there is clearly more to it than that. George Steiner comes nearer the mark when he links the Russian novelist's anti-Shakespearean animus with Wittgenstein's thought that Shakespeare should perhaps be considered a *Sprachschöpfer* rather than a *Dichter*:

that is, as a wordsmith – a creator of language – rather than, as Steiner says in his attempt to translate what he admits is an untranslatable word, 'a truth-sayer, an explicitly moral agent, a visible teacher to and guardian of imperilled, bewildered mankind', a true poet.[77] For Wittgenstein, Shakespeare is too abandoned to words to see beyond or through them into truth. And this resonates with Tolstoy's feeling that Shakespeare promiscuously and irresponsibly abandoned himself to the muse regardless of truth, goodness or even reason. Tolstoy portrays Shakespeare as so distracted by the multiple forms of language and life that he is not able to see the better life beyond them. After reading Wittgenstein and Tolstoy on Shakespeare, Steiner offers the following reflection: 'There is a very real sense, awesome to apprehension, in which Shakespeare does know and say everything; does he know and say anything *else*?'[78] George Orwell sees the issue very clearly, explaining that 'what at bottom' Tolstoy probably most dislikes about Shakespeare is 'simply' his 'interest in the actual process of life'. He concludes: 'The saint, at any rate Tolstoy's kind of saint, is not trying to work an improvement in earthly life: he is trying to bring it to an end and put something different in its place.'[79] What reading Tolstoy's attack on Shakespeare helps us see is that Shakespeare's worldly orientation amounts to a freedom in and of the world, which, at the same time, acts as a limitation on freedom.

I have written elsewhere about the ways in which the apparently mad language of *King Lear*'s hovel scenes actually works insistently to expose the complex, reciprocal immanence of self and world which obtains in our mortal condition.[80] This is the deeper truth of the Fool addressing a chair as Goneril, or of Poor Tom calling himself 'hog in sloth, fox in stealth, wolf in greediness' and so on (*King Lear*, 3.4.82–88). Human self and physical world are interpenetrating in Shakespeare's play. And this is perfectly consistent with its dramatic revelation of the 'bare, forked animal' that Poor Tom presents as the bedrock of human being (3.4.99–100). For the mad dance of language into which the hovel scenes lead us at the same time shows how this 'thing itself' is dispersed and found again and again in the restless imagination it plays host to (3.4.98).

Poor Tom: Shakespeare's compassion reaches deep into this dark territory of our dying lives. Tolstoy does not want to go there, and who can blame him? But of course he did very much enter such depths in his greatest novels. Let us say, then, that Tolstoy does not want to *stay* there.

But, in his attack on Shakespeare, Tolstoy showed us that Shakespeare is always deeply and compassionately (in the literal sense of *feeling with*) responsive to being. For all the power of transcendence in his plays, Shakespeare's language, and not just in *King Lear*, continuously reaches, often with shocking power, into the deeper physical strata of our humanity in its cultural as well as its natural forms. 'It smells of mortality,' says Lear of his hand (4.6.131); but so too do cultural conventions, such as kingship or patriarchy. 'To be, or not to be' (*Hamlet*, 3.1.58): as the Prince knows, human being is haunted and conditioned by not being. And not being is death, but it is also, potentially, an opening for being *otherwise*, and not in the afterlife alone. But any such otherwise will have to contend with the positivity and recalcitrance of this life and, if it succeeds, cope with its loss. Shakespeare's complex worldliness, his endless imaginative investment in life, helps us reckon with this. At the same time, as Tolstoy insisted, it takes us into the darkness of life and history, such darkness as obtained in America in Astor Place and Ford's Theatre. In the twentieth century, after the exposure to Western culture of human being at its worst in Nazism and World War II, two writers have attempted to articulate and explore a Shakespearean freedom of 'complete being' in the hope of coming to terms with and perhaps even overcoming its darkness. That is the subject of the next and final chapter.

9

The Freedom of Complete Being

§

1   Civilization and Its Discontents?

Tolstoy, writing in 1906, felt that Shakespeare was too much in hock to the world, and therefore an obstacle in the way of its much needed reformation. By 1929, when Sigmund Freud sat down to write *Civilization and Its Discontents* (first published in German in 1930 as *Das Unbehagen in der Kultur* ("The Uneasiness in Culture"), Hitler was rising to power in the background and the world was on the brink of its second twentieth-century convulsion. In that context, it would prove difficult to see the darker shades of Shakespearean drama in positive terms of existential enrichment and moral realism, as we have seen a tradition of German critics from Goethe to Gervinus had. The basic flaw in civilisation, according to Freud, derives precisely from the ambivalent instability of freedom. 'What makes itself felt in a human community as a desire for freedom,' he explains, 'may be their revolt against some existing injustice, and so may prove favourable to a further development of civilization; it may remain compatible with civilization.' But Freud equally sees, 'The liberty of the individual is no gift of civilization.' And that: 'It was greatest before there was any civiliza- tion.' Primeval human nature, 'still untamed by civilization', Freud con- tends, may 'become the basis . . . of hostility to civilization'. The 'urge for freedom', he concludes, is at one and the same time the engine of civilisa- tion and its nemesis.[1]

Freud is preoccupied, therefore, in *Civilization and Its Discontents*, with whether 'an accommodation' between 'the liberty of the individual' and human culture 'can be reached by means of some particular form of civilization or whether this conflict is [ultimately] irreconcilable'.[2] He is doubtful about the prospects for an accommodation:

Men are not gentle creatures who want to be loved, and who at the most can defend themselves if they are attacked; they are, on the contrary, creatures among whose instinctual endowments is to be reckoned a powerful share of aggressiveness. As a result, their neighbour is for them not only a potential helper or sexual object, but also someone who tempts them to satisfy their aggressiveness on him, to exploit his capacity for work without compensation, to use him sexually without his consent, to seize his possessions, to humiliate him, to torture and kill him. *Homo homini lupus.*

This of course is much more pessimistic than Tolstoy's view. Human nature construed in this way cannot be redeemed and renovated as the Russian novelist wished it to be. But on the brink of the German catastrophe, Freud believes it is impossible to see life otherwise: 'Who, in the face of all his experience of life and history,' he asks, 'will have the courage to dispute this assertion?'[3] And note that Freud expresses this conviction not just in political but equally in personal terms. Historical crisis reveals a fundamental truth of human inwardness.

But, we might ask, if human beings really are essentially wicked and uncivilised, how does civilisation hold together at all? Freud's rather brilliant answer is that it does so by turning man's aggressive energy against himself: 'His aggressiveness is introjected, internalised; it is, in point of fact, sent back to where it came from – that is, it is directed towards his own ego.'[4] Primordial aggression turns inward, as civilised guilt, self-censure and self-loathing. On one hand, as Freud says, this leaves us with the question 'whether and to what extent . . . cultural development will succeed in mastering the disturbance of . . . communal life by the human instinct of aggression and self-destruction': whether and to what extent political freedom can be protected from the violence of desire.[5] On the other, as Freud bravely confesses, 'when one surveys the aims of cultural endeavour and the means it employs, one is bound to come to the conclusion that the whole effort is not worth the trouble, and that the outcome of it can only be a state of affairs which the individual will be unable to tolerate.'[6]

It is well known that Freud was a great lover of Shakespeare, and in Shakespeare as in life he encountered what Macbeth calls 'black and deep desires' (*Macbeth*, 1.4.51).[7] Famously, he evolved his Oedipus concept in *The Interpretation of Dreams* from his reading of *Hamlet* – Hamlet delays not because he's a shrinking sissy but because, at a deep and disavowed level, he identifies with his uncle's usurping sexual possession of his mother.[8] Hamlet of course has to get over this sort of thing, as we all do in Freud's model, because 'black and deep desires' threaten civilised freedom as such. We see this particularly clearly in *Macbeth*. There Duncan's murder is 'the great doom's image', the means by which Scotland in general becomes not our mother but our grave (2.3.75, 4.3.167). And yet, Freud, like Shakespeare, insists our desires are *deep* as well as dark. You're damned if you act on them, and you're damned if you don't. Their containment is also an intolerable crime against human freedom, and one which inevitably leads to psychosis. Civilisation is sick, perhaps terminally so; what is intended to safeguard our freedoms in fact wrecks them. And so Freud calls for psychoanalysis of human culture in general, 'a pathology of cultural communities'.[9]

In Freud's book, the violence repressed by civilisation returns in the self-mutilating violence of repression. After the Second World War, in 1949, Theodor Adorno presented the more historical view that civilisation had gone bad and was getting worse. Auschwitz was not the *ne plus ultra* of suffering, but instead a shockingly extreme manifestation of the still developing culture of technological capitalism, which subordinates human beings and their needs to its own 'purposeless purposiveness'. As it gets more and more efficient, life gets more and more clueless about what it is actually for. According to Adorno, this enabled the astonishing insensibility of Auschwitz. Because it is so complicit in that process of inhuman abstraction, reason lost its power to resist it; hence Adorno's notorious remark that to write poetry after Auschwitz is barbaric. And if poetry is doomed, cultural criticism is even more so. Because critical detachment turns life into an object of thought, it is related all the more clearly to the death camps. And it has to be admitted that if, in 1949, Adorno could say, 'Absolute reification is now preparing to absorb the mind entirely', today we live in a much more bureaucratic and technologised world.[10]

Adorno finds the conjunction of civilisation and barbarism which Tolstoy found in Shakespeare in civilisation as such. He developed his view in conjunction with Thomas Mann in their intimate collaboration on Mann's 1947 novel, *Doctor Faustus*.[11] That great and forbidding work offers nothing less than a comprehensive diagnosis of the crisis in Western culture, identifying the exuberant abstraction of Shakespeare's writing (in *Love's Labour's Lost* of all plays!) as a demonic turning point on the road to Auschwitz. Such abstraction, according to Mann's novel, is a great opening for creative freedom, on the one hand – indeed, in Mann's *Doctor Faustus*, it signals nothing less than the breakthrough into modern art. But, on the other hand, it enables human beings to treat, manipulate and dispose of life as a thing. And this abstracted distance from life then stimulates a perversely intense hunger to repossess it. As his proof-text for this process, Mann takes the following suggestive couplet from *Love's Labour's Lost:* 'The blood of youth burns not with such excess / As gravity's revolt to wantonness' (5.2.73–4). Of course *Love's Labour's Lost* is a long way from Hitler, but Mann insists, in a passage in *Genesis of a Novel* he lifted from his diaries, that there is a mysterious relationship: 'The Shakespeare play is pertinent. It falls within the magic circle – while around it sounds the roar of the world.'[12] In the mad remoteness from and compensatingly perverse engagement with existence that Shakespeare expresses, Mann finds the tragic image of our modernity.[13] It is not that different from Tolstoy's reading of *King Lear* as discussed in the previous chapter. Shakespeare's expressive freedom in the end makes him desperately unfree and leads into serious moral danger.

From a consideration of Freud, Adorno and Mann, then, we are left with something like the following picture. Civilisation represses barbarism, but civilisation is barbarism. Poetry is civilisation, which is barbarism; and critical intelligence, too, is part of the problem of a barbaric displacement from life. We have lost our original, wild freedom, but we are unable to rise above it; we are radically unfree, and at the same time morally degenerate. Shakespeare is part of the picture, but the freedom which for so long he proffered to Western culture now is nowhere to be seen.

So how do we break the deadlock? Can we recover Shakespearean freedom? This chapter explores two answers.

One. We undo the original repression and start building human culture again, this time hoping to make a better job of it. Such is the project which the Irish philosopher and mystic, John Moriarty, calls for in his remarkable autobiography *Nostos.*

Two. We suffer, honestly, through the whole process of barbarism and repression in the direction of a new dispensation. That's the project recommended by Ted Hughes.

Although Hughes is more centrally and exclusively concerned with the Bard, both of them proceed by reading Shakespeare.

2   Nostos / Poor John

John Moriarty was born in County Kerry in 1938 and by the time he died in 2007 he had returned to the place of his birth. His major work is an autobiographical effort to understand and perhaps even circumvent civilisation and its discontents in the interests of a comprehensive ontological emancipation. It is called *Nostos*: homecoming. Moriarty wants us to come home to ourselves.

In Shakespeare as in other great art, Moriarty finds evidence of a bestial savagery in human nature which resonates with the horrors and disillusionment of the twentieth century. As Andreas Höfele writes, Shakespeare doesn't so much involve 'the invention of the human', as Harold Bloom would have it, as open up 'the *question* of the human'.[14] In a moment which becomes a kind of icon and *leitmotiv* for 'the question of the human' in *Nostos*, Moriarty reflects that 'the hand with which I was turning a page of the Bible was structurally homologous to the fin of a shark'.[15] In relation to this, he quotes Nietzsche: 'I have discovered for myself that the human and animal past, indeed the whole primal age and past of all sentient being works on, loves on, hates on, thinks on in me.'[16] Moriarty emphasises that 'Nietzsche discovered that dinosaur and trilobite weren't only instinctively active in him', deep down, at some buried, subconscious level; instead, they were inseparable from his most conscious and deliberate, which is to say his most *human* passions.[17] The technical whiff of 'trilobite' in Moriarty's gloss indicates that, for this Irish philosopher, the shock Nietzsche experienced comes explosively together with scientific discoveries in modernity that make our kinship with savage nature unarguable. We are not dealing in metaphor anymore. We know *scientifically* that the hand that turns a leaf of scripture – the hands typing this sentence, the hands turning the pages of this book – are in point of fact structurally homologous to the fin of a shark.

This opens Moriarty's ear to an earlier prophetic provocation from Shakespeare:

In its portentous vicinity I hear the Fool's question. Unhoused not just out in the heath, unhoused at home, I hear it:

'How now, nuncle?'[18]

How *now*, nuncle? The fool's insinuating question becomes urgent for Moriarty partly because God has died in our epoch, to the effect that we have become unaccommodated, alienated and unhoused not just in evacuated creation, but even within our own minds. We have become our own bestial remainder, and this of course also evokes the suffering subjectivity of Hamlet. But it is in *Lear*, according to Moriarty, that Shakespeare affords an objective dramatic image of such intimate pain and disturbance. 'Epistemologically,' Moriarty writes, 'I was out-of-doors, and the Fool was still asking his question.'[19]

To review the hovel scenes through Moriarty's eyes after Tolstoy's deconstruction of them is to bring them back from incoherence and to see why *Lear* has come so vividly to life in our times. This perhaps more than any other play of Shakespeare's anticipates the truth of complete human being as it has been revealed by the travails, horrors and guilt of the twentieth century. For Moriarty, this 'cheerless, dark and deadly' old play expresses the essence of modern homelessness (*King Lear*, Conflated Text, 5.3.289); and it is the very same scenes which Tolstoy found most dispiritingly meaningless in *King Lear* that are especially eloquent of this physical and spiritual vagrancy.

They begin, you will recall, on a blasted heath that affords not even a bush to crouch in. Eerily lit by lightning and bombed by tremendous rains, this is the worst night in living memory. 'Man's nature,' we're told, 'cannot carry the affliction, nor the fear' (3.2.46–7). Patently the thing to do would be to lock the door and wrap yourself in all the love and comfort you can muster. And yet – you have to look twice to credit it – Shakespeare gives us an old onetime king running hither and thither in the eye of the storm, intently addressing the furious elements. With him is a fool, and at least that makes sense, for who but a fool would join him? The old man howls, 'Blow winds and crack your cheeks! rage, blow!' (3.2.1). The fool's cap droops, sodden, his rattle trailing mutely; laughter isn't even a memory. Nature continues with its thunder and lightning till the old man's illuminated pate looks almost unbearably vulnerable. And yet, still he invites more pain: 'Singe my white head!' (3.2.6). The fool is helpless to assist, death surely imminent.

But a deliverer steps from the rains. He brings the old man and the fool to a hovel. 'In boy; go first,' the old man says, at last touched by the fool's unswerving loyalty (3.4.27). But the fool backs out in horror:

> Come not in here, nuncle, here's a spirit.
> Help me, help me!
>
> (3.4.40–1)

He is recoiling from a vision of absolute dereliction, a vision of a naked man, with a matted furze of hair, his face smeared liberally with filth. The forearms this naked man extends to his guest are scarred and bleeding, swollen and stuck with 'pins, wooden pricks, nails, sprigs of rosemary' (2.3.15):

> He says his name's Poor Tom. (3.4.43)

It is given to this creature to speak the truth of the scene. You will recall he made no sense whatever to Tolstoy, but Moriarty perceives that Poor Tom is Shakespeare's laureate of the most profound homelessness. His speech mingles gibberish shot with apocalyptical menace and testimonies to terrible suffering. He tells his listeners how the foul fiend marches him like an army 'through fire and through flame, through ford and whirlpool, o'er bog and quagmire', how he leads him into suicidal desperation, laying 'knives under his pillow and halters in his pew' and setting 'ratsbane by his porridge' (3.4.52–4). But if he is part bogeyman, part martyr, to Lear he is a prophet. The old man leans into him, fascinated and murmuring, 'Consider him well . . . Thou art the thing itself' (3.4.96–8). The more he hears, the more convinced the King becomes that the vagrant is a philosopher, and he starts hurriedly taking his clothes off in order to be more perfectly at one with this revelatory image of 'unaccommodated man' (3.4.98–9).

Tolstoy wanted to raise men above the state which the hovel scenes dramatise; but, for Moriarty, writing after the century's end, it is where and what we are. If 'unaccommodated man' is 'the thing itself', then we are all of us homeless: Poor Tom holds the mirror up to a common condition. Whereas Tolstoy wanted men to rise up into universal brotherhood, Shakespeare's scene finds them huddled together beneath any distinction that might otherwise obtain between the privileged and the wretched.

And nor does the truth of human displacement to which Shakespeare is pointing end with our physical vulnerabilities and eventual deaths, for the sheer derangement of the storm and hovel scenes suggests our *psychological* homelessness as well. Tolstoy recoiled from the scene's crazy and immoral redundancies, although perhaps because at a deeper, unconscious level he recognised what Moriarty sees more positively: that Poor Tom's strange and potent speech speaks for the tormented restlessness of human imagination as such. Edgar comes to life as Poor Tom because he expresses the dark subterraneous truths of human existence beyond the ordinary decorums of any given or even humane identity.

And *King Lear* equally bravely explores our *spiritual* homelessness, which came as a particular shock to Moriarty as a Catholic child of rural Ireland but which *Nostos* presents as an inalienable part of our moral inheritance in modernity. Shakespeare seems to anticipate the end of a secure Christian faith in the West by setting his play before the coming of Christianity. Although Kent says to Cordelia, 'The gods to their dear shelter take thee', they can hardly be said to oblige, and something the Fool says seems truer to the play's religious spirit:

> So, out went the candle and we were left darkling. (1.4.192)

When the cosmos has ceased to be a home, it might be reasonable to want to die. But *King Lear* at least glimpses another possibility. At the very beginning of the play, France falls in love with Cordelia not despite but actually because her father has cast her off. He doesn't quite understand his own feelings or how what he calls the 'cold'st neglect' of the gods has kindled his love 'to inflamed respect' but somehow Cordelia's homelessness has made her more lovable to him (1.1.255).

Of course Tolstoy too moved beyond metaphysical Christianity, but he did so in favour of a sort of purified ethics altogether different from the unaccommodated craziness of *King Lear*. I would suggest that in these remarkable scenes Shakespeare is hinting, ahead of his time, that by evading our death-bound, psychological and spiritual homelessness we only become the more lost, and even that if we come home to our homelessness, we might paradoxically discover a more healthy, happy and abiding home than any we have known before. Certainly that is Moriarty's hope in *Nostos*, and, for him, Shakespeare points the way to a difficult and even obscene but necessary emancipation of complete human being.

And for all the pain of godlessness, the problem, as Moriarty recognises, goes deeper than secular modernity, for God (at least as He has been conceived in the mainstream Judeo-Christian Western tradition) is part of it. Moriarty is troubled by Leviathan's exclusion from hope. And this troubles him not just for the sake of that terrible, excluded creature, but equally because he is aware of it thrashing in his own breast, and not just in the depths of his mind and desire. He can't accept a religion that would damn it to Hell: 'No. However hard I tried, I couldn't accept that the hope of Leviathan is in vain. I couldn't accept that something of me is unre-deemable. I couldn't accept that something of me must suffer eternal exclusion.'[20] As will by now be clear, Moriarty's orientation to 'the ques-tion of the human' is a religious one. And it is *differently* religious from Tolstoy's. Tolstoy wants to raise mankind from the hovel; Moriarty wants a new religion that is so tremendously generous it will wrap around Leviathan, including the Leviathan in ourselves. He wants to reconceive our humanity as it were on a horizontal rather than a vertical axis, answering the question of the human by embracing the extent of our humanity. In the hovel scenes, according to Moriarty, Shakespeare is on the right road. 'To bring Poor Tom, who is a-cold, into the fullness of his humanity':[21] such is the project of *Nostos*.

And Poor Tom is indeed at once pitiable, as his name indicates – a no-mark and derelict, unhoused in his own mind – and, at the same time, demonstrably Leviathan, the subject of incommensurately vast, apocalyptical passions which exceed the bounds of any ordinary human ego. As Swinburne said of *King Lear*, 'the darkness of revelation is here.'[22] As much as his name is Poor Tom, it is also Legion. He is 'hog in sloth, fox in stealth, wolf in greediness, dog in madness, lion in prey' (3.4.86–7). And in this of course he represents the terrible multi-fariousness in us all. Given the canons of our culture, Tolstoy's disgust at this is natural – hence, I think, the honest dignity of his hatred of Shakespeare. In order truly to accommodate Poor Tom, to bring him truly into the fullness of his humanity, Moriarty knows, as Lawrence knew too, that 'our road may have to take a great swerve, that seems a retrogression.'[23]

And that great swerve – that retrogression back beyond the deepest decorums and prohibitions in our culture – will lead us further back than Shakespeare. It leads at least as far back as the classical period. In fact, according to Moriarty, it winds back further yet, into 'the dark backward and abyss of time', since the classical period, according to him, is exactly when things start to go wrong (cf. *The Tempest*, 1.2.50). Classical myth tells the tale of our constitutive and damaging repressions. And yet, in doing so, it equally testifies to the truth they repress.

Thus, if Nietzsche discovered that 'dinosaur and trilobite' were active not just in his instincts but in the highest reaches of his emotional and intellectual life, Moriarty contends that 'Greek myth knows that this is true of all of us, figuring it for us in Centaur and Minotaur.' 'Centaur and Minotaur are outcrops,' he suggests, 'of who we phylogenetically are', images in which we may recognise the repressed truth of our own selves. 'It would,' Moriarty contends, therefore 'be unwise not to include them in an account of who we are, in an estimation of who we prospectively can be.'[24]

Moriarty is a thinker who doesn't just talk the talk; he walks the walk too. Thus, in an attempt to come to grips with the Minotaur, he goes looking for him in Greece. He walks into the original heartlands of Greek myth, drawn all the time on the musky scent of the antique knowledge we outgrew before we grew out of what it knows: that we are all ourselves Centaurs and Minotaurs; that these figures merely represent our own nature, in its Nietzschean double aspect. Moriarty takes himself physically to Greece because this is a truth that cannot just be known theoretically; it has to be possessed existentially, felt on the pulses. In Greece, he comes so literally close to it that time and again it practically overpowers him, as in this instance when he's mugged by this visceral apprehension of Pasiphae's fabled congress with a bull:

I walked along mule tracks and when they ran out I walked in the trackless places beyond them. On the way in, in a narrow place, a sheer mountain wall on one side, I met a girl of no more than eight years of age herding a long flock of goats. As they passed me, the dense, rank smell of the bucks almost suffocated me, and I thought about Pasiphae. For how long afterwards did she smell of the bull? For how long did she smell of him in her hair and in her mind? For how long did her arse smell of him? For how long did it smell of his foaming mouth. And the royal apartment! And the bed-clothes? And Minos? How did they cope? How did they both cope?[25]

This is so powerfully direct as really to need no comment, and it is just one of the shocks that Moriarty receives on his way back into the origins of civilisation. Moriarty wishes *we* could 'suffer our questions and crises with the same sincerity that the Greeks suffered theirs'.[26] He suspects Greek myth is in fact better adapted to life than our own culture is. Because, according to Moriarty, 'Greek myth *knows*, in its own way knows, the whole of our phylogenetic past is in us', whereas we only know this scientifically, refusing to know it in ourselves and our passions. In fact, Greek myth 'sponsored and validated' it, as a truth which it expressed iconically 'as Satyr, as Centaur, as Minotaur'.[27]

This erotic abjection and savagery which Moriarty confronts in Pasiphae isn't that far from Poor Tom, whose speeches reveal a spirit that is fair game for every low and fleeting thing that would take him.[28] This is from the quarto text of *King Lear*:

Five fiends have been in Poor Tom at once, of lust, as Obidicut; Hobbididence, prince of darkness; Mahu of stealing; Modo, of murder; Flibertigibbet, of mopping and mowing, who since possesses chambermaids and waiting-women. (4.1.59–63)

It intimates a demonic sodomitical gang-rape. Contemplating Pasiphae and Clytemnestra as ancestors to Poor Tom – and all of them as avatars of our more real selves – Moriarty recognises that 'our Enlightenments, ancient and modern, took off on a very wide detour' around them, and he suggests in a densely potent image that this attempted circumvention has failed disastrously: 'One of his horns reappearing as our revolutionary guillotine, the other reappearing as our revolutionary gulag, the Minotaur, altogether more terrible for not being acknowledged walked with us.'[29] It may be worth unfolding this a bit. While he walks beside us, Moriarty's Minotaur is laughing a terrible laugh; he is doing so because, although we will not recognise or even look at him, he is irresistibly walking us towards our own catastrophe – the catastrophe of a narrowly rationalist culture, one which will inevitably end up paying him terrible homage. Repression doesn't work, and transcendence doesn't either. The savagery is ineradicable. We can never defeat the beast. Just as he led us to the guillotine and gulag, he led us to the German catastrophe. Kosovo, Rwanda, Syria . . . the catastrophe is not over. When Poor Tom leads Gloucester over Dover Cliff, he leads him into free fall. There is no end to suffering in *King Lear* or history, so we had better come to terms with it, and the Minotaur, Leviathan, Pasiphae and Poor Tom. That is our only hope of making a new beginning.

'The question of the human' for Moriarty is far from only – it is far from *primarily* – an intellectual one; it is an existential and moral, even a sexual question. It is a question of who we are, and what we might become. And, consequently, it is a question of what to *do*: an urgent question of what to do *now*. 'How now, nuncle?' Should we kill our dragons, or invite them in?

In *The Marriage of Heaven and Hell*, Moriarty notes, Blake says the roaring of lions, the howling of wolves, the raging of a stormy sea and the destructive sword are 'portions of eternity' that man cannot recognise.[30] Not man as he has been in Western civilisation, in any case. But in his quest for a new humanity, Moriarty does not just push back into our ancient beginnings, he also pushes *away*: he pushes beyond the pale of Europe, where he discovers the alternative myth of the Blackfoot, who 'won the good will of the Bull' and by means of their mysterious and slow buffalo dance 'went on to ritually institute that good will not just at, but as, the beginning of their culture'.[31] But how, even if we wanted to, could we turn the whole European tradition round in that direction? One proposal Moriarty makes is to, in antique terms, move the centre of civilisation from the stoa of purely rational exchange to the more holistically human environment of the theatre. This in fact, Moriarty suggests, is a move we don't need to initiate since it has 'already come to pass in the epistemological sufferings of poets and novelists such as Coleridge, Melville, Arnold and Wallace Stevens'. 'Questions asked in the stoa,' he insists, 'become different questions when they are *suffered* in a theatre whose patron and first and continued protagonist is a suffering god.' In the theatre, we find 'an alternative kind of intelligence', not the new intelligence which Wallace Stevens called for, but 'a kind of intelligence we need to grow *back* into'.[32]

And so we return to Shakespeare. After all, there are clear indications that Shakespeare can accommodate savage nature. We might, despite Tolstoy's disgust, recall 'the head-lugg'd bear' who Albany imagines licking Lear's reverence (4.2.41–2). We might also recall the ass-headed Bottom, whose dream which 'hath no bottom' is so paradoxically central to the social world and whirl that is constructed in *A Midsummer Night's Dream* (4.2.209). But, according to Moriarty, Shakespeare really breaches 'the Wall' of our European civilisation in *Macbeth*, which involves 'the awakening of all those dimensions and moods of our minds that the Wall was built against'.[33] It is a major epistemological, indeed spiritual breakthrough. As Moriarty puts it:

And one thing is sure. In spite of our best civilising efforts, the world will always be
what it has always been – in its strange and mysterious ways it will always be extra-
mural. And so will our minds. At their best, so will our minds.

> Birnam Wood.
> Birnam World.
> Birnam mind.[34]

Thus Shakespeare, according to Moriarty, beckons us beyond the stoa, but
we will not yet follow him. According to Moriarty, 'for the sake of being
citizens, Roman citizens, we are willing to be cut off from Birnam Wood,
the Birnam Wood of our minds and the Birnam Wood of the world.'[35]

Moriarty says what he says 'knowing the risks', but can *Macbeth* really
be read as utopian prophecy? Wouldn't one of the festive comedies –
As You Like It, say – serve better, stand a better chance of drawing us
optimistically out of our city walls? Come to think of it, doesn't
A Midsummer Night's Dream explicitly play with such questions, enter-
taining the desire to remain walled in as well as the desire to break out, and
rather brilliantly suggesting in its most comic episode that 'Wall' as what
stands between us and our yearnings may itself become a sort of fetish?
'And thou, O wall, O sweet O lovely wall' (*A Midsummer Night's Dream*,
5.1.172)! Maybe, but it still remains the case that none of the festive
comedies really gets to grips with the savagery in human nature as
Macbeth does. *Dream* has its vision of a man with an ass's head making
love with the Fairy Queen, but the threatening edge of this bestial encounter is taken off by the prevailing comic tone. Not so in *Macbeth*, where the
hero himself really and terrifyingly becomes a sacred monster set loose
both within and beyond the city limits. For this reason, The Scottish Play
does truly, as Moriarty claims, mark a break with the tidy ring-fencing of
civilisation as we have traditionally constituted it.

And it certainly shows he isn't ducking or sentimentalising the issue that
Moriarty chooses *Macbeth* of all Shakespeare's plays to enlarge 'the question of the human'. It also shows he isn't minimising the risks that he
agonises over in this choice. For Moriarty is intimately disturbed by
Macbeth, writing as follows:

In *Macbeth*, Shakespeare metaphorically assimilates two terrible moments:
Tarquin going to rape Lucrece, and Macbeth going to murder Duncan.

In unconscious elaboration, Tarquin's phallus hallucinates itself right there in the hall before him, pointing the way he should go, and Macbeth's dagger, that also hallucinates itself before him and it points the way he should go.

In the way that Tarquin's going and Macbeth's going are assimilated one to the other, so are phallus and dagger assimilated one to the other.

Admittedly this is still merely criticism, picking up on the fact that Macbeth goes 'with Tarquin's ravishing strides' to murder Duncan (2.1.55). But it is written with a lean directness that makes it refreshingly different. In the wake of a dream of sex in his parents' yard in rural Kerry, Moriarty goes on to confess, 'More horrendously in my case it was an assimilation between phallus and pig-killer's knife.' And, having said so, he admits, 'a whole symphony of sexual trouble had simmered to the surface.'[36]

At one point in *Nostos*, Moriarty suggests Macbeth's tragedy is 'that he somehow found and walked through a breach in Hadrian's Wall, but since he didn't know it he behaved in the real world as he would in our constructed world, he behaved in Birnam Wood as he would in a Roman *castra*'.[37] This echoes Adorno: civilised violence might be worse than the uncivil violence it disavows, but it also seems an evasion of that original uncivil violence, a pretence that the world beyond civilisation which *Macbeth* breaks into could be anything other than violent. Elsewhere Moriarty seems to admit that original violence, in Birnam and himself:

Waking every night at the hour of my wolf, my room would be thick with moral pollution. In the oldest parts of who I was, no, what I was, I was on the boil. I pictured it. Down there somewhere among my oldest roots there was a witch's cauldron hanging over a fire of deadwood gathered from the floor of Birnam Wood, and it was bubbling, toiling, troubling:

> Fillet of a fenny snake,
> In the cauldron boil and bake:
> Eye of newt and toe of frog,
> Wool of bat and tongue of dog,
> Adder's fork and blind worm's sting,
> Lizard's leg and howlet's wing,
> For a charm of powerful trouble,
> Like a hell-broth boil and bubble.[38]

It is of course in this cauldron from *Macbeth* that the 'whole symphony of sexual trouble had simmered to the surface.' The literary picture of Moriarty hugging it into himself – almost literally gathering it into his breast – presents a shockingly powerful response to Shakespeare's play. In *Macbeth*, this poisonous stew of dismembered nature very accurately represents the state of its hero's soul, but, unlike most professional commentators, Moriarty doesn't hold Macbeth at arm's length. Instead, he finds Macbeth in himself; he *is* Macbeth. 'It was as if my very blood, all of it, was a hell-broth,' he writes, 'And all my humours too, in the Elizabethan sense, they were a hell-broth, varieties of the hell-broth, and now they had come to the boil and I didn't have to go to a blasted heath to find fog and filthy air, it was here in my room, condensing on my window, condensing on sclera and cornea.'[39] And in case you're wondering, yes, this means and portends for Moriarty exactly what it means for Shakespeare's hero: 'There were awful impulses simmering in me and maybe when I was off guard in the night they'd take over and I'd somnambulate to murder.'[40]

Moriarty gives us an exceptionally naked, unprotected form of literary response, one where the terrors of myth and literature compel an immediate and dreadful recognition. Shakespeare's tragedy seems to speak a truth to the author of *Nostos* that he is powerless to resist. He confesses, 'It was in me to commit the unspeakable crime.' As a result, he writes, 'I saw three great doors in front of me: one into a monastery, one into a mental home, and one into a high security prison.' Worst of all, he says, 'ask anyone and they'd say I was a decent enough sort of bloke, and if you asked me, if you asked me a few months ago, that's what I'd say too, I'm a decent enough sort of bloke.' I should say that Moriarty lived without the supports that sustain most of us – career, marriage, a mortgage, a professorship and so on. Still, his point is that he isn't, in any essential way, different from you or me, that none of us, really, is that different from Macbeth, his soul, like his destiny, a savage shambles; his hands stained indelibly with Duncan's blood: hands which are, as by now Moriarty has told us often enough, structural refinements of the fin of a shark. The question of the human is under real pressure. Again Moriarty quotes Lawrence: 'every new conquest of life means a harrowing of hell.'[41]

So, what do you do, where does this terrible identification with Macbeth lead Moriarty? It leads him back to Christianity, although this is a Christianity of a very different stripe from Tolstoy's morally dignified, reasonable holiness. Moriarty's Christianity is one which above all 'has integrated dereliction, making it religiously respectable'. He goes on: 'And not only that. Iconographically, down the centuries, it has integrated it luridly, sensationally. So sensationally that if it was a film there is hardly a national censor that would give it screening permission.'[42] Moriarty presents Christ in the darkness of Gethsemane, reintegrating our darkness into a redeemed humanity: 'In us as trilobite he prayed, in us as stegosaurus he prayed. In us as cormorant and great owl and satyr and vulture he prayed.'[43] This is something other than metaphysical religion; it is something other even than civilised religion. Christ is the answer and redemption in *Nostos* of 'the question of the human' as it is posed by Poor Tom and Macbeth.

This rediscovery and new vision of traditional religion leads Moriarty through the door of a monastery: the Carmelite monastery at Boar's Hill, Oxford, where he lived and worked, for some years, as a gardener. It wasn't a refuge from the struggle with the question of the human that he had always waged. The boar which, time out of mind, gave Boar's Hill its name was always present to him. After all, he reflects, 'Whatever very difficult chance we have with the boar we acknowledge, we have no chance at all with the boar that we don't acknowledge.' And yet, even as he says this, he has his doubts. He wonders whether, in his life, he has gazed upon the boar with excessive fascination. 'Had I looked as often and as long at the elevated Host,' he asks, 'how would I be now?'[44] He recalls that in Greece, somewhere on the road to the Labyrinth, 'it occurred to [him] that, once disturbed, once exasperated, the phylogenetic depths of the psyche mightn't come to rest again, not sufficiently to live an ordinary civil life.'[45] Maybe, after all, he took the wrong road.

In *Nostos*, Moriarty attempts to break the deadlock which Freud says dooms men and women to choose between an unsatisfactory civilised life and a total if vital chaos. By offering his own alternative interpretation of Western culture, and by having the courage and commitment to live his life in accordance with this, Moriarty attempts to undo the original repression which Freud contends constitutes the personal and civic life we know. He does this in the hope of reintegrating what is presently repressed into a new, more hopeful subjectivity and culture, one which at last will liberate human beings into their own complete, completely integrated being. He finds this emancipation as it were negatively foreshadowed in *Macbeth*. The more positive realisation he leans towards would effect a return from the damaging abstraction which Thomas Mann exposed in modern culture, and which according to Adorno is what at once drives and is reinforced by the hectic development of capitalism. Mann found such dangerous abstraction in *Love's Labour's Lost*, albeit with a correspondingly perverse hunger to repossess the material bodily life it loses. Moriarty is more in tune with that mainstream German tradition stretching from Goethe to Gervinus which emphasises Shakespeare's unusual worldliness, a quality which Tolstoy took to reveal the Bard's culpable capitulation to the debasement of what merely exists. But for Moriarty as for Höfele in *Stage, Stake, and Scaffold: Humans and Animals in Shakespeare's Theatre*, the cultural crises of the twentieth century, including two bloody World Wars, reveal a savagery that is thoroughly ineradicable in human being, contributing 'renewed urgency' to Shakespeare's enquiry into 'what it means to be an animal that considers itself human';[46] and for Moriarty as for Tolstoy, this is a question which demands a real, a really liveable answer. The effort to find one which *Nostos* documents demands our respect because it is so grand and ambitious. In its sheer existential, cultural and spiritual seriousness, it goes well beyond most academic criticism. And whereas Tolstoy chose a purifying transcendence in the face of Shakespeare's worldliness, Moriarty discerns in Shakespeare a comprehensive embrace of human being which could have positive political as well as personal consequences.

But the quest remains a somewhat quixotic one, because Moriarty undertakes it so very much on his own. It provides only an epiphanic glimpse of the new politics it yearns for: a fantasy of a new civic dispensation that is symbolised by a sculpture of Pasiphae giving suck to her bull-headed baby above the city gate. Its reimagined Christianity will hardly appeal to everybody in today's multicultural and secularised society. Perhaps instead of the orthodox Christ, Moriarty should have even more squarely founded the new psychological and political dispensation he wants on the figure of Poor Tom. And then there are the risks of Moriarty's project: given what, after Auschwitz, we know about the scale and scope of human savagery, lifting the lid on it – even letting it in through the city gate – might be heroic, but it could also be just plain and culpably crazy.

3   Shakespeare and the Goddess of Complete Being

Moriarty on Boar's Hill, where a terrible identification with Macbeth has
brought him, struggling with the boar within: this strikes lights with Ted
Hughes's idiosyncratic as well as enormously extended interpretation of
the Bard in *Shakespeare and the Goddess of Complete Being*, because
Shakespeare for Hughes is, believe it or not, essentially and almost always
about a spiritual struggle with a mythical boar. According to Hughes,
Shakespeare explicitly admits this when a fatal boar actually charges into
Venus and Adonis, but Hughes suggests that the boar's tusked and grizzled
face is discernible everywhere in Shakespeare's work, and it is the boar we
have to integrate into our personal and political lives if we are to attain
a new and complete being.

It isn't hard to see what he means at such moments as when Richard III is
called an 'elvish-mark'd, abortive, rooting hog!'(*Richard III*, 1.3.225). And
Hughes also points to 'Falstaff, the Bartholomew Boar Pig of the Boar's
Head'; and Caliban, 'the child of Sycorax ('swine-crow')', particularly when
he's grubbing for his 'pig nuts'.[47] We may also remember that Lear 'hovels'
with swine on his blasted heath (*King Lear*, 4.7.38–40). But the boar in *Venus
and Adonis* is clearly associated with sex and sexual problems, sheathing its
tusk in the frigid hero's groin, and Hughes tends to feel its force and
presence in Shakespeare's work in moments of erotic violence. By means
of what he describes as an 'occult crossover', Tarquin, he suggests, actually
becomes the boar in Shakespeare's second narrative poem *The Rape of
Lucrece*.[48] And this is emblematic of Shakespeare in general, where Adonis-
like rejection of sex and the female all-too-readily flips into Tarquin-style
sexual violence.

Hughes wasn't unaware of the resistance his book was likely to
encounter:

It might be thought a kind of sacrilege to drag Shakespeare back into capering
about in a public arena (on a stage!) to a drum (a jig!), not in a goatskin, like the
forerunners of the Greek tragedians, but in the bristly pelt of that holiest of Celtic
and Anglo-Saxon beasts – the wild boar.[49]

But in the event if his detractors did feel any sense of sacrilege, they warded
it off with scorn. Of course when, at the beginning of his book, Hughes
announced, with frankly impressive insouciance – 'I rely on hand-torch

and divining-rod through the tunnels of the wild pig' – he was asking for it
so far as academics were concerned, particularly at a time, in the early 1990s,
when the most energetic criticism was impatient to cut the crap and intervene politically.[50] The headlines in the papers spoke for themselves. The
Guardian ran a piece by Terry Eagleton called 'Will and Ted's Bogus
Journey' (2 April 1992); and Terence Hawkes's review in *The Times Higher*
ran under the banner 'A Porker-wise Bard' (19 June 1992). And if the book
fared ill with prominent radical critics, it fared scarcely better with more
establishment types. In the *Sunday Times* (5 April 1992), John Carey, then
Merton Professor of English at Oxford, also put the boot in, taking Hughes
to task for an 'enormous and glaring self-contradiction', which Carey rather
nastily described as 'most Hughes-ish of all' – I don't like the sneering
distaste for the poet's name. Eagleton and Hawkes are right that
Shakespeare and the Goddess can, at times, be hieratic, humourless, even
absurd. And Carey, too, was onto something. He demonstrates that
Hughes's attempt to rescue 'complete being' in Shakespeare was doomed
to fail since its own method was so maniacally and systematically single-
minded. But if the *Shakespeare and the Goddess* detractors were right that
the book can be wrongheaded, wearying and oppressive, they were wrong
not to recognise that at its best it is powerful and suggestive. And it may be
that this was more a matter of resistance than neglect. Consciously or
unconsciously, these reviewers may not have wanted to know what
Hughes – sometimes awkwardly, sometimes effectively, always urgently –
wanted to tell them.

   Writing some five years later, Neil Rhodes struck a more sensitive and
humane note. He recognised 'a terrible honesty' in *Shakespeare and the
Goddess of Complete Being*, picking out in particular 'the anxieties' it
expresses 'both about gender and the broader cultural antagonisms with
which those are ensnared'. He insisted that 'whatever the merits of *Goddess*
as a reading of Shakespeare it is not an enterprise that should simply be
mocked.' I strongly agree but note that phrase 'whatever the merits of
Goddess as a reading of Shakespeare'. Though Rhodes honours Hughes's
'terrible honesty' about sex and society, he reserves the right to keep
Shakespeare out of it.[51] In a more recent piece, published in 2011,
Jonathan Bate suggests, 'Shakespeare was the absolute centre of Ted
Hughes's sense of the English literary tradition.' 'The world of Hughes's
verse,' he goes on, 'is one in which, as Macbeth puts it, "light thickens, and

the crow / Makes wing to the rooky wood.'"[52] This is especially true of Hughes's extraordinary 1970 collection *Crow*, which can fairly be read as an extended poetic riff on the lines Bate quotes from *Macbeth* (3.2.51–2).[53]

Hughes presents an alternative Shakespeare, unlocking what he calls the 'power-house and torture chamber' of the complete works.[54] This isn't at all the Shakespeare who in the course of Stephen Greenblatt's *Will in the World* becomes a rather smugly justified social success.[55] This Shakespeare is a 'misfit', whose work, 'in its elemental otherness and ferocity, suggests an almost pathological alienation from the culture within which his plays triumphed'.[56] As Bate suggests, Hughes's early, essayistic attempt to explain his theory about Shakespeare in the Introduction to *With Fairest Flowers while Summer Lasts*, the American edition of his choice of Shakespeare's verse, offers the quickest and easiest handle on it.[57] Hughes tells there how when he brought the most powerful bits of Shakespeare together in preparing his anthology, he suddenly recognised their 'strong family resemblance', their powerful and 'particular knot of obsessions'. Reading them together was like 'plucking out Shakespeare's heart', discovering it had 'a black look'.[58] And yet, even as they reveal Shakespeare, Hughes insists, we simultaneously 'look through them into our own darkness'.[59] For Shakespeare's 'poetry has its taproot in a sexual dilemma of a particularly black and ugly sort', deriving not from any particular thing Will did with the Fair Youth or the Dark Lady but instead from a deep structure of sexuality in our culture.[60] This recognition sheds dark light through many major episodes of the canon, according to Hughes, as he goes on to indicate in urgent, lean clauses. 'Hamlet, looking at Ophelia, sees his mother in bed with his uncle and goes mad.' 'Lear, looking at Cordelia, sees Goneril and Regan, and goes mad.' 'Leontes, looking at his wife, sees Polixenes' whore, and begins to act like a madman; Posthumus, looking at his bride, who of his "lawful pleasure oft restrained" him, sees the one Iachimo mounted "like a full-acorned boar," and begins to act like a madman.'[61]

Such dramatic moments of misogynistic madness are so central, so essential to Shakespeare that, borrowing the phrase from Patrick Cruttwell, Hughes calls them '*the* Shakespearean moment'.[62] According to Hughes, this is the moment of spiritual ignition in Shakespeare, albeit a spiritual ignition of a perverted, misogynistic kind. Nature's maddened force, figured in *Venus and Adonis* as the ravening boar, invades the deepest being of the one who rejects her and Adonis turns into Tarquin. It troubles as well as fascinates Hughes as he meditates on this in *Shakespeare and the Goddess of Complete Being* that, far from being a diminishing thing, this is such a grand transfiguration. Indeed, until it happens the hero is 'merely another dramatic character':

> But once the Boar has arrived, and transformed him, he suddenly embodies the unique thing: Shakespeare's revelation. Immediately he overflows with inner riches. King Lear, for instance, is a mechanical, foolish despot till the Boar arrives. Timon is a deluded, idealistic prodigal till the Boar arrives. Without the Boar, Adonis is simply stuck in his rules of ego behaviour (something like Prospero). Once the Boar has taken possession, and shattered Adonis, the hidden, potential spirituality reveals itself in the poetry.[63]

This dark 'spirituality' which Hughes finds in Shakespeare resonates with the dark spirituality Thomas Mann found in both Shakespeare and the German catastrophe. Confronting the terrible beauty of these energetic ravings, Hughes suggests that they express a 'massive thunderbolt of Divine Love' in perverted form. The complete love and being of the Goddess cannot be rejected inasmuch as it is one with the energy and reality of the world; it can only be diverted and will always return, however unpropitious the circumstances. According to Hughes, it returns as the Boar. But the Boar still gleams with and expresses the beauty of the Goddess. That is why the most vicious and tragic verse in Shakespeare is nevertheless disturbingly beautiful.

It's compelling stuff which touches a vein of violence that is unquestionably there in Shakespeare, and Hughes goes on to fold in the cultural trauma of the Reformation. Sex and religion shade into each other, and the rejection of the Goddess is redolent of the rejection of Marian Catholicism in Protestant England. But given the terrible charisma of the Goddess violators, this can't be a simple matter of Catholic nostalgia. As Neil Corcoran writes, 'the formula secreted in Shakespeare is a myth at once defensive of Catholicism and exacerbatedly intimate with the strained subjectivities of Puritanism.'[64] Or, as Hughes puts it himself, Shakespeare was 'a shaman, a prophet, of the ascendant, revolutionary, Puritan will . . . just as surely as he was a visionary, redemptive shaman of the Catholic defeat'.[65] He articulates a continuing crisis of English culture.

And if there's a recalcitrant localism in *Shakespeare and the Goddess of Complete Being* – one which, I must admit, I find rather refreshing in the context of the current vogue for global Shakespeare – that hardly damages its larger meaning. For Hughes also says that the 'Shakespearean moment', though it emerges from the particular agonies of English history, may nonetheless be read as embodying 'the inevitable crime of Civilisation, or even the inevitable crime of consciousness'.[66] In other words, *Shakespeare and the Goddess of Complete Being* is directly addressing the problem which Freud defined in *Civilization and Its Discontents*, a problem which Hughes suggests is always specific to and often worsened by our historical circumstances, even if it ultimately goes deeper than history.

Hughes's title takes no pains to conceal that he derives something of the world-view he presents from Robert Graves's *The White Goddess*. This was once a very influential book but now looks just as eccentric as Hughes's. Graves mentions in passing that Shakespeare 'knew and feared' the Goddess, whom he discerns in sportive mood in Titania, as well in her more serious aspect in Lady Macbeth and Cleopatra. Her ultimate manifestation, for Graves, is as Sycorax in *The Tempest*.[67] Hughes shared with Graves a 'sustained interest in the mythologies and folklores of the world', 'which', he says, 'had long preceded my interest in poetry and had in a way led me to poetry'.[68] He had also worked as an 'ideas man' for Peter Brook and he offers *Shakespeare and the Goddess* 'as a continuation of his dream (which was also mine) of a theatre simultaneously a revelation of spiritual being and an explosive image of life's infinite animal power and psychological abundance'; this recalls Moriarty's view that theatre could once again be a vehicle of renewal and regeneration.[69] We have seen that Hughes is not at all uninterested in history – *Goddess*, indeed, is centrally an analysis of the simultaneously psychosexual and spiritual effects of the Reformation – but Hughes agrees with Yeats, who furnishes one of his epigraphs: 'There is only one history, and that is the soul's.'

One advantage of Hughes's approach is that it captures something of the extra charge of meaning with which Shakespeare invests dialogue, scene and plot. This, as Hughes puts it, 'is recognized as a charisma strobing from everything the characters say and do – a radiant medium in which they move, like Yeats' Sages in "God's holy fire, as in the gold mosaic of a wall"'. 'This bigger effect,' he insists, 'comes from something more profoundly organized and substantial than a poetic effulgence from his electrified realism.'[70] *Goddess* makes it possible to recognise Shakespeare as a mythic poet. And the myth, Hughes contends, serves as 'a natural form of deep therapy, where the mythic plane holds the key to health, vitality, mean-ingfulness and psychic freedom' in the 'real' everyday world. 'The deeper understanding, the instinctive prompting, of ritual drama' recognises, he suggests, 'that a human being is only half alive if their life on the realistic, outer plane does not have the full assent and co-operation of their life on the mythic plane'. The artistic challenge 'is to objectify the mythic plane satisfactorily – so that it produces those benefits of therapeutic catharsis, social bonding and psychological renewal – without becoming unintelli-gible, and without spoiling the audience for adaptive, practical life on the realistic plane'.[71]

Hughes suggests that we nowadays have an urgent need of such ritual or mythic nourishment, because we increasingly live the thinned out and brittle life of the purely realistic plane, and this resonates to a degree with Adorno's diagnosis of an excessively mechanical rationalisation of life. Shakespeare offers mythic nourishment, but also an X-ray diagnosis of our predicament. *Goddess* in fact remarkably anticipates Iain McGilchrist's influential thesis in *The Master and His Emissary* that the rational and instrumental left brain's progressive dominance through human history over the more physically, emotionally and other orientated right brain has effected a grave impoverishment of human life.[72] According to Hughes, Shakespeare was onto this already: 'The Goddess myth is in the right side, while the (ultimately rational and secularizing) myth of the Goddess-destroyer is in the left side.'[73] Shakespeare, in other words, furnishes a myth that expresses the dangerous blockade on mythic nourishment that modern, left-brain attitudes entail. But Hughes also goes further than this. According to him, Shakespeare's poetry also, each time it's experi-enced, enacts a new, dialectical fusion between self-centred left-brain rationality and right-brain vision, emotion and identification with the world. In the process of reading Shakespeare, a metaphor, for instance, will effect 'a sudden flinging open of the door into the world of the right side, the world where the animal is not separated from either the spirit or the real world or itself'.[74] Moving between reason and passion, thought and image, Shakespeare achieves a 'balanced and sudden perfect co-operation of both sides of the brain', which constitutes 'a momentary restoration' of what Hughes calls 'perfect consciousness'. We feel this, Hughes suggests, 'as a convulsive expansion of awareness, of heightened reality, of the real truth revealed, of obscure joy, of crowding indefinite marvels, a sudden feeling of solidarity with existence, with oneself, with others, with all the possibilities of being'.[75] This extraordinary sensation of a sudden identification with being in all of its extensiveness is a tremendous experience of freedom, and who wouldn't want to partake of it? Shakespeare doesn't so much address 'the question of the human' here as he at least momentarily resolves it.

But if Shakespeare operates as deep therapy in this way, and therapy not just for personal life but for Western culture more broadly, criticism potentially rolls back all its gains into the sort of left-brain dominance which originally presented the problem. Hughes was mocked by critics for seeing boars in Shakespeare where there aren't any. Fair enough, except that the Boar which Hughes sees is an image, a right-brain apprehension of a powerfully felt truth. It has a clear Shakespearean origin, as the fatal antagonist in Shakespeare's most explicitly mythic poem; and, as Hughes argues, its tusks glint here and there throughout the canon. As we have seen, Hughes also feels its rushing charge in many other places. He discerns the Boar at the centre of the canon. Instead of describing it abstractly, he imagines it poetically as Shakespeare might have done. He is, after all, himself a poet.

I would suggest that Hughes's work deserves attention because it offers a thrillingly intense and serious picture of human existence which gives us a really significant Shakespeare: Shakespeare as the liberator of complete being. This works the darkness of the twentieth century into the tradition of Shakespearean freedom we have been examining in this book, and in the process produces powerfully exciting readings both of Shakespeare's total achievement and of specific plays. All we have to do is accept or entertain its terms. Thus when Hughes writes –

In *Hamlet* the suffering Adonis factor predominates, resisting the Boar for almost the entire play, keeping the centre of gravity within the Adonis point of view. In *Macbeth* the uncontrollable Boar predominates and the Adonis factor is helpless almost before Macbeth properly understands what the Witches are saying, letting the centre of gravity drop with a shock to the Boar's point of view.[76]

– he is saying something powerfully illuminating, something much more than just that Hamlet resists violence whereas Macbeth becomes its vehicle. Hughes's imagery of the Boar gives back the ontological threat and thickness to Shakespeare's plots which they already have in themselves, and which more abstract critical language is not well adapted to convey. Similarly, when Hughes writes of Macbeth 'living out, as none of the others does, that full subjective awareness of the Boar', it's not really the case that this corresponds in any very empirical way to Macbeth's agonised self-expression, but rather that Hughes's transgressive *incorporation* of the Boar into Shakespeare expresses something that does truly correspond with the menace, the adventure and the existential loneliness of Macbeth.[77] And when Hughes writes of 'the King's murder, when Tarquin "rapes" the Crown, and the Boar climbs into Duncan's slashed skin and stands up King of Scotland', it says more than you could get into paragraphs of standard-issue critical prose, powerfully resonating with the poet's creative response to *Macbeth* in *Crow*, and picking up on the demonstrable link between Tarquin and Macbeth who goes to murder Duncan 'with Tarquin's ravishing strides'. When the doomed Macbeth sees a flower child rising from the cauldron, Hughes remembers the resurrection of Adonis as a flower which Venus plucks and hugs between her breasts, suggesting that Macbeth is thereby afforded a brief and tragic glimpse of a redemption in fact reserved for later Shakespearean heroes: 'And so it is Macbeth and not Lear who actually makes the first breakthrough on to the spiritual plane – without understanding it. He is the Moses, who glimpses the Promised Land that he himself will never enter.'[78]

And Hughes is illuminating on *Lear* as well. He suggests that Lear is too weak and too old to become the Boar as Macbeth does, and as Tarquin did before him. 'Because he cannot surrender to it,' Hughes writes, 'Lear has to go on enduring its attack – untransformed. As if Adonis were clinging to the Boar's head, hanging on to its ears, wrestling with it, while it tears at him and flails about the heath.'[79] And yet, the force of the Boar cannot be dissipated; its pressure has to be somehow expressed, and so this first blocked trans-formation eventuates in another, a new version of the Adonis-like transfor-mation that Macbeth foresaw but could not attain. Thus Lear is reborn 'not a Tarquin, but the opposite of a Tarquin', 'not a Jehovan Goddess-killing tyrant, but an infantile, frail, brain-washed idiot savant, the child of his daughter': 'a new type in Shakespeare'.[80] It is not that Lear does not, first, reject the Goddess of Complete Being. Indeed, he of all Shakespeare's characters utters the most violently misogynistic speech:

> Down from the waist they are Centaurs,
> Though women all above.
> But to the girdle do the gods inherit.
> Beneath is all the fiends'; there's hell, there's darkness
> There is the sulphurous pit, burning, scalding,
> Stench, consumption! Fie, fie, fie! pah, pah!
>
> (*King Lear*, 4.6.121–6)

And yet, Hughes writes, 'he emerges, as on the opposite side of a Black Hole, into a new universe, punished, corrected, enlightened and transfigured, as a grey-haired babe, and the Goddess embraces him, correspondingly transformed, and wakens him with a kiss, as Cordelia.' As he movingly concludes, 'It is the same tableau that Shakespeare placed at the end of *Venus and Adonis*, but in this case Adonis is not only a flower, and is *alive*.'[81]

What Moriarty and Hughes ultimately find in Shakespeare is that we have given the wrong answer to 'the question of the human', making what amounts to a horrible cultural and religious error, which Hughes presents in terms of culpable and profound misogyny. It compromises who we are both individually and collectively; it constitutes a cramping and appalling unfreedom. But, according to *Shakespeare and the Goddess of Complete Being*, that, tragically, is our life, the life we inherit. There is no short cut to the right answer, not in life, not in thought which is honestly responsive to life. Moriarty wishes to undo the original repression and re-enter a larger human life and culture through a gate upon which Pasiphae is suckling her bull-headed baby: itself an honourable, monumental restitution of the female. But Hughes suggests we can only suffer our way through to the right answer, as Lear does. And, as Shakespeare makes plain, the road will be a perilous one. 'At bottom of both the Greek tragedy and Shakespeare's Tragic Equation' Hughes saw 'the same thing: "total, unconditional" Divine Love rejected'.[82] In less religious terms, he saw this as the tragic rejection of our own complete being, and specifically as rejection of the female. Like Moriarty, Hughes is honest enough to thrill to that dreadful rejection; and, given the gender spin he puts on it, it acquires a shocking gravity when we consider the tragedies of his own life. At the same time, and with corresponding intensity, Hughes yearns towards reconciliation and a better life, which he finds exemplified in Shakespeare's later plays.

For Hughes, 'only Shakespeare took the next step and discovered the second part of the Equation, in which Pentheus and Hippolytus, surviving the terrors of the Goddess, and having atoned, would be, like Leontes, spiritually transformed by their sufferings and his love.'[83] According to him, the human in Shakespeare is consummated as the actual realisation of complete being; and this isn't a wishful or sentimental thing because if on the one hand it represents a reconciliation with the Goddess, it is equally a reconciliation with the Boar. Hughes also encourages us to see such self-enlargement and integrity as at the same time politically hopeful – an augury of the end of violence, and above all of new and better relations between guilty men and male culture and the women whose lives and sheer spiritual and existential amplitude they have systematically violated and repressed.

With regard to what Hughes says about this simultaneously hopeful and dangerous emancipation, and particularly as we approach the end of this book, it seems appropriate to admit that there is an armchair aspect to literary criticism and, indeed, other aesthetic experience – an unedifying quality of taking at least some of the experiential thrill and all the cognitive gains involved in extreme experience without really risking anything. Maybe this vicarious type of encounter with life, often understood and discussed as catharsis, is really a sort of repression. But it seems clear that, in their respective books, both Moriarty and Hughes really are facing up to and wrestling with their own private terrors, Moriarty explicitly, Hughes less so; but then the catastrophes of Hughes's private life – the suicides of both Sylvia Plath and Assia Wevill, who also killed the daughter she had with Hughes – are so much public knowledge as to be painfully involved throughout the extraordinary story Hughes finds in Shakespeare of Goddess-violating, repentance and reconciliation.[84] And I am suggesting that in reading and responding to Shakespeare as they do, both Moriarty and Hughes are simultaneously struggling to understand, and even to see beyond, the horrors of the twentieth century that all of us in modernity inherit. Once again, Moriarty is more explicit about this, but Hughes's book is unmistakeably a twentieth-century production directly addressed to a dark, indeed a murderous cultural crisis. Moreover, the way that history, psychology and sexuality become one in Moriarty and Hughes suggests the nightmares of history may be powerfully at work in our personal histories even when we aren't aware of it. After what we have learned about ourselves from the gulags and the death camps, not to mention more recent crises such as Syria and Rwanda, perhaps these authors tell the story of Shakespearean freedom in the only way in which it can now be told. Certainly both men manifest, via their deeply engaged interpretations of Shakespeare, something of the 'pathology of cultural communities' Freud called for in *Civilization and Its Discontents.*

'Both *men*': I am aware that the story I have been telling in this final chapter is an especially male one, albeit that for Hughes it is about a desperate and guilty reconciliation with 'the Goddess'. In her classic critical study *The Haunting of Silvia Plath*, Jacqueline Rose suggests 'the logic of blame which seems to attach itself so relentlessly to the story of Sylvia Plath needs once and for all to be left behind.'[85] That is partly because the story of Plath, Hughes and their tragic marriage is just part of a bigger story of sex and sexual difference in which each of them and all of us are inextricably involved; no ascription of personal blame can threaten or even lay bare this larger narrative, which requires a more comprehensive structural analysis. Still, Rose does something less than justice to Hughes's interpretation of Shakespeare when she describes his Shakespearean 'Goddess of Complete Being' as an 'idealisation', 'an image of female purity'.[86] This doesn't even match the description of the Goddess which Rose herself quotes from Hughes as an 'overwhelmingly powerful, multiple, primaeval being'.[87] Hughes is intent on recovering the Goddess of *Complete Being*; his really isn't a pristine, patriarchal and thinned-out concept of the feminine.

In Rose's much more recent book *Women in Dark Times* (2014), the only Hughes referenced is to Howard, not Ted; but the 'scandalous feminism' Rose develops for a new century in fact recalls surprisingly closely the terms of Hughes's attempted recovery of the feminine by means of reading Shakespeare. 'One reason women are often so hated, I would suggest,' Rose writes, 'is because of their ability to force to the surface of the everyday parts of the inner life – its visceral reality, its stubborn unruliness – which in the normal course of our exchanges we like to think we have subdued.'[88] This is perfectly continuous with Hughes's Shakespearean diagnosis of a Tarquin-style violence in modern culture against a goddess who exposes too much of the teeming amplitude of complete being. 'But we kid ourselves,' Rose also writes, 'if we think that human fear of sexuality, and then the hatred of women which is so often its consequence, is something that the so-called reason of our modern world can simply and safely dissipate'; this well-made point accords with Hughes's grim insistence that the rehabilitation of the Goddess both in and beyond Shakespeare cannot but be grievously, indeed violently difficult.[89] Finally, when Rose says –

Let feminism, then, be the place in our culture which asks everyone, women and men, to recognise the failure of the present dispensation – its stiff-backed control, its ruthless belief in its own mastery, its doomed attempt to bring the uncertainty of the world to heel. Let feminism be the place where the most painful aspects of our inner world do not have to hide from the light, but are ushered forth as handmaidens to our protest.[90]

– she articulates a creed which closely mirrors that which Hughes expresses via his reading of the *Complete Works*. When he was most under attack by feminists, Hughes was in the habit of making defensive, rather bizarrely old-fashioned remarks about 'women's libbers', but, strange though it may seem to say so, *Shakespeare and the Goddess* is a book which yearns for women's liberation and what Rose wants in *Women in Dark Times* is very much in line with what Hughes wants too.[91]

Of course it makes an enormous difference for a woman rather than a man – let alone an especially guilty one – to say the sort of things which both Rose and Hughes, in their different ways, say about women. And what Rose says, unmediated as it is by Shakespeare, poetry or mythology, has the advantage of directness. But I would maintain that what Hughes says also has value. Hughes finds his Goddess of Complete Being at the heart of our most valued (male) writer. And because for him and Shakespeare (as men) identification with the Goddess has to involve transcendence of their (male) selves and atonement with what they (as men within patriarchal culture) have violated and repressed, this acquires an exemplary ethical power. But I should stress at this point that the plays themselves do not just affirm the feminine from a male point of view. As we saw in Chapter 2, Rosalind is a prime exemplar of Shakespearean freedom; and just as she so easily surpasses her male love-interest Orlando, Juliet is the great exemplar of the phenomenon in Shakespeare's master-piece of free love, *Romeo and Juliet*. Moreover, *Antony and Cleopatra* actually reverses Hughes's pattern. Of all Shakespeare's protagonists, Cleopatra already *is* the Goddess of Complete Being. She doesn't need rescuing; it is she who fishes out or perhaps invents and upholds a latent *God* of Complete Being in Antony, one whose arm crests the globe and whose delights are dolphin-like and so on (*Antony and Cleopatra*, 5.2.78 ff.). That said, Hughes does offer something important by bringing us back to the misogynistic violence that really is there in the plays and by showing us that Shakespeare is working through it towards a realistic and hard-won emancipation both of women and of human being and culture more broadly. In its own, idiosyncratic way, it opens the way for a credible recovery of Shakespearean freedom in dark times.

4   Conclusion

One of the best-known and most important things ever said about Shakespeare is this:

> At once it struck me what quality went to form a Man of Achievement, especially in Literature, and which Shakespeare possessed so enormously – I mean Negative Capability, that is, when a man is capable of being in uncertainties, mysteries, doubts, without any irritable reaching after fact and reason.[92]

Thus wrote John Keats in a letter to his brothers George and Thomas Keats, on 21 December 1817, and it remains an astonishingly brilliant and cherishable formulation, one which encourages us to see Shakespeare better, and to recognise his tremendous potential to unsettle and transcend conventional habits of thought. But there remains, at least to my mind, one big problem with Keats's dictum. Given my feminist reflections, the phrase 'Man of Achievement' perhaps already gives it away. Keats's formulation is like the theological argument from design, working back from creation to reveal the mind of the creator. I propose that instead we should stick with the creation directly manifest to us – stick, that is, with the plays which can never be identified with one agency or mind, but instead are forged and sustained precisely in the complex negotiation between different minds and agencies. If we do stick with the plays in this way, we will arrive not at Keats's bardolatry and the 'Man of Achievement' but rather at better appreciation of an art which encourages us to remain always, indefatigably open to the mobile, indeterminable possibilities engendered by the ongoing interaction of human selves. Such, I propose, is Shakespeare's politics of freedom. It is a politics that is necessarily vested in the individual freedom which Shakespeare as a great artist exemplifies; and which, as the creator of supremely lively dramatic characters, he dramatises: but it is equally a politics that is insistently tested by such individual freedom, and at times wrecked by it, as in *Macbeth*. Freedom, in Shakespeare, remains an irreducibly provisional thing, dangerous as well as promising.

The reckless, sometimes destructive way in which personal freedom sheers off from the politics of freedom in general has been a major theme of this book. According to Hegel, it is Shakespeare's commitment to personal freedom at all costs that marks the moral limit of his achievement, and we have seen how Shakespearean freedom precipitated real-world catastrophe when John Wilkes Booth assassinated Abraham Lincoln. Tolstoy felt Shakespeare was too free, too complicit with a degraded world that we should reject in favour of a better one. In the midst of the Second World War, Thomas Mann considered that Shakespeare's expressive freedom had effected a dangerous unmooring from real-world responsibility. It is in order to circumvent such wild excesses that Hegel wants the individual subject to identify his or her own subjectivity with the prospect of freedom for all. In *Civilization and Its Discontents*, Freud is not confident that individual freedom can ever be reconciled with the politics of freedom, while Adorno, for his part, can't see a way out of the rampant, barbaric culture of technological capitalism. Hughes doesn't minimise the difficulty and danger of trying to resolve what he sees as the crisis of contemporary culture, but he does offer a glint of hope. For him, Shakespeare's plays teach that the dark and dangerous kind of freedom which prevents the fruition of freedom in general has to be lived out to the end; but at that point it might be reconciled to a progressive ethics and politics of freedom for all, by means of what has traditionally been called repentance.

Reading Freud, Adorno and Mann strongly suggests that a Romantic view of Shakespearean freedom is unsustainable after the horrors of the twentieth century, and that no doubt is one of the salient reasons for the eclipse of Shakespearean freedom in our times; but I have suggested that Moriarty and Hughes can begin to help us imagine an integration of even the dark potentialities of freedom into the general good. Both writers, however, remain focused on major protagonists. And as we have seen in earlier chapters, the political breadth and promise of Shakespeare's dramatic polyphony cannot be restricted to this. In Chapter 7, I suggested that reading Shakespeare alongside Hegel's political philosophy can freshly reveal both, as well as that Hegel's vision of the ideal society needs only minimal adjustment to serve as an illuminating description of the politics of Shakespearean form. We can readily recognise a play of Shakespeare's as 'a fragmented being, self-sacrificing and benevolent, in which each character accomplishes his own work, rends asunder the universal being, and takes from it his own share'.[93] At another point in the *Phenomenology*, the philosopher describes the ideal society as a constellation of stars, 'countless self-luminous points' which are 'explicitly for themselves' and yet remain together 'through the sacrifice of their particularity'.[94] But a play of Shakespeare's, with its human characters struggling through dramas of desire and power, in fact brings this politics of freedom much more fully and completely to life than does Hegel's image, and not just in the mind's eye, but on a raised stage in the presence of a real audience.

It is natural to concentrate on Shakespeare's big stars; their freedom is realised most richly and spectacularly. But I have also tried to emphasise in these pages that Shakespeare has his little lights as well, such as the eunuch Mardian, who says in *Antony and Cleopatra*, 'Yet have I fierce affections and do think what Venus did with Mars' (1.5.17–18). In Chapter 3, I offered a new reading of *Romeo and Juliet* in terms of the interplay between the big stars (R and J themselves, of course) and the play's constant aspiration towards a broader, more inclusive freedom that is briefly embodied at its beginning as the spectre of an offstage 'Freetown' (1.1.100). In the context of Hegel's starry, constellated image of political freedom, one particular speech of Juliet's calls for additional comment:

> Come, gentle night, come, loving black-brow'd night,
> Give me my Romeo, and when I shall die
> Take him and cut him out in little stars,
> And he will make the face of heaven so fine
> That all the world will be in love with night
> And pay no worship to the garish sun.
>
> (3.2.20–24)[95]

In wanting to cut the big star Romeo out 'in little stars' after her death, the big star Juliet gestures towards a broader, more multifarious world not only such as Hegel describes, but also such as is more humanly embodied in the populous artifice of the very play she is presently playing in. I have argued that *Romeo and Juliet* struggles to imagine a free world not just for Romeo and Juliet but also for the outsider Mercutio – and, for that matter, the much more excluded, impecunious Apothecary, who has little choice but to sell to the hero the poison which kills both Romeo and his lover. Hegel helps us see that a larger, more accommodating politics of freedom is implied by the structure of an art form where a range of characters struggle to realise themselves more fully and freely, and Juliet's speech invites us to reflect on the interplay between the splendidly manifest albeit frustrated freedom of the tragedy's big stars and the more dispersed subjectivity of freedom in general. Juliet encourages us to see in this broader franchise a finer, more heavenly and ravishing prospect of con-stellated 'little stars', one which might even eclipse the big stars insofar as it makes them look just a touch 'garish' or vulgar. I have been arguing in this book that such dialectical interplay between flamboyant big stars and freedom in general generates the idea of 'Freetown' not just in *Romeo and Juliet* but in all of Shakespeare.

And such dramatic poetry of freedom isn't just a lovely image to delight what Hegel witheringly calls 'the beautiful soul'; no, it has inspired, as we have seen, real-world struggles for material change, from Cooper to Kossuth, from Kossuth to Mandela. At the first important Shakespeare celebration in 1769, Garrick was ridiculed for not including any Shakespeare, and I have suggested that it'd be difficult to celebrate Shakespeare today without at least doing one of the plays or reciting some poems. But I've also suggested that what Garrick did at Stratford presents Shakespeare less as heritage to be preserved at all costs than as a stimulus to new life. And the historical record shows that this inspiring power can't be neatly cordoned off in some separated aesthetic realm because it is just as much an existentially and politically motivating force. When he read Shakespeare for the first time, the young Goethe felt he had leapt into new being and discovered he had hands and feet. Boswell came to Stratford for the Garrick Jubilee dressed as a Corsican chief in solidarity with the international liberation movement. And for many other readers and theatre goers, Shakespeare has been a beacon for freedom, his characters positively exemplifying not just freedom of a personal kind but the struggle for political freedom for all. Cooper and Kossuth and other charismatic leaders in history have deliberately channelled and displayed to the world an explicitly Shakespearean condition of freedom which they were fighting to win for others. I think we need to get some of this inspiring power of Shakespearean freedom back. Hegel writes, 'everything depends on the spirit's self-awareness; if the spirit knows that it is free, it is altogether different from what it would be without this knowledge.' 'It is the sensation of freedom alone,' he goes on, 'which makes the spirit free.'[96] The ethical and ideological scepticism about freedom which is a major feature of our contemporary intellectual climate does not ultimately invalidate Shakespearean freedom. It makes it more important. Today, I'd suggest, it is more important than ever to learn from Shakespeare that we're free.

The plays, as we have recognised, are not in any simple way utopian. They are politically unstable, always in process. If they are sometimes ethically promising, at others they are undeniably dangerous. But I want to end this book by holding them up as an artifice and image of freedom as itself an inherently volatile and ambivalent but nonetheless extremely precious phenomenon. This – for me, for now – is why they matter. 'Workers need poetry more than bread,' writes Simone Weil, 'They need that their life should be a poem.'[97] I suggest that Shakespeare's plays are a dramatic poem of freedom, and not just for their heroes, but for us all.

What we do or do not make of them, in contemporary life and politics, is our responsibility.

Notes

1 Reclaiming Shakespearean Freedom

1. Jonathan Bate, *The Genius of Shakespeare* (London: Picador, 1997).
2. Bate, pp. 327–35.
3. Shakespeare references are, unless otherwise indicated, to the *Norton Shakespeare*, ed. Stephen Greenblatt (New York: Norton, 2008).
4. John Carey, *What Good Are the Arts?* (London: Faber and Faber, 2005).
5. Carey, p. 29.
6. Carey, p. 101; see also Hans and Shulamith Kreitler, *Psychology of the Arts* (Durham, NC: Duke University Press, 1972).
7. Carey, p. 135.
8. See Marghanita Laski, *Ecstasy: A Study of Some Secular and Religious Experiences* (London: The Cresset Press, 1961).
9. Frederic Spotts, *Hitler and the Power of Aesthetics* (London: Hutchinson, 2002).
10. Carey, p. 214.
11. Carey, pp. 216, 217.
12. Carey, pp. 247–8.
13. See Paul Prescott, 'Shakespeare and the Dream of Olympism', in *Shakespeare on the Global Stage: Performance and Festivity in the Olympic Year*, ed. Paul Prescott and Erin Sullivan (London: Bloomsbury, 2015), p. 4. For more on Shakespeare and the 2012 Olympics, see Erin Sullivan, 'Olympic Performance in the Year of Shakespeare', in Paul Edmondson, Paul Prescott and Erin Sullivan (eds.), *A Year of Shakespeare: Reliving the World Shakespeare Festival* (London: Bloomsbury, 2013), pp. 3–11; Stephen Purcell, '"What Country, Friends, Is This?": Cultural Identity and the World Shakespeare Festival', *Shakespeare Survey* 66 (2014), 155–65; Richard Wilson, 'Like an Olympian Wrestling: Shakespeare's Olympic Game', *Shakespeare Survey* 66 (2014), 82–95.
14. Sullivan, p. 4.
15. Sullivan, p. 4.
16. Colette Gordon writes, 'Shakespeare's mawkish appearance both as architect-apologist for modernization and the voice of the slave, asked audiences to mind the gap' ('Mind the gap': Globalism, Postcolonialism and Making up Africa in the Cultural Olympiad', in Prescott and Sullivan (eds.), pp. 191–227; p. 195).
17. See Aimé Césaire, *Une tempête: d'après "la Tempête" de Shakespeare; Adaptation pour un théâtre négre* (Paris: Seuil, 1969).
18. Bate, pp. 248–9.
19. Laurence M. Porter, 'Aimé Césaire's Reworking of Shakespeare: Anticolonialist Discourse in "Une Tempête"', *Comparative Literature Studies* 32.3 (1995), 360–81, 375.
20. Harold Bloom, *Shakespeare: The Invention of the Human* (New York: Riverhead Books, 1998), p. 662.

21. Leslie A. Fiedler, 'Caliban as the American Indian', in *Shakespeare, the Tempest: A Selection of Critical Essays*, rev. edn., ed. D. J. Palmer (London: Macmillan, 1991), p. 172; extracted from the same author's *The Stranger in Shakespeare* (London: Croom Helm, 1973).

22. Derek Walcott, *Collected Poems* (London: Faber, 1992), p. 483.

23. Prescott has observed that in 2009–10 the Royal Mint issued its 'Celebration of Britain Silver Proof Collection', including 'a coin devoted to "Tolerance"'. This 'featured a well-dressed black man in late Georgian / early Victorian clothes, an unidentifiable book in his right hand, and to his left the words "Abolition of SLAVERY" and "BRITISH DOMINION, January the 24th 1825". That was not all. Between the man's head and the mandatory 2012 logo were the words "To thine own self be true"' (pp. 16–17). The figure pictured was 'Olaudah Equiano, a former slave who managed to earn enough money to buy his own freedom and campaigned assiduously against slavery' (p. 18). But this was too early to make much impact on the Olympics. And as with the materials I analyse here, the potential association of Shakespeare and freedom is partly obscured and nominated as something else: 'Tolerance'. Prescott, in addition, troublingly juxtaposes it with the report of 'a Royal Marine sergeant murdered a severely wounded Afghan insurgent … [breaking] the Geneva Convention and saying, "There you are, shuffle off this mortal coil you cunt"' (p. 20). I shall argue in this book that such wicked freedom cannot, alas, be entirely dissociated from the struggle for political freedom in Shakespeare, and perhaps more generally.

24. 'Intriguingly,' writes Sullivan, 'the origin of these rather bemusing lines … remains unclear' (p. 6). Purcell's remarks show how central this episode was animated by a political impulse: 'the ceremony's climax featured both McKellen and Miles-Wildin waving placards for "Equality" (in a clear nod to McKellen's activism as a gay rights campaigner) while Graeae Theatre Company played the song "Spasticus Autisticus"' (p. 164). He sees the whole thing as keyed to 'progressive politics and social optimism' (p. 164).

25. Prescott, p. 2.

26. See Frank Cottrell Boyce, 'Foreword', in Humphrey Jennings, *Pandæmonium: The Coming of the Machine as Seen by Contemporary Observers*, ed. Marie-Louise Jennings and Charles Madge (London: Icon, 2012), p. xii.

27. Frank Cottrell Boyce, Tom Bird and Tracy Irish, in Prescott and Sullivan (eds.), 'Performing Shakespeare in the Olympic Year: Interviews with Three Practitioners', pp. 43–79; p. 48.

28. William Shakespeare, *William Shakespeare: The Complete Works*, ed. Peter Alexander (London: Collins, 1951). A picture of this page appears on page 269 of Jonathan Bate and Dora Thornton, *Shakespeare: Staging the World* (Oxford: Oxford University Press, 2012).

29. Bate and Thornton, p. 269.

30. Katherine Duncan-Jones agrees that Mandela's name being beside the passage suggests 'that he didn't expect to emerge alive, but was characteristically stoical about that prospect' (Katherine Duncan-Jones, 'The world Shakespeare festival – authentic or eccentric?' (www.the-tls.co.uk/tls/public/article1099143.ece (accessed 16 September 2014)).

31. Neil MacGregor, *Shakespeare's Restless World: An Unexpected History in Twenty Objects* (London: Penguin, 2012), p. 284.
32. David Schalkwyk, *Hamlet's Dreams: The Robben Island Shakespeare* (London: Arden, 2012), p. 13.
33. In his pioneering *Shakespeare Against Apartheid*, Martin Orkin argued that the supposedly non-political Shakespeare who was taught in South Africa during apartheid had facilitated the white supremacism of that regime (Martin Orkin, *Shakespeare Against Apartheid* (Craighall, Johannesburg: Ad. Donker, 1997)). David Johnson's *Shakespeare in South Africa* argued that this guilt extended even to the engagement with Shakespeare of native South Africans such as Sol T. Plaatje (David Johnson, *Shakespeare and South Africa* (Oxford: Clarendon, 1996)). But Natasha Distiller's later, revisionary account argues, contra Orkin and Johnson, that Shakespeare, humanism and liberalism had also made a positive contribution to the resistance against apartheid and to black South African identity (Natasha Distiller, *South Africa, Shakespeare, and Post-Colonial Culture* (New York: Edwin Mellen Press, 2005)).
34. Quoted in MacGregor, p. 283.
35. Schalkwyk, p. 34.
36. See Schalkwyk, p. 34; see also Ashwin Desai, *Reading Revolution: Shakespeare on Robben Island* (Pretoria: UNISA Press, 2012), pp. 13–14.
37. Schalkwyk, p. 23.
38. Schalkwyk, p. 63.
39. Quoted in Schalkwyk, p. 63; see also Nelson Mandela, *Long Walk to Freedom* (London: Holt, Rinehart and Winston, 2000), p. 445.
40. Schalkwyk, pp. 65–6.
41. Schalkwyk, p. 72.
42. Schalkwyk, p. 73.
43. Schalkwyk, p. 72.
44. Schalkwyk, p. 159.
45. Schalkwyk, p. 24.
46. Schalkwyk, p. 159.
47. Schalkwyk, p. xiii.
48. Gordon has shown how the emphasis on 'the old unity of the struggle' that was encapsulated by the story of the Robben Island Bible 'suited the mood and intellectual agenda of the "Mbeki years" (1999–2008) following Mandela's presidency' but that Jacob Zuma's rise to power exposed 'tensions, refusals, uncertainties and shifts of allegiance' within the ANC and between those who had fought for freedom with Mandela undermined this (pp. 210–11).
49. Quotations are from 'Presentation of the Shakespeare Testimonial to Kossuth'. The source appears to be the *Illustrated London News*, 15 May 1853, page number unknown. See Lemuel Matthews Griffiths, *Newspaper Cuttings Relating to Shakespeare* at the Library of Birmingham, vol. 11, p. 88; see also Andrew Murphy, *Shakespeare for the People: Working-Class Readers, 1800–1900* (Cambridge: Cambridge University Press, 2008), p. 149, which originally led me to Griffiths. I supplement this with the speech that Douglas Jerrold gave when presenting the Shakespeare Testimonial to Kossuth and the account of the event

as given in Walter Jerrold's *Douglas Jerrold, Dramatist and Wit*, vol. 2 (London: Hodder and Stoughton, 1918).

50. Tibor Frank, '"Give Me Shakespeare": Lajos Kossuth's English as an Instrument of International Politics', in Holgar Klein and Péter Dávidházi (eds.), *Shakespeare and Hungary*, A Publication of the Shakespeare Yearbook, vol. 7 (Lewiston /Queenston/Lampeter: The Edwin Mellen Press, 1996), pp. 47–75.

51. Frank, pp. 54–5. See also Istvan Deak, *The Lawful Revolution: Louis Kossuth and the Hungarians 1848–1849* (New York: Columbia University Press, 1979), p. 13.

52. Deak, pp. 40–41.

53. Deak, p. 36.

54. Christopher Clark, *Iron Kingdom: The Rise and Downfall of Prussia 1600–1947* (London: Penguin, 2007), p. 499.

55. Dezső Keresztury, 'Shakespeare and the Hungarians', *The New Hungarian Quarterly* (13, Spring 1964), 3–9; 19.

56. Deak, pp. 314–15.

57. See ER149/33: 'Our Representatives. XXII. – The School Board (Continued), Mr George Dawson', *Volume of newspaper cuttings related to local, national and international events: includes obituaries of Mazzini, J. S. Mill and David Livingstone as well as accounts of political and religious events in Birmingham*, Misellanous Cuttings, 1872–1875, p. 92 (Shakespeare Centre Library and Archive). Dawson sustained his serious commitment to Shakespeare in tandem with his serious commitment to Kossuth. The Shakespeare Centre Library and Archive holds a note in Kossuth's hand which reads 'received from Revd. George Dawson as the proceeds of my lectures at Birmingham, London May 14, 1856' together with a small photographic portrait of himself that Dawson had evidently presented to the Hungarian in which he looks at once gravely committed and leonine (DR1136/3/2/ 89: Kossuth note: Garside collection; other letters, 14 May 1856 (Shakespeare Centre Library and Archive)).

58. John Alfred Langford, *Modern Birmingham and Its Institutions: A Chronicle of Local Events, from 1841–71*, vol. 1 (Osbourne: Birmingham, 1873), pp. 401–4.

59. I quote from The Project Gutenberg EBook of *Select Speeches of Kossuth, by Kossuth, Condensed and Abridged, with Kossuth's Express Sanction* by Francis W. Newman: www.gutenberg.org/cache/epub/10691/pg10691.html (accessed 30 October 2014).

60. Abraham Lincoln, *Lincoln on Democracy*, ed. Mario Matthew Cuomo and Harold Holzer (New York: Fordham Universty Press, 2004), p. 376.

61. See Misha Glenny, *The Balkans 1804–1999: Nationalism, War and the Great Powers* (London: Granta, 2000), p. 49. A contemporary account which argues that Kossuth risked Serbian and Croatian interests by flirting with a Russian alliance is Anon, *Kossuth. Six Chapters. By a Hungarian* (London: Robert Hardwicke, 38, Carey Street, Lincoln's Inn, 1854). And it is worth noting that this text tries to turn Kossuth's Shakespearean celebrity against him by taking liberties with *Othello* as an epigraph: 'Nothing extenuated, nor set down aught in malice.'

62. See Deak, p. 314.

63. See Deak, p. 349.

64. See Deak, pp. 344–5.
65. Ralph Waldo Emerson, 'Address to Kossuth at Concord, May 11, 1852', in *The Complete Works of Ralph Waldo Emerson with a Biographical Introduction and Notes by Edward Waldo Emerson and a General Index*, vol. XI: Miscellanies (Cambridge, MA: The Riverside Press, 1906), p. 399.
66. Emerson, p. 400.
67. Emerson, p. 399.
68. Peter Ackroyd, *Dickens* (London: Minerva, 1991), p. 224.
69. *Harper's New Monthly Magazine*, vol. IV, 1852, 277.
70. www.accessible-archives.com/collections/african-american-newspapers/frederick-douglass-paper/ (accessed 30 July 2015).
71. Jerrold, pp. 595–6.
72. 278973: Autograph letter signed from Douglas Jerrold, Putney, to Thornton Hunt, Leader [manuscript] (The Folger Shakespeare Library). The Folger dates this MS 21 November 1850; but I suggest that 1852 is much more likely.
73. 260328: Autograph letter signed Douglas Jerrold, West Lodge, Putney, to Charles Gilpin [manuscript], 19th century (The Folger Shakespeare Library). The Folger dates this 5 December; I suggest, again, that it dates from 1852.
74. 281474: Autograph letter signed from Lajos Kossuth, Regent's Park, London, to Charles Gilpin [manuscript], 1853, 3 May (The Folger Shakespeare Library).
75. Jerrold, p. 596.
76. Jerrold, p. 599.
77. Frank has shown that Kossuth's claim to have learned English from Shakespeare was so much repeated and embellished over the course of the nineteenth century as to come 'closest to a literary *topos*, almost Shakespearean in nature', one by means of which Shakespeare became 'identified with freedom itself, and found his place in both Kossuth lore and in the realm of international political symbolism' (p. 47).
78. Jonathan Dollimore, *Radical Tragedy: Religion, Ideology and Power in the Drama of Shakespeare and His Contemporaries*, 3rd edn. (1984; Basingstoke, Hampshire: Palgrave, 2004), p. xv.
79. Jerrold, p. 599.
80. Jerrold, p. 599.
81. 'Kossuth was recently presented with a copy of Shakespeare, paid for by subscriptions of one penny each, by 20,000 English workmen', *Frederick Douglass' Paper* (10 June 1853): www.accessible-archives.com/collections/african-american-newspapers/frederick-douglass-paper/ (accessed 13 July 2015).
82. Dollimore, p. 271
83. See Eric Hobsbawm, *The Age of Revolution 1789–1848* (1962; repr. London: Abacus, 2014).
84. Hobsbawm, p. 141.
85. Thomas Mann, *The Genesis of a Novel*, trans. Richard and Clara Winston (London: Secker and Warburg, 1961), p. 89.
86. See Hannah Arendt, *Between Past and Future: Eight Exercises in Political Thought* (New York: Penguin Books, 1977), pp. 169, 156.

87. Jonathan Bate, *Shakespearean Constitutions: Politics, Theatre, Criticism, 1730–1830* (Oxford: Clarendon Press, 1989), p. 213.

88. Ania Loomba and Martin Orkin, 'Introduction', in *Post-Colonial Shakespeares*, ed. Ania Loomba and Martin Orkin (London and New York: Routledge, 1998), p. 19.

89. Alexander [now Alexa] C. Y. Huang, 'Global Shakespeares as Methodology', *Shakespeare* 9.3 (2012), 273–90; 284.

90. Simon Winder, *Danubia: A Personal History of Habsburg Europe* (London: Picador, 2014), p. 331.

91. Clark, pp. 486–7.

92. Edwin Morgan, 'Louis Kossuth', *London Review of Books* 24.11 (6 June 2002).

93. Morgan, Letters, *London Review of Books* 24.14 (25 July 2002).

94. Morgan, 'Louis Kossuth'.

95. See, for example, G. Wilson Knight, *The Wheel of Fire: Interpretations of Shakespearean Tragedy, with Three New Essays*, 4th rev. and enl. edn. (London: Methuen, 1949), p. 271.

96. Quoted in Deak, pp. 345–6; cf. Karl Marx to Bertalan Szemere (London, 26 September 1859), and Marx, 'Patrons and Vagrants', in *Herr Vogt*, both of which Deak cites from John Komlos's unpublished manuscript, 'Karl Marx's Critique of Louis Kossuth'. See Jonathan Sperber, *Karl Marx: A Nineteenth-Century Life* (New York: Liveright, 2013) pp. 275–6.

97. Terry Eagleton, *Why Marx Was Right* (New Haven and London: Yale University Press, 2011), pp. 86–7.

98. Sperber, p. 209.

99. See Sperber, p. 489.

100. Quoted in R. S. White, 'Marx and Shakespeare', *Shakespeare Survey* 45 (1992), 89–100; p. 95. See also Karl Marx and Friedrich Engels, *Werke* (Herausgegeben vom Institut für Marxismus beim ZK der SED, Berlin, 1956–68) pp. 40, 420.

101. See, for example, 'A Short Organum for the Theatre', in Bertholt Brecht, *Brecht on Theatre: The Development of an Aesthetic*, ed. and trans. John Willett (London: Methuen Drama, 1978), p. 189.

102. 'Bertolt Brecht's entire attempt to rewrite tragedy – literally to rewrite past tragedies and in the process to evolve a new conception of it – can be seen as an attempt to overcome the Western theology of failure' (Jonathan Dollimore, 'Shakespeare and Theory', in Loomba and Orkin (eds.), p. 267). See also Herbert Marcuse, 'The Ideology of Death', in *The Meaning of Death*, ed. H. Feifel (New York: McGraw Hill), pp. 64–75.

103. Ryan presents Shakespearean tragedy as dramatising 'the heartbreaking contradiction between what men and women could be, and what time and place condemn them to become, in spite of the superior selves and fuller lives struggling within them for realization' (Kiernan Ryan, *Shakespeare*, 3rd edn. (Houndmills, Basingstoke: Palgrave, 2002), p. 71).

104. Jerrold, p. 595.

105. Jerrold, p. 598.

106. Jerrold, p. 599.

107. Deak, p. 350.

2   Shakespeare Means Freedom

1. Sir Philip Sidney, *A Defence of Poetry*, in *Miscellaneous Prose of Sir Philip Sidney*, ed. Katherine Duncan Jones (Oxford: Clarendon Press, 1973), p. 78.
2. Ben Jonson, *Timber, or Discoveries*, in *The Works of Ben Jonson*, ed. C. H. Herford and P. and E. Simpson (11 vols, Oxford: Oxford University Presss, 1925–52), vol. 8, pp. 583–4.
3. Matthew Arnold, 'Shakespeare', in *The Poems of Matthew Arnold*, ed. Kenneth Allot (London: Longman, 1965), p. 48.
4. See Richard Wilson, *Free Will: Art and Power on Shakespeare's Stage* (Manchester: Manchester University Press, 2013), p. 8. See also Michel Foucault, '25 February 1976', in *'Society Must Be Defended': Lectures at the Collège de France, 1975–6*, ed. Mauro Bertini and Allesandro Fontana, trans. David Macey (London: Allen Lane, 2003), pp. 172–7 and 'Dream, Imagination and Existence', in *Dream and Existence: Michel Foucault and Ludwig Binswanger*, trans. and ed. Keith Hoeller (Atlantic Highlands, NJ: Humanities Press, 1993), pp. 53–4.
5. See Jonathan Dollimore and Alan Sinfield (ed.), *Political Shakespeare*, 2nd edn. (Manchester: Manchester University Press, 2012). Margot Heinemann's essay, 'How Brecht Read Shakespeare', includes the quotation from Nigel Lawson (p. 227).
6. Alvin Kernan, *Shakespeare the King's Playwright* (New Haven: Yale University Press, 1995), p. 95.
7. Jonathan Bate, *The Genius of Shakespeare* (London: Picador, 1997), p. 230.
8. Peter Holbrook, *Shakespeare's Individualism* (Cambridge: Cambridge University Press, 2010), p. 137.
9. See Richard Wolin, *Walter Benjamin: An Aesthetics of Redemption* (New York: Columbia University Press, 1982). I take the notion of 'counter-memory' from Michel Foucault, *Language, Counter-Memory, Practice: Selected Essays and Interviews*, ed. Donald F. Bouchard, trans. Donald F. Bouchard and Sherry Simon (Ithaca, NY: Cornell University Press, 1977). For a discussion from within Shakespeare studies of counter-memory as a force which works against the better-known totalising tendency in Foucault, see Hugh Grady *Shakespeare's Universal Wolf: Studies in Early Modern Reification* (Oxford: Clarendon, 1996), pp. 47–52 and *Shakespeare, Machiavelli, and Montaigne* (Oxford: Oxford University Press, 2002), p. 195.
10. Walter Benjamin, *Illuminations*, ed. and intro. Hannah Arendt, trans. Harry Zorn (London: Pimlico, 1999), pp. 247.
11. Benjamin, p. 254.
12. Hugh Grady is good on this aspect of the Henriad and *Hamlet* in *Shakespeare, Machiavelli and Montaigne*.
13. Benjamin, p. 249.
14. Virginia Woolf, 'On Being Ill', in *Selected Essays*, ed. David Bradshaw, Oxford World Classics (Oxford: Oxford University Press, 2008), p. 108.
15. Conversation with Friedrich von Müller, 1827, in *Goethes Gespräche*, ed. W. fhrh von Biedermann, 5 vols (Leipzig: Biedermann, 1909–11), vol. 4, p. 477: 'Ein Kunstwerk, besonders ein Gedicht, das nichts zu erraten übrig liesse, sei kein

wahres, vollwürdiges. Seine höchste Bestimmung bleibe immer, zum Nachdenken aufzuregen, und nur dadurch könne es dem … Leser recht lieb werden, wenn es ihn zwänge, nach eigener Sinnesweise es sich auszulegen und gleichsam ergänzend nachzuschaffen.' I am grateful to David Fuller for this quotation.

16. John Russell Brown, *Free Shakespeare* (London: Heinemann, 1974), p. 3.
17. Theodor Adorno, *Aesthetic Theory*, ed. Gretel Adorno and Rolf Tiedmann, trans. Robert Hullot Kentnor (Minneapolis: University of Minnesota Press, 1997), p. 213; G. W. F. Hegel, 'Dramatic Poetry', from *Aesthetics: Lectures on Fine Art*, in *Philosophers on Shakespeare*, ed. Paul Kottman (Stanford: University of Stanford Press, 2009), p. 70. The Kottman collection makes the most pertinent portion of the *Aesthetics* conveniently available for Shakespeareans, and I quote from it where possible. It is excerpted from the culminating section of G. W. F. Hegel's *Aesthetics: Lectures on Fine Art*, trans. T. M. Knox, vols 1 and 2 (Oxford: Clarendon Press, 1975), vol. 2, pp. 1158–237.
18. See Jonathan Dollimore and David Jonathan Y. Bayot, *Jonathan Dollimore in Conversation* (Manila: De La Salle University Publishing House, 2013), p. 45.
19. Quoted in Jonathan Dollimore, *Radical Tragedy: Religion, Ideology and Power in the Drama of Shakespeare and his Contemporaries*, 3rd edn. (Basingstoke, Hampshire: Palgrave, 2004), p. xxxv.
20. Wilson, p. 58. Shakespeare references are, unless otherwise indicated, to the *Norton Shakespeare*, ed. Stephen Greenblatt (New York: Norton, 2008).
21. See Stephen Greenblatt, *Renaissance Self-Fashioning: From More to Shakespeare* (Chicago: University of Chicago Press, 1980) and Bate, pp. 327–35.
22. For an excellent suggestive essay on gender and Shakespearean verse, see Margaret Tudeau-Clayton, '"The Lady shall say her mind freely": Shakespeare and the S/Pace of Blank Verse', in *Shakespeare and Space: Theatrical Explorations of the Spatial Paradigm*, ed. Ina Habermann and Michelle Witen (Houndmills, Basingstoke: Palgrave, 2016), pp. 79–102.
23. A. C. Bradley, 'The Rejection of Falstaff', in *Shakespeare: King Henry IV Parts 1 and 2*, Casebook Series, ed. G. K. Hunter (London: Macmillan, 1970), p. 69.
24. Robert Graves and Laura Riding, *Contemporary Techniques of Poetry: A Political Analogy*, Hogarth Essays No. 8 (London: The Hogarth Press, 1925), p. 24.
25. George Saintsbury, *A History of English Prosody from the Twelfth Century to the Present Day* (London: Macmillan, 1906–1910), 3 vols, vol. I, p. 345.
26. George T. Wright, *Shakespeare's Metrical Art* (Berkeley: University of California Press, 1988), p. 257.
27. Wright, p. 282.
28. Wright, p. 257.
29. Heinrich von Kleist, 'The Puppet Theatre', in *Selected Writings*, ed. and trans. David Constantine (1810; Indianapolis/Cambridge: Hackett Publishing, 2004), pp. 411–16.
30. See John Gray, *The Soul of the Marionette: A Short Enquiry into Human Freedom* (Allen Lane: London, 2015). Gray uses the phrase 'the harlequinade of politics' apropos of the philosopher Leopardi on page 36. He bemoans the poor prospects for political freedom in times where civil liberty is being eroded and there is unprecedented surveillance: 'If freedom of any kind can be found in these

conditions, it is some version of the inward variety that was prized by thinkers of the ancient world' (p. 162). Shami Chakrabarty has recently given a cogent and disturbing overview of the parlous state of personal and political freedom in our time in *On Liberty* (London: Allen Lane, 2014). For the quotation about Übermarionettes, see Gray, pp. 165–6. For an intelligent and suggestive treatment of puppet theatre in relation to Shakespearean theatricality, see Kenneth Gross, 'Puppets Dallying: Thoughts on Shakespearean Theatricality', *Comparative Drama* 41.3 (2007), pp. 273–96. See also Kenneth Gross, *Puppet: An Essay on Uncanny Life* (Chicago: University of Chicago Press, 2011).

31. On this point, see especially Robert Weimann, *Shakespeare and the Popular Tradition in the Theater: Studies in the Social Dimension of Dramatic Form and Function*, ed. Robert Schwarz (Baltimore and London: Johns Hopkins University Press, 1978) and Robert Weimann, *Author's Pen and Actor's Voice: Playing and Writing in Shakespeare's Theatre* (Cambridge: Cambridge University Press, 2000).

32. Quoted in Wilson, p. 372. See also Jürgen Habermas, *The Structural Transformation of the Public Sphere*, trans. Thomas Burger and Frederick Lawrence (Cambridge: Polity Press, 1989), pp. 38–9, 49.

33. See Wilson, p. 376. See also the Swiss tourist Thomas Platter's observation in 1600 that 'everyone has a good view' (Thomas Platter, *Thomas Platter's Travels in England*, trans. Clare Williams (London: Jonathan Cape, 1937), p. 167).

34. Stephen Greenblatt, *Shakespeare's Freedom* (Chicago and London: University of Chicago Press, 2010), p. 1.

35. Greenblatt, *Shakespeare's Freedom*, p. 58.

36. Greenblatt, *Shakespeare's Freedom*, pp. 18–48.

37. Holbrook, p. 23.

38. John Middleton Murray, *Shakespeare* (London: Jonathan Cape, 1936), pp. 19–21; quoted in Holbrook, pp. 145–6; Holbrook's emphasis.

39. See Chakrabarty.

40. Coppélia Kahn, *Roman Shakespeare: Warriors, Wounds and Women* (London: Routledge, 1997), p. 116.

41. See, for example, Leonard Tennenhouse, *Power on Display: The Politics of Shakespeare's Genres* (New York and London: Methuen, 1986).

42. Dympna Callaghan argues that Webster's Duchess, purely by dint of being female, in fact isn't qualified to represent the supposedly 'universal human situation'. Her response is comprehensively to reject tragic universalism, asserting political particularity instead (*Women and Gender in Renaissance Tragedy: A Study of King Lear, Othello, The Duchess of Malfi and The White Devil* (Hemel Hempstead: Harvester Wheatsheaf, 1989), p. 68).

43. Susan Snyder considers the 'de-characterization of Helen' and different interpretations of it in her Oxford edition of *All's Well that Ends Well* (Oxford: Oxford University Press, 1998), 'Introduction', p. 40.

44. Hegel, p. 59. So far as aesthetics goes, that is; in religion, modern individuality emerges with the Reformation: see G. W. F. Hegel, *The Philosophy of History*, trans. J. Silbree (New York: Dover, 1956), pp. 416–17.

45. See Kottman's introduction to Hegel's 'Dramatic Poetry', p. 12.

46. Peter Holbrook, *English Renaissance Tragedy: Ideas of Freedom* (London: Bloomsbury, 2015), p. 4; see also, R. H. Tawney, *Equality* (London: Unwin Books, 1964), p. 235.

47. See Andrew Hadfield, *Shakespeare and Republicanism* (Cambridge: Cambridge University Press, 2005).

48. Jonathan Dollimore, *Radical Tragedy*, p. xxxv.

49. Gray, p. 6; Erich Fromm, *Escape from Freedom* (New York and Toronto: Rinehart & Company, Inc., 1941), p. 32.

50. Jean-Paul Sartre, *Being and Nothingness*, trans. Hazel E. Barnes (New York: Philosophical Library, 1956), p. 440.

51. This is a main theme of *Escape from Freedom*.

52. See Jean Paul Sartre, *Kean or Disorder and Genius*, trans. Kitty Black, in *Three Plays: Kean, Nekrassov, The Trojan Women* (Penguin: London, 1969), 4.1, pp. 76–7.

53. John Stuart Mill, *On Liberty: With, The Subjection of Women* and, *Chapters on Socialism*, ed. Stefan Collini (Cambridge: Cambridge University Press, 1989).

54. Mill, p. 20.

55. Mill, p. 8.

56. Mill, p. 35.

57. See William Hazlitt, 'A Letter to William Gifford, Esq.' (1819), *Complete Works*, ed. P. P. Howe, 21 vols (London: Frank Cass and Company, 1967), vol. 9, p. 50; and *Characters of Shakespear's Plays* (1817), vol. 4, p. 214.

58. Hazlitt, *Characters of Shakespear's Plays*, pp. 214–15.

59. Jonathan Bate, *Shakespearean Constitutions: Politics, Theatre, Criticism 1730–1830* (Oxford: Clarendon Press, 1989), p. 168.

60. Hazlitt, *Characters of Shakespear's Plays*, p. 214.

61. Jacques Derrida, *Specters of Marx: The State of the Debt, the Work of Mourning, and the New International*, trans. Peggy Kamuf (London: Routledge, 1994), p. 168.

62. Jacques Derrida, *Acts of Religion*, ed. and trans. Gil Anidjar (London: Routledge, 2002), p. 289.

63. See, for instance, Slavoj Žižek, *The Puppet and the Dwarf: The Perverse Core of Christianity* (Cambridge, MA: MIT Press, 2003), which reads the Incarnation in Christianity as a signal that we have to fight the good fight politically here and now.

64. Gillian Rose, *The Broken Middle: Out of Our Ancient Society* (Oxford: Blackwell, 1992).

65. See Jacqueline Rose, *Women in Dark Times* (London: Bloomsbury, 2014), p. 41. Hannah Arendt writes, 'To destroy individuality is to destroy spontaneity, man's power to begin something new out of his own resources.' Hannah Arendt, *The Origins of Totalitarianism* (1951; New York: Harcourt Brace Jovanovich, 1979), p. 455.

66. Quoted in Jacqueline Rose, p. 79; see also Marion Milner, *On Not Being Able to Paint* (1950; London: Heinemann, 1957), p. 143.

67. Quoted in Jacqueline Rose, p. 41. See also Adrienne Rich, 'Raya Dunayevskaya's Marx', *Arts of the Possible* (New York: Norton, 2001), p. 85.

68. Quoted in Jacqueline Rose, p. 41; see also Rosa Luxemburg, 'The Russian Revolution' (1918), in *The Russian Revolution and Leninism or Marxism?*,

Introduction by Bertram B. Wolfe (Ann Arbor: University of Michigan Press, 1961), p. 70.

69. David Pan, 'Preface to the English Translation', in Carl Schmitt, *Hamlet or Hecuba: The Intrusion of Time into the Play*, trans. David Pan and Jennifer Rust (New York: Telos Press Publishing, 2009), p. vii. For an overview of Schmitt's influence on Shakespeare studies to 2009, see Jennifer R. Rust, 'Political Theology and Shakespeare Studies', *Literature Compass* 6.1 (2009), 175–90. For a critical response to this work, see Andreas Höfele, 'Hamlet in Plettenberg: Carl Schmitt's Shakespeare', *Shakespeare Survey* 65 (2012), 378–97.

70. Carl Schmitt, *Political Theology: Four Chapters on Sovereignty* (Cambridge, MA: MIT Press, 1985), p. 5.

71. Rodney Symington, *The Nazi Appropriation of Shakespeare. Cultural Politics in the Third Reich* (Lewiston, NY: Mellen, 2005), p. 190.

72. See Nietzsche on *Macbeth*: Friedrich Nietzsche, *Daybreak: Thoughts on the Prejudices of Morality*, trans. R. J. Hollingdale, intro Michael Tanner (Cambridge: Cambridge University Press, 1982), pp. 140–41.

73. Howard Barker, 'The House of Infection: Theatre in the Age of Social Hygiene', in *Arguments for a Theatre*, 3rd edn. (Manchester: Manchester University Press, 1997), p. 186.

74. See Fyodor Dostoevsky, *Crime and Punishment*, trans. Richard Pevear and Larissa Volokhonsky (New York: Knopf, 1993).

3   'Freetown!' (*Romeo and Juliet*)

1. Michael Dobson, *Shakespeare and Amateur Performance: A Cultural History* (Cambridge: Cambridge University Press, 2011), p. 2.

2. Bernice Kliman, 'At Sea About *Hamlet* at Sea: A Detective Story', *Shakespeare Quarterly* 62.2 (2011), 180–204.

3. Dobson, p. 3.

4. *Romeo and Juliet* references, unless otherwise indicated, are to the Arden edition of *Romeo and Juliet*, ed. René Weis (London: Bloomsbury, 2012).

5. According to the Arden editor, p. 131.

6. Notable recent readings such as Simon Palfrey's in *Romeo and Juliet* (Chippenham: Connell Guides, 2012) and Paul A. Kottman's in 'Defying the Stars: Tragic Love as the Struggle for Freedom in *Romeo and Juliet*', *Shakespeare Quarterly* 63.1 (2012), 1–38 have argued in their different ways that the play turns, with its lovers, emphatically away from the civic. That also is Wagner's reading in *Tristan und Isolde*, but Wagner had to excise the civic from Shakespeare, and I argue that a central interest of *Romeo and Juliet* remains its exploration of free love in relation to the possibilities of civic flourishing. Kottman's 'new interpretation of the play' as he says 'yields a deeper understanding of our struggle for freedom and self-realization as lovers'. He argues that *Romeo and Juliet* 'mutes' the 'conflict between the individual desires and the reigning demands of family, civic and social norms shaping those desires' (5). But, though it is famous for its notion of 'star-cross'd lovers', the Prologue to

Romeo and Juliet in fact firmly subordinates the idea of doomed love to civic crisis, beginning thus:

> Two households both alike in dignity
> (In fair Verona, where we lay our scene)
> From ancient grudge breaking to new mutiny
> Where civil blood makes civil hands unclean.
> (Prol., 6, 1–4)

Susan Snyder clearly defined the communal aspect of the play in '"Romeo and Juliet": Comedy into Tragedy', *Essays in Criticism* 20.4 (1970), 391–402; 400–1. And Hugh Grady has argued that 'the play presents a civil space with density enough to provide a social context to a young couple's love and marriage' as well as that 'it is within this carefully sketched civic space – a representation of early modern European life that is capable of constant updating – that the legendary love of Romeo and Juliet is kindled, and it is precisely love that challenges the power of the social' (Hugh Grady, *Shakespeare and Impure Aesthetics* (Cambridge: Cambridge University Press, 2009), pp. 208, 210). Jonathan Goldberg observes that *Romeo and Juliet* has come to dominate American high school curricula: '*Julius Cesar* has been usurped; the sexual revolution has replaced the civics lesson'. But, like Grady, he insists that 'love, from the start of the play, is implicated in the social not separate from it' ('*Romeo and Juliet*'s Open Rs', in *Romeo and Juliet*, ed. R. S. White, New Casebook Series (London: Palgrave, 2001), pp. 194, 199).

7. Goldberg repeats a contemporary critical truism when, in his reading of the play, he says, 'hetero- and homosexuality are profound misnomers in Shakespeare's time' (p. 203), but since (1) the play, as I shall argue, asks to be read in such terms, and (2) only such terms – rather than a more historically alienated vocabulary – can really bring it home to us, I defy that embargo here.

8. *Romeo and Juliet*'s male valentines have, for the most part, been overlooked by criticism. Joseph A. Porter deserves credit for properly noticing Mercutio's Valentine, who, he observes, does not appear in Brooke. He asks, 'what is he doing in the play at all, where does he really come from, what are we to make of him?' ('Mercutio's Brother', *South Atlantic Review* 49.4 (1984), 32). Though you get the impression he knows the answers, what he actually says is somewhat coy: 'Mercutio develops a brother, however ghostly and evanescent, in *Romeo and Juliet* because of the increased brotherliness and decreased amorousness he also develops there'; 'Valentine is there to begin the characterization of Mercutio as fraternal'; 'Who is he really? In a sense Valentine is a possibly subliminal double of the play's lover-hero Romeo' (37). Porter develops his case for this last judgement in *Shakespeare's Mercutio* (Chapel Hill, NC: University of North Carolina Press, 1988), pp. 1–10, 145–63. There is something in it, given Mercutio's frustrated passionate friendship for Romeo; but I prefer to see 'brother Valentine' as a figure in his own right for the amorous fulfilment that, though it is not available in Verona to Mercutio, surely would be in Freetown. It is left to Goldberg to notice that his name 'resonates (assonates) with another name down the list, "*Signor Valentio and his cousin Tybalt*"'. 'This second Valentine', he concludes, 'participates in a cousinship that, like the brotherhood of Mercutio and Valentine, may name properly what cannot be said' (Goldberg, p. 206).

9. Palfrey, p. 27.
10. Stanley Wells, *Shakespeare, Sex, and Love* (Oxford: Oxford University Press, 2010), p. 152.
11. See, for instance, Dympna Callaghan's reading of the play in terms of 'apparently unchangeable structures of oppression, particularly compulsory heterosexuality and bourgeois marriage' (in 'The Ideology of Romantic Love: The Case of *Romeo and Juliet*', in *The Weyward Sisters: Shakespeare and Feminist Politics*, ed. Dympna Callaghan, Lorraine Helms and Jyotsna Singh (Oxford: Blackwell, 1994), pp. 59–60).
12. Shakespeare references are, unless otherwise indicated, to the *Norton Shakespeare*, ed. Stephen Greenblatt (New York: Norton, 2008).
13. Quoted by Peter Holding, *Romeo and Juliet*, Text and Performance series (Basingstoke, Macmillan, 1992), p. 55.
14. For the Porter reference and a comment on the case he makes, see note 8. Roger Allam, 'Mercutio in *Romeo and Juliet*', in *Players of Shakespeare* 2nd edn. ed. Russell Jackson and Robert Smallwood (Cambridge: Cambridge University Press, 1988), p. 114.
15. See Kottman, 'Defying the Stars'. I go on to discuss his reading.
16. Wells, pp. 154, 155.
17. See Russell Jackson (ed.), *Romeo and Juliet*, Shakespeare at Stratford series (London: Arden Shakespeare, 2003), p. 99.
18. For Brooke's poem, see Geoffrey Bullough, *Narrative and Dramatic Sources of Shakespeare*, vol. 1 (London: Routledge and Kegan Paul 1957–75), pp. 284–363.
19. The Capulet ball of course above all presents an erotic scene but to the extent that it undoes established strife and erases social markers and privileges and predicates in favour of human potential, it has something in common with 'the original position' offered by the American philosopher John Rawls as foundation for the most important and influential contemporary theory of justice (see *A Theory of Justice* (1971; Cambridge, Massachussetts: Harvard University Press, 2005)).
20. Both lovers see the other in terms of amazing illumination, with Romeo saying that the brightness of Juliet's cheek shames the stars, and so on (2.2.1 ff.) and Juliet describing him as a 'day in night' (3.2.17); presumably the golden statues their fathers intend to erect for the lovers after their deaths also bear witness to this.
21. Paul Hammond notes that the 'open arse' simultaneously evokes 'both vaginal intercourse and sodomy (Paul Hammond, *Love between Men in English Literature* (New York: St Martin's Press, 1996), p. 59); and Goldberg concurs that 'anyone – man or woman – might be in the place marked by the open Rs of *Romeo and Juliet*' (p. 208).
22. Arden edition, p. 184.
23. Palfrey, p. 47.
24. Quoted in Roger Paulin, *The Critical Reception of Shakespeare in Germany 1682–1914: Native Literature and Foreign Genius* (Georg Olms Verlag: Hildesheim, 2003), p. 292.
25. Kottman interestingly argues that the initial violence in *Romeo and Juliet* is an important evolutionary stage in the 'struggle for freedom' it stages: *I risk my life in a battle to the death – say the men – not for prestige, or as an act of tribal duty or animal aggression; but rather to show that the desire to stay alive (mere instinct) does not drive me absolutely ('Draw if you be men' [1.1.59])'* (7). 'This,' he notes, 'is exactly

how Hegel describes the motivation for life-and-death struggle' (7, n 17): see
G. W. F. Hegel, *The Phenomenology of Spirit*, trans. A. V. Miller (Oxford: Oxford
University Press, 1977), p. 114. 'Subverting the philosophical preoccupation with
life-and-death struggles', Kottman proceeds to argue, 'Shakespeare begins his love
tragedy with an *aborted* duel' (9; my emphasis).

26. Arden edition, p. 136.
27. As Goldberg suggests, 'he reads his emotional state as the reflection of the public
brawl' (p. 199).
28. Palfrey, pp. 4–5.
29. Julia Kristeva, 'Romeo and Juliet: Love-Hatred in the Couple' ['Le couple amour-
haine selon *Roméo et Juliette*'], in White, p. 74.
30. Quoted in Catherine Belsey, 'The Name of the Rose in *Romeo and Juliet*', in White,
p. 56; see also Jacques Derrida, *The Post Card: From Socrates to Freud and Beyond*,
trans. Alan Bass (Chicago: University of Chicago Press, 1987), p. 39.
31. Jacques Derrida, 'Aphorism, Countertime', in *Philosophers on Shakespeare*, ed.
Paul Kottman (Stanford: University of Stanford Press, 2009), p. 173.
32. Derrida, p. 178.
33. Palfrey, p. 75.
34. See Palfrey, p. 75.
35. Kottman, 25.
36. As Kottman observes, 'The young Hegel referred to these lines as the paradigmatic
expression of mutual self-recognition and earthly happiness, and it is difficult to
disagree' (23): see G. W. F. Hegel, 'Love', in *Early Theological Writings*, trans. T. M.
Knox (Philadelphia: University of Pennsylvania Press, 1971), p. 307.
37. August Wilhelm Schlegel, 'Zueignung des Trauerspiels Romeo und Julia', in *August
Wilhelm von Schlegel's sämmtliche Werke*, ed. Eduard Böcking, 12 vols (Leipzig:
Weidmann, 1846–47), vol. 1, pp. 35–7; quoted in Roger Paulin, 'A Poem by August
Wilhelm Schlegel: "Zueignung des Trauerspiels Romeo und Julia"', in *The Present
Word: Culture, Society and the Site of Literature: Essays in Honour of Nicholas Boyle*,
ed. John Walker (London: Legenda, 2013), pp. 52–9. I am indebted to Roger Paulin
for alerting me to this poem, and for his translation, which I quote.
38. Kristeva, p. 75.
39. Kottman, 29.
40. Kottman, 25. Also worth reading is Kottman's earlier analysis of the balcony scene
in 'A Scene of Speaking: Convocation and the Suspension of Tragedy in *Romeo and
Juliet*' in *A Politics of the Scene* (Stanford: Stanford University Press, 2008), pp. 166–
84. 'The freedom of the scene,' Kottman argues, 'is a freedom that arises from the
initiative taken in the action itself. In this sense, the freedom promised by the scene
is a freedom that arises precisely through unpredictable and contingent interaction
among at least two actors' (p. 184).
41. Kristeva, p. 76.
42. Hazlitt defended it against the expurgators in *Characters of Shakespear's Plays*, 2nd
edn. (1817; London: Taylor and Hessey, 1818).
43. See Helmut Rehder, 'Novalis and Shakespeare', *PMLA* 58 (1948), 604–24, esp. 616–
20. Wagner also turned up the volume on the night-loving poetry of *Romeo and
Juliet* in *Tristan und Isolde*.

44. Hegel, *Phenomenology*, pp. 359, 360.
45. I follow the Arden 2 editor Brian Gibbons in rendering this speech (see *Romeo and Juliet* (London: Methuen, 1986)). The Folio doesn't print 'ay' or 'I' but has just I throughout, which makes the play in this speech between the speakable ay or affirmation, the objective first person pronoun, and the alternative I-beyond-I that is discovered in negation and death all the more dense and dizzying. Gibbons, I think, brings out the more profound semantic possibilities more helpfully than Weis does, in this instance.
46. Denis de Rougement argues that in the twelfth century heretical mysticism, by confusing divine eros with human desire, begins that long obsession which is nothing less than an 'impossible love … a truly devouring ardour, a thirst which death alone could quench'. He sees *Romeo and Juliet* as 'the most magnificent resuscitation of the myth that the world was to be given' until Wagner's *Tristan und Isolde* (*Love in the Western World* [1940], trans. Montgomery Belgion, rev. and augmented edn. [1956] (New York: Fawcett, 1966), pp. 145, 178–9, 201, 243); see also Jonathan Dollimore, *Death, Desire and Loss in Western Culture* (London: Routledge, 2001), p. 108). Norman Rabkin also regards the lovers as inherently doomed by 'the self-destructive yearning for annihilation we recognize as the death-wish' (Norman Rabkin, *Shakespeare and the Common Understanding* (New York: Free Press, 1967), p. 151); but I argue that more than love's climax is at stake in their 'civil night'. The play has hinted as much since the Prologue:

> The fearful passage of their death-mark'd love
> And the continuance of their parents' rage,
> Which, but their children's end, nought could remove,
> Is now the two hours' traffic of our stage.
>
> (Prologue, 9–12)

'Which, but their children's end, nought could remove' seems to mean nothing other than that the tragedy of Romeo and Juliet could have redeemed their parents, but there's another possibility. The line could, admittedly more obscurely but also more suggestively, mean that 'nought' could do this redeeming work *even without Romeo and Juliet*. And this starts to make sense when we recognise that what's valuable about the love of Romeo and Juliet as the Prologue presents it is its rush (its 'fearful passage') towards death, to the 'children's end'. Romeo and Juliet serve to bring their parents face-to-face with 'nought'; and of course there are many ways there, for all the terrible beauty of this one – even if you believe that there is another, eternal life, every way is the way to 'nought'. What I argue in what follows is that death is inextricably involved not just in achieving but in the very essence of the politics of freedom.
47. For more on this point, see Ewan Fernie, *The Demonic: Literature and Experience* (London: Routledge, 2012), p. 4.
48. Dostoevsky engages perhaps more profoundly than any other writer with the links between revolution and the demonic; see Fernie, 'Dostoevsky's Demons', in Fernie, pp. 87–115.
49. Again I follow Arden 2 and Gibbons here, but Arden 3 and Weis do not exclude the meaning which Gibbons's punctuation implies.

50. Derrida, p. 174.
51. Kristeva, p. 74.
52. Kottman, 'Defying the Stars', 32.
53. Kottman, 'Defying the Stars', 32. See also Paul A. Kottman, *Tragic Conditions in Shakespeare: Disinheriting the Globe* (Baltimore: The Johns Hopkins University Press, 2009), p. 50.
54. See Kottman, *A Politics of the Scene.*
55. Kottman, 'Defying the Stars', 36.
56. The fact that it isn't fully possible to imagine the nature of Freetown, or (following Kottman) its rituals, might be related to the late Derrida's interest in the 'messianic promise' of a perfect democracy discussed in the previous chapter. But I argue that *Romeo and Juliet* does partly realise what it promises: in the Capulet ball and that hint of its ghostly analogue and perfect consummation in Freetown; as Romeo and Juliet's 'death-marked love'; as their radical achievement in the family tomb and as its challenge to us to make a new tradition. Kottman, who is impressively well versed in Hegel's writings, follows on from Hegel's reflections on death and human society (see, for example, Hegel, *Phenomenology*, p. 270). But Hegel, as Kottman well knows, is centrally concerned with how to marry freedom and society to the point that society becomes freedom's perfect expression and vehicle. Likewise, one of the concerns of this book will be to bring Shakespeare and Hegel into dialogue on these issues: see especially Chapters 6 and 7.
57. G. W. F. Hegel, *Aesthetics: Lectures on Fine Art*, trans. T. M. Knox, vol. 2 (Oxford: Clarendon, 1975), p. 464.
58. Jacques Lacan offers a particularly progressive reading of *Antigone* in terms of freedom. He argues that Antigone inaugurates a radical humanism, first, in the name of her own, self-authorising act – 'That's how it is because that's how it is' – which is related to Polynices' transgressions; and, second, in the name of her brother's absolute value in spite of anything he has done or been. He relates this to the abstracted, originating signifying power of which 'the human being ... happens to be the bearer' (Jacques Lacan, *The Ethics of Psychoanalysis 1959–60: The Seminar of Jacques Lacan*, ed. Jacques-Alain Miller, trans. Dennis Porter (London: Routledge, 1999), pp. 278, 282). This is a powerful reading but the liberated humanism Lacan finds in Sophocles has to be uncoupled from family, as in 'Defying the Stars' Kottman suggests it is in *Romeo and Juliet.*
59. Chris Fitter, *Radical Shakespeare: Politics and Stagecraft in the Early Career* (London: Routledge, 2012), p. 169. In his chapter on *Romeo and Juliet*, '"The Quarrel Is Between Our Masters and Us Their Men": *Romeo and Juliet*, Dearth and the London Riots', Fitter seeks to 're-embed this play in events and conditions in London between 1594–96 – the escalating inter-class youth violence, the dearth of 1594–7, and the sensational London riots of 1595 which the combination precipitated' (pp. 144–73; p. 145).
60. 'In the grotesque parody of the wedding night that follows, Romeo seeks a repetition in the tomb of the original darkness, silence, and secrecy invoked so eloquently in Juliet's epithalamion,' writes Belsey (p. 59).

4   Freetown-upon-Avon

1. Christian Deelman, *The Great Shakespeare Jubilee* (London: Michael Joseph, 1964); Martha Winburn England, *Garrick's Jubilee* (Columbus: Ohio State University Press, 1964); Johanne M. Stochholm, *Garrick's Folly: The Shakespeare Jubilee of 1769 at Stratford and Drury Lane* (London: Methuen, 1964). I have drawn on all of these sources in what follows. For a recent account of the Jubilee in a book described on its blurb as 'the definitive biography of William Shakespeare's afterlife', see Jack Lynch, *Becoming Shakespeare: The Unlikely Afterlife That Turned a Provincial Playwright into The Bard* (New York: Walker and Company, 2007). Kate Rumbold is good on the curious and shifting ambiguities of the festival ('The Stratford Jubilee' in *Shakespeare in the Eighteenth Century*, ed. Fiona Ritchie and Peter Sabor (Cambridge: Cambridge University Press, 2012), pp. 254–76).

2. See Keats's letter to Richard Woodhouse, 27 October 1818, in *Letters of John Keats: A Selection*, ed. Robert Gittings (Oxford: Oxford University Press, 1970), pp. 157–8.

3. David Garrick, *An essay on acting: in which will be consider'd the mimical behaviour of a certain fashionable faulty actor, … To which will be added, a short criticism of his acting Macbeth* (London: Printed for W. BICKERTON, at the *Gazette*, in the *Temple Exchange*, near the *Inner Temple Gate, Fleet-street*. M, DCC, XLIV [1744]), p. 14.

4. Quoted in Alan Kendall, *David Garrick: A Biography* (London: Harrap, 1985), p. 31.

5. Quoted in Kendall, p. 33.

6. Fanny Burney, *Evelina; or the History of a Young Lady's Entrance into the World* (Oxford: Oxford University Press, 1982), p. 26.

7. Shakespeare references unless otherwise indicated are to the *Norton Shakespeare*, ed. Stephen Greenblatt (London and New York: W. W. Norton, 2008).

8. Garrick, pp. 8–9.

9. Denis Diderot, *The Paradox of Acting*, trans. Walter Herries Pollock (London: Chatto & Windus, 1883).

10. See Jenny Uglow, *Hogarth, A Life and a World* (London: Faber, 1997), p. 589.

11. See R. Evan Sly, *Garrick and Hogarth or the Artist Puzzled*, 1845, Coloured Lithograph of 28 × 37 cm, Trustees of the British Museum, in *Every Look Speaks: Portraits of David Garrick, with an essay by Desmond Shawe-Taylor: An exhibition at the Holburne Museum of Art, Bath 16th September to 7th December 2004* (Bath: The Holburne Museum of Art, 2003), c. 59, pp. 87–9; the same catalogue refers to the Gainsborough obituary, p. 14.

12. Quoted in Hugh Tait, 'Garrick, Shakespeare and Wilkes', *British Museum Journal*, 24 (1961), 102.

13. ER1/82:Watercolour drawing of David Garrick as Steward at the Stratford-upon-Avon Jubilee, c.1769 in 'An Account of the Jubilee celebrated at Stratford-upon-Avon in honour of Shakspeare, 1769'. Saunders papers, c.1813, p. 78 (Shakespeare Centre Library and Archive).

14. See Deelman, p. 184; and Stochholm, p. 21. The quotation from Johnson derives from the lines he wrote to be spoken by Garrick at the opening of Drury Lane on 15 September 1747.

15. Quoted in England, p. 58.
16. Written by Garrick, and set by Dibdin, according to Deelman this 'at once became the hit tune of the whole festival' (p. 184). The communal emphasis, and indeed achievement, of the Stratford Jubilee resonates with the fact that in 1901 the Stockport Garrick Society became the first community organisation to own its own playhouse. For more on the Stockport Garrick Society, see Michael Dobson, *Shakespeare and Amateur Performance: A Cultural History* (Cambridge: Cambridge University Press, 2011), pp. 92–101.
17. Quoted in Deelman, p. 261; on the religious aura surrounding the communal drinking from the mulberry goblet, see Péter Dávidházi, *The Romantic Cult of Shakespeare: Literary Reception in Anthropological Perspective* (Houndmills, Basingstoke and London: Macmillan, 1998), p. 40 ff.
18. *The Public Advertiser* (16 September 1769), 3; quoted in Stochholm, p. 58. 'No company, so various in character, temper, and condition, ever formed, at least in appearance, such an agreeable group of happy and congenial souls', according to Tom Davies (quoted in Deelman, p. 183). Looking back in 1964, Martha England wrote, 'Hairdressers and earls, townspeople, runaway apprentices, lords and ladies and actors all rejoiced together' (p. 46).
19. See Dávidházi, p. 39.
20. See *Lloyds Evening Post* (4–6 September 1769), 25, 231, 2; quoted in Stochholm, p. 47.
21. David Garrick, *An Ode upon Dedicating a Building, and Erecting a Statue, to Shakespeare, at Stratford upon Avon. By D. G.* (London: Printed for T. Becket, and P.A. de Hondt, in the Strand, 1769), p. 5.
22. Garrick, *Ode*, p. 9.
23. Garrick, *Ode*, p. 10.
24. *1 Henry IV*, 2.5.438. Jonathan Bate notes that Edward Thomas's anthology, *This England: An Anthology from Her Writers Compiled by Edward Thomas* (Oxford: Oxford University Press, 1916) includes Falstaff in praise of sack. 'Consider', he asks, 'what it would mean to make Falstaff into the true embodiment of England' (*The Genius of Shakespeare* (London: Picador, 1997), p. 204).
25. Edward Thompson, *Trinculo's trip to the Jubilee* (London: printed for C. Moran; W. Flexney; and R. Riddley, 1769), p. iv.
26. See Johan Zoffany, *Mr and Mrs Garrick by the Shakespeare Temple at Hampton*, 1762, The Lambton Trustees, in *Every Look Speaks*, c. 16, p. 49.
27. Carola Oman, *David Garrick* (London: Hodder and Stoughton, 1958), p. 352.
28. Quoted in Tait, p. 106. On links between Garrick and Wilkes, see Michael Dobson, *The Making of the National Poet: Shakespeare, Adaptation and Authorship, 1660–1769* (Oxford: Oxford University Press, 1992), pp. 218–19, n. 48. The following is evidence of an association between Wilkes and Shakespeare before the Jubilee: *The three conjurors: a political interlude, stolen from Shakespeare, as it was performed at sundry places in Westminster; on Saturday the 30th of April, and Sunday the 1st of May: most humbly dedicated to John Wilkes, Esq* (London: printed for E. Cabe, 1763).
29. Deelman, p. 264. See also *Shakespeare's Garland. Being A Collection of New Songs, Ballads, Roundelays, Catches, Glees, Comic-Serenatas, &c. Performed at the*

JUBILEE at STRATFORD UPON AVON. THE MUSICK BY DR. ARNE, MR. BARTHOLOMEW, MR. ALLWOOD, AND MR. DIBDIN (London: Printed for T. Becket, and P.A. de Hondt, in the Strand, 1769).

30. *The Patriot's Jubilee, being songs proper to be sung on Wednesday, the 18th of April, 1770; the day of Mr Wilkes's enlargement from the King's-Bench* (London: Printed for T. Evans, No. 54, Paternoster-Row; and to be had of all booksellers, 1770), p. iii.

31. *The Patriot's Jubilee*, pp. 26, 3 ff.

32. *The Patriot's Jubilee*, p. 18.

33. See, for example, Katherine Eisaman Maus's introduction to the play in the *Norton Shakespeare*, pp. 973–4. Blair Worden has disputed that it was in fact Shakespeare's play which was performed in 'Which Play Was Performed at the Globe Theatre on 7 February 1601?', *London Review of Books*, 25.13 (10 July 2003).

34. Andrew Hadfield, *Shakespeare and Republicanism* (Cambridge: Cambridge University Press, 2005), pp. 36–8.

35. Hadfield, p. 214.

36. Hadfield, p. 221.

37. On Milton and freedom, see Quentin Skinner, 'What Does It Mean to Be a Free Person?' *London Review of Books* (22 May 2008); Satan rebels because he can no longer bring himself to pronounce 'forced Hallelujahs' (John Milton, *Paradise Lost*, ed. David Scott Kastan (Indianapolis: Hackett Publishing, 2005), 2.243).

38. Quotations are from 'Presentation of the Shakespeare Testimonial to Kossuth'. The source appears to be the *Illustrated London News*, 15 May 1853, page number unknown. My source is Lemuel Matthews Griffiths, *Newspaper Cuttings Relating to Shakespeare* at the Library of Birmingham, vol. 11, p. 88.

39. Maximillian E. Novak, 'The Politics of Shakespeare Criticism in the Restoration and Early Eighteenth Century', *English Literary History* 81.1 (2014), 115–42.

40. Dobson, *The Making of the National Poet*, p. 36.

41. See *Drury Lane Journals, Selections from James Winston's Diaries, 1891–27*, ed. Albert L. Nelson and Gilbert B. Cross (London: The Society for Theatre Research, 1974).

42. See Andrew Murphy, *Shakespeare for the People: Working-Class Readers, 1800–1900* (Cambridge: Cambridge University Press, 2008), p. 141; Antony Taylor, 'Shakespeare and Radicalism: The Uses and Abuses of Shakespeare in Nineteenth-Century Popular Politics', *The Historical Journal* 45.2 (2002), 357–79; 367.

43. Anne Janowitz, *Lyric and Labour in the Romantic Tradition* (Cambridge: Cambridge University Press, 1998), p. 146.

44. Janowitz, p. 146.

45. See Murphy, p. 144.

46. Quoted from *Reasoner*, II, 277, in Stephen Roberts, *Thomas Cooper: Radical and Poet*, c. 1830–1860, 1986, A thesis submitted to the Faculty of Arts of the University of Birmingham for the degree of MASTER OF LETTERS, School of History, Faculty of Arts, p. 31.

47. Quoted from *Reasoner*, II, 277, in Roberts, p. 31.

48. Thomas Cooper, *The Life of Thomas Cooper*, with an introduction by John Saville (1872; Leicester: Leicester University Press, 1971), p. 64.

49. Quoted in Bate, *Genius*, p. 215; see also *Cooper's Journal: or, Unfettered Thinker and Plain Speaker for Truth, Freedom, and Progress*, published in book form (London: James Watson, 1850), No. 21, Vol. 1, FOR THE WEEK ENDING SATURDAY, MAY 25, 1850, p. 328.

50. Roberts quotes *Reasoner* V, 308 on p. 32.

51. Cooper, pp. 64, 68; my emphasis.

52. Cooper, p. 160. This was a familiar vein for Cooper. His own 'Chartist Chaunt' includes these lines:

> TRUTH is growing – hearts are glowing
>   With the flame of Liberty:
> Light is breaking – Thrones are quaking –
>   Hark! – the trumpet of the Free!

(Thomas Cooper, *The Poetical Works of Thomas Cooper* (London: Hodder and Stoughton, 1877), p. 283).

53. See Cooper, *The Life*, p. 163.

54. See Roberts, p. 32. This splinter group of Leicester Chartists called themselves Shakespeareans not only because the room in which they met in Humberstone Gate was so called, but also because Cooper 'liked the name of Shakespeare' (see the letter written by Cooper to R. G. Gammage, dated 26 February 1855, and printed in *Gammage's History of the Chartist Movement* (1854; New York: A. M. Kelly, 1969), p. 405).

55. Cooper, *The Life*, p. 166.

56. Cooper, *The Life*, p. 166.

57. Cooper, *The Life*, p. 165.

58. Cooper, *The Life*, p. 169.

59. Cooper, *The Life*, p. 324.

60. Murphy, p. 147; see also Thomas Cooper's letter, dated 29 August 1842, to the *Northern Star* (3 September 1842), 6.

61. See Philip Collins, 'Thomas Cooper, The Chartist: Byron and the "Poets of the Poor"', Nottingham, Byron Lecture, 1969 (Hawthorne: Nottingham, 1969), p. 11; and R. J. Conklin, *Thomas Cooper, The Chartist* (Manila, 1935), pp. 97–8.

62. Cooper, *The Life*, pp. 228–9.

63. Cooper, *The Life*, pp. 228–9.

64. Cooper, *The Life*, p. 252.

65. Thomas Cooper, *The Purgatory of Suicides: A Prison Rhyme*, in ten books, 3rd edn. (London: Chapman and Hall, 1853), p. 2.

66. Cooper, *The Life*, pp. 256–7.

67. *Cooper's Journal*, No. 22, Vol. 1, FOR THE WEEK ENDING SATURDAY, JUNE 1, 1850, p. 345.

68. *Cooper's Journal: or, Unfettered Thinker and Plain Speaker for Truth, Freedom, and Progress*, published in book form (London: B. Steil, 1849) No. 8, Vol. 1, *Saturday 10 March, 1849*, p. 57.

69. Cooper, *The Life*, p. 291.

70. Cooper, *The Life*, pp. 301, 310.

71. William Whitmore, 'To Mazzini and Kossuth', *Cooper's Journal*, No. 4, Vol. 1, FOR THE WEEK ENDING SATURDAY, JANUARY 26, 1850, p. 56.

72. John Alfred Langford, 'To Kossuth', *Cooper's Journal*, No. 13, Vol. 1, FOR THE WEEK ENDING SATURDAY, MARCH 30, 1850, p. 198.

73. Quoted in Taylor, 366; see also *Cooper's Journal*, No. 21, Vol. 1, *Saturday June 9, 1849*, p. 170. It should be admitted Cooper is fired up by Milton as much as Shakespeare in this passage.

74. *Cooper's Journal*, No. 15, Vol. 1, *Saturday April the 28th, 1849*, p. 118.

75. *Cooper's Journal*, No. 1, Vol. 1, *Saturday January the 20th, 1849*, p. 6.

76. *Cooper's Journal*, No. 8, Vol. 1, *Saturday March the 10th, 1849*, p. 58.

77. *Cooper's Journal*, No. 10, Vol. 1, *Saturday March the 24th, 1849*, p. 82.

78. *Cooper's Journal*, No. 13, Vol. 1, *Saturday April the 14th, 1849*, p. 106.

79. *Cooper's Journal*, No. 13, Vol. 1, Saturday *April the 14th*, 1849, p. 106.

80. Taylor, 361; see also the memoir of Ernest Jones's life in the *Manchester City News* (18 January 1919), 4.

81. 'George Julian Harney', *National Reformer* (30 April 1876), 278.

82. Taylor, 369; see also Tom Mann, *Tom Mann's Memoirs* (1923; London: Gibbon and Key, 1967), pp. 17–19 and 176.

83. Taylor, 373.

84. Reproduced in Richard Foulkes, *The Shakespeare Tercentenary of 1864* (London: The Society of Theatre Research, 1984), pp. 35–6.

85. Taylor, 374.

86. Taylor, 374.

87. Taylor, 374; see also E. L. Burney, 'George Linnaeus Banks 1821–1881', *Manchester Review*, 12 (1971), 1–21.

88. See Susan Brock and Sylvia Morris, 'Enchanted Ground: Celebrating Shakespeare's Birthday in Stratford-upon-Avon', in *Shakespeare Jubilees 1769–2014*, ed. Christa Jansohn and Dieter Mehl (Münster: LIT Verlag, 2015), p. 40.

89. Murphy, p. 151; see also *Illustrated London News* (30 April 1864), 422.

90. Taylor, 377.

91. Taylor, 377; Foulkes, p. 43.

92. Taylor, 378.

93. Taylor, 378; see also *The Commonwealth* (26 May 1866), 1.

94. See Murphy, p. 152.

95. T. Evans, 'Shakespeare and Secularism in Birmingham', *National Reformer* (7 May 1864), 123. 'Shakespeare … featured in J. M. Wheeler's *Biographical Dictionary of Freethinkers*' (Taylor, 365; see J. M. Wheeler, *Biographical Dictionary of Freethinkers* (London: Progressive Publishing, 1889), pp. 298–9).

96. Taylor, 364–5; see Robert Ingersoll and Charles Bradlaugh, *Will Shakespeare, Tom Paine* (London: National Secular Society, 1890), p. 29.

97. Dobson, *Shakespeare and Amateur Performance*, p. 167.

98. See Sheila Stowell, 'Suffrage Critics and Political Action: a Feminist Agenda', in *The Edwardian Theatre*, ed. Michael R. Booth and Joel Kaplan (Cambridge: Cambridge University Press, 1996), p. 176; see also the review in *The Suffragette* (18 October 1912), p. 5.

99. Susan Carlson, 'The Suffrage Shrew: The Shakespeare Festival, "A Man's Play", and New Women', in *Shakespeare and the Twentieth Century: The Selected Proceedings of the International Shakespeare Association World Congress, Los Angeles, 1997*, ed. Jonathan Bate, Jill L. Levenson and Dieter Mehl (London: Associated University Presses, 1998), p. 87.
100. Carlson, p. 87; see also *Birmingham Gazette* (9 April 1909), quoted in 'Press Comments,' *Votes for Women* 2 (30 April 1909), 601.
101. Carlson, p. 88.
102. Carlson, p. 86.
103. Carlson, p. 97, n. 2; see 'Stratford-on-Avon', *Votes for Women* 2 (30 April 1909), 601.
104. Carlson, p. 94; see also, 'Shakespeare as Suffragist', *The Vote* 3 (29 July 1911), 180.
105. Susan Carlson draws attention to 'The Shakespeare Festival: Sellers Wanted at Stratford-on-Avon' in *The Suffragette* (10 April 1914) in 'Politicizing Harley Granville Barker: Suffragists and Shakespeare', *New Theatre Quarterly* 22.2 (2006), 124.
106. See Jonathan Dollimore and Alan Sinfield (ed.), *Political Shakespeare*, 2nd edn. (Manchester: Manchester University Press, 2012).
107. Peter Holbrook, 'Shakespeare, "The Cause of the People", and *The Chartist Circular* 1839–42', *Textual Practice* 20.2 (2006), 203–29; 204; see also Arnold Kettle, 'Introduction', in *Shakespeare in a Changing World*, ed. Arnold Kettle (London: Lawrence and Wishart, 1964), pp. 13–14.
108. Holbrook, 223.
109. See Dobson, *The Making of the National Poet*, p. 219.
110. *The Public Advertiser* (16 September 1769), 3; quoted in Stochholm, p. 58.
111. See James Boswell, *Boswell in Search of a Wife, 1766–69*, ed. Frank Brady and Frederick A. Pottle (Melbourne, London, Toronto: William Heinemann Ltd, 1957), p. xvi.
112. See Boswell, p. xvii.
113. Boswell, p. 288.
114. Boswell, pp. 291–2.
115. Boswell, p. 293.
116. Boswell, p. 299.
117. *The London Magazine* (September 1769), 38, 455–6. The explicit link which Boswell makes between Shakespearean freedom and Corsica in these lines rather gives the lie to Peter Barnes's more cynical representation of Boswell in his play about what Garrick did at Stratford, *Jubilee* (London: Methuen, 2001), which was performed by the RSC in the same year: '*Garrick* James Boswell will appear as a Corsican patriot. What Shakespeare play is that from? *Boswell* It's got nothing to do with Shakespeare. I'm promoting my new book, Travels in Corsica. I have a few signed copies left. Not at Jubilee prices' (p. 82).
118. Walter Benjamin, 'Theses on the Philosophy of History', in *Illuminations*, ed. and intro. Hannah Arendt, trans. Harry Zorn (London: Pimlico, 1999), pp. 245–55. See also Ronald Beiner, 'Walter Benjamin's Philosophy of History', *Political Theory* 12.4 (Aug. 1984), 423–34.

5   Freetown-am-Main

1. The Free Imperial Cities of the Holy Roman Empire enjoyed relative autonomy, subordinate only to that of the emperor.
2. Martha Winburn England, 'Garrick's Stratford Jubilee: Reactions in France and Germany', *Shakespeare Survey* 9 (1956), 90–100; 96.
3. See Martha Winburn England, *Garrick's Jubilee* (Columbus: Ohio State University Press, 1964), p. 233. In fact, as England notes, the Stratford Jubilee had a surprisingly pervasive influence in Europe: 'Paul van Tieghem has recorded various evidences of that impact in other countries. In Italy, Holland, Sweden, Russia, Denmark, and Spain there were accounts of the Jubilee, productions on the stage of Shakespeare's plays, translations, critical essays, and discussions of literary theory with reference to Shakespeare' (*Garrick's Jubilee*, pp. 229–30; see also Paul van Tieghem, *Le Préromantisme* (Paris: Alcan, 1947), vol. 3, pp. 196–8). Garrick's own background was European. 'The young man who conquered London in 1741,' writes Christian Deelman, 'was of French Huguenot descent, his grandfather having come to England from Bordeaux in 1685', and he had married a 'beautiful Viennese dancer', who had come to England in the most Shakespearean fashion: 'disguised as a boy' (*The Great Shakespeare Jubilee* (London: Michael Joseph, 1964), pp. 77, 83).
4. Quoted in Jennifer Ann Bates, *Hegel and Shakespeare on Moral Imagination* (Albany: State University of New York Press, 2010), p. 12. As Bates notes, 'This was the climax of Lessing's involvement with Shakespeare … At heart, Lessing was a classicist and in sympathy with Voltaire's conception of tragedy' (p. 12).
5. See Roger Paulin, *The Critical Reception of Shakespeare in Germany 1682–1914: Native Literature and Foreign Genius* (Hildesheim: Georg Olms Verlag, 2003), p. 21. And see England, 'Garrick's Stratford Jubilee', 94; see also *Mercure de France* (December 1769), pp. 180–6.
6. See John Alexander Kelly, *German Visitors to English Theatres in the Eighteenth Century* (Princeton: Princeton University Press, 1936), pp. 50–6.
7. See England, *Garrick's Jubilee*, pp. 93–4.
8. Terry Pinkard, *Hegel: A Biography* (Cambridge: Cambridge University Press, 2000), p. 24.
9. See Paulin, p. 203; see also Georg Christoph Lichtenberg, *Briefe aus England*, in *Georg Christoph Lichtenberg, Schriften*, ed. Franz H. Mautner (Frankfurt am Main: Insel, 1983), vol. 2, p. 34. England recalls Lichtenberg's description of Garrick's acting in conjunction with amazingly pervasive Shakespeare idolatory in Germany, with children learning 'To be or not to be' before they even learned their ABC or the Creed (see *Garrick's Jubilee*, p. 236).
10. August Wilhelm Schlegel, *Etwas über William Shakespeare bei Gelegenheit Wilhelm Meisters* (*Some Remarks on William Shakespeare Occasioned by Wilhelm Meister*) is discussed in Paulin, p. 280. See also Jonathan Bate, *The Genius of Shakespeare* (London: Picador, 1997), 'The German National Poet', pp. 180–4.
11. England, 'Garrick's Stratford Jubilee', 96.

12. On the religious atmosphere of the original Jubilee, see Péter Dávidházi, *The Romantic Cult of Shakespeare: Literary Reception in Anthropological Perspective* (Houndmills, Basingstoke and London: Macmillan, 1998).

13. For the two letters quoted here, see *Der junge Goethe*, ed. Max Morris (Leipzig: Insel-Verlag, 1909–12), vol. 2, pp. 111 and 115; quoted in England, 'Garrick's Stratford Jubilee', 95. Paulin writes, 'The evidence that he actually read the jubilee Ode or the oration in honour of Shakespeare rests on the mention in a letter of Garrick's 'Will of all Wills' (p. 161).

14. Quoted in Deelman, p. 261.

15. See *Olney Hymns, in Three Books. Book I. On Select Texts of Scripture. Book II. On Occasional Subjects. Book III. On the Progress and Changes of the Spiritual Life* (London: Printed and sold by W. Oliver, No. 12, Bartholomew Close, 1779).

16. Johann Wolfgang von Goethe, 'Zum Shakespeares-Tag / In Celebration of Shakespeare', trans. Michael Hoffmann, in *Goethe on Shakespeare / Goethe über Shakespeare: A parallel text edition of Goethe's essays on Shakespeare* (London: Globe Education, 2010), pp. 11–13.

17. Goethe, pp. 12–13; in this case, my translation.

18. Goethe, pp. 14–15.

19. Goethe, pp. 10–11; my emphasis.

20. See David Garrick, *An Ode upon Dedicating a Building, and Erecting a Statue, to Shakespeare, at Stratford upon Avon. By D. G.* (London: Printed for T. Becket, and P.A. de Hondt, in the Strand, 1769), p. 1.

21. Goethe, pp. 10–11.

22. *King Lear*, Conflated Text, 3.4.100. References unless otherwise indicated are to the *Norton Shakespeare*, ed. Stephen Greenblatt (London and New York: W. W. Norton, 2008).

23. See 'Thou soft-flowing Avon' in Garrick's *Ode*, pp. 12–13.

24. Goethe, pp. 14–15.

25. 'In Europe in 1769', writes England, 'it was said that the Jubilee was a spontaneous folk movement, a glorious example of the citizenry rising as one man to do honour to a Bard' (England, *Garrick's Jubilee*, p. 68). 'For the German idolaters,' she writes in her article specifically devoted to the impact of the Jubilee in Europe, 'the Jubilee was a true folk movement' ('Garrick's Stratford Jubilee', 95). Deelman concurs (p. 291).

26. Goethe, pp. 10–11; my emphasis.

27. *Henry V*, Prologue, 1.

28. According to Thomas Mann, 'the coming of Goethe was a new confirmation of the legitimacy of the individual being'; but Goethe is ultimately 'nonpolitical', glad to profit from the patronage of princes, doing much to establish the German metaphysical version of freedom, which was also at least in part Shakespeare derived (see *Reflections of a Nonpolitical Man*, trans. and intro. Walter D. Morris (1918; New York: Frederick Ungar Publishing Co., 1983), p. 202). Certainly, Goethe's most famous critical reflection on Shakespeare – his reading of *Hamlet* in terms of 'a soul which is not adequate to cope', an 'oak tree planted in a precious pot which should only have held delicate flowers' – is not very redolent of political activism (see Johann Wolfgang von Goethe, *Wilhelm Meister's Apprenticeship*, ed. and trans.

Eric A. Blackall in cooperation with Victor Lange (Princeton: Princeton University Press, 1989), p. 146). But the young man on Shakespeare's Day we are contemplating here clearly *is* fired up with a much more politically progressive vision, one which this book hopes to show constitutes a major tradition of Shakespeare reception.

29. Ernst Beutler (ed.), *Goethes Rede Zum Schäkespears Tag* (Weimar: Schriften der Goethe Gesellschaft, 1938), pp. 3–4; quoted in England, 'Garrick's Stratford Jubilee', 97–8.

30. Goethe, pp. 14–15.

31. See England, *Garrick's Jubilee*, p. 96.

32. J. G. Herder, 'Shakespeare, in *Philosophers on Shakespeare*, ed. Paul A. Kottman (Stanford: Stanford University Press, 2009), pp. 21–39; p. 37. Herder fears at this point in his essay that, in spite of Garrick's heroic efforts, Shakespeare's greatness may be becoming irrevocably remote.

33. See Kottmann, p. 199, n. 1.

34. Herder, p. 21.

35. Herder, p. 27.

36. England, *Garrick's Jubilee*, p. 234.

37. Herder, p. 28.

38. Paulin, p. 152. It may be worth remarking that in his late essay, '*Shakespeare und kein Ende*', Goethe presents Englishness as a thing so opaque and abstracted that it can accommodate all humanity: 'Sea-washed, wrapped in fog and cloud, active into all the quarters of the earth'. For Goethe, Englishness expressly opens onto the universal, just as he wants Germanness to. He is not after a narrow, essentialist nationalism: 'Shakespeare is a companion of the world spirit.' See '*Shakespeare und kein Ende* / No End to Shakespeare', trans. David Constantine, in *Goethe on Shakespeare / Goethe über Shakespeare*, pp. 24–5.

39. Herder, p. 31; my emphasis.

40. Shakespeare is for Herder, as Paulin puts it, 'a unique phenomenon', 'a representative of creative forces never before or since seen in such wholeness, a microcosm of the very "Eins und Alles" of creation itself, giving insight not merely into "Geschichte der Menschheit" ("history of humanity") but the very "menschliche Seele" ("human soul") itself' (p. 147). Alexander Gillies suggests that Shakespeare turned Herder on to history, and that as a corollary Herder started to see God as a dramatist and His world as a stage (Alexander Gillies, *Herder* (Oxford: Basil Blackwell 1945), p. 57). Shakespeare is also seen as an elemental historical force in Friedrich Gundolf's *Shakespeare und der deutsche Geist* (Berlin: Bondi, 1911). England mentions both Gillies and Gundolf in 'Garrick's Stratford Jubilee', 99.

41. Herder, p. 37; his exclamation.

42. Herder, p. 35.

43. Johann Wolfgang von Goethe, *Faust, Part 2*, 1.5; for an English translation, see for instance *Faust: Parts I and II*, a new version by Howard Brenton from a literal translation by Christa Weisman (London: Nick Hern Books, 1995).

44. Herder, p. 29.

45. Herder, p. 29.

46. Roger Paulin writes of Johann Georg Hamann's *Aesthetica in nuce* (1762): 'Analagous to Socrates' or Paul's wisdom in unwisdom, it is an expression of freedom from the law, indeed it cannot be divorced from religious experience proper, and its utterances might seem to fall within the theological category of "general or special operations of the spirit"' (p. 139). Paulin also shows how, for the young Hegelian critic Julian Schmidt as well as for Hermann Ulrici, Shakespeare's 'Protestantism' enables a union of the historical, the experiential and the divine (p. 409). Gervinus explains, so Paulin recounts, 'that "Protestant" is not to be understood in any sectarian sense; it follows Schiller's definition, "guardian of nature"' (p. 412; see also Georg Gottfried Gervinus, *Shakespeare*, 4 vols (Leipzig: Englemann, 1849–50), vol. 4, p. 398).

47. Herder, p. 34.
48. Garrick, *Ode*, p. 10.
49. Goethe, '*Zum Shakespeares-Tag*', pp. 16–17.
50. Goethe, '*Zum Shakespeares-Tag*', pp. 15–17.
51. Herder, p. 38.
52. Garrick, p. 4. An interesting detail of cultural history is that, as England notes, 'much that ramified from these German writings came back into English criticism by way of the German readings of Coleridge and Carlyle' (*Garrick's Jubilee*, p. 140; see also 'Garrick's Stratford Jubilee', 99).
53. Friedrich Schlegel, from *Dialogue on Poetry*, trans. Ernst Behler and Roman Struc, *German Romantic Criticism*, ed. A. Leslie Wilson, foreword by Ernst Behler (New York: Continuum, 1982), p. 94.
54. See Victor Hugo, *William Shakespeare*, trans. M. B. Anderson (1864; Chicago: A. C. McClurg, 1899), pp. 374, 373. For Hugo's radical reading of Shakespeare, see Jonathan Bate, 'Shakespeare without a Muzzle', in *The Genius of Shakespeare* (New York: Oxford University Press, 1998), pp. 230–9 and Peter Holbrook, *Shakespeare's Individualism* (Cambridge: Cambridge University Press, 2010), p. 13.
55. Edward Dowden, *Shakespeare: A Critical Study of His Mind and Art* (London: H. S. King, 1875), p. 420.
56. Quoted in Bate, p. 232; see also, Hector Berlioz, *The Memoirs of Hector Berlioz*, trans. David Cairns (New York: A. A. Knopf, 1969), p. 95.
57. Quoted in Zdeněk Stříbrný, *Shakespeare and Eastern Europe* (Oxford: Oxford University Press, 2000), p. 36.
58. See Stříbrný, p. 32.
59. Quoted in Stříbrný, p. 34.
60. Quoted in Stříbrný, pp. 44, 45–6.
61. Dezső Keresztury, 'Shakespeare and the Hungarians', *The New Hungarian Quarterly* 5.13 (Spring 1964), 5.
62. Christopher Clark, *Iron Kingdom: The Rise and Downfall of Prussia 1600–1947* (London: Penguin, 2007), p. 455.
63. Stříbrný, p. 69.
64. Quoted in Stříbrný p. 62.
65. Stříbrný, p. 62.
66. Keresztury, p. 17.

67. Keresztury, p. 23.
68. Quoted in Stříbrný, p. 64; for the full text of Petőfi's essay, see the Shakespeare anniversary issue of the *New Hungarian Quarterly* 5.13 (1964).
69. Stříbrný, p. 70.
70. Quoted in Istvan Deak, *The Lawful Revolution: Louis Kossuth and the Hungarians 1848–1849* (New York: Columbia University Press, 1979), p. 71.
71. See Richard Wilson, *Free Will* (Manchester: Manchester University Press, 2013), p. 308. Wilson cites Peter Hoffmann, *Stauffenberg: A Family History, 1905–44* (Cambridge: Cambridge University Press, 1995), pp. 235 and 43.
72. Tibor Frank, "'Give Me Shakespeare': Lajos Kossuth's English as an Instrument of International Politics', in *Shakespeare and Hungary, A Publication of the Shakespeare Yearbook*, ed. Holgar Klein and Péter Dávidházi, vol. 7 (Lewiston /Queenston/Lampeter: The Edwin Mellen Press, 1996), p. 65; cf. Endre Sebestyén, *Kossuth: A Magyar Apostle of World Democracy* (Pittsburgh: Expert Printing Co., 1950), p. 136.
73. See George Steiner, *Language and Silence: Essays 1958–66* (London: Faber, 1967). A possible if admittedly fugitive reconnection between Shakespeare and Kossuth in English culture is in the drama of Christopher Fry. As verse drama, this was unavoidably associated with Shakespeare, and in *The Dark Is Light Enough: A Winter Comedy* (Oxford: Oxford University Press, 1954) Fry took the Hungarian revolution of 1848 as his subject matter. Here are some pertinent lines:

> When pride of race has been pent up
> In a tyrannous disregard, and valued liberties
> Have been lost for long enough, what comes in the way
> Of dignity's free and natural flowing
> Is nothing but rocks to be blasted.
>
> (Act 1, pp. 14–15).

74. Stříbrný, p. 115.
75. Stříbrný, pp. 118–19.

6   Free Artists of Their Own Selves!

1. Terry Pinkard, *Hegel: A Biography* (Cambridge: Cambridge University Press, 2000), p. 5.
2. Pinkard, p. 551.
3. G. W. F. Hegel, 'Dramatic Poetry', from *Aesthetics: Lectures on Fine Art,* in *Philosophers on Shakespeare*, ed. Paul Kottman (Stanford: University of Stanford Press, 2009), p. 70. The Kottman collection makes the most pertinent portion of the *Aesthetics* conveniently available for Shakespeareans, and I quote from it where possible. It is excerpted from the culminating section of G. W. F. Hegel's *Aesthetics: Lectures on Fine Art*, trans. T. M. Knox, vols 1 and 2 (Oxford: Clarendon Press, 1975), vol. 2, pp. 1158–237. Where I quote from elsewhere in the *Aesthetics*, this is the

translation I use, unless otherwise indicated. The next chapter includes reflection on Hegel's broader interest in freedom.

4. Harold Bloom, *The Western Canon: The Books and School of the Ages* (London: Papermac, 1995), p. 70; my emphasis.

5. Bloom, p. 70.

6. Bernard Williams, *Moral Luck: Philosophical Papers, 1973–80* (Cambridge: Cambridge University Press, 1981), p. 29.

7. See Terry Eagleton, *Why Marx Was Right* (New Haven and London: Yale University Press, 2012), pp. 86–7.

8. See Jonathan Dollimore and David Jonathan Y. Bayot, *Jonathan Dollimore in Conversation* (Manila: De La Salle University Publishing House, 2013), p. 45.

9. Quoted in Jonathan Dollimore, 'Introduction to the Third Edition', in *Radical Tragedy: Religion, Ideology and Power in the Drama of Shakespeare and His Contemporaries*, 3rd edn. (1984; Basingstoke, Hampshire: Palgrave, 2004), p. xxxv.

10. Pierre Bourdieu, *Outline of a Theory of Practice*, trans. Richard Nice (Cambridge: Cambridge University Press, 1977), p. 79.

11. Michel de Certeau, *The Practice of Everyday Life*, trans. by Steven F. Rendall (Berkeley: University of California Press, 1988), pp. xiv–xv.

12. See Jacques Derrida, *The Gift of Death*, trans. D. Wills (Chicago and London: University of Chicago Press, 1995) and Søren Kierkegaard, *Fear and Trembling and The Sickness unto Death*, trans. Walter Lowrie (Garden City, New York: Doubleday, 1955).

13. See Jacques Lacan, *The Ethics of Psychoanalysis 1959–60: The Seminar of Jacques Lacan*, ed. Jacques-Alain Miller, trans. Dennis Porter (London: Routledge, 1999), p. 251.

14. Slavoj Žižek, Judith Butler and Ernesto Laclau, *Contingency, Hegemony, Universality: Contemporary Dialogues on the Left* (London: Verso, 2000), p. 122.

15. See Thomas Middleton, *The Changeling*, in *Thomas Middleton: Five Plays*, ed. Bryan Loughrey and Neil Taylor (London and New York: Penguin, 1988).

16. Jacob Burckhardt, *The Civilization of the Renaissance in Italy* (1860; New York: Random House, 2002).

17. See A. C. Bradley, 'Hegel's Theory of Tragedy', in *Oxford Lectures on Poetry* (London: Macmillan, 1909), pp. 67–97. In 'Bradley and Hegel on Shakespeare', *Comparative Literature* 6 (1964), Anne Paolucci writes, 'The refusal of critics to take seriously A. C. Bradley's emphatic acknowledgement of his debt to Hegel must appear as an embarrassing paradox to anyone examining the matter today' (211).

18. Stephen Greenblatt, *Renaissance Self-Fashioning: from More to Shakespeare* (Chicago: University of Chicago Press, 1980), pp. 256, 257.

19. In his career after *Renaissance Self-Fashioning*, Greenblatt has continued to struggle to affirm human freedom. *Shakespearean Negotiations* explores how apparent freedom cannot only be 'contained' by ideology but can even be produced by ideology as a way of defusing real freedom. Bravely, Greenblatt also shows how critical freedom is itself contained, since 'we find "subversive" in the past precisely those things that are *not* subversive to ourselves, that pose no threat to the order by which we live and allocate resources' (Stephen Greenblatt, *Shakespearean*

Negotiations: The Circulation of Social Energy in Renaissance England (Berkeley and Los Angeles: University of California Press, 1988), p. 39). *Learning to Curse* sounded a more hopeful note:

> Indeed if there is any inevitability in the new historicism's vision of history it is this insistence on agency, for even inaction or extreme marginality is understood to possess meaning and therefore to imply intention. Every form of behaviour, in this view, is a strategy: taking up arms or taking flight is a significant social action, but so is staying put, minding one's own business, turning one's face to the wall. Agency is virtually inescapable.
>
> (Stephen J. Greenblatt, *Learning to Curse: Essays in Early Modern Culture* (Routledge: New York and London, 1990), p. 164)

But the struggle to affirm freedom remains a struggle: 'A gesture of dissent may be an element in a larger legitimation process, while an attempt to stabilize the order of things may turn out to subvert it'; 'there are no guarantees, no absolute, formal assurances that what seems progressive in one set of contingent circumstances will not come to seem reactionary in another' (p. 165). In 2010, Greenblatt echoed Hegel and pronounced that 'Shakespeare as a writer is the embodiment of human freedom' (*Shakespeare's Freedom* (Chicago and London: University of Chicago Press, 2010), p. 1) thereby belatedly trumpeting what he had failed to find in his seminal *Renaissance Self-Fashioning*. But, as I have already suggested in these pages, *Shakespeare's Freedom*, by Greenblatt's standards, is a slight book.

20. In his recent interview with David Jonathan Bayot, Dollimore quotes Marx's comparable sixth thesis on Feuerbach: 'Feuerbach resolves the essence of religion into the essence of man. But the essence of man is not an abstraction inherent in each particular individual. The real nature of man is the totality of social relations' (p. 9).

21. See Dollimore, *Radical Tragedy*, pp. 248–9; my emphasis.

22. See Claire Colebrook, *New Literary Histories: New Historicism and Contemporary Criticism* (Manchester and New York: Manchester University Press, 1997), p. 194.

23. See Catherine Belsey, *The Subject of Tragedy: Identity and Difference in Renaissance Drama* (London: Methuen, 1985); Francis Barker, *The Tremulous Private Body: Essays on Subjection* (London: Methuen, 1984); John Lee, *Shakespeare's Hamlet and the Controversies of Self* (Oxford: Clarendon Press, 2000), p. 151.

24. Herbert Marcuse, *The Aesthetic Dimension: Towards a Critique of Marxist Aesthetics* (Boston: Beacon, 1978), pp. 3–4.

25. See Dollimore and Bayot, p. 16.

26. Lisa Jardine, *Still Harping on Daughters*, 'Morningside Edition' (New York: Columbia University Press, 1989), pp. viii–ix.

27. In *Sexual Dissidence: Augustine to Wilde, Freud to Foucault* (Oxford: Clarendon Press, 1991), Dollimore suggested, for instance, 'straying is the original (if unintended) act of demystification, one which reveals the coercive "nature" of the prescribed path, the straight and narrow. The path we thought we were on naturally, or by choice, we are in fact on by arrangement, and in straying we discover alternative ways to alternative futures.' Dollimore secures the point with a

Shakespearean reference. "'The wiser, the waywarder", observes Rosalind in *As You Like It*' (4.1.129–30, pp. 106–7).

28. Judith Butler, *Gender Trouble: Feminism and the Subversion of Identity* (London and New York: Routledge, 1990).

29. See for one such treatment Marjorie Garber, *Vested Interests: Cross-Dressing and Cultural Anxiety* (London: Penguin, 1993). And for the article that introduced Butler to Shakespeare scholarship, see Linda Charnes, 'Styles that Matter: On the Discursive Limits of Ideology', *Shakespeare Studies* 24 (1996), 118–47.

30. See Madhavi Menon (ed.), *Shakesqueer: A Queer Companion to the Complete Works of Shakespeare* (Durham, NC: Duke University Press, 2011).

31. Jonathan Dollimore, *Sex, Literature and Censorship* (Cambridge: Polity, 2001), p. 38.

32. Dollimore, *Sex, Literature and Censorship*, pp. 38–9.

33. See Hugh Grady, *Shakespeare's Universal Wolf* (Oxford: Clarendon, 1996); 'On the Need for a Differentiated Theory of (Early) Modern Subjects', in *Philosophical Shakespeares*, ed. John J. Joughin (London and New York: Routledge, 2000), pp. 34–50; *Shakespeare, Machiavelli and Montaigne: Power and Subjectivity from* Richard II *to* Hamlet (Oxford: Oxford University Press, 2002).

34. Grady, *Shakespeare, Machiavelli and Montaigne*, p. 53.

35. Richard Wilson, *Free Will: Art and Power on Shakespeare's Stage* (Manchester: Manchester University Press, 2013).

36. See Charles Nicholl, *The Lodger: Shakespeare on Silver Street* (London: Allen Lane, 2007). Nicholl's book both begins and ends with this detail.

37. Edward Bond, *Bingo* (London: Eyre Methuen, 1974), scene 1, pp. 6–7.

38. Wilson, p. 64; James Shapiro, *1599: A Year in the Life of William Shakespeare* (London: Faber and Faber, 2005).

39. Wilson, p. 58.

40. Wilson, p. 443.

41. See Wilson, pp. 113 and 67, as well as Judith Halberstam, *The Queer Art of Failure* (Durham, NC: Duke University Press, 2011).

42. See Wilson, p. 354.

43. Wilson, p. 443. Hannah Arendt, 'What Is Freedom?' in *Between Past and Future* (Harmondsworth: Penguin, 1968), p. 165; Martin Heidegger, *Existence and Being* (Washington, DC: Gateway, 1949), p. 305.

44. John Stuart Mill, *On Liberty: With, The Subjection of Women* and, *Chapters on Socialism*, ed. Stefan Collini (Cambridge: Cambridge University Press, 1989), p. 115.

45. Howard Barker, 'The House of Infection: Theatre in the Age of Social Hygiene', in *Arguments for a Theatre*, 3rd edn. (Manchester: Manchester University Press, 1997), p. 186.

46. See Bradley, 'Hegel's Theory of Tragedy', pp. 88.

47. Peter Holbrook, *Shakespeare's Individualism* (Cambridge: Cambridge University Press, 2010), p. 23.

48. Holbrook, p. 228.

49. Quoted in Holbrook, p. 56.

50. See Erich Fromm, *Escape from Freedom* (New York and Toronto: Rinehart & Company, Inc., 1941). Sartre says we are 'condemned to be free' (*Being and Nothingness*, trans. Hazel E. Barnes (New York: Philosophical Library, 1956), p. 631). Walter Kaufmann explains, 'Condemned, because [man] did not create himself, yet is nevertheless at liberty, and from the moment that he is thrown into this world he is responsible for everything he does' (*Existentialism from Dostoevesky to Sartre* (New York: Penguin, Meridian, 1975), p. 353). It is from this overwhelming responsibility, according to Sartre, that we escape into the 'bad faith' of compliance and unfreedom.

51. Holbrook, p. 229.

52. Holbrook, p. 60.

53. George Orwell, *Nineteen Eighty-Four* (1949; London: Penguin, 2000), p. 33; quoted in Holbrook, p. 229.

54. Shakespeare references are, unless otherwise indicated, to the *Norton Shakespeare*, ed. Stephen Greenblatt (New York: Norton, 2008).

55. Bloom, p. 71.

56. For more on Poor Tom, see Ewan Fernie, *The Demonic: Literature and Experience* (London: Routledge, 2012), pp. 223–35; and Simon Palfrey, *Poor Tom: Living* King Lear (Chicago: University of Chicago Press, 2014).

57. Bradley, 'Hegel's Theory of Tragedy', p. 69.

58. G. W. F. Hegel, *Phenomenology of Spirit*, trans. A. V. Miller (Oxford: Oxford University Press, 1979), p. 471.

59. Novalis, 'Aphorisms and Fragments', trans. Alexander Gelley, in *German Romantic Criticism*, ed. A. Leslie Wilson (New York: Continuum, 1982), p. 174.

60. Arthur Rimbaud, *Lettre du Voyant, in Œuvres Poetiques Complètes*, ed. Alain Blottières (Paris: Laffont, 1980).

61. S. T. Coleridge, 'Marginalia on Othello', in *Shakespeare: Othello*, ed. John Wain (London: Macmillan, 1971), p. 53.

62. Howard Barker, p. 186.

63. See Holbrook, p. 68; Bloom, p. 73.

64. Hegel, 'Dramatic Poetry', p. 81; my emphasis.

65. Margreta de Grazia has recently offered a provocatively materialist reading of *Hamlet*, one where the Prince of Denmark is seen above all in relation to issues of land and its ownership (Margreta de Grazia, *Hamlet without Hamlet* (Cambridge: Cambridge University Press, 2007)). Kottman has objected, 'I would suggest that precisely the contrary is the case; it is only in dialectical relation to historical principles of social organization like property rights and land owner-ship (as Hegel makes clear) that Hamlet's self-alienation/subjectivity – subjectivity in general – arises, and remains, a demanding problem' (Paul A. Kottman, *Tragic Conditions in Shakespeare: Disinheriting the Globe* (Baltimore: The Johns Hopkins University Press, 2009), p. 177, n. 24). I agree with Hegel that Hamlet is lost in the world he finds himself in, and with Kottman that he is defined against it. Shakespeare seems to point to this first by calling him Hamlet like his very different father, and second by giving us Laertes as the standard type of worldly son and heir which Hamlet is not.

66. Harold Bloom, *Hamlet: Poem Unlimited* (New York: Riverhead Books, 2003), p. 134.
67. Søren Kierkegaard, *Fear and Trembling*, p. 49.
68. Hegel, 'Dramatic Poetry', p. 77.
69. See the Knox translation of the *Aesthetics*, vol. 2, p. 1188. It's worth noting here that Hegel is writing in something of a German tradition.
70. See Roger Paulin, *The Critical Reception of Shakespeare in Germany 1682–1914: Native Literature and Foreign Genius* (Hildesheim: Georg Olms Verlag, 2003), pp. 230, 236.
71. See William Hazlitt, *Selected Writings*, ed. Jon Cooke (Oxford: Oxford University Press, 1991), p. 328.
72. Bradley, 'Hegel's Theory of Tragedy', p. 77.
73. See Georg Wilhelm Friedrich Hegel, *Vorlesungen über die Aesthetik*, ed. H. G. Hotho, 3 vols, vol. 3, p. 572; quoted in Paulin, p. 402. Such an independence of character can only occur when the fullest importance is given to what is external to the Divine, that is, to the particular element in man. For the relevant passage in the Knox translation of the *Aesthetics*, see vol. 1, p. 577.
74. Hegel, 'Dramatic Poetry', p. 79; my emphasis.
75. Bradley, 'Hegel's Theory of Tragedy', p. 78.
76. Bradley, 'Hegel's Theory of Tragedy', p. 88.
77. Howard Barker, p. 186.
78. Bradley, 'Hegel's Theory of Tragedy', p. 86.
79. See the Knox translation of the *Aesthetics*, vol. 1, p. 582.
80. See the Knox translation of the *Aesthetics*, vol. 1, p. 418.
81. Paulin, pp. 404–5.
82. See the Knox translation of the *Aesthetics*, vol. 1, p. 419.
83. See the Knox translation of the *Aesthetics*, vol. 1, p. 418.
84. See the Knox translation of the *Aesthetics*, vol. 1, p. 586.
85. Bates, p. 150.
86. Hegel, 'Dramatic Poetry', p. 73.
87. Bradley, 'The Rejection of Falstaff', *Oxford Lectures on Poetry*, p. 262.

7   Freetown Philosopher

1. G. W. F. Hegel, 'A Conversation of Three: A Scene from *Julius Caesar*', intro. H. S. Harris, trans. Christiane Seile, *Clio* 7.2 (1978), 247–50. For original German text, see G. W. F. Hegel, *Documente zu Hegels Entwicklung*, ed. Johannes Hoffmeister (Stuttgart: Frommann, 1936), pp. 3–6. I am grateful to Patrick Gray for putting me on to this.
2. References unless otherwise indicated are to the *Norton Shakespeare*, ed. Stephen Greenblatt (London and New York: W. W. Norton, 2008).
3. As Simon Critchley and Jamieson Webster admit, it is not unproblematic to move from the early Hegel of the *Phenomenology* to the late Hegel of the *Aesthetics*, but Hegel's achieved system is clearly the background for his contemplation of and judgement on Shakespeare towards the end of his career (*The Hamlet Doctrine*

(London: Verso, 2013), p. 84). That said, it is also true that the less systematic side of his reflections on Shakespeare arguably enrich his achieved system. And given that Hegel wrote about Shakespeare as a boy, it isn't unreasonable to suppose that Shakespeare influenced his system in the first place.

4. Jennifer Ann Bates, *Hegel and Shakespeare on Moral Imagination* (Albany: State University of New York Press, 2010), p. 194.

5. Andrew Shanks, *Hegel and Religious Faith: Divided Brain, Atoning Spirit* (London: Bloomsbury T and T Clark, 2012), p. 10.

6. Terry Pinkard, *Hegel: A Biography* (Cambridge: Cambridge University Press, 2000), p. 24.

7. Pinkard, p. 24.

8. Pinkard, p. 556.

9. Pinkard, p. 152.

10. Quoted in Christopher Clark, *Iron Kingdom: The Rise and Downfall of Prussia 1600–1947* (London: Penguin, 2007), p. 431.

11. G. W. F. Hegel, 'Dramatic Poetry', from *Aesthetics: Lectures on Fine Art,* in *Philosophers on Shakespeare*, ed. Paul Kottman (Stanford: University of Stanford Press, 2009), pp. 84–5. The Kottman collection makes the most pertinent portion of the *Aesthetics* conveniently available for Shakespeareans, and I quote from it where possible. It is excerpted from the culminating section of G. W. F. Hegel's *Aesthetics: Lectures on Fine Art*, trans. T. M. Knox, vols 1 and 2 (Oxford: Clarendon Press, 1975), vol. 2, pp. 1158–237. Where I quote from elsewhere in the *Aesthetics*, this is the translation I use, unless otherwise indicated.

12. Roger Paulin, *The Critical Reception of Shakespeare in Germany 1682–1914: Native Literature and Foreign Genius* (Hildesheim: Georg Olms Verlag, 2003), pp. 281–2.

13. Hegel, 'Dramatic Poetry', pp. 73, 74, 59, 68 (my emphasis). 'Shakespeare becomes the paradigmatic modern dramatist because his characters are wholly absorbed in their own individual aims' (Pinkard, pp. 600 ff.).

14. See Søren Kierkegaard, *The Concept of Dread*, trans. Walter Lowrie (Princeton: Princeton University Press, 1957), p. 119.

15. Hegel speaks of 'the self-subsistent inherently infinite personality of the individual' in *The Philosophy of Right* (trans. T. M. Knox (Oxford: Oxford University Press, 1967), para. 185: paragraph references are given for this work because various translations are widely used.

16. Jonathan Bate writes, 'The effect of such a reading is that the aesthetic is placed in opposition to the quotidian and political. For Hegel, this is the difference between classical and Romantic tragedy' (*The Genius of Shakespeare* (London: Picador, 1997), p. 261). But what he doesn't say is that Hegel is complaining about this.

17. G. W. F. Hegel, *Phenomenology of Spirit*, trans. A. V. Miller (Oxford: Oxford University Press, 1979), p. 110.

18. 'According to Hegel, the Greeks stood in an essentially unthinking and unreflective relation to the customs and mores of their community, whereas modern Europeans refuse to recognize any demand or obligation as valid that they do not perceive as rational' (Alan Patten, *Hegel's Idea of Freedom* (Oxford: Oxford University Press, 2002), p. 59).

19. G. W. F. Hegel, *The Philosophy of History*, trans. J. Silbree (New York: Dover, 1956), p. 416.

20. See Hegel, *The Philosophy of Right*, para. 185.

21. Hegel, *The Philosophy of History*, pp. 416–17.

22. Margreta de Grazia, *Hamlet without Hamlet* (Cambridge: Cambridge University Press, 2007), p. 18.

23. See Peter Singer, *Hegel: A Very Short Introduction* (Oxford: Oxford University Press, 1983), p. 33.

24. Hegel, 'Dramatic Poetry', p. 84.

25. Quoted in Singer, p. 1.

26. Hegel, *Phenomenology*, pp. 359, 360.

27. Quoted in Singer, p. 2.

28. Quoted in Singer, p. 2. In relation to the tradition of German response to Shakespeare, it is interesting to note that Bismarck identified with Coriolanus: see Otto Fürst von Bismarck, *Gedanken und Erinnerungen*, Neue Ausgabe (Stuttgart: Cotta, 1942), vol. 1, p. 69; vol. 2, p. 353.

29. Andrew Shanks, *Against Innocence: Gillian Rose's Reception and Gift of Faith* (London: SCM Press, 2008), p. 36.

30. Hegel, *Phenomenology*, p. 361.

31. Working after Hegel, German historians developed the view that the reformed Prussian monarchy represented an apex of human freedom, reconciling individual freedom with social integration. This 'German idea of freedom' was contrasted with the more atomistic ideas of 1789 (cf. Peter Watson, *The German Genius: Europe's Third Renaissance, the Second Scientific Revolution, and the Twentieth Century* (London: Simon and Schuster, 2010), p. 270).

32. See Hegel, *Philosophy of Right*, para. 15. He opposes Thomas Hobbes's definition of freedom as 'the absence of opposition [or] external impediments'. 'A Freeman,' according to Hobbes, 'is he that, in those things which by his strength and wit he is able to do, is not hindered to do what he has a will to.' See *Leviathan*, ed. A. P. Martinich (Ontario: Broadview, 2002), p. 190.

33. Hegel writes of 'the free will which wills the free will' (*Philosophy of Right*, para. 27).

34. See Mark Evan Bonds, *Music as Thought: Listening to the Symphony in the Age of Beethoven* (Princeton: Princeton University Press, 2006), pp. 35–40.

35. Friedrich Schlegel, 'Talk on Mythology', *Dialogue on Poetry*, trans. Ernst Behler and Roman Struc, in *German Romantic Criticism: Volume 21*, ed. A. Leslie Wilson, foreword by Ernst Behler (New York: Continuum, 1982), p. 100.

36. Friedrich Nietzsche, *The Birth of Tragedy and Other Writings*, ed. R. Geuss and R. Spiers, trans. R. Spiers (Cambridge: Cambridge University Press, 1999), p. 76.

37. See G. K. Hunter, 'Introduction', in *Shakespeare Henry IV Parts I and II: A Casebook*, ed. G. K. Hunter (Houndmills: Macmillan, 1988), p. 11.

38. See Watson, *The German Genius*, p. 492; see also Ulrich Weinzerl, *Hofmannsthal: Skizzern zu seinem Bild* (Vienna: Zsolnay, 2005), pp. 147 ff.

39. See Watson, *The German Genius*, p. 775; see also Hans Georg Gadamer, *The Relevance of the Beautiful*, ed. Robert Bernasconi, trans. Nicholas Walker (Cambridge: Cambridge University Press, 1986), pp. 123–30.

40. See Richard Wilson, *Free Will* (Manchester: Manchester University Press, 2013), p. 299.
41. See Jonathan Dollimore, *Radical Tragedy: Religion, Ideology and Power in the Drama of Shakespeare and his Contemporaries*, 3rd edn. (1984; Basingstoke, Hampshire: Palgrave, 2004), pp. 260–1. Though his analysis of post-Bradleyan criticism is acute, I think Dollimore here is somewhat unfair to Bradley himself. In his Introduction to *Philosophers on Shakespeare*, Paul Kottman notes Bradley's view that 'Shakespeare's dramatic representations are the fullest reconciliation of the fate of the individual and the collective (or universal) that we have' (p. 12).
42. Hegel, *Phenomenology*, p. 227.
43. Graham Bradshaw, *Shakespeare's Scepticism* (Brighton: The Harvester Press, 1987), pp. 138–9.
44. Hegel, *Aesthetics*, vol. 2, p. 1061.
45. See Hugh Grady, *Shakespeare's Universal Wolf: Studies in Early Modern Reification* (Oxford: Clarendon Press, 1996).
46. Hegel, *Phenomenology*, p. 117.
47. Hegel, *Phenomenology*, p. 117.
48. See Hegel, *Phenomenology*, p. 117.
49. *Romeo and Juliet* references are to the Arden edition of *Romeo and Juliet*, ed. René Weis (London: Bloomsbury, 2012).
50. Quoted in Patten, p. 128. See also G. W. F. Hegel, *Hegel's Philosophy of Mind*, trans. William Wallace and A. V. Miller (Oxford: Oxford University Press, 1971), para. 431A.
51. Hegel, *Phenomenology*, p. 138.
52. Hegel, *Phenomenology*, p. 409.
53. Friedrich Schlegel, 'Epochs of Literature', from *Dialogue on Poetry*, p. 86.
54. Martin Buber, *I and Thou*, trans. W. Kaufman (New York: Touchstone, 1970).
55. Hegel, *Phenomenology*, p. 111.
56. Hegel, *Phenomenology*, p. 111.
57. See Paul A. Kottman, '*Shakespeare's Individualism* by Peter Holbrook (review)', *Shakespeare Quarterly* 64.1 (Spring 2013), 107–10.
58. Hegel, *Phenomenology*, p. 111.
59. Hegel, *Phenomenology*, p. 10.
60. See Slavoj Žižek, *Less Than Nothing: Hegel and the Shadow of Dialectical Materialism* (London and New York: Verso, 2012) p. 321; see also Judith Butler and Catherine Malabou, *Sois mon corps. Une lecture contemporaine de la domination et de la servitude chez Hegel* (Paris: Bayard, 2010).
61. Hegel, *Phenomenology*, p. 19.
62. Hegel, *Phenomenology*, p. 19.
63. G. W. F. Hegel, *Faith and Knowledge*, trans. Walter Cerf and H. S. Harris (Albany: State University of New York Press, 1977), p. 191.
64. Hegel, *Phenomenology*, p. 27.
65. Hegel, *Phenomenology*, p. 264.
66. Hegel, *Phenomenology*, pp. 212–13.
67. Hegel, *Philosophy of Right*, para. 260. Hegel's idealisation of the state is what stimulated Rudolf Haym's classic attack, *Hegel und Seine Zeit* (Berlin: Rudolf

Gaertner, 1857); and Karl Popper seized on it in his polemical charge that the origins of totalitarianism are to be found in Hegel's thought: see *The Open Society and Its Enemies*, vol. 2 (London: Routledge and Kegan Paul, 1966), Chapter 12. The quotation given, however, makes it abundantly clear that what Hegel has in mind is a sustainably *liberal* state. As Patten writes, 'Hegel's procedure leaves open the possibility that oppressive social orders can be condemned for failing to actualize the capacities for free and rational agency of their members' (p. 137).

68. See Johann Wolfgang von Goethe, *Shakespeare und kein Ende* / No End to Shakespeare', trans. David Constantine, in *Goethe on Shakespeare / Goethe über Shakespeare: A Parallel Text Edition of Goethe's Essays on Shakespeare* (London: Globe Education, 2010), pp. 20–46; see also Watson, *The German Genius*, p. 708.

69. Marx's biographer observes that the 'sole description of a communist society' in *The Communist Manifesto* was the assertion that it would be 'an association in which the free development of each is the condition of the free development of all' (Jonathan Sperber, *Karl Marx: A Nineteenth-Century Life* (Liveright: New York, 2013), p. 209). De Grazia observes that both Hegel and Marx conceptualise the modern breakthrough as the 'old mole' that works 'i'th'earth so fast' in *Hamlet* (1.5.164), in the *Philosophy of History* in Hegel's case, in *Capital* in Marx's: see de Grazia, '"Old mole": the modern *telos* and the return to dust', pp. 23–44. 'In 1600,' de Grazia writes, 'the liberating movement Hegel requires of the mole would have been precluded by the word's homonymic kinship with *mold*' (29). I disagree with this. The old mole Hamlet addresses is also his father's spirit, and for Hegel spirit is always evolved in dialectical relation to corporeality. Hence his extraordinary and telling maxim, 'the Spirit is a bone' (*Phenomenology*, p. 208).

70. See Stephen Greenblatt, *Shakespeare's Freedom* (Chicago and London: University of Chicago Press, 2010), p. 80.

71. Hegel, *Phenomenology*, p. 400.

72. Gillian Rose, *The Broken Middle: Out of Our Ancient Society* (Oxford: Blackwell, 1992), pp. 236–7.

73. Hegel, *Phenomenology*, p. 328.

74. Quoted in Christian Deelman, *The Great Shakespeare Jubilee* (London: Michael Joseph, 1964), p. 285.

75. Péter Dávidházi, *The Romantic Cult of Shakespeare: Literary Reception in Anthropological Perspective* (Houndmills, Basingstoke and London: Macmillan, 1998), p. 48.

76. Martha Winburn England, *Garrick's Jubilee* (Columbus: Ohio State University Press, 1964), p. 92.

77. Hegel, *Phenomenology*, pp. 356–7.

78. Hegel, *Phenomenology*, p. 461.

79. Žižek, p. 320; see also Rebecca Comay, *Mourning Sickness: Hegel and the French Revolution* (Stanford: Stanford University Press, 2011), p. 149.

80. Hegel, 'Dramatic Poetry', p. 73; Shanks, *Against Innocence*, p. 150.

81. Hegel, *Phenomenology*, p. 455.

82. Hegel, *Phenomenology*, p. 456; my emphasis.

83. Hegel, *Phenomenology*, p. 456.

84. Quoted in Patten, p. 124. See also G. W. F. Hegel, *Lectures on the Philosophy of World History*, trans. H. B. Nisbet (Cambridge: Cambridge University Press, 1975), p. 48.

8   Against Shakespearean Freedom

1. *Ode to Shakespeare*, in Bodleian Library MS Mus d 14; quoted in Michael Dobson, *The Making of the National Poet: Shakespeare, Adaptation and Authorship, 1660–1769* (Oxford: Oxford University Press, 1992), p. 227.
2. For more on the way in which imperialism can in fact yoke together 'the classically incompatible ideas of liberty and empire', see David Armitage, *The Ideological Origins of the British Empire* (Cambridge: Cambridge University Press, 2001), p. 8 and *passim*. But of course the trouble with freedom as justification for Empire is that it eventually furnishes imperial subjects with a motive for revolt.
3. Jonathan Bate, *The Genius of Shakespeare* (London: Picador, 1997), p. 196; see also Walter Raleigh, Sir Sidney Lee and C. T. Onions, *Shakespeare's England*, vol. 1 (Oxford: Clarendon Press, 1916), p. xxii.
4. Nigel Cliff, *The Shakespeare Riots: Revenge, Drama and Death in 19th-Century America* (London: Random House, 2007), p. 131.
5. Quoted in Cliff, p. 20.
6. See Cliff, p. 90.
7. See Michael Dobson, 'Let him be Caesar!' *London Review of Books* (2 August 2007).
8. Quoted in Cliff, p. 88.
9. *Public Ledger*, 22 November 1848, quoted in Cliff, p. 167 ff.
10. See Cliff, pp. 175–6.
11. See *Macbeth*, 5.4.57–8. References unless otherwise indicated are to the *Norton Shakespeare*, ed. Stephen Greenblatt (London and New York: W. W. Norton, 2008).
12. See Cliff, p. xx.
13. See Cliff, pp. 211–12.
14. See Pauline Maier, *From Resistance to Revolution: Colonial Radicals and the Development of American Opposition to Britain 1765–7* (New York: W. W. Norton, 1992); see also, Jack Lynch, 'Wilkes, Liberty, and Number 45', *Colonial Williamsburg Journal* (Summer 2003).
15. Albert Furtwangler, *Assassin on Stage: Brutus, Hamlet and the Death of Lincoln* (Urbana and Chicago: University of Illinois Press, 1991), p. ix.
16. Carl Sandburg, *Abraham Lincoln: The War Years* (New York: Harcourt, Brace, 1939), vol. 4, p. 301.
17. Here's a choice memory of Edmund Kean: 'Kean requested the rehearsal might not be till twelve as he should get drunk that night – said he had frequently three women to stroke during performances and that two waited while the other was served … That night he had one woman (Smith) though he was much infected' (James Winston, *Drury Lane Journal: Selections from James Winston's Diaries 1819–27*, ed. Alfred L. Nelson and Gilbert B. Cross (London: Society for Theatre Research, 1974), p. 4). See also Jean Paul Sartre, *Kean or Disorder and Genius*, trans. Kitty Black, in *Three Plays: Kean, Nekrassov, The Trojan Women* (Penguin: London, 1969).

18. Quoted in Gene Smith, *American Gothic: The Story of America's Legendary Theatrical Family, Junius, Edwin, and John Wilkes Booth* (New York: Simon and Shuster), p. 80.

19. See Gordon Samples, *Lust for Fame: The Stage Career of John Wilkes Booth* (Jefferson, NC and London: McFarland & Company, Inc, 1982), p. 105.

20. Asia Booth Clarke, *John Wilkes Booth: A Sister's Memoir* (Jackson: University Press of Mississippi, 1996), p. 89.

21. Walt Whitman, 'Death of Abraham Lincoln: Lecture deliver'd in New York, 14 April 1879 – in Philadelphia, '80 – in Boston, '81', in *Prose Works 1892, Vol. 2: Collect and Other Prose*, ed. Floyd Stovall, *The Collected Writings of Walt Whitman* (New York: New York University Press, 1964), p. 505.

22. Whitman, 'Death of Abraham Lincoln', p. 508.

23. Furtwangler, p. 141.

24. Thomas Goodrich, *The Darkest Dawn* (Bloomington: Indiana University Press, 2005), p. 62. 'One of his theatrical friends even claimed that the actor's admiration for the classical Brutus was the "mainspring" of the assassination' (John Rhodehamel and Louise Taper, 'Introduction', in John Wilkes Booth, *'Right or Wrong, God Judge Me': The Writings of John Wilkes Booth*, ed. John Rhodehamel and Louise Taper (Urbana and Chicago: University of Illinois Press, 2001), p. 8). The footnote to this sentence reads: 'The remarks of John T. Ford, owner of Ford's Theatre, were quoted in a letter (signed 'A MARYLANDER') to the editor of the *Philadelphia Press*, 27 November 1881' (n. 10). 'Within days of the shooting, newspapers began to report that an anonymous source had once heard Booth talk about killing the president. Asked why he would do such a thing, he had quoted a couplet from the Colley Cibber version of *Richard III*:

> The daring youth that fired the Ephesian dome
> Outlives in fame the pious fool that reared it.'

(Michael W. Kauffman, *American Brutus: John Wilkes Booth and the Lincoln Conspiracies* (New York: Random House, 2004), p. 245).

25. Quoted in Smith, pp. 197–8; see also Booth, p. 155.

26. *Macbeth*, 3.4.16.

27. See Stephen Dickey, 'Men of Letters: Lincoln, Booth, and Shakespeare', *Folger Magazine* (Spring 2009), 4–10.

28. See Philip B. Kunhardt III, 'Lincoln's Contested Legacy', *Smithsonian*, Smithsonian Institution 39.11 (February 2009), 34–5.

29. Booth, p. 155. See *Macbeth*, 5.7.2.

30. George Bernard Shaw, *Shaw on Shakespeare*, ed. Edmund Wilson (New York: Arno, 1980), p. 56.

31. George Orwell, 'Lear, Tolstoy and the Fool', in *Collected Essays* (London: Secker and Warburg, 1961), p. 433.

32. G. Wilson Knight, *The Wheel of Fire: Interpretations of Shakespearean Tragedy, with Three New Essays*, 4th rev. and enl. edn. (London: Methuen, 1949), pp. 270, 291.

33. G. Steiner, 'A Reading against Shakespeare', W. P. Kerr Lecture, 1986 (Glasgow: Glasgow University Press, 1987), p. 5. For more on great Shakespeare detractors, see

Erin Sullivan, 'Anti-Bardolatry through the Ages – Or, Why Voltaire, Tolstoy, Shaw and Wittgenstein Didn't Like Shakespeare', *Opticon 1826*, 2 (2007).

34. Leo Tolstoy, 'Shakespeare and the Drama', in *Tolstoy on Shakespeare*, ed. and trans. V. Tchertkoff (London: Free Age Press, 1907), p. 7.
35. Tolstoy, p. 9.
36. Tolstoy, p. 9.
37. Tolstoy, pp. 9, 77.
38. Tolstoy, pp. 21–3.
39. Tolstoy, p. 25.
40. Frank Kermode (ed.), *Shakespeare: King Lear*, Casebook Series (London: Macmillan, 1969), p. 21; Stanley Cavell, *Must We Mean What We Say?: A Book of Essays* (Cambridge: Cambridge University Press, 1987), p. 280; Tolstoy, p. 28.
41. Tolstoy, pp. 62–3.
42. Jonathan Bate, *The Genius of Shakespeare* (London: Picador, 1997), p. 150.
43. Wilson Knight, pp. 274, 295.
44. Tolstoy, p. 67.
45. Tolstoy, p. 68.
46. Tolstoy, pp. 71–72.
47. Tolstoy, p. 73.
48. Tolstoy, p. 60.
49. Tolstoy, p. 54.
50. Tolstpy, p. 56.
51. Quoted in Tolstoy, p. 56.
52. Tolstoy, p. 57.
53. Tolstoy, pp. 56, 60–1.
54. Tolstoy, p. 61.
55. Tobias Döring, 'A Note on Mann's Shakespeare', in *Thomas Mann and Shakespeare: Something Rich and Strange*, ed. Tobias Döring and Ewan Fernie (New York: Bloomsbury, 2015), p. 15.
56. G. G. Gervinus, *Shakespeare Commentaries*, translated under the author's superintendence by F. E. Bunnètt, 6th edn. (London: Smith, Elder, & Co., 1903), p. 909.
57. Gervinus, p. 909.
58. See Roger Paulin, *The Critical Reception of Shakespeare in Germany 1682–1914: Native Literature and Foreign Genius* (Hildesheim: Georg Olms Verlag, 2003), pp. 139, 409, 412.
59. Gervinus, p. 910.
60. Gervinus, pp. 913, 912; see also Karl Marx and Friedrich Engels, *The German Ideology*, ed. C. J. Arthur (New York: International Publishers, 2004).
61. Arthur Schopenhauer, *The World as Will and Idea: Abridged in One Volume*, ed. David Berman, trans. Jill Berman (1819, rev. edn. 1859; London: Everyman, 1995), pp. 161–2.
62. See Ferdinand Freiligrath, *Werke*, ed. Julius Schweing, vol. 2 (Berlin, etc.: Bong 1909), pp. 71–3. For Gervinus's comparison of Germany with Hamlet, see Gervinus, p. 575 ff.
63. Gervinus, p. 917.
64. Gervinus, pp. 917–18.
65. Brandes is quoted in Tolstoy, pp. 60–1.

66. Gervinus, p. 913.
67. Gervinus, p. 914.
68. Gervinus, p. 923.
69. Gervinus, p. 924.
70. Gervinus, p. 924.
71. Gervinus, p. 925.
72. Gervinus, p. 920.
73. Gervinus, p. 930. Roger Paulin writes, 'we sense that for him Shakespeare is a "man for all seasons"' (p. 411).
74. Gervinus, p. 921.
75. Gervinus, pp. 925, 924.
76. See, for instance, Knight, p. 271; or Yury D. Levin, 'Shakespeare and Russian Literature: Nineteenth-Century Attitudes', in *Russian Essays on Shakespeare and His Contemporaries*, ed. Alexandr Parfenov and Joseph G. Price (London: Associated University Presses, 1998), p. 92. The quotation is from Zdeněk Stříbrný, *Shakespeare and Eastern Europe* (Oxford: Oxford University Press, 2000), p. 92.
77. Steiner, p. 13; see also Ludwig Wittgenstein, *Culture and Value*, ed. G. H. von Wright, trans. P. Winch (Oxford: Blackwell, 1998), pp. 95–6.
78. This is part of the final peroration of Steiner's lecture on pages 16–17.
79. George Orwell, 'Lear, Tolstoy and the Fool', in *Collected Essays* (London: Secker and Warburg, 1961), pp. 424, 429.
80. See Ewan Fernie, 'Poor Tom', in *The Demonic: Literature and Experience* (London: Routledge, 2013), pp. 223–37.

9   The Freedom of Complete Being

1. Sigmund Freud, *Civilization and Its Discontents*, ed. and trans. James Strachey (New York: Norton, 1962), pp. 42–3.
2. Freud, pp. 42–3.
3. Freud, p. 58.
4. Freud, p. 70.
5. Freud, p. 92.
6. Freud, pp. 91–2.
7. Unless otherwise noted, Shakespeare reference are to the *Norton Shakespeare*, ed. Stephen Greenblatt (New York: Norton, 2008).
8. See Sigmund Freud, *The Interpretation of Dreams*, trans. James Strachey, ed. Angela Richards, The Penguin Freud Library, vol. 4 (London: Penguin, 1991).
9. Freud, *Civilization and its Discontents*, p. 91.
10. Theodor W. Adorno, 'Cultural Criticism and Society', in *Prisms*, trans. Samuel Weber and Shierry Weber Nicholsen (Cambridge, MA: MIT Press, 1991), p. 34.
11. See Thomas Mann, *Doctor Faustus: The Life of the German Composer Adrian Leverkühn as Told by a Friend*, trans. H. T. Lowe-Porter (Harmondsworth: Penguin, 1968); see also Thomas Mann, *The Genesis of a Novel*, trans. Richard and Clara Winston (London: Secker and Warburg, 1961) and Lorenz Jäger, *Adorno:*

A Political Biography, trans. Stewart Spencer (New Haven: Yale University Press, 2004), p. 129 ff.

12. Thomas Mann, *The Genesis of a Novel*, pp. 26–7.
13. For more on Mann and Shakespeare, see Ewan Fernie, *The Demonic: Literature and Experience* (London: Routledge, 2013), pp. 115–42; and Tobias Döring and Ewan Fernie (eds.), *Thomas Mann and Shakespeare: Something Rich and Strange* (New York: Bloomsbury, 2015).
14. Andreas Höfele, *Stage, Stake, and Scaffold: Humans and Animals in Shakespeare's Theatre* (Oxford: Oxford University Press, 2011), p. 2; my italics. Moriarty is writing outside Shakespeare studies about Shakespeare in the context of the Western tradition more broadly. His work has not previously been considered by Shakespeareans; but *Nostos* does strike lights with Höfele's recent intervention. For more on the resonance between Höfele's book and Moriarty, see Ewan Fernie, 'Lighten Our Darkness', in *Acts of Crime: Lawlessness on the Early Modern Stage. Essays in Honour of Andreas Höfele*, ed. Bettina Boecker, Daniella Jancsó, Stephan Laqué, Enno Ruge and Gabriela Schmidt (Würzburg: Königshausen und Neumann, 2015), pp. 43–65.
15. John Moriarty, *Nostos* (2001; Dublin: The Liliput Press, 2011), p. 221.
16. Quoted by Moriarty for example on p. 551.
17. Moriarty, p. vi.
18. Moriarty, p. vii; see also *King Lear*, Conflated Text, 1.4.89–90.
19. Moriarty, p. 89.
20. Moriarty, p. 74.
21. Moriarty, p. 341.
22. Quoted in A. C. Bradley, *Shakespearean Tragedy*, 2nd edn. (London: Macmillan, 1966), p. 228.
23. This is Moriarty's epigraph to *Nostos*.
24. Moriarty, p. vi.
25. Moriarty, p. 131.
26. Moriarty, p. 133.
27. Moriarty, p. 145.
28. For more on sex and possession, see Fernie, *The Demonic*; and Lyndal Roper, *Oedipus and the Devil: Witchcraft, Sexuality and Religion in Early Modern Europe* (London: Routledge, 1994), p. 175.
29. Moriarty, p. 145.
30. Moriarty, p. 289.
31. Moriarty, p. 243.
32. Moriarty, p. 183; my emphasis.
33. Moriarty, p. 465.
34. Moriarty, p. 510.
35. Moriarty, p. 463.
36. Moriarty, p. 576.
37. Moriarty, p. 463.
38. Moriarty, p. 586; see also *Macbeth*, 4.1.12–19.
39. Moriarty, p. 586.
40. Moriarty, p. 587.

41. Moriarty, pp. 587–9.
42. Moriarty, p. 547.
43. Moriarty, p. 552.
44. Moriarty, p. 614.
45. Moriarty, p. 632.
46. Höfele, p. 278.
47. Ted Hughes, *Shakespeare and the Goddess of Complete Being* (London: Faber and Faber, 1992), pp. 88–9, 467.
48. Ted Hughes (ed.), *With Fairest Flowers While Summer Lasts: Poems from Shakespeare* (New York: Doubleday, 1971), p. xvii.
49. Hughes, *Shakespeare and the Goddess*, p. 92.
50. Hughes, *Shakespeare and the Goddess*, p. 34.
51. Neil Rhodes, 'Bridegrooms to the Goddess: Hughes, Heaney and the Elizabethans', in *Shakespeare and Ireland: History, Politics, Culture*, ed. Mark Thornton Burnett and Ramona Wray (Basingstoke, Hampshire: Macmillan, 1997), p. 155.
52. Jonathan Bate, 'Hughes on Shakespeare', in *The Cambridge Companion to Ted Hughes*, ed. Terry Gifford (Cambridge: Cambridge University Press, 2011), p. 135. See also Jonathan Bate, *Ted Hughes: The Unauthorised Life* (London: William Collins, 2015), p. 457.
53. See Ted Hughes, *Crow: From the Life and Songs of the Crow* (London: Faber and Faber, 1972). 'Carrion King' is just one example of a poem which can be read as a gloss on *Macbeth* (p. 85).
54. Hughes, *Shakespeare and the Goddess*, p. xvii.
55. Stephen Greenblatt, *Will in the World: How Shakespeare Became Shakespeare* (London: Jonathan Cape, 2004).
56. Hughes, *Shakespeare and the Goddess*, p. 504.
57. See Bate, *Ted Hughes*, p. 461.
58. Hughes, *With Fairest Flowers*, p. viii.
59. Hughes, *With Fairest Flowers*, p. v.
60. Hughes, *With Fairest Flowers*, p. viii. See also Bate, *Ted Hughes*, p. 461.
61. Hughes, *With Fairest Flowers*, p. xvii.
62. Patrick Cruttwell, *The Shakespearean Moment and Its Place in the Poetry of the Seventeenth Century* (London: Chatto and Windus, 1954).
63. Hughes, *Shakespeare and the Goddess*, p. 253.
64. Neil Corcoran, *Shakespeare and the Modern Poet* (Cambridge: Cambridge University Press, 2010), p. 203.
65. Hughes, *Shakespeare and the Goddess*, p. 91.
66. Hughes, *Shakespeare and the Goddess*, p. 47.
67. Robert Graves, *The White Goddess: A Historical Grammar of Poetic Myth* (London: Faber and Faber, 1948), p. 426.
68. Hughes, *Shakespeare and the Goddess*, p. xi.
69. Hughes, *Shakespeare and the Goddess*, p. xv.
70. Hughes, *Shakespeare and the Goddess*, p. 38.
71. Hughes, *Shakespeare and the Goddess*, p. 106.
72. Iain McGilchrist, *The Master and His Emissary: The Divided Brain and the Making of the Western World*, 2nd edn. (New Haven: Yale University Press, 2012).

73. Hughes, *Shakespeare and the Goddess*, p. 161.
74. Hughes, *Shakespeare and the Goddess*, p. 159.
75. Hughes, *Shakespeare and the Goddess*, p. 160.
76. Hughes, *Shakespeare and the Goddess*, p. 250.
77. Hughes, *Shakespeare and the Goddess*, p. 249.
78. Hughes, *Shakespeare and the Goddess*, p. 400.
79. Hughes, *Shakespeare and the Goddess*, p. 260.
80. Hughes, *Shakespeare and the Goddess*, p. 261.
81. Hughes, *Shakespeare and the Goddess*, p. 264.
82. Hughes, *Shakespeare and the Goddess*, p. 375.
83. Hughes, *Shakespeare and the Goddess*, p. 375.
84. Bate writes, 'The gestation of the Shakespeare book was inseparable from the shock of Assia's death and his belief that the terrible news of her suicide had killed his mother' (*Ted Hughes*, p. 459). He also says of Hughes, 'He is supposed to be writing about Shakespeare and he cannot stop writing about Plath' (p. 474). I wouldn't disagree when he says, 'the Shakespeare book was also Ted's veiled autobiography', but I think that Bate presses on this autobiographical element to an extent that undersells the critical achievement of *Shakespeare and the Goddess* (p. 457).
85. Jacqueline Rose, *The Haunting of Silvia Plath* (London: Virago, 1991), p. 68.
86. Rose, p. 151.
87. Quoted in Rose, p. 151. See also Ted Hughes, Note, in *A Choice of Shakespeare's Verse*, selected with an introduction by Ted Hughes (London: Faber and Faber, 1971), p. 187.
88. Jacqueline Rose, *Women in Dark Times* (London: Bloomsbury, 2014), p. 5.
89. Rose, *Women in Dark Times*, p. xi.
90. Rose, *Women in Dark Times*, p. 268.
91. See, for Hughes on 'women's libbers', Mark Ford, 'Sorrows of a Polygamist: *Ted Hughes: The Unauthorised Life* by Jonathan Bate' London Review of Books 38.6 (17 March 2016), 21.
92. John Keats, *The Complete Poetical Works and Letters of John Keats* (Boston: Houghton, Mifflin and Company, 1899), p. 277.
93. G. W. F. Hegel, *Phenomenology of Spirit*, trans. A. V. Miller (Oxford: Oxford University Press, 1979), p. 264. As in Chapter 7, I have added the word 'character'.
94. Hegel, *Phenomenology*, pp. 212–13.
95. *Romeo and Juliet* references, unless otherwise indicated, are to the Arden edition of *Romeo and Juliet*, ed. René Weis (London: Bloomsbury, 2012).
96. G. W. F. Hegel, *Lectures on the Philosophy of World History*, trans. H. B. Nisbet (Cambridge: Cambridge University Press, 1975), p. 48.
97. Simone Weil, *Gravity and Grace* (London and New York: Routledge, 2002), p. 180.

Index

Characters (cont.)

Albany, 230, 232

Angelo, 237

Antony, 60–4, 214, 271

Apothecary, 274

Barnardine, 193

Benvolio, 84, 94, 98

Bolingbroke, 206

Bottom, 253

Brutus, 224, 226

Caesar, 17, 21, 23

Caliban, 10–12, 14–15, 157, 259

Capulet, 95, 108

Cleopatra, 63, 65, 188, 213, 263, 270

Coriolanus, 6

Edgar, 176, 229–30, 240, 248, 249, 250, 252, 257, 258

Edmund, 4–5, 175–7

Falstaff, 2–5, 122–3, 124, 155, 157, 189–93, 214, 217, 259

Faulconbridge, 237

Fool, 229–30, 240, 247, 249

France, 249

Ganymede. *See* Rosalind

Gloucester (*King Lear*), 229, 230, 231

Goneril, 175

Guildenstern, 197

Hal, 171, 190, 191–2, 212, 237, 238

Hamlet, 76, 171, 175, 178–80, 189, 197–8, 204, 206, 209, 211, 212, 213, 214, 226, 236, 237, 241, 243, 261, 265

Helena, 65

Henry V. *See* Hal

Hotspur, 189–90, 193

Iago, 171, 175, 177–8, 213

Jack Cade, 124, 125, 221

Juliet, 82, 83, 84, 86–8, 90, 94, 97, 98–108, 109, 110, 111–12, 142, 186–7, 206, 213, 270, 273–4

Kent, 229–30, 249

Lady Capulet, 87

Lady Macbeth, 263

Lear, 229–30, 231, 241, 259, 261, 266–7

Leontes, 261

Macbeth, 182, 185, 227, 254–5, 256, 257, 265–6

Mardian, 213, 273

Mercutio, 82, 84, 86, 88–94, 95–7, 102, 103, 152, 274

Nurse, 86–7, 88

Oliver, 5

Othello, 178, 182

Paris, 94

Parolles, 9

Percy. *See* Hotspur

Poor Tom. *See* Edgar

Posthumus, 261

Regan, 175

Richard II, 187–8, 206

Richard III, 259

Richmond, 224

Romeo, 82, 83, 84–6, 88, 90, 94, 97, 98–101, 103–6, 107, 108, 109, 110–12, 207, 273

Rosalind, 4–5, 63–4, 65, 70, 71, 73, 74, 95, 173, 212, 214, 270

Rosaline, 85

Rosencrantz, 197

Shylock, 70, 71, 72, 73

Stephano, 157

Sycorax, 263

Tarquin, 259, 266

Titania, 263

Tybalt, 82, 90, 93, 95, 97, 110

Vincentio, 21, 23

Chartism, 128–32, 134, 135–6

Shaksperean Association of Leicester Chartists, 130, 131

Shaksperean Chartist Hymn Book, 130

Shaksperean General. *See* Cooper

Christ, 160, 212, 257, 258

resurrection of, 192

Christianity, 192–3, 199, 249–50, 256–7, 258

Catholicism, 207, 262

Protestantism, 147, 150, 155, 207, 236, 262

Churchill, Charles, 114

Churchill, Winston, 15, 16

civilisation, 242, 243–4, 245, 252, 253, 255